C3

# A DICTIONARY OF
# MOTTOES

*Also by L. G. Pine*

The Stuarts of Traquair
The House of Wavell
The Middle Sea
The Story of Heraldry
Trace Your Ancestors
The Golden Book of the Coronation
They Came with the Conqueror
The Story of the Peerage
Tales of the British Aristocracy
The House of Constantine
Teach Yourself Heraldry and Genealogy
The Twilight of Monarchy
A Guide to Titles
Princes of Wales
American Origins
Your Family Tree
Ramshackledom, A Critical Appraisal of the Establishment
Heirs of the Conqueror
Heraldry, Ancestry and Titles, Questions and Answers
The Story of Surnames
After Their Blood
Tradition and Custom in Modern Britain
The Genealogist's Encyclopedia
The Story of Titles
International Heraldry
The Highland Clans
Sons of the Conqueror
The New Extinct Peerage
The History of Hunting

# A DICTIONARY OF
# MOTTOES

L. G. PINE

ROUTLEDGE & KEGAN PAUL
London, Boston, Melbourne and Henley

First published in 1983
by Routledge & Kegan Paul Plc,
39 Store Street, London WC1E 7DD,
9 Park Street, Boston, Mass. 02108, USA,
296 Beaconsfield Parade, Middle Park,
Melbourne 3206, Australia, and
Broadway House, Newtown Road,
Henley-on-Thames, Oxon RG9 1EN
Set in Optima and Palatino by
Rowland Phototypesetting Ltd, Bury St Edmunds, Suffolk
and printed in Great Britain by
St Edmundsbury Press, Bury St Edmunds, Suffolk
© L. G. Pine 1983

Library of Congress Cataloging in Publication Data
Main entry under title:

A Dictionary of mottoes.

English and Latin.
Includes index.
1. Mottoes – Dictionaries.
I. Pine, L. G. (Leslie Gilbert), 1907–
PN309.D5   1983        080        82-21463

ISBN 0-7100-9339-X

To Dr Martin Lings
Keeper Emeritus of Oriental
Manuscripts & Printed Books,
British Museum
and author of
*Ancient Beliefs and Modern Superstitions*,
in appreciation

# CONTENTS

# PREFACE

Which the user of this work is respectfully requested to read

The definition of the word 'motto' is given comprehensively in the *Concise Oxford Dictionary* thus: 'Sentence inscribed on some object and expressing appropriate sentiment; word or sentence accompanying coat of arms or crest; maxim adopted as rule of conduct; verses etc. in paper cracker; quotation prefixed to book or chapter; (Mus.) recurrent phrase having some symbolical significance.' *Chamber's Twentieth Century Dictionary* concurs with *Oxford* in a derivation of the word from Low Latin of *muttum* – *muttire*, to mutter, no doubt correct philologically but somewhat obscure.

Of the six classes of meaning above, the present work is concerned with the first three and for the vast majority of instances with the second class only, that in which the motto accompanies a coat of arms. The reason is that in ancient history, either classical or scriptural, a motto was in most cases associated with some particular event. Only very occasionally did a sentence enter permanent usage. Obvious examples are the Roman wording, *Senatus populusque Romanus*, which survived the transformation of the Republic into the Empire. As mentioned in due course, SPQR even appeared on 'arms' attributed to Julius Caesar; and this alleged 'coat of arms' was included in the grand armorial achievement of Queen Elizabeth I, a matter beyond human learning to explain, since among all the kings and princes from whom the great sovereign had descent, Caesar was neither king nor ancestor.

Or again one might consider as a permanent expression of a maxim the famous 'Know thyself' of the Delphic Oracle; or the inscription about the importance of mathematics and music as prime factors in education over the Athenian Academy.

The real development of the motto comes with the civilization of medieval Europe; consequently the overwhelming majority of the mottoes listed are connected with coats of arms. A caveat needs to be remembered here. A motto is very frequently found in the description of an arms grant when the latter comes from a heraldic authority such as the College of Arms, or Lyon Office. From this it would be natural to assume that the motto is part of the grant along with the coat of arms. This is incorrect. A coat of arms, once granted, cannot be varied save by agreement with the grantor, but a motto can be altered at the wish of the owner. Those who edit works illustrated with drawings of arms as a rule strongly discourage any alterations of motto in the illustration; it would mean an entirely new block – an expensive matter.

As the word 'crest' is mentioned above and as if distinct from the coat of arms, and since the term 'crest' is of

frequent occurrence in the book, it is as well to remember
that a crest cannot have what may be termed a dis-
embodied existence. Armorial bearings, heraldic achievement, coat of arms or, poetically, a shield, are all correct
terms. A crest is part of a coat of arms; it cannot exist by
itself. There is one exception, which few will wish to
emulate, in which a citizen of London received the draft
of a grant of arms. He did not like the shield but approved
the crest. The latter was registered but, while the heralds
reconsidered the main device, the prospective grantee
died.

Conversely, however, a perfectly legitimate coat of
arms can exist without a crest. Crests are comparatively
late in the history of heraldry. The great boom period in
the granting of crests came in Tudor times.

No apology is required for this note on heraldry because mottoes are in Europe very closely connected with
the development of heraldry. In fact they can tell us a
great deal about the rise of medieval civilization. It will be
observed that the majority of the mottoes are in Latin, as
the latter was the language of all educated men and
women in western Europe until very recent times. All
over this half of the European continent, from Sweden to
Sicily, from Poland to Ireland, Latin was the lingua franca
of the educated. Newton's *Principia* is usually described
as the greatest scientific work ever written. It was set out
in Latin precisely because the author wanted scientific
men all over Europe and America to be able to read his
work.

Mottoes then are a feature in the Renaissance of western Europe. Some of the oldest, like *Crom a boo*, are
war-cries. It was indeed a society beleaguered on three
sides which had until the 11th century to face a siege of
Vikings, Mongols and Arabs. Warfare, defensive warfare, was necessary. During the period after the destruc-
tion of the western Roman Empire, say from 500 to 1100,
while brilliant cultures flourished in Constantinople and
in Moslem Spain, the western Europeans experienced the
Dark Ages.

But with the conversion to Christianity of the North-
men, the worst external danger was over. From 1100
Europe developed a high civilization. It commenced its
counter-attack; Spain began to be won back from the
Moslem; Malta, Sicily, southern Italy, were likewise re-
claimed for Christendom. For a century even the distant
Holy Land became a Latin kingdom.

This last was achieved by the Crusades, the first international movement in Europe. Men from a dozen coun-
tries found themselves associated in armies. They needed
distinctive signs to tell English from French, Danes from
Italians. The supposition must not be pressed too far, but
it is likely that heraldry took its rise in the Crusades. The
First Crusade captured Jerusalem in 1099. Within the
succeeding fifty years we have evidence of heraldic devices. In the Third Crusade, *c.* 1190, we find the first
instance of an English king using armorial bearings (details of arms borne by Edward the Confessor, Alfred the
Great and Saint Edmund of East Anglia are charming and

hallowed by association with famous buildings, but have no historical validity whatsoever).

Richard I also supplied the motto of our royal house, and it is highly interesting to note that it was a batlle-cry. As he rode out to thrash the French, Richard gave his war-cry – *Dieu et mon droit*.

Many of the original mottoes were thus in all probability war-cries, or clan slogans. With the exception of the latter as still used by Highland, Welsh or Irish clans, few mottoes listed here are war-cries. The reason is simple to understand. Many of the old recorded families died out; more of them became transformed and adopted maxims more suited to reflect the spirit of the family.

In short, mottoes accompanied heraldry in its development. Dating the appearance of heraldry in the twelfth century, it very soon passed from purely warlike to other and peaceful uses. Corporate bodies took arms and mottoes. Many ancient institutions, episcopal sees, abbeys, cities, guilds, acquired arms and, with these, mottoes. As regards families, a very large number, who were strangers to the tourney and the battle, obtained arms and mottoes.

Latin was the language generally used, probably in many cases of the warriors, with their chaplains' help. It is amusing to ponder, did the Dymokes' mass-priest persuade them to use *Pro rege dimico*? One can imagine a medieval knight saying in such a case: 'Are you sure this is right?'

Next to Latin a fair number of mottoes follow that of Richard I, and are in French. This is quite normal, for French was the language of gentlemen for some centuries. It was natural for Edward III (d. 1377) to use French for his Garter motto. Only in his time did English come into general use as the speech of the Court, Parliament and the schools. Anyone who feels slightly jingoistic or chauvinistic (I am using the latter word correctly, nothing whatever to do with sex!!) may console himself with the reflection that Dante's earlier works are in Latin. Fortunately for all subsequent lovers of poetry, Dante after grave consideration decided to use his native tongue. So did Geoffrey Chaucer.

The reasons for the preponderence of Latin and French will explain the comparative paucity of mottoes in English. Many excellent mottoes do appear in modern English; by a merciful dispensation we have only a few of what have been termed 'Ye olde Englyshe'. By some aberration of the English educational system, Old English (formerly known as Anglo-Saxon) appears to have been largely neglected after the time of Camden and Hakluyt. In consequence such abominations as *semni ne semni* were perpetrated.

The meaning of mottoes is very often obscure. Wherever possible a note has been given on the meaning, and for this reason references to the coats of arms are included. Some detail in the arms is carried over into the motto. What of the meaning of the charge in the shield or crest? No more unprofitable field of inquiry exists than the attempt to explain the meaning of heraldic bearings.

In the case of modern grants (e.g. over the last 150 years),
the meaning can be discovered by long and toilsome
research. But of the older arms we simply do not know
the circumstances in which they arose. We were not
present when Dethick showed Master Shakespeare the
draft (still existing) of his arms, and the poet did not leave
us a diary. So it is then with many mottoes, their orig-
ination is lost.

In translations from Latin one is inclined to echo Gibbon's famous remark that they would be better left in the
obscurity of a learned language. In Latin they have the
usual power of that strong and sonorous language. In
English they often appear very wooden.

Many mottoes are puns and thus self explanatory. This
applies to mottoes used by corporate institutions as much
as those of individuals or families.

It will be observed that a large proportion of the mottoes express religious faith, which is a reflection of the
Christian past of continental Europe and of Britain. The
ethical standard shown in the maxims is naturally high.

Although institutions have used mottoes from the middle ages onward, the greatest employment of them has
been in the last forty or fifty years. The reason is the very
considerable extension of heraldic devices which has
taken place in the same period. Nor is this limited to
Britain and Ireland. Heraldry now flourishes in Canada,
Australia, South Africa and the USA. Several hundreds of
the entries are taken from the arms of various bodies,
associations and federations. There are also a large number of mottoes of the armed forces, especially the RAF. In
the instance of the RAF, translations were in almost all
cases provided at source. I mention this because some of
the versions from Latin are not exact, though they do
express the general sense of the mottoes.

In the numerous references to *NEP*, 1972, this is an
abbreviation of a book by the author, namely *The New
Extinct Peerage* published in 1972, which takes up the
account of extinct peerages from 1 January 1884 to 1971,
Sir Bernard Burke in his *Extinct Peerage* having carried the
story up to the end of 1883. He had similarly published in
1844 an Extinct Baronetcies.

An index has been included to enable the user to find
the motto of a person or body when the actual motto is
not known.

I wish to thank several people who have helped me
with translations, as I do not know the Celtic languages.
Major Francis Jones, CVO, TD, Wales Herald Extra-
ordinary; Mr Gerard Slevin, Chief Herald of Ireland; Mr J.
Haulfryn Williams, Hon. Secretary, the Hon. Society of
Cymmrodorian; Mr William Matheson, Reader in Celtic,
Edinburgh University, and Mr D. E. Ivall, of the Cornish
Guild of Heralds. I would add that while all the above
have been most helpful in rendering translations of the
various Celtic tongues, they are not responsible for any
comments which have been added by myself.

On the large portion of the work dealing with mottoes
of the Royal Air Force, it gives me great pleasure to thank
Squadron Leader Graham J. S. Gardner, PI b. (Cer) RAF,

Ministry of Defence, for his courteous and ready assistance.

I also wish to thank the reference book staff of the Suffolk County Library, Bury St Edmunds, for their assistance. Finally, I thank most heartily my wife who has not only typed the whole manuscript but whose help in its compilation deserves one adjective – invaluable.

# ABBREVIATIONS

| | |
|---|---|
| AAF | Auxiliary Air Force |
| AHQ | Air Headquarters |
| all. | allusion |
| Assn. | Association |
| Bd. | Board |
| Bldg. Soc. | Building Society |
| *BLG* | *Burke's Landed Gentry* |
| Bn. | Battalion |
| *B.P.* | *Burke's Peerage* |
| Bt., Bts. | Baronet(s) |
| *c.* | circa, about |
| CC | County Council |
| Cmd. | Command |
| Corp. | Corporation |
| Cttee. | Committee |
| E.R. | East Riding (of Yorkshire) |
| Est. | Established |
| Gram. | Grammar |
| HEH | His Exalted Highness |
| HNAFV | Her Majesty's Auxiliary Fighting Vessel |
| HQ | Headquarters |
| Inc. | Incorporated |
| k. | killed |
| KOLI | King's Own Light Infantry |
| KOSB | King's Own South Borderers |
| KRRC | King's Royal Rifle Corps |
| LI | Light Infantry |
| ME | Middle East; Mining Engineers |
| Mil. | Militia |
| MT | Motor Transport |
| Mus. | Musical |
| *NEP* | *New Extinct Peerage* |
| N.R. | North Riding (of Yorkshire) |
| RAAF | Royal Australian Air Force |
| RAF | Royal Air Force |
| RAFVR | Royal Air Force Volunteer Reserve |
| RCAF | Royal Canadian Air Force |
| RDC | Rural District Council |
| RMLI | Royal Marine Light Infantry |
| RN | Royal Navy |
| Roy. | Royal |
| Tech. | Technical |
| UDC | Urban District Council |
| VRC | Volunteer Rifle Corps |
| Ven. | Venerable |
| W.R. | West Riding (of Yorkshire) |
| WRAF | Womens' Royal Air Force |

# A

| | |
|---|---|
| A BIRD IN THE HAND IS WORTH TWO IN THE BUSH | Walthall. |
| A BLESSING TO THE AGED | Spectacle Makers' Co., used since 1810 at least. |
| A BON DROIT | With good right. Slade, Bts. |
| A BONIS AD MELIORA | From good things to better. Royston (Herts.) UDC, 1952. |
| A CHACUN SON TOUR | Each in his turn. Motto generally of Dukes of Guise and of 3rd Duke, Henri de Lorraine, murdered in 1588, who had captured Calais 1558 and finally driven the English from their last territory in France. |
| A CLEAN HEART AND A CHEERFUL SPIRIT | Viscount Portman. |
| A CRUCE SALUS | Salvation from the Cross. Bourke, Burgh, Lord Connemara (Bourke) (NEP), De Burgh, Downes, Dunnington-Jefferson, Bts., Glencross, Jefferson, co. York., Earls of Mayo (Bourke). |
| A CUSPIDE CORONA | By a spear a crown. Broderick, Chapman, Earls of Midleton (Broderick). |
| ADDIODDEFURS A ORFU | Who suffers conquers. Glam. CC. |
| A DEO ET PATRE | From God and my father. Treherne. |
| A DEO ET REGE | By God and the king. Earls of Chesterfield (Stanhope) (NEP), Fawkes, Earls of Harrington (Stanhope), Lewis, Richmond (Surrey), Bor. of, Scudamore, Bts., Stanhope, Strachy, Bts. |
| A DEO ET REGINA | By God and queen. Frimley & Camberley (W. Surrey) UDC, Reading, Co. Bor. of. |
| A DEO FASCES | High office from God. Mitchell. |
| A DEO FLORUIT | It flourished from God. Lord Thankerton (Watson) (NEP), Watson. |
| A DEO GLORIA MEA | My glory is from God. Hewson. |
| A DEO HONOR ET FORTUNA | From God honour and fortune. Sandys of Dublin, Bt. |
| A DEO OMNIA | All things from God. Goodhart, Bts. |
| A DEO REX, A REGE LEX. | The king is from God, the law is from the king. Jenner. |
| A DEO VICTORIA | Victory from God. Graeme of Inchbrakie. |
| A DEUX PLUS FORTS | Two are stronger than one. No. 83 Group HQ, RAF. |
| A DOMINO POSTULAVI | I have asked of the Lord. Samuel, Bt. |
| A FAVORE REGIS NOMEN | My name is by the favour of the king. Kingan. |
| A FIN TO THE END | Earls of Airlie (Ogilvy). |
| A FLUMINE IMPUGNAMUS | From the river we strike. RAF station, Linton-on-Ouse, Cambs. |

| | |
|---|---|
| A FYNO DUW A FYDD | What God wills will be. Chambres, co. Denbigh, Cowbridge (Glam.) RDC, Hope-Edwardes, Hughes, Matthew, Walsham, Bts. |
| A FYNO DUW DERID | What God wills will be. Edwards of Hrew Bury, Bts. |
| A GAR Y GWIR A GYFYR | Who loves the truth, matters. Edwards of Knighton, Bt. |
| A GOOD NAME ENDURETH | Hornchurch (Essex) UDC. |
| A JAMAIS | For ever. James, Bts. (dormant). |
| A L'ABRI COTIER | Shelter under the tree. Jacques Coictiers, physician to Louis XI of France (1461–83). |
| A L'AMI FIDÈLE POUR JAMAIS | Always faithful to one's friend. Marquesses of Hertford (Seymour). |
| A LA VOLONTÉ DE DIEU | At the will of God. Strickland-Constable, Bts. |
| A MA PUISSANCE | To my power. Gray of Carn Park, Thomas Grey, 1st Marquess of Dorset, 1512, Hale (Ches.) UDC, Earls of Stamford (Grey). |
| A MAGNIS AD MAIORA | From great things to greater. Stepney, London Bor. of. |
| A MARI AD ASTRA | From the sea to the stars. 212 Sq., RAF. |
| A MARI USQUE AD MARE | From sea to sea. Canada. This motto refers to the title of the Dominion of Canada, made in 1867. There had been much discussion among the British committee as to the title of the country; should it be the Kingdom of Canada? This was rejected because of possible offence to US opinion. That night one of the British members, reading his Bible, came upon Psalm 72: 8: 'He shall have dominion also from sea to sea'. The next day he suggested the term 'Dominion', and this was adopted. |
| A MINIMIS INCIPE | Begin from the least. St Benedict's Sch., Ealing, 1902. |
| A NODDO DUW A NODDIR | Who supports God will be protected, or What God protects shall be protected. The Earl of Snowdon (Armstrong-Jones). |
| A PETITE CLOCHE GRAND SON | Small clock, great sound. Grandison. |
| A PLEDGE OF BETTER TIMES | Samuel, Bts. |
| A POSSE AD ESSE | From possibility to actuality. Pierrepont Sch., nr. Farnham, Surrey. |
| A PRUDENT MAN GOD WILL GUARD | Jones-Parry, Bt. |
| A REGE ET VICTORIA | From the king and from victory. Ligonier, Otter-Barry, Symes-Bullen, Thatchell. |
| A TEMPERANCE | In temperance. Joan of Navarre, d. 1437, 2nd wife of Henry IV of England, dau. of Charles II, King of Navarre, and widow of John V de Montfort, Duke of Brittany. |
| A TOT BIEN ESTRAINZ | Aim for all good. Latter. |
| A TOUT POUVOIR | To provide for everything. Oliphant, co. Perth |
| A TOUT VENANT BEAU JEU | A fair game coming to all. Beaujeu. |
| A TRIBULACIONE | By tribulation. Cokayne, Bt. |

A VAILLANS RIEN E IMPOSSIBLE — To the valiant, nothing is impossible. Jacques Coeur, *c.*1461, a financial genius under Charles VII, condemned by his enemies but escaped to take service under Pope Calixtus III.

A VO PENN BIT PONT — He who would be leader, let him be a bridge. Bridgend (Glam.) UDC.

A VOUS ENTIER — To you entirely. John, Duke of Bedford, brother of Henry V and Regent of France, d. 1435.

AB ALIIS VIRTUTE VALEMUS — From other (sources) we prevail in valour. Pedro di Navarro, a Spanish general very skilled in military mining. Served Spain and then France. Blew up Castel dell 'Uovo at Naples, but being captured by Charles V was smothered in 1528 in the rebuilt 'Egg Castle'.

AB INSOMNI NON CUSTODITA DRACONE — Not guarded by a sleepless dragon. Cardinal Ferrara, *c.*1572, Ippolito d'Este, Papal Legate when Henry IV of France was thinking of being converted to catholicism. The motto taken in compliment to the Gallic Hercules and the Gardens of the Hesperides.

AB INITIO — From the beginning. No. 1 Elementary Flying Training Sch., RAF.

AB OBICE SUAVIOR — More smooth from an obstacle. Galbraith, Lords Strathclyde (Galbraith).

AB UNO DISCE OMNES — From one teach all. 59 Sq., RAF.

ABAL BREOTAN — A. Ababrelton. Motto of arms registered in Lyon Office. Jon Davies, *Armorial Families.* Thought by Lyon Office to be a play on surname.

ABARTH KERNOW (CORNISH) — For Cornwall. Evelby.

ABEUNT STUDIA IN MORES — Studies go out (i.e. show themselves) in manners. Coll. St Mark and St John (formerly in Chelsea). Motto is a saying quoted by Francis Bacon in his essay on Study.

ABILITY AND AMBITION OF THE HIGHEST (ORIGINAL IN CHINESE SCRIPT) — RAF station, Hong Kong, formerly Kai Tak.

ABOVE ALL — 542 Sq., RAF. On badge is a terrestrial globe because sq. operated all over the world.

ABSCISSA VIRESCIT — Cut off, yet it blossoms. Bisset, co. Aberdeen. Has for crest the trunk of an oak tree sprouting afresh.

ABSQUE LABORE NIHIL — Nothing without labour. Darwen (Lancs.) Bor. of, Down CC, Edwards of Treforest, Bts., Stalybridge (Ches.) Bor. of, Steele Bts.

ABUNE THE LAVE — Above the rest. St Andrew's Univ. Air Sq., RAFVR.

ABUNE THE LAVROCK — Higher than the lark. East Lowlands Univ. Air Sq., RAFVR.

ACCEDIT NEMO IMPUNE — No one approaches with impunity. HQ, RAF, Malta.

ACCENDIT CANTU — He animates by crowing. Cockburn. Motto above crest of a cock crowing.

ACCEPT — RAF Inspectorate of Recruiting.

ACCURACY — 578 Sq. RAF (bombing sq.).

| | |
|---|---|
| ACER AD HOSTEM | Eager for the enemy. 54 Base, RAF. |
| ACER ET EXACTUS | Bold and exact. Assn. of Consulting Engineers. |
| ACER NON EFFRENUS | Bold not unbridled. Viscount Milner *(NEP)*. |
| ACHIEVE | Speaight, No. 3 Flying Training Sch., RAF. |
| ACHIEVE YOUR AIM | 97 Sq., RAF. Badge is an ogress pierced by an arrow. |
| ACIEM ACRUNT ACULEI | Stings sharpen his keeness. Italian Literary Academy of the Offuscati. |
| ACHIEVEMENT | No. 73 Operational Training Unit, RAF. |
| ACQUIRITUR QUI TUETUR | He who defends, obtains. Hingley Bts., Mortimer of Auchenbody. |
| ACRA SEMPER ACRIA | The peninsula is always eager. RAF station, Akrotiri, Cyprus. |
| ACTA NON VERBA | Acts not words. Jameson. |
| ACTION | Bognor Regis (W. Sussex) UDC. |
| ACTION REACTION | 26 Sq., RAF Regt. |
| ACTIVE IN REPOSE | 3513 Fighter Control Unit, RAAF. |
| ACUIT UT PENETRAT | It sharpens as it goes in. John I (1385–1433) King of Portugal who m. 1386 Philippa, dau. of John of Gaunt and Blanche of Castile. Under this king began the Portuguese alliance with England as her oldest ally. |
| A'CUMAIL SUAS N'AS FHEARR | Best maintenance only. RAF station, Greenock, Renfrew. |
| AD ALAUNAN AD NASHUAM | From the Alauna to the Nashua. Lancaster, Mass. This town is on the river Nashua; Alauna was the Latin form of Lune, the river on which is the English Lancaster. |
| AD ALIOS ADJUVANDO POTENS | Powerful in helping others. Contingency Insurance Co. Ltd. |
| AD ALTA | To high things. Cairnie, Lord Cautley *(NEP)*. |
| AD ALTIORA | To higher things. Kirton. |
| AD AMUSSIM | Exactly (i.e. to a carpenter's rule). Cuninghame of Caprington, co. Ayr. This wording is in a scroll over the first crest of this family, i.e. a hand holding a plumb rule (crest of Cuninghame, 2nd crest being that of Dick), Dick Cunningham, Bts. |
| AD ARMA PARATI | Ready for battle. 93 Sq., RAF (badge is an escarbuncle, a heraldic charge which arose from the metal bands radiating from the shield and used to strengthen it). |
| AD ASTRA | To the stars. The Viscounts Astor (part play on the name, and part allusion to three mullets in the crest), also used by the Lords Astor. |
| AD ASTRA SEQUOR | I follow the stars. Tottenham, co. Wexford. |
| AD ASTRA VIRTUS | Virtue rises to the stars. Saltmarshe. |
| AD AURORAM | To the dawn. 255 Sq., RAF. |
| AD DEI GLORIAM | To the glory of God. Southend High Sch. for Girls, Essex. |

| | |
|---|---|
| AD EXTREMUM TENAX | Tenacious to the end. Macready, Bts. |
| AD FINEM | To the end. 238 Sq., RAF. |
| AD FINEM FIDELIS | Faithful to the end. Colville, Daubeney, Gilroy, Howson, Kerslake, Peto, Bts., Wedderburn, Whitehead. |
| AD GLORIAM PER SPINAS | To glory through the thorns. Shebbear Coll., nr. Holsworthy, Devon, 1841. |
| AD HONOREM INDUSTRIA DUCIT | Industry leads to honour. Joynson. |
| AD LIBERATEM VOLAMUS | We fly to liberty. 86 Sq., RAF. |
| AD LUCEM | Towards the light. Goudhurst Coll., Ltd., nr. Cranbrook, Kent, Ophthalmological Soc. of UK. |
| AD MAJOREM DEI GLORIAM | To the greater glory of God. The Soc. of Jesus, commonly called Jesuits, Roman Catholic religious order founded in 1534 by a Spaniard, St Ignatius Loyola, and approved by the Pope in 1540. The order was suppressed in 1773 but revived in 1814. St Ignatius Coll., Tottenham, Middx. |
| AD MELIORA | To better things. Mellor. |
| AD METAM | To the mark. Bower, Bt. (had an archer as crest), Combrey, Comrie, Comry, 415 Sq., RCAF. |
| AD MOREM VILLAE DE POOLE | In the custom of the town of Poole. Poole (Dorset), Bor. of. |
| AD OMNIA ORDINANDA | For the purpose of arranging everything in order. RAF Record Office, RAF Personnel Management Centre. |
| AD OMNIA PARATUS | Ready for anything. Air Traffic Control Centre, RAF. |
| AD PATRIAM FIRMANDAM | For the strengthening of the country. WRAF depot. |
| AD PONTES PROSPICIMUS | We look to the bridges. Staines (Middx.) UDC, 1951. |
| AD REM | To the point. Osmaston, Wright of Wootton Court. |
| AD REPUGNANDUM RENATUS | Reborn to hit back. RAF station, Krendi, Malta. |
| AD SALTUM PARATUS | Ready for the jump. 416 Sq., RCAF. |
| AD SANGUINEM | To the blood. Goodenough, Bts. |
| AD SERVIENDUM NITOR | I strive to serve. No. 90 Maintenance Unit, RAF. |
| AD SIDERA TOLLITE VULTUS | Raise your countenance to the stars. Carr, co. Norfolk. |
| AD SUAM QUISQUE OPERAM | Each to his own affairs. No. 28 Group HQ, RAF. |
| AD SUMMA NITAMUR | Let us strive for the heights. Croydon, London Bor. of. |
| AD VIGILAMUS UNDIS | We watch (in) the waves. 413 Sq., RCAF. |
| ADDECET HONESTE VIVERE | It much becomes us to live honourably. Addison. |
| ADDERE LEGI JUSTITIAM DECUS EST | It is an ornament to add justice to law. Adderley, Lords Norton (Adderley). |
| ADDIMUS VIM VIRIBUS | We add strength to strength. 256 Sq., RAF. |
| ADDIT FRENA FERUS | He puts bridles on wild beasts. Milner, Bts. |
| ADESTE COMITES | Rally round, comrades. 32 (fighter) Sq., RAF. |
| ADHAEREO VIRTUTI | I cling to virtue. Kennedy, Bts., Kennedy, co. Lancs. |

| | |
|---|---|
| ADHUC HIC HESTERNA | Thus far here yesterday. Chichester (W. Sussex) RDC. |
| ADHUC STAT | It still stands. Queen Dowager of Scotland, Mary of Lorraine, widow of James V and mother of Mary Queen of Scots. |
| ADJIDAUMO (CHIPPEWAY INDIAN) | Tail-in-the-Air. 268 Sq., RAF (a tomahawk, which is part of the badge, was in connection with Tomahawk aircraft used at one time). |
| ADJUTORES MULTORUM | In support of many. RAF station, Watton, Norfolk. |
| ADJUVAMUS TUENDO | We assist by watching. 13 Sq., RAF. |
| ADJUVANTE DEO | God my helper. Acton, Lords Kindersley, Kindersley-Porcher, Malins, Nicholson, Philips. |
| ADJUVANTE DEO IN HOSTES | God aiding against enemies. O'Donovan. |
| ADJUVATE ADVENAS | Help strangers. Deal (Kent), Bor. of. |
| ADORIENS DEFENDE | In striking defend. RAF station, Turnhouse, Edinburgh. |
| ADSIT DEUS | May God be present. Lords Balfour of Inchrye (Balfour). |
| ADSTANTES | Standing by them. 111 Sq., RAF. |
| ADSURGENTES PUGNAMUS | Rising we fight. RAF station, Horsham St Faith, Norfolk. |
| ADVANCE | Birkmyre, Bts., Brand, Ferrier of Belsyde, Goole (W.R. Yorks.) UDC, Sayer, Spiers of Eldershe. |
| ADVANCE DARNGLE | Dukes of Richmond and Gordon (Gordon-Lennox). Motto above 1st crest of Duke. Darngle is corruption of Arkyll, legendary founder of ancient feudal Earls of Lennox. |
| ADVANCE WITH COURAGE | Marjoribanks of Lees, Bts., Lords Tweedmouth (Marjoribanks) (NEP). |
| ADVANCEZ | Advance. Chalmers, Bt. |
| ADVERSA VIRTUTE REPELLO | I repel adversity by virtue. Denison, Dennistoun, Lords Londesborough (Denison) (NEP), Medhurst. |
| ADVERSIS MAJOR | Greater in adversity. Queen Elizabeth Training Coll. for the Disabled, Leatherhead, Surrey, 1946. |
| ADVERSIS MAJOR, PAR SECUNDIS | Greater in adversity, equal in prosperity. Bulwer, Lord Dalling and Bulwer (Bulwer) (NEP), Hudson of North Hackney, Bt. |
| AEDIFICIUM NOSTRUM BENE STAT | Our building stands well. Abbey National Bldg. Soc. |
| AEGIS FORTISSIMA HONOS | Honour is the strongest shield. Inst. of Heraldry (part of US army). |
| AEGIS FORTISSIMA VIRTUS | Virtue is the strongest shield. Aspinall, co. Lancs. |
| AEQUABILITER ET DILIGENTER | By consistency and diligence. Mitford, Moore, Earl of Redesdale (Freeman-Mitford) (NEP), Lords Truro (Wilde) (NEP). |
| AEQUAM SERVARE MENTEM | To preserve an equal mind. Green, Bts., Hoyle, Mathew, Moon of Portman Square, Bts., Raymond, Rivers, Treacher. |
| AEQUANIMETER | With equanimity. Harbord, Lords Suffield (Harbord-Hamond), Shuttleworth. |
| AEQUITAS ACTIONUM REGULA | Equity is the rule of actions. Inst. of London Underwriters. |

| | |
|---|---|
| AEQUO ADESTE ANIMO | Be present with mind unchangeable. Cope of Hanwell, Bts. |
| AEQUO ANIMO | With equanimity. Jones, Pennant, Lords Penrhyn (Douglas-Pennant), Repton, 464 Sq., RAAF. |
| AEQUO PEDE PROPERA | Hasten with steady pace. East of Calcutta, Bts., Leigh (Lancs.) Bor. of. |
| AEQUUS IN ARDUIS | Equal in hard times. Thomas-Stanford, Bt. |
| AERE ET TERRAM IMPERARE | To govern the air and the earth. 193 Sq., RAF. |
| AERE INVICTI | Invincible with the brass. Central Band, RAF, Halton, nr. Aylesbury, Bucks. |
| AERE PERENNIUS | More lasting than bronze. Norman of Moor Place, Lord Norman (NEP). |
| AEQUORA DIVIDUNT CONJUNGIT CAELUM | The seas separate, the sky unites. RAF Empire Central Flying Sch. |
| AET MEA MESSIS ERIT | My life will be a harvest. Denny of Castle Moyle, Bts. |
| AETERNA CONJUGE | With eternal union. Anne of Austria, d. 1580, 4th wife of Philip II of Spain. |
| AETHEREM VINCERE | To conquer the upper air. Signals Command RAF, no. 90 Group, RAF. |
| AFGANISTAN | Montagu-Pollock, Bts. Derived from victories of 1st Bt., Field Marshal Sir George Pollock, who forced the Khyber Pass, relieved Sir Robert Dale at Jellalabad and captured Kabul 1842. He received thanks of Parliament for his services, and was cr. 1872 Bt. 'of the Khyber Pass'. |
| AGE OFFICIUM TUUM | Act your office. Abbott. |
| AGE OMNE BONUM | Do all good. Allgood of Nunwich (an obvious pun). |
| AGE PRO VIRIBUS | Do your utmost. RAF station, Colerne, nr. Chippenham, Wilts. |
| AGE QUOD AGIS | Do what you are doing. Birmingham Coll. of Commerce, Prevost of Westbourne Terrace, Bt. |
| AGGRESSIVE IN DEFENCE | RAF station, Coltishall, Norfolk. |
| AGINCOURT | Earls of Kimberley (Wodehouse), Lenthall, co. Oxon., Walker, Waller (Ázincourt), Wodehouse. The legendary origin of this motto is that the families concerned had an ancestor at the battle in 1415. As far as Wodehouse is concerned there is no evidence; the first of the family known to fame was John Wodehouse, Constable of Castle Rising, 1402. |
| AGMINA DUCENS | Leading the armies. Lords Strathcona & Mount Royal (Howard), cr. 1900, Strathcona & Mount Royal (Smith) (NEP). |
| AGNOSCAR EVENTU | I shall be known by the results. Ross of Arnage. |
| AGRICULTURE AND COMMERCE | Maidstone (Kent), Bor. of. |
| AIDANT SE JE PUIS | Helping if I can. Allhusen, co. Bucks. |
| AIDE TOI LE CIEL T'AIDERA | Aid thyself, Heaven will aid thee. Massie of Coddington. |

| | |
|---|---|
| AIDES DIEU | Help, O God. Aubert, Mill (formerly Barker), Bt. |
| AIDONS NOUS MUTUELLEMENT | Let us aid each other. Lord Tomlin *(NEP)*. |
| AIM STRAIGHT | Fletcher, Bt., Scott of Witley Bts. |
| AIM SURE | 15 Sq., RAF. |
| AIM TO SUCCEED | Coastal Cmd. Fighter Affiliation Training Unit, RAF. |
| AIME TON FRÈRE | Love thy brother. Freer, Frere. |
| AIMEZ LOYAULTÉ | Love loyalty. Lord Bolton, Cowan, Bt., Marquess of Winchester (Paulet). |
| AINSI ET PEUT ESTRE MEILLEUR | Thus and perhaps better. Rolleston, Bt. |
| AINSI IL EST | Thus it is. Bellingham, Bts. |
| AIR FHAIRE (GAELIC) | On watch. 3612 Fighter Control Unit, RAAF. |
| AIR MUIR'S AIR TIR (GAELIC) | From land and sea (*also given as* Victory or death). Macalister, Mackean, RAF station, Port Ellen, Argyll. |
| AIRM A DHIONADH NA FAIRGEACHAN (GAELIC) | Arms to defend the seas. RAF station, Machrihanish, Kintyre. |
| AKE AKE KIA KABA (MAORI) | For ever and ever. 75 Sq., RAF, composed of NZ personnel. |
| AL-I' TIMAD'ALA AK-NAFS | The reliance is on one's own self. RAF station, Masirah, Oman. |
| AL PARECER DE L'ALBA S'ASCONDAN LAS ESTRELLAS | At the appearance of the dawn, the stars hide themselves, *or*, At my appearance, al mio paracer, etc. Alba, more generally Alva, Duke of. Fernando Alvarez de Toledo. Great Spanish general, 1508–82. Motley, the American historian, gave full account of Alva's cruelties (*Rise of the Dutch Republic*, Pt. 3) in revolt of the Netherlands against Spain. At the end of his life, he, whose diet Motley said had been of blood, had to be nourished on woman's milk. |
| AL WORSHIP BE TO GOD ONLY | Fishmongers' Co., 1512, Gresham's Sch., Holt, Norfolk, founded 1555. |
| ALA MINANS | The threat of the wing. No. 26 Operational Training Unit, RAF. |
| ALACRES ILLO COLUERUNT | Eager ones attended to that. East Elloe (Parts of Lindsey, Lincs.) RDC, 1955. |
| ALAE DEFENDUNT AFRICAM | Wings defend Africa. 223 Sq., RAF. |
| ALAS EOAS DIRIGIMUS | We direct the eastern wings. Air HQ, RAF, Hong Kong. |
| ALAS TIBI PARA | Equip yourself with wings. No. 14 Elementary Flying Training Sch., RAF. |
| ALATOS RECREAMUS | We restore to health the wingborne men. RAF No. 5 Hospital, Middle East. |
| ALBAM EXORNA | Adorn Albion. St Dunstan's Coll., Catford (re-founded 1888). |
| ALBAN, ALBAN | Used by the largely Celtic warriors of the King of Scots at the Battle of the Standard, 1138, when the Scots were beaten by the English at Northallerton. |
| ALBANICH | Galloway (Kirkcudbright & Wigtown) Volunteer Rifles. |

| | |
|---|---|
| ALBERTUS ANIMOSIS | Albert to the brave. Order of Albrecht the Brave, Saxony. |
| ALERE FLAMMAN | To feed the flame. 358 Sq., RAF. |
| ALERT | RAF station, Pucklechurch. |
| ALERT THE EAGLE | 3701 County of Sussex Radar Reporting Unit, RAF. |
| ALES VOLAT PROPRIUS | The bird flies to its kind. Eley, Lords Hothfield (Tufton), Merton, Tufton. |
| ALGIERS | Viscounts Exmouth (Pellew), Pellew. Motto taken because the 1st Viscount in 1816 bombarded and destroyed the fleet and arsenal of the pirates of Algiers. In the arms is a chief of honourable augmentation showing a British warship before Algiers. |
| ALIFERO TOLLITUR AXE CERES | Ceres rising in a winged car. 610 Co. of Chester Sq., RAF. |
| ALIGEROS ALIMUS | We nourish the wing bearers. No. 53 Maintenance Unit, RAF. |
| ALIMUS | We maintain. No. 23 Maintenance Unit, RAF. |
| ALIOS ALIS ALO | With my wings I nourish others. No. 46 Group HQ, RAF. The group was engaged in the Berlin air lift. |
| ALIOS DELECTARE JUVAT | It helps to please others. Hunstanton (Norfolk) UDC. |
| ALIOS SEMPER ADJUVARE | Always to aid others. Phillips of Burnworthy Manor, Churchin-ford, nr. Taunton, Devon. |
| ALIS APTA SCIENTIS | Ready for the wings of knowing. Royal Aircraft Establishment. |
| ALIS NOCTURNIS | With night's wings. 58 Sq., RAF (has owl badge as night bombing unit). |
| ALIS VOLAT PROPRIIS | He flies on his own wings. Parker, Bt. |
| ALITUM ALTRIX | Nurturer of the winged. RAF Coll., Cranwell. |
| ALIUD AGERE QUAM NIHIL | To do anything rather than nothing. Beale, Bt. (advice given by Field Marshall Viscount Montgomery). |
| ALL FOR THE BEST | Waley-Cohen, Bts. |
| ALL POINTS WE DEFEND | 16 Sq., RAF Rgt. |
| ALL THINGS ARE OVERCOME BY DILIGENCE | Hicking of Southwell, Bts. |
| ALL THIS BEAUTY IS OF GOD | Isle of Wight CC. |
| ALL'S FOR YE BESTE | Stephens, co. Glos. |
| ALL'S WELL | Camberwell, London Bor. of. |
| ALLA CORONA FIDISSIMO | To the crown most faithful. Leche. |
| ALLA TA HARA | God my help. St John-Mildmay, Bts. (dormant). |
| ALLAH AKBER | God is great. Middleton of Bradford Peverell. |
| ALLELUIAH (SAME HEBREW EXCLAMATION AS HALLELUJAH) | Praise ye the Lord. Tuite, Bts. |
| ALLIANCE IS WISDOM | Alliance Perpetual Bldg. Soc. |

| | |
|---|---|
| ALNUS SEMPER FLOREAT | May the alder always flourish. Aldersey of Aldersey, co. Chester (a pun, *alnus* being alder in Latin). |
| ALONE ABOVE ALL | 541 Sq., RAF. |
| ALTA PETE | Aim at high things. Fletcher of Atherton Hall, Glen. |
| ALTA PETENS | Seeking high things. The Barons Addington. |
| ALTA PETIT | He seeks high things. Martin (formerly Stott), Stott, Bts. |
| ALTA PETO | I seek the heights. Lords Daresbury (Greenall) |
| ALTA SENTENTIA | High thought. Arnold (Notts.) UDC. |
| ALTE VOLO | I fly aloft. Heywood Bts., Heywood of Haresfield Court, Stonechurch, co. Glos., Heywood (Lancs.), Bor. of. |
| ALTERA LEVATUR | The other is raised. Cardinal Ascanio Piccolomini. Also used *Plena luna proxima* (The full moon is near) as he expected to be elected Pope, which he was not. |
| ALTERA MERCES | Another reward. Maclean of Ardgour. |
| ALTERA SECURITAS | A second security. Henry VII (1485–1509), alluding to his portcullis badge, sign of his descent from John of Gaunt. |
| ALTERI SI TIBI | To another if to thyself. Lords Harvey of Tasburgh, Levy, Ohlson, Bts., Saville-Onley. |
| ALTIOR ADVERS(I)O | Higher than misfortune. Order of the Griffin, Mecklenburg-Strelitz. |
| ALTIORA IN VOTIS | Higher things are in my wishes. Des Voeux, Bts., Highgate Sch., London, N6 (founded in 1565 by Sir Roger Cholmeley, Lord Chief Justice). |
| ALTIORA PETAMUS | Let us seek higher things. Univ. of Salford. |
| ALTIORA PETIMUS | We seek higher things. Finsbury, London Bor. of. |
| ALTIORA PETO | I seek higher things. No. 1 Armament Training Station, RAF, HMS *Hermes*, King's Sch., Warwick (existed *temp.* Edward the Confessor), Oliphant of Condie, Wellingborough Sch., Northants. |
| ALTIORA SEQUIMUR | We follow the higher things. Poad, Pode. |
| ALTIUS IBUNT QUI AD SUMMA NITUNTUR | They will rise highest who strive for the highest place. Forbes of Newe, Bts., Fordyce. |
| ALTIUS TANDO | I aim higher. Kinloch of Gilmerton, Bts. |
| ALTO NOMINE | With a high name. Alton (Hants.) RDC. |
| ALTRINCHAM EN AVANT | Altrincham forward. Altrincham (Ches.), Bor. of. |
| ALWAYS ADVANCING | Thornaby-on-Tees (W.R. Yorks.), Bor. of. |
| ALWAYS FAITHFUL | Andrews Bt., Andrews of co. Down, Andrews of Comber, Mackenzie of Fawley Court, Mackenzie of Hilton, Mackenzie, co. Inverness. |
| ALWAYS READY | Glanford Brigg (Lincs.) RDC, South Shields (Durham), Bor. of. |
| ALWAYS YOUR BEST | King. |
| AMA ET DAS MULTUM | Love and give much. Amadas. |
| AMAN JUST PIET FID | Order of St Anne (Russia). |

| | |
|---|---|
| AMANTES ARDUA DUMOS | The thorns which love the hills. Davie-Thornhill (motto comes from Virgil, *Georgics* iii, 315, and is a play on the name). |
| AMAT VICTORIA CURAM | Victory loves care. Clark Bts., Clerk of Norwich, Francesco de Medici, d. 1587, 2nd Grand Duke of Tuscany, Mathias, Bts., Stephenson, co. Lancs., Victoria Coll., Jersey (founded to commemorate visit of Queen Victoria, and opened 1852; bears the arms of Jersey). |
| AMENITY, PROGRESS, STABILITY | Inst. of Municipal and Co. Engineers. |
| AMICI VETERRIMI OPTIMI | The oldest friends are best. Lucas of Hitchin. |
| AMICIS NON DEFICIT AEQUIS | He is not wanting to just friends. Buckle, formerly of Chaceley, co. Worcs. (George Earle Buckle was editor of *The Times* 1884–1912). |
| AMICITIA PROGREDIMUR | We progress in friendship. Water Supply Industry Training Bd, 1967. |
| AMICITIA REDDIT HONORES | Friendship returns honours. Pringle, Bts. |
| AMICITIAE PERFICIAMUS | Let us perfect the art of friendship. Brit. Fed. of Univ. Women, Ltd. |
| AMICITIAE VIRTUTUSQUE FOEDUS | The league of friendship and virtue. Hippisley, Bts. (the motto is also that of the Grand Order of Württemberg; the Duke of Württemberg granted to the 1st Bt., Sir John Coxe Hippisley, the right to bear the arms of Württemberg because he had been instrumental in arranging the marriage in 1796 of the Princess Royal with the reigning Duke), Nelson of Beeston, co. Norfolk. |
| AMICITIAM TRAHIT AMOR | Love draws friendship. Gold and Silver Wyre Drawers' Co., inc. 1693. |
| AMICUS CERTUS | A sure friend. Ambler, co. Yorks., Peat, Peit, co. Kent. |
| AMICUS HUMANI GENERIS | Friend of the human race. Assn. of Public Health Inspectors, 1957. |
| AMO | I love. Dukes of Buccleuch (Montagu-Douglas-Scott), Hoops, MacKindlay, Scott, Swan. |
| AMO UT INVENIO | I love as I find. Perrott, Bts. |
| AMOENIORA LITORA NOSTRA | Our shores are more pleasant. Mablethorpe & Sutton (Lincs.) UDC. |
| AMOENITAS ET ANTIQUITAS | Pleasantness and antiquity. North Westmorland RDC. |
| AMOENITAS QUIES | Pleasantness is quiet. Whitby (N.R. Yorks.) RDC, 1958. |
| AMOENITAS SALUBRITAS URBANITAS | Pleasantness, healthiness and urbanity. Ryde (IOW), Bor. of. |
| AMOR ANGLIAE RUSTICAE | Love of rural England. Osgoldcross (Yorks.) RDC. |
| AMOR DEI ET PROXIMI SUMMA BEATITUDO | The love of God and our neighbour is the highest happiness. Dobbs. |
| AMOR DUCIT PATRIAE | Love of country leads. Keating. |
| AMOR E FIDELIDADE | Love and fidelity. Order of the Rose (Brazil), cr. in 1829 when Brazil was an empire under the House of Braganza. |
| AMOR ET PAX | Love and peace. Ireland of Oldfield Lodge. |

| | |
|---|---|
| AMOR PATRIAE | The love of country. Barran Bts., Brazier-Creagh, Pinney, Pretor-Pinney. |
| AMOR QUEAT OBEDIENTIAM | Love is (able to produce) obedience. Painter Stainers' Co., inc. 1581. |
| AMOR VINCIT OMNIA | Love conquers all. Ussher. |
| AMORE ET LABORE | With love and labour. St George's Coll., Weybridge, Surrey, 1869. |
| AMORE NON VI | By love not force. Viscount Amory, Heathcoat-Amory, Bts. (play on the name). |
| AMORE SITIS UNITI | Be ye united in love. Plate Workers' and Wire Workers' Co., charter 1568. |
| AMORE VICI | I have conquered by love. M'Kenzie. |
| AMOUR DE LA BONTÉ | Love of goodness. Barrie, Bts., Cowell. |
| AMSER YU'N GOLUD | Time brings riches. Ystradgynlais (Pembroke) RDC, 1951. |
| AN DEN | The man (Cornish). Endean. |
| AN GER WELLA YN AN GWYR | The best fortress is the truth (Cornish). Angear. |
| AN GOLONNEGYON A BEW PUPTRA | To the brave belong all things (Cornish). Whether. |
| ANGWYR ERLYN AN BYS | The truth against the world (Cornish). Rawe, Hambly. |
| AN HONEST MANS THE NOBLEST WORK OF GOD. | Lees, Bt. |
| AN I MAY | De Lyle, Lyle of Greenock, Bt., Montgomery, Lyle of Glendelvine Bts., Lords Lyle of Westbourne. |
| ANCHOR FAST | Gray (having an anchor as crest), Gray-Cheape (formerly Gray), co. Angus, Groat. |
| ANCHOR FAST ANCHOR | Lords Gray, Gray of Graymount. |
| ANCHORA SALUTIS | The anchor of safety. Commercial Union Assurance Co. Ltd., O'Loghlen, Bts. |
| ANCIENT AND LOYAL | Wigan (Lancs.), Bor. of. |
| ANCILLA DOMINI | The handmaid of the Lord. St Mary's Soc., Durham, 1957 (quotation from the Magnificat or Song of the Blessed Virgin Mary). |
| ANCORA IMPARO | With unequal anchor. Reading Coll. of Technology, 1960. |
| ANE STAY | Lang of Paisley. |
| ANGELIS SUIS PRAECIPET DE TE | He shall give His angels charge over thee. Power, co. Hereford (quoted from St Matthew 4:6, part of the devil's words to Christ, but originally from Psalm 91:11). |
| ANGLIAE COR | The heart of England. Hinckley (Leics.) UDC. |
| ANIMA IN AMICUS UNA | One feeling among friends. Powell. |
| ANIMIS ET FATI | By boldness and by fortune. Threipland, Bts. |
| ANIMO ET CONSILIO | With heart and counsel. Clarke of Gatcombe Park. |

ANIMO ET FIDE — With spirit and faith. 18 Sq., RAF (Pegasus badge, sq. being first to co-operate with cavalry on the Somme, 1914–18).

ANIMO ET FIDE — By courage and faith. Burroughs, co. Norfolk, Cornock, co. Wexford, Dill, Lords Essendon (Lewis), Grotrian, Bts., Earls of Guildford (North), Humphreys, co. Cork, Lords Leighton of St Mellons (Seagar), Lever, Bts., Levy, Bts., Lords North *(NEP)*, North of Southwell, Bts., North of Eltham, North, co. Lancs., Phillips-Scourfield, Bts., Seagar, Stockport (Lancs.), Co. Bor. of, Ward of Wellington, Bts.

ANIMO ET PRUDENTIA — By courage and prudence. Jowitt.

ANIMO ET SCIENTIA — By spirit and knowledge. Clark-Maxwell of Speddoch.

ANIMO FIDE ET HONORE — With soul, faith and honour. Richardson of Yellow Woods, Bts.

ANIMO ET LABORE — By spirit and labor. Lord Marks *(NEP)*.

ANIMO LIBERO DIRIGIMUR — We are guided by the mind of liberty. 320 Sq., RAF, Netherlands, 1941.

ANIMO NON ASTUTIA — By courage not by craft. Conway-Gordon, Gordon, co. Down, Gordon of Northcourt, Bts., Viscounts Hudson *(NEP)*, Marquesses of Huntley (Gordon), Pedlar, Smith-Gordon, Bts.

ANIMUM REGE — Rule thy mind. Alcock-Beck, Day, Keith, Bts., Moore.

ANIMUS NON DEFICIT AEQUUS — Equanimity is not wanting. Lords Gwyder (Burrell) *(NEP)*.

ANIMUS NON RES — Mind not circumstance. Huth.

ANIMUS TAMEN IDEM — Yet our mind is unchanged. Cuffe, Bts., Fearnley-Whittingstall, Wheeler, Bts.

ANNETH GOTH AGAN TASOW — Old dwelling of our fathers Nancarrow, Hendra (Cornish).

ANORCHFYGOL — Irresistible. Montgomeryshire Yeomanry.

ANTE EXPECTATEM DIEM — Before the expected day. Kemmis-Steiman.

ANTE FERIT QUAM FLAMMA MICIT — Before the flame sparkles, it strikes. Philip the Good, Duke of Burgundy *c*.1467, founder of the Order of the Golden Fleece.

ANTE HONOREM EST HUMILITAS — Humility is before honour. Battersby, co. Westmeath.

ANTE LUCEM — Before the dawn. 38 Sq., RAF, formed in E. Anglia (hence heron badge, as this bird seeks its prey early).

ANTE OBITUM NEMO FELIX — Call no man happy before his death. Witts. Famous Greek saying attributed to Solon; used by André Maurois as title of one of his books.

ANTE OMNIA DEUS — God before all things. Inman of Highmoor Hall.

ANTIQUA CONSTANS VIRTUTE — Constant in ancient virtue. Arundel (Sussex), Bor. of.

ANTIQUAE FAMAE CUSTOS — Guardian of ancient renown. HMS *Renown*.

ANTIQUI COLANT ANTIQUUM DIERUM — Let men of the ancient virtues worship the Ancient of Days. Chester, City of.

| | |
|---|---|
| ANTIQUUM DECUS FLOREAT | May old time honour flourish. Oldbury (Worcs.) UDC. |
| ANTIQUUM OBTINENS | Holding our ancient honour (*honorem* being understood). Bagot of Galway, Bagot, Bts., the Lords Bagot, Beaumont, Colgreave, Warwick, Bor. of. |
| ANTURIAF | I venture. Jones of Liverpool. |
| ANYWHERE, ANY TIME | No. 10 Flying Training Sch., RAF. |
| AP ITHEL | Lords Westbury (Bethell). |
| APERTO VIVERE VOTO | To live without a wish concealed. Chamier, The Earls of Aylesford (Finch-Knightly), Gould, Wright. |
| API SOYA PARAGASAMU (Sinhalese) | (We seek and strike. 160 Sq., RAF (unit operated from Ceylon, badge Sinhalese lion). |
| APPETITUS RATIONI PAREAT | Let your desires obey your reason. Earls Fitzwilliam, Custance, co. Norfolk. |
| APPRENDRE ET TENIR | To learn and to hold. Lord Willoughby de Eresby, *temp.* Elizabeth I (*B.P.* Earl of Ancaster). |
| APRÈS MOI LE DELUGE | After me, the deluge. 617 Sq., RAF. This was the famous saying of Louis XV of France, 'Le bien-aimé', referring to the coming revolution; nothing could be more appropriate to this sq., which has a broken wall pierced by flashes of lightning to commemorate sq.'s successful attack on enemy dams, May 1943. |
| AQUAM EDUXISTI EIS | You have brought water to them. Doncaster & District Water Bd. |
| AQUILA NON (CAPTAT) CAPIT MUSCAS | The eagle catcheth not flies. Bedingfield, Buller, Chinn, Viscount Dilhorne (Manningham-Buller), Drake, Graves, Greaves, Gothard, Illidge, Keevil, Simpson, Steel, Trant, Weddeburn, Weston, Wright, co. Yorks., Lords Churston (Yarde-Buller). |
| AQUILA SUPRA VOLAT | The eagle flies above. Kingsford. |
| AQUILIS OSTENDERE PRAEDAM | To show the eagles their prey. 3618 Co., Sussex Fighter Control Unit, RAAF. |
| AR DDUW Y GYD | All depend on God. Lewis, Lloyd, Phillips. |
| AR DUW Y GYD | All on God. Price of Trengwainton, Bts. |
| AR ESGYLL DYSG | On the wings of learning. Univ. of Wales Air Sq. |
| AR NYD YW PWYLL PYD YW | Lords Baden-Powell. |
| AR OL GWAITH GORPHVYS | After toil rest. Lloyd of Cowesby. |
| ARA FEJN HU (PRESUMABLY MALTESE) | Look where it is. 185 Sq., RAF (Maltese cross as part of badge; sq. in Malta during severe enemy attacks in World War II). |
| ARATE SULCO RECTE | Plough rightly in a furrow. Rochford (Essex) RDC. |
| ARBOR NE CAREAT NUCE | Let the tree never lack a nut. Nussey, Bts. |
| ARBOR VITAE CHRISTUS, FRUCTUS PER FIDEM GUSTAMUS | Christ, the tree of life, we taste the fruit by faith. Fruiterers' Co., 1607. |
| ARCUI MEO NON CONFIDO | I trust not to my bow. Wilks, Bt. |
| ARDENS FIDE | Burning with faith. Brentwood (Essex) UDC. |

| | |
|---|---|
| ARDENS IN IGNIS | Burning in fire. N. Ireland Fire Authority. |
| ARDENT | Lawrence. |
| ARDUA PETIT ARDEA | The heron seeks the heights. Heron of Newark, Bts. |
| ARDUA SEMPER | Always the heights. Dr William's Sch., Dolgelly, Merioneth. |
| ARDUA TENDO | I rise on high. Malcolm, Bts. |
| ARDUA VINCE MERENDO | Conquer hard things by deserving. Winchester RDC. |
| ARDUA VIRTUTEM | The heights produce virtue. Giovanni Battista Cybo, Pope Innocent VIII. |
| ARDUIS SAEPE METU NUNQUAM | Often in difficulties, never in fear. Lords Brassey of Apethorpe (NEP). |
| ARDUUS AD SOLEM | Arduous to the sun. Univ. of Manchester. |
| ARF DOETH YW PWYLL | The weapon of the wise is care. No. 19 Maintenance Unit, RAF. |
| ARISE TO PROTECT | RAF station, Manston, Kent. |
| ARM WELL AIM WELL | No. 11 Operational Training Unit, RAF. |
| ARMA PACIS FULCRA | Arms the levers of peace. The Hon. Artillery Co., North Somerset Imperial Yeomanry, HAC Territorials. |
| ARMARE IN PROELIA FRATRES | To equip our brethren for the fray. No. 280 Maintenance Unit, RAF. |
| ARMATUS NON LACESSITUR | An armed man is not attacked. RAF station, Scampton, Lincs. |
| ARMÉ A TOUS POINTS | Armed at all points. Byrom, Eden. |
| ARMÉ DE FOI HARDI | Armed with strong faith. Earls of Cranbrook (Gathorne-Hardy), Hardy, Bts., Hardy of Broughton Court. |
| ARMED BY KNOWLEDGE | No. 15 Sch. of Technical Training, RAF. |
| ARMET NOS ULTIO REGUM | Let vengeance for princes arm us. Viscount Portal of Hungerford (NEP). The pedigree of the Lords Portal is traced to 1456 in France; it is related that an earlier Raymond de Portal was a member of the expedition into Spain under Bertrand du Guesclin to avenge the death of Blanche of Bourbon, queen of Pedro the Cruel, King of Castile. |
| ARMING TO STRIKE | No. 7 Flying Training Sch., RAF. |
| ARMIS DIVERSIS UNANIMO IMPETU | With different arms but united in attack. HQ Army Co-op. Cmd., RAF. |
| ARMIS ET INDUSTRIA | By arms and industry. Cochran of Ashkirk. |
| ARMS AND THE MAN | No. 2 Air Armament Sch., RAF (motto is the title of one of Bernard Shaw's best-known plays). |
| ARRIVERETTE | Cameron of Fassiefern, Bt. The motto which is borne above the crest commemorates the gallant leadership of Col. John Cameron in 1813 in securing the passage of the River Gave at Arriverette, nr. Bayonne. Col. Cameron d. 1815 at Quatre Bras, but a baronetcy was bestowed on his father, Sir Ewen Cameron, in consideration of his son's services. |

| | |
|---|---|
| ARROYO DOS MOLINOS | Stream of the mills. 34th Foot (the Border Regt.), Royal Cumberland Militia. |
| ARS EST CELARE ARTEM | The art is to conceal the art. Central Signals Est., RAF. |
| ARS IMPRESSÓRIA GENTIUM CONCORDIA | Art expressed is concord of nations. Viscount Southwood (Elias) *(NEP)*. |
| ARS LENIT ITER | Skill smooths the journey. RAF Movements Sch. |
| ARS LONGA VITA BREVIS | Art is long, life is short. Millais, Bts. The original baronet was the famous Victorian painter. |
| ARS NON HABET INIMICUM NISI IGNORANTIUM | Art has no enemy except that of the ignorant. British Antique Dealers' Assn. Ltd. |
| ARS SCIENTIA MORES | Art, science and morals. British Dental Assn. |
| ARSO IL MORTAL, AL CIEL N'ANDRA L'ETERNO | The mortal burns, the eternal will go to heaven. Academy of Infiammati of Padua, Leone Orsini, Bishop of Fréjus, Var, France. |
| ART AND INDUSTRY | Trevithick of Gt. Trevemedoc, St Eval, Cornwall. |
| ART, INDUSTRY, CONTENTMENT | Basildon Development Corp., Essex. |
| ARTE CONSERVATUS | Saved by art. Christopher of Norton, co. Herts. |
| ARTE ET ANIMO | By art and mind. Ferguson of Kilmundy, Fergusson, Ground Radio Servicing Sq., RAF. |
| ARTE ET INDUSTRIA | By art and industry. Sowerby (Lancs.) UDC. |
| ARTE ET LABORE | By art and labour. Blackburn, Co. Bor. of. |
| ARTE ET SCIENTIA DITAMUR | We are enriched by art and science. Mid-Essex Tech. Coll. & Sch. of Art. |
| ARTE FAVENTE NIL DESPERANDUM | Supported by skill, there is no cause for despair. Leek (Staffs.) UDC. |
| ARTE, MARTE, VIGORE | By art, by war, by vigour. Wednesbury (Staffs.), Bor. of. |
| ARTE UTILE FACIO | I act usefully by art. Craig of Alsager, Bt. |
| ARTEM TUAM AMA | Love thy art. Wontner. |
| ARTES DANT GLORIAM | Accomplishments add lustre. No. 66 Maintenance Unit, RAF. |
| ARTIBUS ET ARMIS | By arts and arms. Harwood-Elton, Bt. |
| ARTS AND TRADE UNITED | Fanmakers' Co., inc. 1709. |
| ARVORUM CULTUS PECORUMQUE | The culture of fields and cattle. Royal Agricultural Coll., Wye, Kent. |
| ARX CELEBRIS FONTIBUS | A stronghold famed for its springs. Harrogate (W.R. Yorks.), Bor. of. |
| AS GOD WILL SO BE IT | Worshipful Co. of Blacksmiths (ancient motto). |
| AS GOD WILLS | Lord Winterstoke (Wills) *(NEP)*. |
| ASCENDAM | I shall rise. Kennaway, Bts. |
| ASGRE LAN DIOGEL EI PHERCHEN | A good conscience is the best shield. Herbert, Lord Treowen (Herbert) *(NEP)*, Vaughan of Nannau, Williams-Vaughan. |

| | |
|---|---|
| ASK OF THE BEASTS AND THEY SHALL TEACH THEE | Bristol Zoological Soc., 1834. |
| ASPERA ME JUVANT | Difficulties delight me. Low, Morrison-Low, Bts. |
| ASPICE ET IMITARE | Look and imitate. No. 6 Flying Training Sch., RAF. |
| ASPICE FINEM | Look to the end. West Penwith (Cornwall) RDC 1953. |
| ASPICE RESPICE | Behold, look back. Wellingborough (Northants.) UDC 1949. |
| ASPICE UT ASPICIAR | Behold me that I may be beheld. Louise de Vaudémont, d. 1601, wife of Henry III of France – see *Manet ultima coelo* – a wife completely neglected, he being homosexual. |
| ASPICIT ET INSPICIT | It looks at and into. Giambattista della Porta, using it as member of Neapolitan branch of natural history Academy of the Lincei (Rome, 1603). |
| ASPIRE | Chesterfield (Derbys.), Bor. of. |
| ASPIRE, PERSEVERE AND INDULGE NOT | Adams, co. Carmarthen. |
| ASPIRO | I aspire. Bolton, Curry, M'Feil, Ramsey of Balmain, Bts. |
| ASPIRO ET PERSTO | I aspire and persist. Johns. |
| ASSHER DURE | Phonetic rendering of the French *acier dure* = steel is hard (wrongly given as *assez dure*, sufficiently hard), Ironmongers' Co., inc. 1463. |
| ASSIDUE EXQUIRENDO SERVIRE | Assiduously to serve by seeking out. Inst. of Gas Engineers. |
| ASSIDUE PORTAMUS | We carry with regularity. 147 Sq., RAF (transport). |
| ASSIDUITATE | By assiduity. Albert, Archduke of Austria, d. 1621, Gov. of Spanish Netherlands, m. Isabella, dau. of Philip II of Spain. |
| ASSIDUITATE NON DESIDIA | By diligence, not by sloth. King William's Coll., I. of Man (founded by Bishop Isaac Barrow, 1668), Lords Loch, Loch of Drylaw and Rachan, No. 23 Service Flying Training Sch., RAF. |
| ASTRA CASTRA, NOMEN LUMEN | The stars are my camp, (Thy) name my light (sometimes varied to *lumen munimen* – thy light my guard). Earls of Crawford & Balcarres, Lord Wantage (Loyd-Lindsay) (NEP). |
| ASTRA, CASTRA NUMEN LUMEN MUNIMEN | Stars, camps, deity, light and help. Lindsay (formerly Trotter), Bts. |
| AT COMMAUNDEMENT OF OWRE SUPERIORS | Waterman & Lightermens' Co., inc. 1827. |
| AT FIRST SIGHT | 627 Sq., RAF. |
| AT SPES INFRACTA | Yet my hope is unbroken. Conyngham, Bts., Dick, Dick-Cunningham, Bts., Hood, Hope of Craighall, Bts., Hope, co. Hants., Dukes of Newcastle under Lyme (Hope), Lords Rankeillour (Hope). |
| AT SPES NON FRACTA | But my hope is not broken. Blaenavon (Mon.) UDC, Hope of Kinnettles, Bt., Earls of Hopetown, Kennard, Bts., Marquesses of Linlithgow (Hope) (the crest of Hope is a globe fractured at top under a rainbow). |

| | |
|---|---|
| ATTACK | 174 Sq., RAF. |
| ATTACK AND PROTECT | RAF station, Leuchars, Fife. |
| ATTACK TO DEFEND | RAF station, Tangmere, Sussex (a lion is a principal charge in the badge, from the arms of Chichester, Tangmere being 5 miles away). |
| ATTENDE ET VIGILA | Be alert and on guard. 283 Sq., RAF, formed 1943 at Algiers. |
| ATTINGO RURA | I touch country matters. Thingoe (Suffolk) RDC, 1958. A good instance of a punning motto. |
| AU BON DROIT | With good right. Dalling, Bts., Lords Egremont & Leconfield (Wyndham), Windom, Wyndom of Orchard Wyndom. |
| AU COURANT | Well informed. No. 409 Signals Unit, RAF. |
| AU GUET, AU GUET! | To watch, to watch! Genlis. |
| AU PLAISIR FORT DF DIEU | To the powerful pleasure of God. Earls of Mount Edgcumbe, Sir Percy Edgecombe. |
| AU ROY DONNE DEVOIR | Give duty to the king. Royden, Bts. |
| AUCTO SPLENDORE RESURGO | I rise again with increased splendour. 85th Foot, Shropshire L.I. |
| AUCTOR PRETIOSA FACIT | The Giver makes them valuable. Earls of Buckinghamshire (Hobart-Hampden), Hobart, Bts., Lubbock, Bt., Parker of Hanthorpe, Raymond. |
| AUCTORE DEO | With God for Author. Campion Sch., Hornchurch Essex. |
| AUDACES FORTUNA JUVAT | Fortune favours the bold. Barrow, Bloxham, Bowen, Bts., Burroughs, Carpenter, Chamberlaine, Charles, Archduke of Austria (3rd son of Ferdinand I and a suitor of Elizabeth I), Cosby of Stradbally, Costello, Forster, Bts., Davenport of Bramhall, Hayes, Kemble, King, Bts., King of Corrard, Morgan, Roberts, Bt., Stewart, Turnbull, Woulfe Flanagan. |
| AUDACES PRORSUM | Forward the bold. Boldon (Durham) UDC. |
| AUDACITER | Boldly. Ewen of Craigton, Orr Ewing, Bts., Orr Ewen of Hendon, Bts. |
| AUDACTER | Boldly. HMS *Amazon*. |
| AUDACTER ET APERTE | Boldly and openly. Lords Stratheden and Campbell (Campbell). |
| AUDACTER ET SINCERE | Boldly and sincerely. Castleford (W.R. Yorks.), Bor. of, Clive of Whitfield, co. Hereford, Earls of Powis (Clive), Essex Imp. Yeo., Essex Yeo. Dragoons. |
| AUDACTER ET STRENUE | Boldly and earnestly. Blyth, Crawfurd-Pollok, Bt., Viscount Hanworth (Pollock), Montagu-Pollock, Bts., Pollock of Hatton, Bts. |
| AUDACTER TOLLE | Bear boldly. Guthe. |
| AUDAX ERO | I will be bold. Boldero. |
| AUDAX ET CELER | Audacious and swift. Pearce of Cardell, Bts. |
| AUDAX IN RECTO | Bold in the right. Stewart of Blackhouse. |

| | |
|---|---|
| AUDAX OMNIA PERPETI | Bold to endure anything. 54 Sq., RAF. |
| AUDAX VINCENDO | Bold in conquering. Ashwin, co. Worcs. |
| AUDE ET PRAEVALEBIS | Dare and thou shalt prevail. Rochdale Grammar Sch., 1966. |
| AUDEMUS DUM VAVEMUS | Wallasey (Ches.), Bor. of, 1910. |
| AUDENTES FORTUNA JUVAT | Fortune favours the bold. Davenport, Mackinnon, Moubray. Mowbray, Turing. |
| AUDENTIOR | Bolder. Watford, Bor. of, 1922. |
| AUDENTIOR ITO | Forward more valiantly. Bristol Univ. Air Sq., RAFVR. |
| AUDEO | I dare. Rose of Hardwick House, Bts., Rose of Montreal, Bts., Rose of Houghton Conquest, Trelawny-Ross. |
| AUDI CONSILIUM | Heed counsel. West Riding of Yorks. CC, 1927. |
| AUDI, VIDE, TACE | Hear, see, keep silence. United Grand Lodge of Freemasons. (Motto is often accompanied by sketch of three wise monkeys, each with gesture appropriate to the words of the motto.) |
| AUDIENT SURDI MULTIQUE LOQUENTUR | The deaf shall hear and many shall speak. Royal National Throat, Nose and Ear Hosp., London, 1951. |
| AUDIO SED TACEO | I hear but say nothing. Lords Kesteven (Trollop) *(NEP)*, Trollop, Bts. |
| AURIS VITALIBUS VESCI | To feed on vital airs. British Oxygen Co. Ltd. |
| AUSPICE CHRISTO | Under the guidance of Christ. Ferguson Davie, Bts., Lawley, Bt., Lords Wenlock (Lawley) *(NEP)*. |
| AUSPICE TEUCRO | Under the auspices of Teucer. Tucker (Virgilian quotation or adaptation of same). |
| AUSPICIUM MELIORIS AEVI | A pledge of better times. Dukes of St Albans (de Vere Beauclerk), Order of St Michael & St George, Raffles. |
| AUSTRALIA | Commonwealth of Australia, 1912. |
| AUT AGERE AUT MORI | Either do or die. Barclay-Harvey. |
| AUT CAESAR AUT NIHIL | Either Caesar or nothing. Cesare Borgia, bastard son of Pope Alexander VI, k. in 1507, had many titles and offices, including cardinalate. Ladislaus of Durazzo, d. 1414, had vision of conquering all Italy and of becoming Emperor, styled himself King of Rome. |
| AUT DISCE AUT DISCEDE | Learn or depart. No. 6 Sch. of Tech. Training, RAF. |
| AUT INVENTIAM VIAM AUT FACIAM | I will either make or invent a way. Lord Snow (Life Baron). |
| AUT MAXIMA PARATI MINIMAVE | Prepared for the greatest or the least. Northern Rock Bldg. Soc. |
| AUT MORS AUT LIBERTAS | Either death or liberty. Braddon. |
| AUT MORS AUT VICTORIA | Death or victory. Jackson of Stansted, Bts. |
| AUT MORS AUT VITA DECORA | Either death or honourable life. Barclay-Harvey, Gordon, Shaw. |
| AUT NUMQUAM TENTES AUT PERFICE | Either never attempt, or accomplish. Bennet, Cresswell, co. Gloucs., Crouch, Day, Dorset, Greenaway, Bts., Hustler, Nuttall, Bts., Parkin-Moore, Marquesses of Reading (Isaacs), Sackville. |

| | |
|---|---|
| AUT NUNC AUT NUNQUAM | Now or never. Charles V, Duke of Lorraine, d. 1690. |
| AUT PAX AUT BELLUM | Either peace or war. Lord Donaldson of Kingsbridge (Life Baron), Donaldson of Kinnardie, Gunn, Hall, Heaton, Morris, Tweedie. |
| AUT PORTARE AUT PUGNARE PROMPTI | Ready to carry or fight. RAF station, Northolt, Middx. |
| AUT PUGNA AUT MORIRE | Either fight or die. 92 Sq., RAF (East Indian). Sq. was associated with East India; during World War I was a Canadian unit. |
| AUT SUAVITATE AUT VI | By gentleness or by force. Hopkins, Bts. |
| AUT VIAM INVENIAM AUT FACIAM | Either I will find a way or I will make a way. Chigwell Sch., Essex (founded 1629 by Samuel Harsnett, Archbishop of York). |
| AUT VINCAM AUT PERIBO | I will either conquer or perish. Chudley, Tacon. |
| AUT VINCERE AUT MORI | Victory or death. Fitzgerald-Lombard, Power, Wrekin Coll., Salop, 1880. |
| AUX GRANDS MAUX LES GRANDS REMÈDES | To desperate evils, desperate remedies. No. 95 Maintenance Unit, RAF. |
| AUXILIIS NOSTRIS DEFENDIMUS | We defend with our aids. RAF Signals Unit, Malta. |
| AUXILIO DIVINO | By divine aid. Devon CC, HMS *Devonshire*, Drake of Buckland, Bts., Ref. to crest of Sir Francis Drake (from the brother of whom this family descended) – a ship drawn round a terrestrial globe with a cable rope by a hand out of the clouds; on a scroll the motto. Drake Bn., Royal Naval Div. |
| AUXILIUM A CAELO | Help from heaven. 228 Sq., RAF. |
| AUXILIUM A DOMINO | Our help is from the Lord. Londonderry CC. |
| AUXILIUM AB ALTO | Aid from above. Lords Clonbrock (Dillon) *(NEP)*, Dillon, Bts., Killett, King, Machin, Martin, Bts., Lord Normand *(NEP)*, Ordell, Earls of Rosscommon (Dillon). |
| AUXILIUM AQUILIS | Aid to the eagles. 3507 Co. of Somerset Fighter Control Unit, RAAF. |
| AUXILIUM DE SUPERIS | Help from above. Lysaght. |
| AUXILIUM MEUM A DOMINO | My help is from the Lord. Collyer, Lloyd, Lords Mostyn, Mostyn, Bts., Price, Bts. |
| AVANCEZ | Advance. Chalmers of Culto, Chambers, Churton, Viscount Hill. |
| AVANT | Forward. Stewart of Allanbank, Bts. Stirling-Stewart, Stuart. |
| AVANT DARNLEY | Forward Darnley. Stewart of Hornhead. |
| AVANT SANS PEUR | Forward without fear. Ker. |
| AVANTI SAVOYA | Forward Savoy. War-cry of Savoy. |
| AVANTUREY ET MARCHEZ AVANT | Advance and march well. Swinnerton of Swinnerton (sometimes the second part of the motto is put as *archez bien* – shoot well). |
| AVE MATER ANGLIAE | Hail, Mother of England, Canterbury, City of. |

| | |
|---|---|
| AVENGE | 94 Sq., RAF. |
| AVI NUMERANTUR AVORUM | A long train of ancestry is enumerated, *or* A long line I follow. Lords Grantley (Norton), Hitch, Lowndes-Stone-Norton, Norton, Pryce, Rede, Turberville. |
| AVIS(E) LA FIN | Look to the end. Marquesses of Ailsa (Kennedy), Clark-Kennedy, Kennedy-Cox, Kennedy of Girvanains, Bts., Kennedy-Skipton, Keydon. |
| AVITA ET AUCTA | Inherited and acquired. Order of the Iron Crown (Austria). The Iron Crown of Lombardy was used in crowning the Holy Roman Emperors from Charlemagne, incl. Napoleon (Lombardy was formerly under Austrian rule). |
| AVITA PRO FIDE | For the ancestral faith. St Edmund's Coll., Ware, Herts. (combination of English Coll., Douai, of 1568, forcibly closed 1793, and Old Hall Green, Acad. of 1662). |
| AVITO VIRET HONORE | He flourishes through the honour of his ancestors. Marquesses of Bute (Crichton-Stuart), Mackenzie, Lords Stewart of Rothesay, Lords Stuart of Decies, Turner, Lords Warncliffe (Stuart-Wortley-Mackenzie), Order of the Wendish Crown (Mecklenberg-Strelitz). |
| AVORUM HAUD IMMEMOR | Not unmindful of our ancestors. Quain, Bt. |
| AVORUM HONORI | For the honour of our ancestors. Barne of Broom Hall. |
| AWN RHAGOM | Let us advance, *or* Forward. Cowbridge (Glam.), Bor. of. |
| AYE BE HONEST | Lords Darling. |
| AYE READY | Galloway, Johnston of Cashel Johnston, Lords Newlands (Hozier) *(NEP)*. |
| AYMEZ LOYAULTÉ | Love loyalty. Lords Bolton, Cowan, Paulett, Stratton, Marquesses Winchester (Paulet). |
| AZINCOURT | Lenthall (according to one account Sir Rowland Lenthall was an officer at Agincourt), Waller. |

# B

| | |
|---|---|
| BALANCE AND CONTROL | Viscount Mills. |
| BARKUMA MUNNOPARA | Support from Edinburgh. Munnopara Dist. RAF Supply Unit, Australia (Edinburgh Field). |
| BARROSA | Viscount Gough. Byron in *Childe Harold* refers to the marvels of Barrosa's fight in which Sir Hugh Gough, later Viscount, greatly distinguished himself. |
| BASIS VIRTUTUM CONSTANTIA | Constancy is the foundation of the virtues. Bass, Bt., Lord Burton (Bass) *(NEP)*, Devereux, Viscount Hereford, Muntz. |
| BE AS GOD WILL | Bracebridge, co. Warwick, Compton-Bracebridge. |
| BE ASSURED | London and Manchester Assurance Co. Ltd. |
| BE BOLD | 229 Sq., RAF. |
| BE CAREFUL | Viscount Caldecote (Inskip). |
| BE FAITHFUL | Vans-Agnew. |
| BE(E) FAST | Compton-Thornhill, Bt., Earls of Mexborough (Savile), Lords Savile of Rufford, Thornhill. |
| BE FIRM | Coates of Glasgow, Ferie, Ferrie, Lords Glentanar (Coats) *(NEP)*. |
| BE FREE | Hitchcock. |
| BE IT FAST | Fotheringham. |
| BE JUST | Finlay of Epping, Bt. |
| BE JUST AND FEAR NOT | Ashby, Atkins, Carlisle, City and Co. Bor. of, Coleman, Hewitt, Viscount Lilford (Hewitt), Lurgan (co. Armagh), Bor. of, Payne, Peacock, Pudsey (W.R. Yorks.), Bor. of, Strange, Tapps-Gervis-Meyrick, Bts., Warren, Wakefield, Bts., Lords Wakefield, Yarrow, Bts., Farnworth (Lancs.) UDC. |
| BE MINDFUL | Budd, co. Suffolk, Calder, Campbell, Bts., Campbell-Preston, Clyde, Earls of Cawdor (Campbell), Hooker, Ismay. |
| BE MINDFUL TO UNITE | Brodie of Lethen, Nairn, Brodie, Bt. |
| BE NOT WEARY IN WELL DOING | Edwards of Longparish. |
| BE PREPARED | Scout Assn., 1908. |
| BE READY | Lords Lawrence, Lord Lawrence of Kingsgate *(NEP)*, Nall, Bts., Nall, co. Notts. |
| BE RIGHT AND PERSIST | Lords Kennet (Young), Young, co. Bucks., Young, Bts. |
| BE STEADY | Lord Danesfort (Butcher) *(NEP)*. |
| BE STILL AND KNOW | Univ. of Sussex, 1962. |

| | |
|---|---|
| BE TRAIST | Be faithful. Innes, Dukes of Roxburghe (Innes-Ker). |
| BE WISE | Lewis of Henllab. |
| BE WATCHFUL | Daroch. |
| BEANNCHOR | Bangor, Bangor (Co. Down), Bor. of. |
| BEAR AND FORBEAR | Balguy, co. Derby, Bernard-Morland, Bts., Bear, Bircham, Burgoyne of the Army, Bt., Langford, Bt., Moreland, Bt., Rowley of Lawton. In cases of Bernard and Bear the allusion is to the crest of a bear's head. |
| BEAR THEE WELL | Bardswell of Chigwell, co. Essex. |
| BEAR UP | Fulford. |
| BEATI MUNDO CORDE | Blessed are the pure in heart (St Matthew 5:8) (One of the beatitudes). Ardingly Coll., Sussex, Birkenhead Sch., Hurstpierpoint Coll., Sussex, 1849, Lancing Coll., Sussex, Sven Silen, Bishop of Vasteras, Sweden, 1692. |
| BEATI PACIFICI | Blessed are the peacemakers (St Matthew 5:9) (Part of the beatitudes in the Sermon on the Mount.) Anderson of Isfield, Sussex, Fitz-Simon, James VI of Scotland and I of England, who used several mottoes: *Fecit eos in gentem unam* – He made them into one people; *Tueatur unita Deus* – May God keep them united; *Henricus rosas regna Jacobus* – Henry (i.e. VII) united the roses and James the kingdoms (allusion to James I's desire to make English and Scots one people), Viscount Waverley (Anderson). |
| BEAU REPEYR | Fine repair (or quiet). Belper (Derbys.) RDC. |
| BEAU SÉJOUR | Fine sojourn. Budleigh Salterton (Devon) UDC. |
| BEAUTY SURROUNDS, HEALTH ABOUNDS | Morecambe & Heysham (Lancs.), Bor. of. |
| BEE FAST | Earls of Liverpool (Fuljambe). |
| BEHOLDE TO YE HENDE | Look to the end. Badenoth, co. Dorset. |
| BEDHOK FYE HA HEB DROH | Let us be wise without guile. Carthew of Woodbridge Abbey. |
| BELABORANT | A. Ababrelton. |
| BELGAE GALLORUM FORTISSIMI | The Belgae are the bravest of the Gauls. 350 Sq., RAF (Belgian), 1941 (motto from Julius Caesar's *De Bello Gallico*). |
| BELL ASSEZ BEL | Bell is fine enough. Bell, co. Northumberland. |
| BELLA HORRIDA BELLA | Wars, horrid wars. Lords Lisle (Lysaght), Lysaght. |
| BELLA MA POCO DURA | Fair but not long lasting. Philibert the Fair of Savoy, one-time Governor of the Netherlands, d. 1504, m. the Duchess Margaret. |
| BELLAMUS NOCTU | We wage war by night. 622 Sq., RAF. |
| BELLATORIS OCULI | The eyes of the fighter. 3602 City of Glasgow Fighter Control Unit, RAAF. |
| BELLEMENT ET HARDIMENT | Handsomely and hardily. Buck, Stucley, Bts. |
| BELLI DURA DESPICIO | I despise the hardships of war. HMS *Warspite* (credited with the largest number of battle honours of any ship). |

| | |
|---|---|
| BELLICUM CECINERE | They have sounded the war trumpet. 421 Sq., RCAF. |
| BELLO PARATI, PACEM VOLENTES | Prepared for war, wishing for peace. 41st Middlesex (Enfield Lock) Rifle Volunteer Corps. |
| BELLUM ET PACEM PARATUS | Prepared for war and peace. No. 12 Sch. of Tech. Training, RAF. |
| BENE | Well. Binney of Pampisford, co. Cambs. |
| BENE AGERE AC LAETARI | To do well and rejoice. Kingston Gram. Sch., Surrey, 1561. |
| BENE AMBULET RES NOSTRA | Let our matter walk well. Lee Conservancy Board. |
| BENE CONSULENDO | Well in counselling. Derbyshire CC. |
| BENE EST TENTARE | It is well to try. Lords Latham. |
| BENE FACTUM | Well done. Weldon, Bts. |
| BENE PRAEPARATUM PECTUS | A heart well prepared. Jex-Blake. |
| BENE QUI SEDULO | He lives well who lives industriously. Arkley, Lords Harmsworth, Harmsworth, Bts., Viscount Northcliffe (Harmsworth) *(NEP)*, Viscount Rothermere (Harmsworth). |
| BENE SERVIENDO | Well in serving. Derbyshire Bdlg. Soc. |
| BENEDICITE FONTES DOMINO | O all ye springs bless ye the Lord. Buxton, Bor. of. |
| BENEDICTUS ES O DOMINE DOCE ME STATUTA TUA | Blessed art thou O Lord, teach me Thy statutes. Bradfield Coll., Berks. (reminiscent of much of Psalm 119). |
| BENEDICTUS QUI TOLLIT CRUCEM | Blessed is he who bears the cross. Bennet, Bt., Woodbridge. |
| BENEFICIORUM MEMOR | Mindful of benefits. Kelham. |
| BENEMERENTUM PRAEMIUM | The reward of the well deserving. Order of the Southern Cross (Brazil). |
| BENIGNO NUMINE | By benign Deity (part of a line in Horace, *Carm*. iv.4). Bently, Earls of Chatham, Copeland, co. Staffs., Davies, Grenville, Hicks, Horsford, Lewis-Barned, Meigh, Pitt, Smith of Dorchester. |
| BENIGNO NUMINE ENISUS | Having struggled with (help of) benign God. Lords Monk Bretton (Dodson). |
| BE THOU DUR | Be bold. Sloggett. |
| BEWARE | Chorley (Staffs.), Bor. of. |
| BEWARE, BEWARE | 611 West Lancs. Sq., RAAF. |
| BEWARE, WARD WELL | Dennys. |
| BIBE SI SAPIS | Drink if you are wise. Brunner, Bts. |
| BIDD LLU HEBB LLYDD | Lewis. |
| BIEN JE ESPOYRE | Well I hope. Sir John Bourchier, 2nd Baron Berners (now represented by Baroness Berners, *B.P.* 1970). |
| BIENFAICTZ PAYERAY, MALFAICTZ VANGERAY | Do good, I will pay; do ill, I will avenge. Walrond. |
| BIND THE TONGUE OR THE TONGUE WILL BIND THEE | Hoskyns, Bts. |

| | |
|---|---|
| BIS DAT QUI CITO DAT | He gives twice who gives quickly. RAF station, Bishopbriggs. |
| BIS VIVIT QUI BENE | He lives twice who lives well. Becher, co. Cork, Wrixon-Becher, Bts. |
| BIS VIVITUR VIRTUTE | He lives twice by virtue. Arnold-Forster, Story-Maskelyne. |
| BOG NAM RADZI | God for Radzi. Radziwill of Poland (Prince of Holy Roman Empire). |
| BOJEM A VZDELANIM K SVOBODE | Through fight and education to freedom. Czechoslovak Depot, RAF. |
| BOLD AND LOYAL | Wycliffe Coll., Gloucester, 1931. |
| BOLD AND TENACIOUS | RAF station, Hemswell, Lincs. |
| BOLD IN SELLING, HONEST IN TELLING | Inst. of Marketing & Sales Management, 1961. |
| BOLDLY AND RIGHTLY | Bexley (Kent), Bor. of. |
| BON CHATEL GUARDE QUI SON CUER GUARDE | Good guard for castle who guards his leather. Secretan. |
| BON I BEL ASSIZ | Good and fine seat. Kerr of Toronto. |
| BON TEMPS VIENDRA | The good time will come. Rokewode-Gage, Bts. |
| BONE ET FIDELIS | Good and faithful. Woodhouse Grove Sch., Bradford. |
| BONI OPERIS CLAVEM HABEMUS | We hold the key of good workmanship. No. 5 Sch. of Tech. Training, RAF. |
| BONNE ET ASSEZ BELLE | Good and rather beautiful. Grubb. |
| BONO ANIMO ESTO | Be in good spirit. Morrell. |
| BONO MALUM SUPERATE | Overcome evil with good. Westonbirt Sch., Glos., 1960. |
| BONO RURIS CONSULERE | To counsel for the good of the country. Burnley (Lancs.) RDC. |
| BOS WYDHEK | The wooded dwelling (Cornish) Beswetherick. The history of this surname has one curious feature: until quite late, i.e. after 1750, the name was often spelt Boswarthick. A change of vowel was very unusual at so late a date. In C. L'Estrange Ewen's *A History of Surnames of the British Isles* in a list of Cornish names, the meaning is given as 'the house by the meadow'. A genealogist who knew a great deal about Cornish families told me that the name was traceable to the reign of Henry VI, when he thought that it had been changed from Williams (*The Story of Surnames*, 1965, p.25). As small landowners, the Beswethericks are found for several centuries in Cornwall. There are large and flourishing branches of the family in New Zealand and South Africa. |
| BOULOGNE ET CADIZ | Heygate, Bts. These place-names commemorate the war service of two ancestors of the Heygate family. Thomas Heygate was Provost Marshal of the army at St Quentin and Boulogne. His son, also Thomas, was Provost Marshal in the Earl of Essex's capture of Cadiz, 1596. |

| | |
|---|---|
| BOUND TO OBEY AND SERVE | Jane Seymour, 3rd wife of Henry VIII and mother of Edward VI. |
| BOUTEZ EN AVANT | Push forward. Barry, co. Chester, Lord Barrymore (Barry) *(NEP)*, Batten, Bury-Barry, Fowle, co. Wilts. |
| BRENHINOL BRIG GWYNEDD | The royal leader of Gwynedd (trans. by a Welsh scholar). Caernarvon, Royal Bor. of. |
| BRYCHEINIOG | Brecon. Brecknockshire Agricultural Soc. |
| BUAIDH NO BAS | Victory or death. Macdougall. |
| BUENA GUIA | A good guide. Alfonso V the Wise, King of Aragon (1416–58), patron of the arts and sciences (motto refers to these as good guides for a king), Henry II of Trastamare, King of Castile (1369–79), bastard brother of his predecessor, Pedro I, whom he killed. |
| BUILD IN DEPTH | No. 61 Group HQ, RAF. |
| BUILD SURE | McAlpine, Bts., Sir Robert McAlpine & Sons Ltd. |
| BUILD TO ENDURE | Airfield Construction Depot, RAF. |
| BURGUS DE NEWBURIE | Borough of Newbury, Newbury Volunteer Training Corps, 1914. |
| BURNING I SHINE | Jehangir, Bts. |
| BUSINESS IN GREAT WATERS | Mersey Docks & Harbour Board. |
| BUTLER A BOO | Butler for ever. Marquesses of Ormonde (Butler). |
| BUTT SICKER | More sure. Lord Duffus (Sutherland, later Dunbar) *(NEP)*. |
| BWY A GADEL BWY | Jenkins, co. Radnor. |
| BY ASSIDUITY | Byass, Bts. |
| BY CONCORD AND INDUSTRY | Droylsden (Lancs.) UDC. |
| BY COURAGE AND ENDEAVOUR | Fraser of Allander, Bts. |
| BY COURAGE AND FAITH | Seaham (Durham) UDC, 1951. |
| BY DESIGN AND ENDEAVOUR | Crawley Development Corp., Sussex. |
| BY FAITH AND INDUSTRY | Grimsby (Lincs.) RDC. |
| BY FAITH AND WORK | Viscount Mackintosh of Halifax. |
| BY FAITH, FORESIGHT AND INDUSTRY | Durham RDC. |
| BY FAITH I OBTAIN | Turners' Co., charter 1604. |
| BY FAITH WE ARE SAVED | Cathcart, Bt., Cathcart-Walker-Heneage. |
| BY FRIENDSHIP AND BY SERVICE | Richardson of Eccesall, Bt. |
| BY HAMMER AND HAND ALL ARTS DO STAND | Blacksmiths' Co., inc. 1571. |
| BY INDUSTRY AND INTEGRITY | Nelson, Bor. of. |
| BY INDUSTRY EVER STRONGER | Enfield, London Bor. of. |
| BY INDUSTRY WE PROSPER | Gavin, Todmorden (Yorks.), Bor. of. |

| | |
|---|---|
| BY LIGHT TO KNOWLEDGE | Inst. of British Photographers. |
| BY NIGHT AND DAY | 119 Sq., RAF. |
| BY PERSEVERANCE | Cunard, Bts. |
| BY PERSEVERANCE TO PERFECTION | HMAFV *Bridlington* (transferred from RN to RAF). |
| BY SEA | Viscount Runciman of Doxford (shipowner). |
| BY SEA AND FOREST ENCHANTED | Lymington (Hants.), Bor. of. |
| BY SERVICE AND JUSTICE | Lord Royle (Life Baron). |
| BY SERVICE, INDUSTRY AND HONOUR | N.E. Coast Inst. of Engineers & Shipbuilders. |
| BY SERVICE LET US GOVERN | Tadcaster (Yorks.) RDC. |
| BY SERVICE WE PROGRESS | Burnley Building Soc. |
| BY SKILL AND INDUSTRY | No. 217 Maintenance Unit, RAF. |
| BY STRENGTH AND COURAGE | Yule, Bt. |
| BY THE STARS | No. 2 Air Navigation Sch., RAF. |
| BY THE SWORD | Atkins, co. Cork. |
| BY TRUTH AND DILIGENCE | Cameron-Ramsay-Fairfax-Lucy Bts., Lucy, Leighton Linsdale (Bucks.) UDC. |
| BY WISDOM AND DESIGN | RAF Central Tactics and Trials Organization. Welwyn Garden City (Herts.) UDC, 1958. |
| BY WORTH | Farnham (Hants.) UDC, Keighley (Yorks.), Bor. of. |
| BYDAND | Remaining. Gordon of Lesmoir, Bts., Gordon-Canning, Ingram, Dukes of Richmond and Gordon (Gordon-Lennox), Wimberley, 92nd Foot, the Gordon Highlanders, 2nd Bn., 6th Volunteer Bn., Gordon Highlanders. |
| BYDD DDIYSGOG | Be steadfast. Earls of Liverpool (Foljambe). |
| BYDD GYFLAWN AC NAG OFNA | Be just and fear not. Williams, Bt. |
| BYDD LEW HEB LID | Be a lion without wrath. Jones, co. Glam. |

# C

**CADARN AR CYFRWYS**
Strong and subtle. Williams of Bodelwyddan, Bts.

**CADARN YW FY FYDD Y PORTHA DUW Y GIGFRAIN**
Great is my faith that God will keep the ravens. Pryse-Rice (possibly ref. to Biblical account of Elijah being fed by ravens).

**CADENTI PORRIGO DEXTRAM**
I extend my right hand to the falling. Meade-King, Pearce.

**CADERE NON CEDERE POSSUM**
I can fall but not yield. Cottingham.

**CADERNID CYFIAWNDER CYNNYDD**
Strength and justice. Barry (Glam.), Bor. of.

**CADERNID GWYNEDD**
The strength of Gwynedd. Caernarvonshire CC.

**CAEDIMUS NOCTU**
We slay by night. 141 Sq., RAF.

**CAELESTIA CANIMUS**
We sing of heavenly things. Synge.

**CAELITUS MIHI VIRES**
Heavenly strengths are mine. Viscount Ranelagh (Jones) (NEP).

**CAELUM NON MUNUS MUTATUM**
The sky has changed but not our duty. No. 34 Service Flying Training Sch., RAF.

**CAELUM TUEMUR**
We watch the sky. RAF station, Neatishead, Norfolk, No. 271 Signals Unit, RAF.

**CAEN, CRECY, CALAIS**
Delme-Radcliffe, Radclyffe. The Radclyffe family was of great distinction in the Hundred Years' War, and Sir John Radclyffe of Ordsall served under Edward III at Crecy (1346) and the siege of Calais (1347), hence the motto.

**CAERVAELOC (CORNISH)**
Nance. Motto is a name from the area Caermaeloc in the Helston–Lizard district where the family of Nance was once located. It is thought that Maeloc was a prince of the Veneti (in Brittany, subdued by Caesar) and name signifies Maeloc's camp or fortress, m and v being often interchanged in compound words in Cornish.

**CAESARIS CAESARI DEI DEO**
Of Caesar to Caesar, of God to God. Order of the Yoke and Arrows (Spain). Motto derived from Christ's saying: Render . . . unto Caesar the things that are Caesar's, and unto God the things that are His (St Luke 20:25).

**CAETERIS MAJOR QUI MELIOR**
He is greater than others who is better. Radcliffe, co. Devon.

**CAFFRARIA**
The motto borne over the crest of the Willshire Bts., the 1st Bt., Sir Thomas Willshire, was Commandant of British Caffraria, 1879. He added to the colony in S. Africa the territory between the Fish River and Keishamma. In the arms there is a mounted Beelochee soldier, and on a chief is a representation of the fortress of Kelat; on a canton is a representation of the badge of

the first class of the Order of the Deoranee Empire bestowed upon Sir Thomas by the King of Afghanistan. The crest is of a Kaffir, while the supporters are soldiers of the 38th Regt. of Foot (dexter) and the 2nd Regt. of Foot (sinister).

CALA RAG WHETHLOW

A straw for stories. Carminow, an ancient Cornish family still represented through the female line, which figured in the famous heraldic controversy in the reign of Richard II. This was the Scrope *v.* Grosvenor case (1385) in which both parties were using the same arms, azure a bend or, although the families were quite unconnected. Grosvenor, ancestor of the Dukes of Westminster was compelled by Richard II's ruling to give up his ancestral arms and to devise another coat of arms; but a little later Carminow was found also to be bearing azure a bend or. The bold Cornishman, however, took the initiative and challenged Scrope's right to the arms. Scrope, the great nobleman, claimed that his arms dated from the Norman Conquest (a historical anachronism, since heraldry began in the twelfth century), to which Carminow replied that his ancestor received his coat of arms from King Arthur. Nonplussed, the investigating commission ruled that Carminow should difference his arms by a canton charged with a cross. Sometimes the Carminows did this, sometimes they did not, but they kept their ancient arms. Hence the significance of the motto.

CALESPULGH

Excalibur (Cornish). Sampson. Excalibur was the name of the famous sword of King Arthur which he told Sir Bedivere, the last of his knights, to cast into the mere. When at last Sir Bedivere obeyed, an arm in white samite rose from the mere to receive the sword.

CALLIDE ET HONESTE

Wisely and honourably. Calley, co. Wilts.

CALLIDE SED HONESTE

Wisely but honestly. Cayley.

CAMERA PRINCIPIS

Chamber or court of the Prince. Coventry, City of. Motto thought to derive from the fact that the Black Prince was much associated with Coventry as Lord of the Manor of Cheylesmore.

CAMPI FERO PRAEMIA BELLI

I bear the rewards of the battlefield. Campbell of Skerrington.

CANDIDA CANDIDIS

White to the white. Claude de France, d. 1524, first wife of Francis I and dau. of Louis XII (no doubt allusion to sincerity (or chastity) as full moon was her emblem).

CANDIDE

Candidly. Stewart of Feddal.

CANDIDE ET CONSTANTER

Fairly and firmly. Allfrey, Earls of Coventry. Irwine. Sassoon, Bts., Warner.

CANDIDE ET SECURE

Candidly and safely. Maxtone-Graham, Murray-Graham.

CANDIDE SECURE

Candidly, securely. Gilstrap, Bt.

CANDIDUS CANTABIT MORIENS

The white (*or* candid) soul shall sing when dying. The Earls Cawdor (Campbell).

| | |
|---|---|
| CANDOR DAT VIRIBUS ALAS | Truth gives wings to strength. Boyd-Rochford, Rochford. |
| CANDOR ILLAESUS | Purity unsullied. Giulio de Medici, Pope Clement VII (1523–34), cousin of Leo X. |
| CANDORIS PRAEMIUM HONOS | Honour is the reward of candour. Dunbar of Mochrum, Bts. |
| CANMOL DY FRO ATHRIG YNO | Praise your homeland and dwell there. Brecknock, Bor. of. |
| CANTIUM NOBIS PRINCEPS | Kent is first with us. Assn. of Men of Kent and of Kentish Men. |
| CAPTA MAJORA | Seek greater things. Lords Geddes, Geddes. |
| CAPUT INTER NUBILA CONDIT | The head is set amongst the clouds (Virgil, *Aeneid* iv. 177; x. 767). Gateshead, Co. Bor. of. |
| CARA FE M'E LA VOSTRA | Your faithfulness is dear to me. Carafa. Family took surname from opening words of motto – itself an allusion to an ancestor having saved his sovereign the Holy Roman Emperor, Henry VI. |
| CARAID SAN AIRC | A friend in difficulty. Alford (a rare motto; according to Irish scholars, but thought to be Irish). |
| CARED DOETH YR ENCILION | Let the wise love the retreats. Cymmrodorion, Hon. Soc. of. |
| CARITAS FRUCTUS HABET | Charity bears fruit. Baron, Bt. |
| CARITAS, HUMILITAS, SINCERITAS | Charity, humility, sincerity. St Swithin's Sch., Winchester. |
| CARPE DIEM | Seize the present opportunity. Berns, Clarke, Finch, Jackson, Langford, Moens, Paynter, Shepperson, Bts., Stern, Bt., Wigan, co. Kent. Wigan, Bts., 576 Sq., RAF. |
| CARRY ON | Lord Stevenson (*NEP*), No. 51 MT Co., RAF. |
| CASSIS TUTISSIMA VIRTUS | The safest helmet is virtue. Armour, Viscount Brentford (Joynson-Hicks), Charrington, Marquesses Cholmondeley, Lords Delamere (Cholmondeley), Helme. |
| CASTELLO FORTIOR CONCORDIA | Union is stronger than a fortress. Northampton, Bor. of, Northampton Citizen Corps, 1914. |
| CASTELLUM SUPRA FLUVIUM | A castle above the river. Flint, Bor. of. |
| CASTIGANDOS CASTIGAMUS | We chastise those who should be chastised. 424 Sq., RCAF. |
| CASTRUM RURI DAT CONSILIUM | The camp gives counsel to the country. Caistor (Lincoln) RDC. In the arms issuing from a tower is a Roman legionary standard, Caistor having been site of a Roman camp. |
| CASU NON MUTATUS | Not changed by chance. Griggs. |
| CAUSE CAUSIT | Cause caused it. Lords Elphinstone. |
| CAUTE SED IMPAVIDE | Cautiously but fearlessly. Cayzer, Bts., of Gartmore. Cayzer of Roffey Park, Bts., Lords Rotherwick (Cayzer). |
| CAUTE SED STRENUE | Cautiously but strenuously. Hamlyn. |

| | |
|---|---|
| CAUTIUS PUGNAT | He fights the more cautiously. Sforza Pallavincino. |
| CAUTUS A FUTURO | Cautious as to the future. Bowen, co. Cork. |
| CAUTUS IN CONSILIO, ALACER IN ACTO | Cautious in counsel, bold in act. Hunting-Clan Air Transport Ltd. |
| CAUTUS METUIT FOVEAM | He who is cautious feared the snare. Caton. |
| CAVE | Beware. Cave, Bts., HMS *Sesame* (destroyer had as badge a key – i.e. to Aladdin's cave), Ware (Herts.) UDC, 1956. |
| CAVE ADSUM | Beware, I am present. Ashmore, Buchanan-Jardine, Bts., Cave, co. Hants., Jardin, Jardine of Applegirth, Bts., Jardine of Godalming, Bts., Jardine of Jardine Hall. |
| CAVE CANEM | Beware of the dog. 49 Sq., RAF. |
| CAVE DEUS VIDET | Beware! God sees. Cave, Viscount Cave *(NEP)*. |
| CAVE ET AUDE | Look out and hear. Darwin. Kindersley (formerly Darwin). |
| CAVE ET SPERA | Look out and hope. Chapel le Frith (Derbys.) RDC. |
| CAVE LEONEM CRUCIATUM | Beware the tormented lion. 602 City of Glasgow Sq., AAF. |
| CAVE LEOPARDUM | Beware the leopard. 132 Sq., RAF (leopard badge). |
| CAVE LUPUM | Beware the wolf. Huband. |
| CAVEAT IRRUMPENS | Let the breaker in, beware. 3511 City of Dundee Fighter Control Unit, RAAF. |
| CAVENDO TUTI | Precaution renders safe. No. 29 Maintenance Unit, RAF. |
| CAVENDO TUTUS | Safe by being cautious. Earls Burlington, Campbell, co. Perth, Cavendish, Lords Chesham (Cavendish), Crookshank, Cruickshank, Dukes of Devonshire (Cavendish), Hardwick, Lords Hayter (Chubb), HMS *Cavendish* (named after Thomas Cavendish who circumnavigated the globe (1586–8), Pope, Renals, Bts., Waring, Lords Waterpark (Cavendish). |
| CAVENDO TUTUS ADVERSA SPERNO | Safe by watching I spurn adverse things. Settle (Yorks.) RDC, 1964. |
| CAVETE PRAEMONITE | Beware, take care. 66 Sq., RAF. |
| C'EST LA VERTU SEUL QUI DONNE LA NOBLESSE | Virtue alone confers nobility. Greame, co. York., Earls of Swinton (Cunliffe-Lister). |
| CE QUE DIEU VEULT | This which God wills. Beauchamp of Woodborough, Bts. |
| CEART LAIDIR ABU | Might and right for ever. Lords Castletown (Fitz-Patrick) *(NEP)*. |
| CEART AGUS NEART | Right justice and strength. Fitzgerald of Cork, Bts. |
| CEDAMUS AMORI | Let us yield to love. Blunden, Bts. |
| CEDANT ARMA | Let arms yield. Barclay, Best. |
| CEDANT ARMA TOGAE | Let arms yield to the gown. Lord Chalfont, Read, Bts., Reade, co. Antrim, Reade of Ipsden, Reade of Ipswich. |

| | |
|---|---|
| CEDE NULLIS | Yield to none. 105th Foot (Madras Light Infantry, 2nd Bn. the Royal Inniskilling Fusiliers), KOLI (South Yorks. Regt. Yorks. L.I.). |
| CEDO NULLI | I yield to none. Desiderius Erasmus *c.*1466–1536 (Dutch), great scholar, produced first edition of Greek New Testament, 1516 (Charles Reade's novel *The Cloister and the Hearth* contains account of Erasmus's parentage). |
| CELER | Swift. 90 Sq., RAF. |
| CELER AD CAEDENDUM | Swift to strike. 547 Sq., RAF. |
| CELER ATQUE FIDELIS | Active and faithful. Hart. |
| CELER ET AUDAX | Quick and bold. Lord Blanesburgh (Younger) *(NEP)*, Jackson of Carramore, Younger of Fountainbridge, Bt., Viscount Younger of Leckie, 60th Foot (changed to KRRC, 1830). |
| CELER ET FIDELIS | Speedy and loyal. N.W. Command Centre, RAF. |
| CELER ET FORTIS | Swift and strong. 260 Sq., RAF. |
| CELER ET VIGILANS | Swift and watchful. No. 2 Signals Sch., RAF. |
| CELER PER AGROS | Swift through the fields. Ruskell. |
| CELER RESPONDERE | Swift to respond. RAF station, Geilenkirchen, Germany. |
| CELERITAS ET VERITAS | Promptitude and truth. Lords Llangattock (Rolls) *(NEP)*, Rolls. |
| CELERITATE ET PRUDENTIA | By speed and prudence. Elwes. |
| CELERITER | Quickly. Lords Herschell, Lane. |
| CELERITER AC DILIGENTER | Swiftly and diligently, Lord Diplock (Life Baron). |
| CELERITER DEFENDERE | Swiftly to defend. 51 Sq., RAF Regt. |
| CELERITER ET JUCUNDE | Quickly and pleasantly. Rogers, co. Salop. |
| CELERITER FERITE UT HOSTES NECETIS | Strike quickly to kill the enemy. 515 Sq., RAF. |
| CEN NATANAC ABU | Earls of Dunraven and Mountearl (Windham-Quinn). |
| CENFIGENA-LADD-EL-HUNAN | – to kill himself (first word unknown to Welsh scholar to whom it was submitted). Lord Maenan (Taylor) *(NEP)*. |
| CENTRAL INDIA | The Prince of Wales's Leinster Regt. (Royal Canadians). |
| CERTAIR ET VICE | Sure and in place. Innes of co. Down. |
| CERTAMINE SUMMO | In the height of conflict. Brisbane, Bt., M'Onoghuy. |
| CERTAVI ET VICI | I have fought and conquered. Innes-Cross, O'Flanaghan, Thunder. |
| CERTIOR IN COELO DOMUS | A surer home in heaven. Adams (formerly of Holyland). |
| CERTUM EX INCERTIS | Sure from uncertainties. Actuaries, Inst. of. |
| CERTUM PETE FINEM | Aim at a sure end. Lords Bilsland *(NEP)*, Bissland, Bundy, Corse, Crosse, Evans, Holt of Liverpool, Bt., Howard, Thompson, Tidswell, Earls of Wicklow. |
| CERTUS ET VIGILANS | Sure and watchful. No. 27 Maintenance Unit, RAF. |
| CERVUS LACESSITUS LEO FIT | A stag when pressed becomes a lion. Jones, co. Mayo. |

| | |
|---|---|
| CERVUS NON SERVUS | A stag not enslaved. Goddard, Hardwicke, Paley, Thorold, Bts. |
| CESTREHUNT | Cheshunt (Herts.) UDC (presumably medieval form of place name). |
| CHA-DI-CHUIMHNICH MI | (?) Shall not forget. MacIver Campbell. |
| CAH TIG IAD 'NAR COIR | They shall not come near us. No. 71 Signals Unit, RAF. |
| CHALLENGE | No. 10 Group HQ, RAF. |
| CHARITY PROVOKES CHARITY | Craig, co. Wicklow, Viscount Craigavon (Craig). |
| CHARITY UNIVERSAL | Bristol Royal Hosp., early 1900s. |
| CHASE | Geary, Bts. (the 1st Bt., Adm. Sir Francis Geary (1710–96), captured several French and Spanish ships, and although never in a great battle, was cr. Bt. for his services; motto probably his favourite order). |
| CHE SARA SARA | What will be will be. Dukes of Bedford (Russell), Lords De Clifford (Russell), Earls Russell, Russell, co. Down, Russell Littleworth, Bts., Lord Russell of Killowen (NEP). |
| CHECK | No. 336 Signals Unit, RAF, RAF station, Partington, Ches. |
| CHERCHE ET TU TROUVERAIS | Seek and thou shalt find. Sawyer. |
| CHERCHE LA VERITÉ | Seek truth. De la Rue, Bts. |
| CHERGAS | Alert. RAF station, Tengah, Malaya. |
| CHERIS L'ESPOIR | Cherish hope. Cherry. |
| CHI LEGGE REGGE | Who bequeaths rules. Amphlett (formerly of Horseley, Staffs.). |
| CHI SI CONTENTA CODE | Who is content waits. Jackson of Wimbledon, Bts. |
| CHINA | Viscount Gough. (Sir Hugh Gough was cr. Bt. for services in China, 1842, hence motto.) |
| CHRISTI CRUX EST MEA LUX | The cross of Christ is my light. Earls of Iddesleigh (Northcote), Lord Northcote (NEP). |
| CHRISTUS PELICANO | Christ is like the pelican. Letchmere, Bts. Ref. to the crest of the family, a pelican vulning herself to feed her young, a type of Christ who gives His blood to His disciples. |
| CHRISTUS VINCIT, CHRISTUS REGNAT, CHRISTUS TRIUMPHAT (OR IMPERIT) | Christ conquers, Christ reigns, Christ triumphs (or rules). Emperor Charlemagne (742–814) first of the Holy Roman Emperors, so cr. 800. |
| CHWILIWN YR AWYR | We search the air. 3614 Co. of Glamorgan Fighter Control Unit, RAAF. |
| CHY LOGH | The house of the pool. Chellew (Cornish). |
| CIÀ'LL AGUS NEART | Reason and power, or Power used with judgment. O'Connell. O'Connell, Bts. |
| CIÒ CHE DIO VUOLE, IO VOGLIO | What God wills, I will. Lords Dormer. |
| CITO NON TEMERE | Quickly not rashly. Northcote. |

| | |
|---|---|
| CIVES OPPIDI FUNDAMENTA | The citizens are the foundations of the town. Kenilworth (Warwicks.) UDC. |
| CIVIBUS SODALIBUSQUE | For citizens and comrades. Sodbury (Glos.) RDC, 1966. |
| CIVITAS CIVI | The state for the citizen. Secretan. |
| CIVITAS IN BELLO, IN PACE FIDELIS | In war and in peace, a faithful city. Worcester, City of. Worcester was always marked by loyalty to the Crown, and suffered severely for admitting Charles II before his defeat in 1651. |
| CIVITAS LINCOLNIA | Lincoln is our city. Lincoln, City of. |
| CIVITATIS FORTUNA CIVES | Citizens are the fortune of the state. Bevington (Warwicks.) Bor. of. |
| CLAMANT NOSTRA TELA IN REGIS QUERELA | Our weapons clash in the King's quarrel. Woolwich, Bor. of. |
| CLARA UBIQUE | Famous everywhere. Isabella, d. 1632, dau. of Philip II of Spain, wife of Archduke Albert. |
| CLARIOR E TENEBRIS | The brighter from previous obscurity. Bright, Gray, Lightbody, Earls of Milltown (Leeson) (NEP), Purves, Purvis. |
| CLARIOR EX IGNIBUS | Clearer from the fires. Silcoates Sch., Wakefield, Yorks. |
| CLARIOR EX OBSCURO | The clearer from the obscure. Burdon-Sanderson, Bt. |
| CLARIOR HINC HONOS | Hence honour is brighter. Carrick-Buchanan, MacCausland, Lord Woolavington (Buchanan) (NEP). |
| CLARIOR VIRTUS HONORIBUS | Virtue is more illustrious than honours. Clay, co. Mon. |
| CLARIORA SEQUOR | I follow brighter things. Buchanan of Ardock, Gray-Buchanan of Scotstown, co. Lanark. |
| CLARIORES E TENEBRIS | The brighter from darkness. Leeson, Polden, Puleston, Bts. |
| CLARIORI E TENEBRIS | From darkness by the clearer. Earls of Milltown (NEP). |
| CLAUDE OS APERI OCULOS | Close your mouth, open your eyes. Potter. |
| CLAUDITER ET APERITUR | It is shut and open to the free. Italian Academy of Chiave of Pavia. |
| CLAVIS FELICITATIS LABOR | Labour is the key of happiness. Kay. |
| CLEANLINESS IS NEXT TO GODLINESS | Launderers' Co. |
| CLEVE FAST | Burdett of Bramcote, Bt. |
| CLOSE TO THE SUN | 250 Sq., RAF, Sudan. The Sudan (British) community donated this squadron. |
| COELESTES PANDITE PORTAE | Open, ye heavenly gates. Lords Ashbourne (Gibson). Perhaps in allusion to three keys in the arms, and to female figures of Mercy and Justice as supporters. |
| COELESTI LUCE CRESCAT | It grows with celestial light. Cheltenham Ladies' Coll. |
| COELESTIA CANIMUS | We sing of heavenly things. Hutchinson, Synge, Bts. |

COELIS EXPLORATIS

The heavens having been explored. Herschel, Bts. Sir William Herschel discovered over 2,000 nebulae as well as making other notable astronomical discoveries, including that of the planet Uranus. His son, the 1st Bt. Sir John Herschel, was equally distinguished as an astronomer. The coat of arms has for principal charge a representation of a 40-ft. telescope with the symbol of Uranus – a tribute to the astronomers as deserved as it is heraldically in appalling bad taste.

COELUM INDICUM PRIMUS

First into Indian skies. 31 Sq., RAF (sq. claims to be first to fly in India).

COELUM IPSUM PETIMUS

We seek heaven itself. Haste, Bts.

COELUM NON ANIMUM

You may change your climate, but not your disposition. Part of the famous line from Horace (*Epistles*, xi. 27), which continues *'mutant qui trans mare currunt'*. Comyn, Harper of Lamberts, Rhodes of Bellsir, Lords Strachie (Strachey), Waldegrave.

COELUM NON SOLUM

Heaven not earth. Hayman, Heyman, Stevenson.

COELUM QUOD QUAERIMUS ULTRA

Heaven which we seek beyond. Hall of Hall Park, Fitzwilliams, Godman.

COEUR FIDELE

A faithful heart. Coats, Bts., Hart.

COGITATIONE ET CONSTANTIA

By thought and constancy. Lord Buckland (Berry) (*NEP*).

COGNOSCE TEIPSUM ET DISCE PATI

Know thyself and learn to suffer. Rawle, Rawlings (the first two words were inscribed above the temple at Delphi, the familiar γνωθι σεαυτον).

COISNIDH SAOTHAIR THOMACHD (GAELIC)

Labour will learn expertness. No. 8 Air Observers' Sch. (badge is a capercaillie, bird found in Scottish district where sch. was located).

COL TEMPO

With time. Sforza of Milan.

COLE DEUM TIME NULLUM

Serve God and fear none. Alkin.

COLLECTOS SPARGERE FONTES

To distribute collected springs. Tees Valley Water Bd.

COLO COMMUNITATEM

I cherish community. Chisholm, Bt.

COLOOMY

Collooney. Viscount Gort (Prendergast-Vereker). Motto derived from defeat by 2nd Vis. Gort of French invaders of Ireland, 1798.

COME ON

Johnson of Marsh Court.

COME ONE, COME ALL

253 Sq., RAF (donated by people of Hyderabad), hence badge of Indian battle-axe upheld by an arm vested in Moghul armour; design suggested by HEH the Nizam.

COME WHO DARES

58 Sq., RAF Regt.

COME UT LEO SUE

Described (*B.L.G.*, 1952) as old Norman, probably untranslatable, but possibly = Wisdom as the lion follows. Blackburne (formerly of Hale and Orford).

COMFORT ET LIESSE

Comfort and mirth. Doncaster, Co. Bor. of.

COMHNADH DO'NT-SEALGAIR

Succour to the hunter. Nimrod Major Servicing Unit, RAF.

| | |
|---|---|
| COMITER SED FORTITER | Courteously but firmly. Sheffield, Bts. |
| COMME JE FUS | As I was. Earls of Dudley (Ward), More, co. Lancs., Ward, Viscount Ward of Witley. |
| COMME JE TROUVE | As I find. Bowden, Blake Butler, Butler of Cloughgrenan, Bts., Carey, Viscount Galmoye, Earl of Kilkenny, Marquesses of Ormonde, Royden, Bts., Shelley, Bts. |
| COMMIT THY WORK TO GOD | (Prov. 16:3) Earls of Caithness. Lords Barrogill (Sinclair) (*NEP*), Sinclair. |
| COMMODUM NON DAMNUM | A convenience not an injury. Backie, Baikie of Kirkwall. The allusion comes from the crest, this being a flame of office. |
| COMMUNE BONUM | The common good. Midland Assurance Ltd. |
| COMPOSITUM JUS FASQUE ANIMI | A mind which respects alike the laws of mutual justice and of God. Lords Ellenborough (Law), Earl of Ellenborough (Law) (*NEP*), Law, Laws, Nightingale. |
| COMPREHENDERE EST ACCINGI | To understand is to be prepared. Joint Services Language Sch., RAF. |
| CONABIMUR | We will try. Birt, Gwynne. |
| CONANTI DABITUR | It will be given to him who strives. Conant, Bts., Conant of Lyndon Hall, Rutland, Pigott. |
| CONANTIA FRANGERE FRANGUNT | They break those striving to break them. Vittoria Colonna, *c.*1547, m. Marquis of Pescara. |
| CONATA PERFICIO | I bring attempts to conclusion. Cooper of Shenstone, Bts. |
| CONCILIO ET ANIMIS | By counsel and spirits. Featherstone (Northumb.) UDC. |
| CONCILIO ET IMPETU | By counsel and energy. Corrigan, Bt. |
| CONCILIO ET LABORE | By counsel and work. Manchester Volunteer Regt., 1914. |
| CONCIPE SPES CERTAS | Conceive sure hopes. Sealy. |
| CONCORDANT NOMINE FACTA | Our deeds agree with our name. Grace, Bts., Sterling Offices Ltd. |
| CONCORDES | Agreeing. Used by Queen Anne on her second great seal, 1707, signifying union of England and Scotland as Great Britain. |
| CONCORDES AD SERVIENDUM | Agreeing to serve. Municipal Mutual Insurance Ltd. |
| CONCORDIA | Concord (*or* By concord). Cobham, co. Berks. |
| CONCORDIA, AMICITIA, CONJUNCTA | Concord, friendship, conjoined. Sawbridgeworth (Herts.) UDC, 1962. |
| CONCORDIA INTEGRITAS INDUSTRIA | Concord, integrity and industry. Nat. Assn. of Goldsmiths, Baron de Rothschild, Lords Rothschild, N. M. Rothschild & Sons. |
| CONCORDIA PARVAE RES CRESCUNT | Small things grow by concord. Merchant Taylors' Co., charter 1502, Merchant Taylors' Sch., Crosby (1620, John Harrison of Merchant Taylors' Co.), The States-General of Holland (motto comes from Sallust, *De Bello Jugurthine*). |

| | |
|---|---|
| CONCORDIA REGNI | Concord of the kingdom. Robert the Good, King of Naples, d. 1343. |
| CONCORDIA RES CRESCUNT | Things increase by union. Bromhead, Bts., Lords Platt. |
| CONCORDIA VINCIT | Agreement conquers. Northam (Devon) UDC. |
| CONCORDIA VICTRIX | Concord the victor. 21st Co. London Bn. (1st Surrey Rifles, Territorials). |
| CONCRETI CORROBORAMUR | Having been collected we are strengthened. Concrete Soc. (arms grant 1967), a very modern example of punning motto. |
| CONCUSSUS SURGO | Struck I rise. Lord Inverchapel (Kerr) *(NEP)*, Philippe de Chabot, Admiral of France *c.*1543. |
| CONDUCO | I bring together. C. S. Cowper, Essex. |
| CONDUCT IS FATE | Browne (formerly De Beauvoir, Bt.). |
| CONFERRE GLADIUM | Collect the sword. Crookshank. |
| CONFIDAS | Thou dost confide. Boyd of Merton, Bts. |
| CONFIDE RECTE AGENS | Doing rightly be confident. Batten-Pooll, Broadhead, Cooke-Hurle, Fellows, Glanville, Jackson of Brisbane, Long, Newdigate. |
| CONFIDO | I trust. Bell, Boyd Bts., Boyd of Middleton Park, Boyd of Ballycastle, Boyd-Rochford, Dury, Lords Kilmarnock (Boyd), Le Bon, Mills, Peters, Winter. |
| CONFIDO CONQUIESCO | I trust and am contented. Earls of Dysart (Tollemache), Hodgetts, Maroy, Lords Tollemache, Tyrner. |
| CONFIDO IN DEO | I trust in God. Backhouse, Bts. |
| CONFIDO IN DOMINO | I trust in the Lord. Catherwood, Peterkin. |
| CONFIDO IN PROBITATE | I trust in my probity. Blake of Langham, Bts., Cadell. |
| CONFIDO NON CONFUNDAR | I trust I shall not be confounded (ref. is to end of the *Te Deum*). Tyndall-Briscoe. |
| CONFITEBOR TIBI DOMINE | I will confess to Thee, O Lord. Milsom. |
| CONFOUND AND DESTROY | No. 100 Group HQ, RAF. |
| CONFUNDEMUS | We shall throw into confusion. 360 Sq., RAF. |
| CONFUSION TO OUR ENEMIES | No. 80 Wing HQ, RAF. |
| CONJUNCTA ET OBSERVATA | Joined together and observed. Langton-Lockton. |
| CONJUNCTIS VIRIBUS | With our united force. 615 Co. of Surrey Sq., RAF. |
| CONJUNCTUS VIRIBUS | United in powers. Instone. |
| CONLAN-A-BU | The family (*or* group) to victory. Leigh, co. Wexford, also O'More of Laois. |
| CONQUIESCO | I am contented. Metcalfe, Bts. |
| CONSEQUITUR QUODCUMQUE PETIT | He hits whatever he aims at. Drummond, Marquesses of Headfort (Taylour), Petit, Bts., Taylor of Pennington. |
| CONSERVA ME, DOMINE | Preserve me, O Lord. Tayler, Wise. |
| CONSERVAMUS UT CONSERVEMUR | We maintain in order that we may be maintained. No. 20 Maintenance Unit, RAF. |

| | |
|---|---|
| CONSIDER THY PURPOSE | Stevenage Development Corp., 1950. |
| CONSILIO ABSIT DISCORDIA | Let discord be absent from counsel. Whitehaven (Cumb.), Bor. of. |
| CONSILIO ET ANIMIS | By wisdom and courage. Eton (Bucks.) RDC, Gibson, Joint Services Medical Rehabilitation Unit, RAF, Kiveton Park (Yorks.) RDC, Earls of Lauderdale (Maitland), Maitland, Bts., Maitland-Titterton, Ramadge, Ramsay-Steel-Maitland, Bts. |
| CONSILIO ET IMPETU | By counsel and by force. Agnew, Agnew, Bts. |
| CONSILIO ET LABORE | By counsel and labour. Manchester, City of. |
| CONSILIO ET PRUDENTIA | By wisdom and prudence. Atherton (Lancs.) UDC, Burgess Hill (Sussex) UDC, Earls of Clancarty (le Poer Trench), Halstead (Essex) UDC, Le Poer Trench, Tyrone CC, 1951. |
| CONSILIO FIRMATA DEI | Strengthened by the counsel of God. Joan of Arc (burnt 1430). |
| CONSILIO NON IMPETU | By counsel, not force. Agnew of Lochnaw, Bts., Neal, Bt., Vans-Agnew. |
| CONSILIO NON VI | By counsel not strength. Macara, Bts. |
| CONSILII TACITURNITAS NUTRIX | Silence is the nurse of counsel. Jessons. |
| CONSILIUM CONTEXAMUS ARTI | We cover counsel in art. Bradford Textile Soc. Ltd. |
| CONSILIUM NON SINE SALE | Counsel not without (a grain of) salt. Lord Salter. |
| CONSILIUM PARIT OPES | Counsel begets wealth. Bridgwater Bldg. Soc. |
| CONSILIUM SCIENTIA | Counsel is knowledge. Chartered Insurance Inst. |
| CONSOCIENT GENTES | Let races come together. CIBA Foundation for Promotion of Internat. Co-op. in Medical and Chemical Research. |
| CONSTANS CONTRARIA SPERNIT | The resolute man despises difficulties. Edgeworth. |
| CONSTANS ET FIDELIS | Constant and faithful. Arnett, Holcroft, Bts., Liddell. |
| CONSTANS FIDEI | Steady to my faith. Aitken, Alderman Cogan's Sch., Hull, Coggan, Coggan, Lords Colborne, Ridley, Viscount Ridley. |
| CONSTANS JUSTITIAM MONITI | St Pancras, London Bor. of. According to R. Crossley (in *London's Coats of Arms*), this is unique among mottoes of London as the author had not discovered anyone who could translate it. If *constans* were replaced by *constantes*, the translation would be 'Standing firm, instructed in justice' (C. W. Scott-Giles, *Civic Heraldry*, 1933, p. 62). |
| CONSTANT AND TRUE | Rose of Leith, Bts., Rose of Montreal, Bts., Rose of Kilravock, Rose of Leweston, Ross of Belfast. |
| CONSTANT BE | Bedfordshire CC. |
| CONSTANT ENDEAVOUR | Coastal Cmd., RAF, No. 18 Group HQ, RAF. |
| CONSTANTER | With constancy. Dukes, Hore, Harperstown, Portal, Bts. |
| CONSTANTER AC NON TIMIDE | Constantly and not fearfully. Lords Hemphill. |

| | |
|---|---|
| CONSTANTER ET PRUDENTER | Constantly and prudently. Campbell of Fairfield, co. Ayr. |
| CONSTANTER ET RECTE | Constantly and rightly. Hemsworth (Yorks.) RDC. |
| CONSTANTIA BASIS VIRTUTUM | Constancy the basis of virtues. Andover, Bor. of. |
| CONSTANTIA ET FIDELITATE | By constancy and fidelity. Clarke-Travers. |
| CONSTANTIA ET LABORE | By resolution and exertion. Kirby, Lord Rushcliffe (Betterton) (NEP), Lord Warrington (NEP). |
| CONSTANTIA ET SPE | By constancy and hope. Horridge. |
| CONSTANTIA ET VIRTUTE | By constancy and virtue. The Earls of Amherst. |
| CONSTANTIA, JUSTITIA ET FIDELITAS | Constancy, justice and fidelity. Lords Coutanche, Coutanche of St Aubyn, Jersey. |
| CONSTANTIS CUSTODES | Constant watchmen. RAF Air Traffic Control Centre, Gloucester. |
| CONSULT, RESOLVE AND ACT | Lord Cole (Life Baron). |
| CONSULTO ET AUDACTER | With prudence and daring. Plummer, Viscount Plumer (NEP), Scott-Plummer. |
| CONTEMNIT TUTA PROCELLAS | Safe, it despises storms. Stefano Colonna, Lord of Palestrina, c.1548. |
| CONTENTEMENT EST ASSEZ | Content is enough. Ashton (formerly of Woolton, Liverpool). |
| CONTENTEMENT PASSE RICHESSE | Contentment is preferable to riches. Bowyer, Lords Denham (Bowyer). |
| CONTRA AUDENTIOR | On the contrary, the more daring. Boden, Lord Mount Stephen (Stephen) (NEP). |
| CONTROL | Co. of Kent Fighter Control Unit, RAAF. |
| COPIA EST LABOR | Labour brings plenty. Norwich UDC. |
| COPIA EX INDUSTRIA | Plenty from industry. Bird, Bts., Comyn. |
| COPIOSE ET OPPORTUNE | Plentifully and in time. Bontein (Bunting) (formerly of Ardoch), No. 61 Maintenance Unit, RAF. |
| COR AD COR LOQUITUR | Heart speaks to heart. The Oratory Sch., nr. Reading, founded 1859 by John Henry (Cardinal) Newman (the above being his own motto). |
| COR DO DEO | I give my heart to God. Cordeaux, co. Lincoln. A very good punning allusion. |
| COR FORTE CALCAR NON REQUIRIT | A strong heart does not require a spur. Mappin, Bts. |
| COR IMMOBILE | A steadfast heart. Hyett, Hussey of Dublin. |
| COR NOBYLE, COR IMMOBYLE | A noble heart, a mind determined. Hussey, Hunt, Symons, Lords Vivian. |
| COR NON JECUR | Heart not liver. Viscount Hyndley (Hindley) (NEP). |
| COR UNUM | One heart. Huntingdon and Peterborough CC. |
| COR UNUM VIA UNA | One heart one way. Lords Amherst of Hackney, Casterton Sch., Kirkby Lonsdale, Cecil, Cory of Coryton, Bts., Marquesses of Exeter (Cecil), Lords Mountsandford, Sandford, Wills. |

| | |
|---|---|
| CORAM DEO LABORAMUS | We work in the presence of God. City and Guilds of London Inst. |
| CORDA SERRATE FERO | I bear locked hearts. Lockhart, Sinclair-Lockhart, Bts. A play on the name of the Scottish family of Lockhart, one of whom went with Sir James Douglas to take King Robert the Bruce's heart to Jerusalem. On Douglas's death in battle in Spain, Sir Simon Lockhart retrieved the heart in its casket and brought it to Dunfermline. |
| CORDA SERRATA PANDO | I lay open locked hearts. Lockhart of Lee, Bts. |
| CORDE ET ANIMO | By heart and soul. Clayhills-Henderson. |
| CORDE, MENTE, MANU | By heart, mind and hand. Farie. |
| CORDE RECTO ELATI OMNES | All are lifted up by a righteous heart. Makers of Playing Cards' Co., inc. 1628. |
| CORDI DAT ROBORA VIRTUS | Virtue gives strength to the heart. Porch. |
| CORIO ET ARTE | By leather and art. Cordwainers' Co., inc. 1439 (derived name from Cordovan leather used in making boots and shoes). |
| CORNUA LEVAT SUPER TERRAS | It raises its horns above the earth. Roy. Central Asian Soc. |
| CORONA MEA CHRISTUS | My crown is Christ. Chetwode, Bts., Chetwood-Aiken, Lapsley, Webb. |
| CORONAM DEFENDO | I defend the crown. Somerville-Large. |
| CORONAT FIDES | Faith crowns all. Dall, Pringle, Bts., Thornbury (Glos.) RDC. |
| CORPUS NON ANIMUM MUTO | I change the body, not the mind. 57 Sq., RAF. Badge is phoenix rising from flames. In 1914–18 all flying personnel of the sq. became casualties in a few days, but it remained in action with new fliers. |
| COSI IO, ALCO DI DIO, IN ITALIA DEI NEMICI FRANCESI | Thus will I the instrument of God deal with the French enemies in Italy. Ludovico Sforza, 'the Moor' (because his device was the *morus* – Latin for mulberry tree). |
| COUNT NOTHING HUMAN INDIFFERENT | RAF Hosp., Uxbridge, Middx. |
| COURAGE | Arrol, Cuming, Cummin, Cumming, Cumming of Coulter, Bt., Gordon Cumming, Bts., Lords Thurlow (Cumming-Bruce). |
| COURAGE À LA MORT | Courage till death. Hutchins. |
| COURAGE AND SKILL | Ampthill (Beds.) RDC. |
| COURAGE, HUMANITY, COMMERCE | South Shields, Bor. of. |
| COURAGE MOUNTETH WITH OCCASION | Eastbourne Training Coll. |
| COURAGE, PATIENCE | Lords Mancroft (Mancroft). |
| COURAGE SANS PEUR | Courage without fear. Aynesworth, Benn of Rollesby, Bts., Butlin, Bt., Viscount Gage, Lord Glenravel (Benn) *(NEP)*, Lancaster, Willoughby. |

| | |
|---|---|
| COURT HOPE | Lord Courthope *(NEP)*. |
| COÛTE QUE COÛTE | Cost what may. Coote, Bts. |
| CRAGAN AN FHITHICH | The rock of the raven. Macdonell of Glengarry. |
| CRAIG ELACHIE | The rock of alarm. Grant (crest of Grant is a rock inflamed), Lords Strathspey (Grant) *(NEP)*. |
| CRAIGACHROCHAN | Place-name beginning 'Rock of'. Grant of Carron. |
| CRAIGNEZ HONTE | Fear shame. Bentinck, Dillwyn, Dukes of Portland (Cavendish-Bentinck), Weston. |
| CRAINS DIEU TANT QUE TU VIVERAS | Fear God as long as you shall live. Earls of Athlone (Cambridge) *(NEP)*. |
| CRAINT REFRAINTE | Fear restrained. Poyntz. |
| CRAS CAELUM | Tomorrow the sky. No. 2 Group HQ, RAF. |
| CRECY, POITIERS, AGINCOURT | Bowyers' Co. inc. 1621, though much older (motto commemorates the three great triumphs of the English bowmen against the gallant knights of France). |
| CREDE BYRON | Trust Byron. Lords Byron (many must have done so to their detriment in the case of the poet!). |
| CREDE CORNU | Trust the horn. Hornby, Bts., Hornby of Pusey House, Phipps Hornby. |
| CREDE CRUCI | Believe (*i.e.* trust in) the Cross. Viscount Cross. |
| CREDE ET VINCE | Believe and conquer. McGildowny. |
| CREDE LE BRETON | Believe the Breton. Le Breton. |
| CREDE MIHI | Believe me. Chadwyck-Healey, Bts., Fitz-Marmaduke. |
| CREDE SIGNO | Believe in the sign. Rochdale, Co. Bor. of. |
| CREDENTIBUS NIL DIFFICILE | Nothing difficult to believers. Hunt of Kensington, Bts., Hunt of Dartmouth. |
| CREDO | I believe. Kirsopp, Lords Sinclair of Cleeve. |
| CREDO ET AMO | I believe and love. Crossley, Bts. |
| CREF HA GWYR | Strong and true (Cornish). Moon. |
| CREF HA LEL | Strong and loyal (Cornish). Charleston. |
| CREIDIMH GAN CEALG | Faith without deceit. Lord Bowles *(NEP)*. |
| CRESCENT | They will increase. Tatton. |
| CRESCENTES DISCIMUS | Growing we learn. No. 1 Sch. of Tech. Training, RAF. |
| CRESCIT EUNDO | It grows in going. Otter. |
| CRESCIT SUB PONDERE VIRTUS | Virtue thrives beneath oppression. Chapman of Whitby, Chapman, Bts., Earls of Denbigh (Fielding), Fielding, Seys, Slater. |
| CRESCITUR CULTU | It grows by cultivation. Barton, co. Lincs. (acorns appear in arms and crest). |
| CRESCO ET SPERO | I grow and I hope. Auden, Hanney. |

| | |
|---|---|
| CROM A BOO | Crom for ever. De Ros, Fitzgerald, Lord Fitzgerald of Kilmarnock *(NEP)*, Dukes of Leinster (Fitzgerald), Purcell-Fitzgerald. Motto originally war-cry used by ancient Norman–Irish family of Fitzgerald. Crom is castle in Limerick, once belonging to the family who, although originally invaders in 1169–72, soon became *Hiberniores ipsis Hibernis*, in short, Irish chieftains. The Irish war-cries were repeatedly prohibited by the English Parliament, but they did not cease until the complete conquest of Ireland under the Stuarts. Also used by De Ros, though their connection with Ireland is post-medieval. |
| CRUX CHRISTI, NOSTRA CORONA | The Cross of Christ is our crown. Barclay, Bts., Mercer, Merser, Tod-Mercer. |
| CRUX CHRISTI SPES MEA | The Cross of Christ my hope. Davidge. |
| CRUX DAT SALUTEM | The Cross gives salvation. Beynon, Bt., Sinclair. |
| CRUX MIHI GRATA QUIES | The Cross is my pleasing rest. Adam, Bt., Adam of Blair Adam, co. Kinross, Adamson, co. Angus, Edie, M'Adam. |
| CRUX PRAESIDIUM ET DECUS | The Cross is my guard and honour. Tyler. |
| CRUX SCUTUM | The Cross my shield. Lords Crook. |
| CU REU BHAID | The hound breaking loose (described by Irish scholars as notoriously difficult to translate; perhaps the form *Cu reuba* would be better). More O'Ferrall. |
| CUI ADHEREO PRAEEST | He to whom I adhere prevails. Henry VIII at Field of Cloth of Gold, 1520, as advice to Francis I of France (and to the Emperor). |
| CUI DEBEO FIDUS | Faithful to whom I ought. Craw, Layland-Barratt, Bts. |
| CUI FIDES FIDE | Place full confidence in whom you trust. Mason, Peard. |
| CUI SERVIRE REGNARE EST | For whom to serve is to reign. Univ. of Kent. |
| CUICUNQUE FERIENTI APERIETUR | It will be opened to him who bears. Lords Sandford (Edmondson). |
| CUIDICH 'N RIGH | Help to the king. 78th Foot, 2nd Bn. Seaforth Highlanders (Ross-shire Buffs, the Duke of Albany's). |
| CUIL RATHAIN | Corner of the fern. Coleraine (co. Londonderry), Bor. of. Name has been anglicized. |
| CUIMHNICH BAS ALPIN | Remember the death of Alpin. Macalpin, Mackinnon. |
| CUIQUE SUUM | Each to his own. Charles V, Holy Roman Emperor and King of Spain, 1600–58 (implication of motto being that he controlled the world in peace or in war). He abdicated two years before his death and rehearsed own funeral. |
| CULTUI AVORUM FIDELIS | Faithful to the cult of my ancestors. Trappes-Lomax. Motto of a family of Old Catholics (i.e. who remained faithful to Catholicism after English Reformation). |
| CUM ALIIS PRO ALIIS | With others for others. Elliot, Bts. |
| CUM CRUCE SALUS | Salvation with the Cross. Mountain, Bts. |

| CUM DEO | With God. Tuck, Bts. |
|---|---|
| CUM GREGE NON GRADITUR | He does not walk with the flock. Cardinal Benedetti Odescalchi, 1676–89, Pope Innocent XI (his device being a lion alone in a field). |
| CUM LABORE ADJUVANTES | With labour helping. No. 24 Operational Training Unit, RAF. |
| CUM LEGE LIBERTAS | Liberty with law. Lord Rhayader (Leif-Jones) *(NEP)*. |
| CUM PRIMA LUCE | At first light. Loveday. |
| CUM SCIENTIA CARITAS | With knowledge charity. Roy. Coll. of General Practitioners. |
| CUM SECUNDO FLUMINE | With favourable stream. Lund. |
| CUNCTI ADSINT, MERITAEQUE EXPECTENT PRAEMIA PALMAE | Let all be present, and expect rewards of the deserved palm. University College London, 1826. |
| CUNCTI PERSEVERAMUS | We persevere together. Viscount Malvern (Huggins). |
| CUPIO, CREDO, HABEO | I desire, I believe, I have. Lords Cawley. |
| CUR ME PERSEQUERIS | Why persecutest thou me? (Acts 9:4; part of the words of Christ to St Paul). Eton, Eustace. |
| CURA DAT VICTORIAM | Care gives victory. Denham, Bts. |
| CURA ET CANDORE | With care and candour. Cunningham, Bt., Forbes of Ardo, Forbes of Foneran, Bts. |
| CURA ET INDUSTRIA | By care and industry. Walker, Lord Wavertree (Walker) *(NEP)*. |
| CURA PII DIIS SUNT | Pious men are a care to the gods. Rees-Mogg. |
| CURA QUIETEM | Care gives repose. Hall of Dunglass, Bts. |
| CURAE GENUS OMNE ANIMANTIUM | Every kind of care of animals. Zoological Soc. of London, 1959. |
| CURAMUS QUOD POPULO SERVIT | We take care because it serves the people. Inst. of Park Administrators (Inc.) |
| CURANDUM OMNIUM BONUM | The good of all to be taken care of. Garstang (Lancs.) RDC. |
| CURSUM PERFICIO | I finish my course. Hunter. |
| CUSTODES RURIS IN URBE | Guardians of the country in the city. Wimbledon & Putney Common Conservators, 1945. |
| CUSTODES URBIS | Guardians of the city. 903 Co. of London Balloon Sq., AAF. |
| CUSTODI CIVITATEM DOMINE | Keep the city, O Lord. Westminster, City of. |
| CYMRU AM BYTH | Wales for ever. Welsh Guards, formed 1915. |
| CYNYDDAF A LLAWENYCHAF | I increase and rejoice. Prestatyn (Flint) UDC, 1964. |

# D

| | |
|---|---|
| D'ACCOMPLIR AGINCOURT | (literally) To accomplish (*or* fulfil) Agincourt. Dalison of Hamptons, Kent, whose pedigree in *B.L.G.*, 1952 is traced to the fifteenth century (the crest of the family is a man in full armour; there may be some legend of an ancestor having been a combatant at Agincourt, 1415), Best-Dalison of Park House, Kent. |
| DA EI FYDD | God will come. Spence-Colby, co. Hereford, Jones, co. Carms. |
| DA GLORIAM DEO | Give glory to God. Dyers' Co. (inc. 1470), Leigh of Adlington. |
| DA MIHI SAPIENTIAM | Give me wisdom. Lords Kenswood (Whitfield). |
| DA PACEM DOMINE | Give peace O Lord. Lord Sanderson *(NEP)*. |
| DA ROBUR FER AUXILIUM | Give strength, bear help (these words, part of Latin hymn used at Benediction, are last line of first verse, which begins: *O salutaris hostia*). Lords Rotherham (Holland) *(NEP)*. |
| DABIT QUI DEDIT | He will give who gives. Smith of Stratford Place, Bts. |
| DAMUS PLUS QUAM POLLICEMUR | We give more than we promise. Pearl Assurance Co. Ltd., 1911. |
| DANGER IS OUR OPPORTUNITY | 124 Sq., RAF, Baroda (badge is a mongoose passant). |
| DANT ANIMOS VICES | Places give spirits. Italian Literary Academy of the Animosi of Milan. |
| DANT VULNERA VITAM | Wounds give life. Lord Collins *(NEP)*. |
| DANTE DEO | By the gift of God. Tyndall. |
| DARE QUAM ACCIPERE | To give rather than to accept. Guys Hosp., London, *c.*1709. |
| DARE TO BE WISE | RAF station, Detling, Kent. |
| DARE TO DISCOVER | 192 Sq., RAF. |
| DAT CURA QUIETEM | Vigilance ensures tranquillity. Medlicott, Medylcott, Bts. |
| DAT DEUS INCREMENTUM | God gives the increase. Allcroft, co. Salop, Crofton, Lords Crofton, Crofton of Longford House, Bts., Crofton of Mohill, Bts., Muggeridge, Plymouth Coll. and Manamead Sch., Tonbridge Sch., Westminster Sch. |
| DAT ET SUMAT DEUS | God giveth and taketh away. Ethelston. |
| DAT GLORIA VIRES | Glory gives strength. Viscount Hailsham (Hogg), Hog, Hogg, Bts., Hogue, Lords Magheramorne (McGarel-Hogg) *(NEP)*. |
| DAT SCIENTIA ALAS | Knowledge gives wings. Durham Univ. Air Sq., RAFVR. |

| | |
|---|---|
| DATA FATA SECUTA | The given fates are followed. Archdale, Bts., Lords St John of Bletso., Streatfield (motto sometimes given with *secutus* – i.e. Having followed the given fates). |
| DAWN DYSG DEALL | The gift of learning (*or* understanding). Univ. of Wales Inst. of Science & Tech., Cardiff. |
| DE BON CUER | Of good heart. Walton-le-Dale (Lancs.) UDC, 1952. |
| DE BON VOULIR SERVIR LE ROY | To serve the king with right good will. Bennet, Lords Glendale (Baring), Grey, Bts., Earls Grey, Lords Grey de Ruthyn (Butler-Bowden) *(NEP)*, Earls of Tankerville (Bennet). |
| DE DEO ET SOLE | From God and Him only. Spence. |
| DE DIEU EST TOUT | From God is all. Mervyn. |
| DE HIRUNDINE | Concerning the swallow. Lords Arundell of Wardour (a play on the surname: Latin *hirundo* = a swallow). |
| DE MI COLOR MI VALOR | Of my colour my value. Amadeus VI, the 'Green' Count of Savoy (referring to his use of money tests); he founded great Order of Annunziati. |
| DE MONTE ALTO | From a high mountain. Maude. |
| DE PRAESCIENTIA DEI | From the foreknowledge of God. Barbers' Co., inc. 1461 (originally until 1745 combined with the surgeons). |
| DE PROFUNDIS | From the depths. Bedlington (Northumb.) UDC. |
| DE RE METALLICA | Concerning the metallic thing. Inst. of Metals, 1953. |
| DE REGE OPTIME MERITO | From the king to him who best merited. Order of St Ferdinand and of Merit of Naples. |
| DE TOUT MON COEUR | With all my heart. Boileau, Bts., Pollen. |
| DE VITA VIS | Strength from life. Devitt, Bts. |
| DEAS DAONNAN DEAS | Ready always ready. No. 45 Maintenance Unit, RAF. |
| DEATH AND LIFE | 271 Sq., RAF (badge a gauntlet holding a cross, the unit carrying paratroops on outward journey and casualties on return). |
| DEBENTUR OMNIA DEO | All things are owing to God. Deben (Suffolk) RDC. |
| DEBONNAIRE | Graceful. Balfour, Bethune. |
| DECENS ET HONESTUM | Becoming and honourable. Fyffe, Viscount Kilmuir (Fyffe) *(NEP)*. |
| DECERPTUS FLOREO | Having plucked away, I flourish. Lorenzo Simmons Winslow of Washington, D.C. (granted by College of Arms). |
| DECIDE | Davis of Well Close. |
| DECORI DECUS ADDIT AVITO | He adds honour to that of his ancestors. Erskine, Kelly, Earls of Mar and Kellie (Erskine). |
| DECRESCERE NON RUBIGINE ATTERI | To decrease but not to be worn away by rust. Webber. |
| DECREVI | I have resolved. Douglas-Nugent, Gadesden, Nugent of Ballinlough, Bts., Nugent of Cloncoskraine, Bts., Nugent of Donore, Bts., Lords Nugent, Lord Nugent of Guildford, Nugent of Portaferry, Bt. Nugent of Waddesdon, Bts., Earls of Westmeath (Nugent). |

| | |
|---|---|
| DECUS ET TUTAMEN | An honour and a protection. Gravesend (Kent), Bor. of, Yeomanry (Dragoons), West Essex Yeo. |
| DECUS ET TUTAMEN IN ARMIS | Honour and safety in arms. Feltmakers' Co., inc. 1604, Vespasiano Colonna, c.1536. |
| DECUS RECTE PETO | Ornament I rightly seek. Jenks, Bt. |
| DECUS SUMMUM VIRTUS | Virtue is the highest honour. Holborne, Bts. |
| DEDERITNE VIAM CASUSVE DEUSVE | Did chance or God direct the way. Godfrey de Bouillon (a castle in Lower Lorraine, now Luxemburg), hero of the First Crusade (1095–9), who refused title of King of Jerusalem, in the place where Christ had died. (Allusion in motto is to legend of Godfrey having transfixed three feetless birds with one arrow.) |
| DEEDS NOT THOUGHTS | Dodds, Bts. |
| DEEDS NOT WORDS | Ashby de la Zouche (Leics.) RDC, Combs, Corby (Northants.) UDC, Dawson of Low Wray, Pirie, Bt., Viscount Pirie (NEP), Rickford of Aylesbury, Sainthill, Lords Westwood. |
| DEEDS SHAW | Deeds show. Laurie, Otway-Ruthven, Lords Ruthven. |
| DEFENCE NOT DEFIANCE | 2nd Co. 21st (Aboyne) Aberdeen Highland Rifle Volunteers, 40th Lancashire (3rd Manchester) Rifle Volunteer Corps. |
| DEFEND | Wood of Boneytown, Wood of Hatherley House, Bts. |
| DEFEND AND STRIKE | Strike Cmd., RAF. |
| DEFEND BY ATTACK | No. 138 Wing, RAF. |
| DEFEND THE FOLD | 918 Co. of Derby Balloon Sq., AAF. |
| DEFEND THE RIGHT | Lord Hatherley (Wood) (NEP), Horncastle (Lincs.) RDC. |
| DEFEND OUR LIBERTY | Dulwich & District Defence League (later 1/12th Bn.) 1st Somersetshire L.I. Militia. |
| DEFENDAM CORONAM | I shall defend the Crown. Richmond. |
| DEFENDAMUS | Let us defend. Taunton, Bor. of, 1934. |
| DEFENDE LE DROIT | Defend the right. Leveson. |
| DEFENDENDO AGGREDIMUR | We attack by defence. No. 13 Air Gunners' Sch., RAF. |
| DEFENDERS OF FREEDOM | Far East Flying Boat Wing, RAF. |
| DEFENSIO NON OFFENSIO | Defence not offence. Harding of Birling Manor. |
| DEFENSORES DEFENDO | I defend the defenders. 27 Sq., RAF Regt. |
| DEFENSORES DIRIGIMUS | We direct the defenders. 3611 West Lancs. Fighter Control Unit, RAAF. |
| DEFFRO MAE'N DDYDD | Awake, it is day. Cardiff, City of, the Welsh Regt. 16th Bn. (Cardiff City – 'Cardiff Pals'), 1914. |
| DEGENERANTI GENUS OPPROBRIUM | To the degenerate, his family is a disgrace. Ashurst, Crewe (formerly Harpur or Harper, Bts.). |
| DEI AUXILIO FABER EST QUISQUE FORTUNA SUAE | By the help of God everyone is the smith of his own fortune. Nottingham and District Tech. Coll. |
| DEI AUXILIO TELIS MEIS | With the help of God and my weapons. 89 Sq., RAF. |

| | |
|---|---|
| DEI DONO SUM QUOD SUM | By the bounty of God I am what I am. Burges-Lumsden, Lumsden, Lundin, Malcolm, Bts. |
| DEI DONUM | The gift of God. Lords Darling, Dundee, Bor. of. |
| DEI GRATIA | By the grace of God. Kingstone. |
| DEI GRATIA GRATA | Grace of God is pleasing. Dixie, Bts. |
| DEI GRATIA PROBEMUR REBUS | By the grace of God we are proved in things. Barking, London Bor. of. |
| DEI GRATIA SUM QUOD SUM | By the grace of God I am what I am (words of St Paul). Ruthin Sch., Denbigh (very ancient origin, refounded sixteenth century), Summerson. |
| DEI GRATIA SUMUS QUOD SUMUS | By the grace of God, we are what we are. Barking, London Bor. of. |
| DEI MANUS MEDICUS | A doctor is the hand of God. Dickinson of Kingweston. |
| DEI MEMOR GRATUS AMICIS | Mindful of God, grateful to friends. Antrobus, Bts. |
| DEI PROVIDENTIA JUVAT | The providence of God is our help. Welman. |
| DEI SUB NUMINE VIGET | It flourishes under the inspiration of God. Princeton Univ. (USA), 1764. |
| DEID SCHAW | Deed shows. Earls of Gowrie (Ruthven). |
| DEIECTA REPARAMUS | We repair what has been cast down. No. 60 Maintenance Unit, RAF. |
| DELECTARE IN DOMINO | To rejoice in the Lord. Bampfylde, Branfill, co. Essex, Lords Poltimore (Bampfylde). |
| DELECTAT ET ORNAT | It is both pleasing and ornamental. Brown of Edinburgh, Cree, Hervey of Glasgow, Macrae, Macrea. |
| DELENTEM DELEO | I destroy the destroyer. 179 Sq., RAF. |
| DEMOURES FERME | Stay firm. Sir Godfrey Foljambe of Derbys., c.1520, Earls of Liverpool (Foljambe). |
| DENIQUE COELUM | Heaven at last. Bonar, Earls of Leven and Melville, Melvile of Raith, Melvill. |
| DENNOCK | For all that. Calburn, co. Surrey (full surname is Reitmeyer Calburn, having originated in Bavaria). |
| DENTES DRACONIS SERIMUS | We sow dragon's teeth. 644 Sq., RAF (one function-troop carrying). In old Greek story of Jason and Argonauts, the dragon's teeth when sown produced warriors (Charles Kingsley, *The Heroes*). |
| DEO ADJUVANTE | With God assisting. Viscount Exmouth (Pellew) (refers to action of 1st Viscount (when a Bt.) in 1814 in saving troops and crew of transport *Dutton* off Plymouth, exploit commemorated in coat of arms), Jones of Abberley, co. Worcs., Pellew. |
| DEO ADJUVANTE ARTE ET INDUSTRIA FLORET | With God's help it flourishes by art and industry. Kidderminster (Worcs.), Bor. of. |
| DEO ADJUVANTE LABOR PROFICIT | With God's help labour is of avail. Lords May, Sheffield, City of. |
| DEO ADJUVANTE NON TIMENDUM | With God assisting we must not fear. Louth (Lincs.), Bor. of, Wellington (Salop) UDC, 1951. |

| | |
|---|---|
| DEO ADJUVANTE VINCAM | God helping I shall conquer. Hart. |
| DEO ADVERSO LEO VINCITUR | The lion is conquered with God opposing. Newenham. |
| DEO AUSPICE, ET CUM SIDERE FAUSTO | God for our guide and with a favouring star. Wragg. |
| DEO CONFIDE | Trust in God. Fison, Bts. |
| DEO CONFIDIMUS | We trust in God. West Ham, London Bor. of. |
| DEO DANTE DAMUS | God giving, we give. Robert Jones and Agnes Hunt Orthopaedic Hosp., Gobowen, nr. Oswestry, 1944. |
| DEO DANTE DEDI | God giving I have given. Charterhouse Sch., Godalming, Surrey (founded 1611 by Thomas Sutton). |
| DEO DATA | (Things) given to God. Lords Arundell of Wardour (NEP). |
| DEO DUCE, COMITE INDUSTRIA | God being my guide, industry my companion. Nicoll, Slaney. |
| DEO DUCE DECREVI | With God as leader I have decided. Harnage (formerly Blackman, Bts.). |
| DEO DUCE, DEO LUCE | With God for leader, God for light. Prior Park Coll., Bath (founded 1830 by Bishop P. A. Baines, Vicar Apostolic of the Western District). |
| DEO DUCE ET FERRO COMITE | With God as leader, and the sword accompanying. Blaise de Montluc, d. 1577, Seigneur de Montluc and Marshal of France. |
| DEO DUCE FERRO COMITANTE | God my guide, my sword my companion. Armitage, Caulfield, Earls of Charlemont (Caulfeild), (NEP), Viscount Charlemont (Caulfeild), Webb of Webbsborough. |
| DEO DUCENTE | God leading. Lords Haldon (Palk) (NEP). |
| DEO DUCENTE NIL NOCET | With God as leader, nothing can injure. East India Co., 1601, Ebrahim, Bts., Pelly, Bts. |
| DEO ET PATRE | With God and father. Goring-Thomas (appears in this form in B.L.G. 1952 both in text and in arms block, but patriae (for country) would seem more correct). |
| DEO ET PATRIAE OMNIA DEBEO | I owe all to God and my country. Milne-Watson, Bts. |
| DEO ET PAUPERIBUS | For God and the poor. Hosp. of Queen Elizabeth, Donnington, Berks. |
| DEO ET REGI FIDELIS | Faithful to God and the king. Atkinson, Daly. |
| DEO FAVENTE | By favour of God. Alves, Benn of Old Knoll, Bts., Boucher of Trenean, Cumberlege-Ware, Dingwall, Mitchell-Innes. |
| DEO FAVENTE ET SEDULITATE | With God favouring and with diligence. Hanson, Bts. |
| DEO FAVENTE PROGREDIOR | God favouring I will progress. Pyke. |
| DEO FIDELIS ET REGI | Faithful to God and King. Daly, Lords Dunsandle and Clanconal (Daly) (NEP). |
| DEO FIDENS PERSISTAS | Trusting in God you remain constant. Hudson-Kinahan, Bts. |

| | |
|---|---|
| DEO FIDENS PROFICIO | Trusting in God I go forward. Chadwick, Mitchell Cotts., Bts. |
| DEO FRETUS ERUMPE | Trust in God and sally. Newark (Notts.), Bor. of. |
| DEO GLORIA | Glory to God. Gennys. |
| DEO GRATIAS | Thanks to God. Lord Estcourt (Sotheron-Estcourt) *(NEP)*, Gault, Lever of Allerton, Marsden, Bts., Senhouse. |
| DEO JUVANTE | God helping. Aikin-Sneath, Duff, Earls of Fife, Forbes-Leith, Bts., Groze, King's Sch., Bruton, Somerset (1519, refounded 1550 by Edward VI), Levis, Maitland, Lords Newall, Pellew, Shatt, Tawse, Wooderspoon. Fifeshire Artillery Volunteers (badge of Thane of Fife with motto below – *Nemo me impune lacessit*). |
| DEO JUVANTE ARTE ET INDUSTRIA FLORET | With God's help it flourishes by art and industry. Kidderminster (Worcs.), Bor. of. |
| DEO JUVANTE FORTIS IN ARDUIS | With God's help I am brave in difficulties. Watson of Dinton. |
| DEO JUVANTE VINCO | By God's assistance I conquer. Stewart of Ardvorlich. |
| DEO NON ARMIS FIDO | I trust in God, not arms. Morse-Boycott. |
| DEO NON FORTUNA | By God, not fortune. Chance, Bts., Earls Digby *(NEP)*, Lords Digby, Elwes, Epsom Coll., Surrey, 1853, Firth, Harrison, Pellew. |
| DEO NON FORTUNA FRETUS | Confident in God not fortune. Viscount Hambleden (Smith). |
| DEO NON SAGITTIS FIDO | I trust in God not in arrows. Cuyler, Bt. |
| DEO OMNIA | All things to God. Harter. |
| DEO OMNIA DEBEO | I owe all to God. Holden of the Firs, Bts. |
| DEO OPERAE SCIENTIAEQUE FISI | Confident in the God of work and knowledge. Luton and Dunstable Hosp. |
| DEO PATRIAE AMICIS | To God, my country and my friends. Arundell, Lords Colchester (Abbot) *(NEP)*, Granville, HMS *Grenville*, Lutwidge, Scrimgeour. |
| DEO, PATRIAE, REGI | For God, my country and my king. Cooper of Abingdon. |
| DEO PATRIA REGE | For God, country, king. Cooper, co. Sligo. |
| DEO PATRIAEQUE FIDELIS | Faithful to God and my country, Fagan. |
| DEO PATRIAE TIBI | For God, your country and yourself. Lambarde. |
| DEO REGE PATRIAE | To God, my king and my country. Duncombe of Cassgrove, Duncombe of Wood Hall, Bt., Earls of Feversham (Duncombe) *(NEP)*, Lords Feversham (Duncombe). |
| DEO REGI VICINO | To God, king and neighbour. Bromsgrove Sch., Worcs. re-organized by Edward VI, 1553. |
| DEO REGIQUE DEBEO | I owe duty to God and the king. Johnson of New York. |
| DEO SOLI GLORIA | Glory to God alone. Kirke. |
| DEO SOLI SERVIO | I serve God alone. Lecky. |

| | |
|---|---|
| DEO VOLENTE | God willing. Palliser. |
| DEPOSITUM CUSTODI | Keep that which is committed to thy trust. No. 5 Radio Sch., RAF (badge of a fish or ichthus was taken from early Christian sign used as a password to denote silence combined with watchfulness; the word 'ichthus' in Greek in its initial letters reads 'Jesus Christ, Son of God, Saviour). |
| DEPRESSUS EXTOLLOR | Though depressed I am raised up. Viscount Mountgarret (Butler). |
| DEPUGNANDUM SEMPER | One must always fight strenuously. Arnold. |
| DERAS DAN BETUL | Speed and accuracy. RAF Communication Centre, Singapore. |
| DES ACTES, NON DES PAROLES | Deeds not words. No. 93 Maintenance Unit, RAF. |
| DESERVE AND HAIF | Deserve and have. MacIver Campbell. |
| DESIGNO OCULIS AD CAEDEM | With my eyes I designate (the victim) for slaughter. 661 Sq., RAAF. |
| DESPICIO TERRENA SOLEM CONTEMPLOR | I despise earthly things and contemplate the sun. Paston-Bedingfeld, Bts. |
| DESPITE THE ELEMENTS | 115 Sq., RAF (bomber). |
| DESTINATA PERFICERE | To accomplish things aimed at. No. 6 Armament Training Station, RAF. |
| DETECT TO DESTROY | 3613 City of Manchester Fighter Control Unit, RAAF. |
| DETECTA DESTRUANTUR | Let that which has been found be destroyed. RAF station, Wartling, Sussex. |
| DETER | RAF station, Markham, Notts. |
| DETERMINATION | 142 Sq., RAF. |
| DETUR GLORIA SOLI DEO | Let glory be given to God alone. Alleyn's Sch., Dulwich Coll., founded by Edward Alleyn, actor, 1619. |
| DEUM COLE, REGEM SERVA | Worship God, revere the king. Cole of Twickenham, Coleridge, Earls of Enniskillen (Cole), Jones, Townshend. |
| DEUM LAUDANS | Praising God. Arbuthnot of Kittybrewster, Bts. |
| DEUM POSUI ADJUTOREM | I have taken God for my helper. Hingston, Kingston. |
| DEUM TIME | Fear God. Hohler, Murray of Blackbarony, Bts., Murray of Clairemont, Bts. |
| DEUM TIME ET DEDECUS | Fear God and it is your ornament. Baddeley of Castle Hale. |
| DEUM TIMEO | I fear God. Hohler, co. Kent. |
| DEUM TIMETE ET REGEM FAVETE | Fear God and favour the king. Holmes (formerly Hill). |
| DEUS ADJUVAT NOS | God assists us. Booth, Bt. |
| DEUS ALIT EOS | God feeds them. Croker, James, Rees, Bts. |
| DEUS CLYPEUS MEUS | God my shield. Baron Adolf Erik Nordenskiold, 1832–1901 (Polar explorer). |
| DEUS DABIT VELA | God will fill the sails. Campbell, Lords Glenconner (Tennant), Norman, co. Sussex. |

| | |
|---|---|
| DEUS DAT INCREMENTUM | God gives the increase. Fruiterers' Co., inc. 1605 (arms, azure on a mount vert the tree of Paradise environed with a serpent, between Adam dexter and Eve sinister all proper), Tonbridge Sch., Kent, 1553, Warrington, Bor. of, Westminster Sch. (re-founded 1560 by Elizabeth I), Lowson, Bts. |
| DEUS DEXTER MEUS | God is my right hand. Dobbin. |
| DEUS EST NOBIS SOL ET ENSIS | God is a sun and sword to us. Kynaston, Powell. |
| DEUS EST NOBIS SOL ET SCUTUM | God is our sun and shield. Gillett Bros Discount Co. Ltd. |
| DEUS EST SUPER DOMO | God is over my house. Straker. |
| DEUS ET LIBERTAS | God and liberty. Evans of Capel End, Godfrey of Bushfield, Bt., Taylor, Bts. |
| DEUS FORTISSIMA TURRIS | God is the strongest tower. Squibb. |
| DEUS FORTITUDO MEA | God is my strength. Jones of Roscommon, Jones of Gerrards Cross. |
| DEUS GUBERNAT NAVEM | God steers the vessel. Leckie, Lecky. |
| DEUS HAEC OTIA FECIT | God hath given this tranquillity. Williams of Stock Hill. |
| DEUS HORAM DAT | God gives the hour. RAF station, Hooton Park, Cheshire. |
| DEUS INCUBAT ANGUI | God lies on the snake. St George's Hosp., London. In the arms there is usual medical symbol of Aesculapius and the serpent, but also St George is represented in the crest slaying the dragon, which may help to explain motto – see Genesis, ch. 3. |
| DEUS INTERSIT | God is with us. Stephens, co. Glos. |
| DEUS JUVAT | God assists. Duke of Fife (Duff) *(NEP)*, McDuff. |
| DEUS MAJOR COLUMNA | God is stronger than a column. Henniker, Bts., Lords Henniker (Henniker-Major). |
| DEUS MEUM SCUTUM EST | God is my shield. Abraham. |
| DEUS MEUS DUX MEUS | My God is my guide. St Albyn, Smith of Kidderminister, Bts. |
| DEUS MEUS ET OMNIA | My God and all things. Greyfriars (Oxford Univ.). |
| DEUS MIHI PROVIDEBIT | God will provide for me. Goold, Bts., Jerrney, Keane, Bts., Lords Keane *(NEP)*. |
| DEUS NOBIS | God with us. Pinkney. |
| DEUS NOBIS HAEC OTIA FECIT | God hath given us this tranquillity (Virgil, *Eclogues* i. 6). Liverpool, City of. |
| DEUS NOBIS PROVIDET | God provides for us. Lords Norrie. |
| DEUS NOBISCUM | God with us. Burton-upon-Trent Gram. Sch., Jaffe, Methodist Coll., Belfast, 1865. |
| DEUS NOBISCUM QUIS CONTRA | If God be with us, who can be against us? Abbey of Greyfriars, Sussex, Baron de Bliss, co. Warwick, Milman, Bts. |
| DEUS NON RELIQUIT MEMORIAM HUMILIUM | God hath not forgotten the memory of the humble. Meynell of Kilvington. |

| | |
|---|---|
| DEUS NOSTER REFUGIUM ET VIRTUS | God is our refuge and courage. Brunton, Bts., Dewsbury, Co. Bor. of. |
| DEUS PASCIT CORVOS | God feeds the ravens. Bridge, co. Sussex, Brydges (formerly Jones, Bt.), Corbet, Corbet, Bts., Corbin, Corbyn, Cornish, Jones, Jones-Brydges, Bt., Lloyd-Johnes, Mowbray, Bts., Protheroe, Ravenshaw, Lords Rowallan (Corbett), Williams of Temple House. Motto is a play on Norman surname of Corbet. *Corbeaus* = ravens, which are a principal charge on shield; a raven also forms the crest. |
| DEUS PASTOR MEUS | The Lord is my shepherd (Psalm 23:1). Bogie, Boggie, David, Bt., Sheppard. |
| DEUS PATRIA REX | God, country, king. Phillips of Middle Hill, Bt. |
| DEUS PER OMNIA | God pervades all things. Islington, London Bor. of. |
| DEUS PRAESIDIUM | God my help. Bevan (formerly of Trent Park, Middx.). |
| DEUS PRAESIDIUM MERCATURA DECUS | God our safeguard, commerce our ornament. Drogheda (Ireland), City of. |
| DEUS PRO NOBIS QUIS CONTRA NOS? | If God be for us who can be against us? Typical of the deeply religious Charles VIII, King of France, welcomed to Italy by Savonarola as 'the new Cyrus'. He d. miserably in 1498 (Villari, *Life of Savonarola*), Pollard. |
| DEUS PROTECTOR MEUS | God is my protector. Humphrey, Bt. |
| DEUS PROTECTOR NOSTER | God is our protector. Emerson-Tennent, Bts., Order of the Lamb of God (Sweden). |
| DEUS PROVIDEBIT | God will provide. Bolger of Wexford, Bolton, co. Sussex, Burton, Bts., Drummond of Blair, Hall of Burton Hall, Lambert of Wexford, Lesley of Aberdeen, Mainwaring Burton, Marshall, Mather, Mein, Munday, Mindy, Prideaux, Bts., Rowley, Lords Selsdon (Mitchell-Thomson), Thomson of Glendarroch, Bts., White-Thomson. |
| DEUS PROVIDEBIT, MI FILI | God will provide, my son (taken from Abraham's words to Isaac: Genesis 22:8). Boger. |
| DEUS REFUGIUM NOSTRUM | God our refuge. Garnett-Orme, Malcolm of Poltalloch. |
| DEUS REX PATRIA | God, king, country. Phillips of Royston. |
| DEUS ROBUR MEUM | God is my strength. Wood, co. Staffs. |
| DEUS SOLAMEN | God is my comfort. Kerr. |
| DEUS SOLUS AUGET ARISTAS | God alone increaseth the harvest. Riddell of Felton. |
| DEUS TUETUR | God defends. Davie of Elmley. |
| DEUS VULT | God wills (motto is famous saying called out by the crowds at preaching of First Crusade, 1095). Gauld. |
| DEUTLICH UND WAHR | Clear and real. Schreiber. |
| DEVANT SI JE PUIS | Forward if I can. Allhusen, Cavenagh-Mainwaring, Lords Gridley, Grindley, Jackson, Mainwaring, Mainwaring, Bts., Scrope. |
| DEVOUEMENT SANS BORNES | Devotion without limits. Ap Roger, Progers, Prodgers. |

| | |
|---|---|
| DEX AIE | God help. Hartley. |
| DEXTRA CRUCE VINCIT | His right hand conquers with the cross. Hurley. |
| DH'AIND DEOIN CO THEIR EADH E | In spite of anyone who would gainsay. Macdonald of Tote. |
| DHANDEON CO. HEIRACHA | In spite of those who would gainsay. Macdonald. |
| DI BENE IN MEGLIO | From well to better. Francesco Cybo, Count of Anguillara, c.1519, son of Pope Innocent VIII and Marinne Maddalina, dau. of Lorenzo de Medici and sister of Pope Leo X. |
| DI OFN YMFFROST | Fearless, boastless. Kyffin. Wynne of Pengwern. |
| DIAS-MO-DHUTHAICH | For God and my country. Mackenzie, Bts. |
| DIC QUID DICERE FAS EST | Say what is right to say. Mallock. |
| DICIENDO Y HACIEND | Saying and doing. Paget of Cranmore, Bts. |
| DICTIS FACTA SUPPETANT | Deeds correspond to words. Liskeard (Cornwall) RDC. |
| DICTUM MEUM PACTUM | My word is my truth (or bond). Lord Mabane (NEP), the Stock Exchange, London, 1801. |
| DIE NOCTUQUE | By day and night. 39 Sq., RAF. |
| DIEU AVEC NOUS | God with us. Earls of Berkeley, Berkeley of Spetchley, Calcraft, Calcott, Lords Segrave. |
| DIEU AYDE | God assists. De Montmorency, Bts., Frankfort de Montmorency, Viscount Mountmorres (de Montmorency) (NEP), Lentaigne. |
| DIEU DEFEND LE DROIT | God defends the right. Blenkinsop, Viscount Churchill (Spencer), Hunter, Seaton, Earls Spenser. |
| DIEU EST MA ROCHE | God is my rock. Fermoy, Roche, Bts. |
| DIEU ET MON DROIT | (Motto of the English and later British sovereigns. Originated in 1198 when Richard I routed Philip Augustus, King of France, and his army at the battle of Gisors. Richard wrote after the victory, 'it is not we who have done it, but God and our right through us.' He had led his men into action with this battle-cry. As long as English kings had possessions in France they were constantly embroiled with the French kings as their overlords. At last in 1340 Edward III declared himself King of France (as by English law he was, in right of his mother) and adopted Richard's battle-cry which thenceforth has been the royal motto.) Sherborne Sch., Dorset (founded eighth century, re-founded by Edward VI; school has royal arms and motto). |
| DIEU ET MON PAYS | God and my country. MacKirdy. |
| DIEU ET MON ROY | God and my king. Seagrave, Stanford. |
| DIEU LE VEUT | God wills it. Lermitte. |
| DIEU LE WARD | God guard it. Ampleforth Coll., Yorks. |
| DIEU ME CONDUISE | God guides me. Hayes of Brumbee Castle, Bts. |
| DIEU NOUS DONNE BONNE AVENTURE | God gives us good venturing. Merchant Adventurers of York. |

| | |
|---|---|
| DIEU POUR NOUS | God for us. Fletcher of Saltoun. |
| DIEU PREMIER DONC MES FRÈRES | God first, then my brothers. Clayesmore Sch., Blandford, Dorset. |
| DIEU AIE | God help. Royal Guernsey Militia. |
| DIFESSA NON DIFFUSA | Weary not hopeless. Italian Academy of Insensati. |
| DII LABORIBUS OMNIA VENDUNT | The gods sell all things to labours. Oslee, Bt. |
| DILIGENCE AND SERVICE | Lord Runcorn (Vosper) (NEP). |
| DILIGENT AND SECRET | College of Arms, 1484. |
| DILIGENTER | Diligently. Bramwell, Bt., Lord Bramwell (NEP). |
| DILIGENTER ET FIDELITER | Diligently and faithfully. Allen, Bts., Inc. Assn. of Rating & Valuation Officers, 1937. |
| DILIGENTER ET FIRMITER | Diligently and firmly. Roberts of Milner Field, Bts. |
| DILIGENTER PERDUCERE | To guide conscientiously. No. 1 HQ (Signals) Wing, RAF. |
| DILIGENTIA ABSQUE TIMORE | Diligently without fear. Viscount Rhondda (Thomas) (NEP). |
| DILIGENTIA DIDAT | Industry renders rich. Ferrier, Newell, Taubman. |
| DILIGENTIA ET HONORE | With diligence and honour. Garnett of Quernmore Park. |
| DILIGENTLY AND FAITHFULLY | Inst. of Builders. |
| DIM NI'N HETYL | Nought shall deter us. No. 38 Maintenance Unit, RAF. |
| DIO VOLENDO IO LO FARO | God willing, I will do it. Kemeys-Tynte. |
| DION'S BUAIL | Protect and strike. No. 15 Group HQ, RAF. |
| DIRECT | 3621 North Lancashire Fighter Control Unit, RAAF. |
| DIRECT EXCHANGE | No. 290 Maintenance Unit, RAF. |
| DIRECT TO KILL | 3506 Co. of Northampton Fighter Control Unit, RAF. |
| DIRIGAT DEUS | May God direct us. Allen, Messel. |
| DIRIGE | Direct us. Aldridge, 651 Sq., RAF (Air Observation Post – hence motto from function of directing artillery fire). |
| DIRIGE GRESSUS MEOS | (Lord) direct my steps. Charles Emmanuel I, Duke of Savoy, 1562–1630. |
| DIRIGE ME DOMINE | Guide me, O Lord. Le Mee-Power. |
| DIRIGERE MINISTRANDO | To direct by serving. Bromsgrove (Worcs.) RDC. |
| DIRIGERE NON DOMINARI | To direct not to rule. Alcester (Warwicks.) RDC. |
| DIRIGET DEUS | God will direct (it). Butler of Pitlochry, co. Perth (crest of two hands issuing out of a cloud and drawing an arrow in a bow). |
| DISCE AUT DESCENDO | Learn or come down. RAF Sch. of Army Co-operation. |
| DISCE MORI UT VIVAS | Learn to die that thou mayest live. Unett. |
| DISCE PATI | Learn to endure. Earls of Camperdown (Haldane-Duncan) (NEP), Donkin of Ripon, Duncan, Ingle. |

| | |
|---|---|
| DISCE PRODESSE | Learn to come forth. Queen Elizabeth's Gram. Sch., Blackburn, 1509. |
| DISCE UT DIRIGAS | Learn in order that you may guide. RAF Sch. of Fighter Control. |
| DISCE UT PROFICIAS | Learn that you may succeed. Inst. of Medical Laboratory Technology, 1960. |
| DISCENDO DUCES | By learning you will lead. Newcastle-upon-Tyne Gram. Sch. 229 Operational Conversion Unit, RAF. |
| DISCERE DOCENDO | To learn through teaching. No. 11 Elementary Flying Training Sch., RAF. |
| DISCERN AND DECIDE | Hambling, Bts. |
| DISCIPLINA FIDE, PERSEVERANTIA | By discipline, faith and perseverance. Duckworth, Bts. |
| DISCITE JUSTITIAM MONITI | Learn justice, being admonished. Russell of Swallowfield, Bts. |
| DISCITE VIGILARE | Learn to be vigilant. No. 1 Air Signallers' Sch., RAF. |
| DISCORDIA FRANGIMUR | We break up discordant matters. Glass-sellers' Co., inc., 1664. |
| DISCRIMINE SALUS | Safety in danger. Traill (according to traditional accounts, motto and crest (column set in the sea) were assumed *c.*1418 when an ancestor was saved in shipwreck by clinging to a rock). |
| DISJUNCTA CONJUNGERE | To connect the disconnected. Radio Engineering Unit, RAF. |
| DISPONENDO ME, NON MUTANDO ME | By influencing me, not by changing me. Dukes of Manchester (Montagu), Montague. |
| DISSIPABO INIMICOS REGIS MEI UT PALEAM | I will disperse the enemies of my king like chaff. Stevans. |
| DISSIPATAE | Dispersed. Earls of Dundee (Scrymgeour-Wedderburn) (motto could refer to dispersal of difficulties which for over 250 years kept this earldom *de jure* not *de facto* until 1953), Scrymgeour. |
| DISTANTIA JUNGIT | It unites the distant. Bernard Stewart, cr. Chevalier d'Aubigny by the King of France, d. 1508. Like several of family before and after him, served in Scots contingent against England, hence motto with allusion to Auld Alliance of Scotland and France. Full account in *B. Ext. P.*, 1883, p.511. |
| DITAT SERVATA FIDES | Tried fidelity enriches. Archbald, Innes of Edinburgh, Papillon. |
| DITAT VIRTUS | Virtue enriches. Cheape. |
| DIU NOCTUQUE PUGNAMUS | We fight by day and night. 145 Sq., RAF (normal Latin for 'by day' = *die*, but in this motto *diu*, normally adverb meaning 'a long time', is used as in Old Latin as ablative case of *dies*). |
| DIVIDE ET IMPERA | Divide and rule. Inst. of Measurement & Control, 1968 (this was famous principle on which Roman conquest and administration was based). |

| | |
|---|---|
| DIVINE | No. 276 Wing, RAF. Badge has diviner's rod, symbolic of the king's function of listening in to enemy communications. |
| DIVINI GLORIA RURIS | Glory of the divine country (Virgil, *Georgics*, i. 169). Foster of Glyde Court, Bts. |
| DIWIDIANT A HARDDWCH | Industry and beauty. Llanelly (Carm.) RDC. |
| DIWYDIANT EIN CADERNID | Industry is our strength. Penybont (Glam.) RDC, 1960. |
| DO DIFFERENT | Univ. of East Anglia. |
| DO IT WITH THY MIGHT | Boyce, Bts., Buxton, Bts., Earl Buxton *(NEP)*, Viscount Cowdray (Pearson), Lords Noel-Buxton. |
| DO NO YLLE QUOTH D'OYLLE | D'Oyly, Bts. |
| DO OR DIE | Douglas of Cavers, Douglas of Springwood, Bts. |
| DO RIGHT AND FEAR NOT | Lord Ferrier (Noel-Paton), Lords Tryon. |
| DO RIGHT AND FEAR NOTHING | Lords Milner of Leeds. |
| DO RIGHT, FEAR NOTHING | Crooks, co. Lancs. |
| DO RIGHT, FEAR NOT | Stancomb. |
| DO RIGHT FEAR NAUGHT | 137 Sq., RAF (badge, white horse's head because of sq.'s association with Kent). |
| DO UT DES | I give that you may give. No. 91 Maintenance Unit, RAF. |
| DO WELL AND DOUBT NOT | Blakeston, Bruce, Bruce of Stenhouse, Bts., Viscount Bryce *(NEP)*, Houston, Kingsmill. |
| DO WELL, DOUBT NOT | Tunbridge Wells (Kent), Roy. Bor. of. |
| DO WELL AND FEAR NOT | Elstree (Herts.) RDC. |
| DOCE UT DISCAS | Teach that you may learn. Cheshire Co. Training Coll., 205 Advanced Flying Sch., RAF. |
| DOCEMUS | We teach. RAF station, Locking, Berks. |
| DOCEMUS ET DISCIMUS | We teach and we learn. RAF station, Newton, Cheshire. |
| DOCEMUS UT REPLEAMUS | We teach that we may replenish. 232 Operational Conversion Unit, RAF. |
| DOCENDO DISCIMUS | We learn by teaching. No. 9 Flying Training Sch., RAF, Stranmills Training Coll., Belfast, 1961. |
| DOCENDO DISCO | I learn by teaching. Courage of Edgcote, co. Oxford. |
| DOCENDO SERVIMUS | We serve by teaching. No. 11 Sch. of Tech. Training, RAF. |
| DOCERE SED DISCERE | To teach but to learn. Taylor of Kennington, Bts. |
| DOCTI DOCERE DISCITE | Ye learned ones, now learn to teach. RAF Sch. of Education. |
| DOCTI SUPERABIMUS AURAS | With instruction we will master the air. Hull Univ. Air Sq., RAFVR. |
| DOCTOREM DICEMUS | We teach the teacher. RAF Central Flying Sch., S. Rhodesia. |
| DOCTINAE LABOR FORMAT DUCEM | The effort of learning makes the leader. RAF Tech. Coll. |

| | |
|---|---|
| DOCTRINAM ACCINGIMUS ALIS | We equip learning with wings. Cambridge Univ. Air Sq., RAFVR. |
| DOE OR DIE | The Border Rifle Volunteers (later, 1887, 1st Volunteer Bn. The King's Own Borderers). |
| DOE WELL AND DOUBT NOT | Blakeston, Bts., Bruce, Houston. |
| DOE WEL EN ZIE NIET OM | Do well and do not look round. Order of the Reunion (Netherlands). |
| DOLE NUMQUAM | Never by fraud. Abrahamson. |
| DOLUERE DENTE LACESSIT | To suffer with a tooth hurts. Arden. |
| DOMINE DIRIGE | O Lord direct. Scotter, Bts. |
| DOMINE DIRIGE NOS | O Lord direct us. City of London, City of London Freemen's Sch., Ashstead Park, Surrey, 1854, 1st City of London Engineer Volunteers, Royal London Militia, City of London Volunteer Regt., 7th City of London Bn., Territorials. |
| DOMINE SALÚUM FAC REGEM | O Lord save the king. King Edward's Sch., Birmingham, 1552. |
| DOMINI EST DIRIGERE | It is for the Lord to direct. Gipping (E. Suffolk) RDC. |
| DOMINUS DEDIT | The Lord hath given. Harries, Harris, Herries, Lord Herries (Constable-Maxwell). |
| DOMINUS FECIT | The Lord hath done it. Baird, co. Fife, Baird, co. Moray, Jackson, Viscount Stonehaven (Baird). |
| DOMINUS FORTISSIMA TURRIS | The Lord is the strongest tower. De Havilland, Tower. |
| DOMINUS FRUSTRA | The Lord in vain. Derby Diocesan Training Coll. |
| DOMINUS ILLUMINATIO MEA | The Lord is my light. Oxford Univ. (a book is the principal charge in the arms and the above is inscribed upon it). |
| DOMINUS IPSE FACIET | The Lord himself will do it. Adam. |
| DOMINUS ME REGIT | The Lord rules me. Jacobs. |
| DOMINUS MIHI ADJUTOR | The Lord is my helper. Douai Sch., Woolhampton, founded 1615 in Paris, as Abbey of St Edmund King and Martyr of East Anglia by English Benedictines. Although a completely English foundation, was twice persecuted by atheistic French governments, but has lasted without a break. |
| DOMINUS NOBIS SOL ET SCUTUM | The Lord is to us sun and shield. Banbury (Oxon.), Bor. of. |
| DOMINUS NON SAGITTA TUTAMEN | The Lord, not an arrow, is the safeguard. Fletcher (the old name for an arrow-maker). |
| DOMINUS PETRA MEA | The Lord is my rock. Dampier. |
| DOMINUS PROVIDEBIT | The Lord will provide Boyle of Limavady, Burton of Burton Hall, Burton of Longnor Hall, Salop, Gordon, Bts., Earls of Glasgow (Boyle), Lords Hacking, Lord Lingen, Masson, M'Laws, M'Vicar. |
| DOMINUS SAPIENTIAM DAT | God gives wisdom. Roy, Sch. for Daughters of Officers of the Army, 1952. |

| | |
|---|---|
| DOMUM ANTIQUAM REDINTEGRARE | To resuscitate an ancient house. Buchan-Hepburn, Bts. |
| DOMUS ARX CERTISSIMA | The home is the most certain citadel. Alliance Bldg. Soc. |
| DONA FERENTES ADSUMUS | We are come bringing gifts. 620 Sq., RAF. |
| DONA PRAESENTE RAPE LAETUS HORAE | Be happy and take in present the gifts of the hour. Cirencester Gram. Sch. |
| DONATE OMNIA | Give all. Kerr, Bt. |
| DONEC IMPLEAT | Until it may fill. Souter. |
| DONEC IMPLEAT ORBEM | Until it fill its orb. Kidd, Kydd. |
| DONEC PURUM | Until clean. Italian Academy of the Travagliati, Italian Literary Academy Ardenti of Viterbo. |
| DONEC TOTUM IMPLEAT ORBEM | Until it fill the whole world. Henry II of France, 1519–59, used motto when Dauphin, a crescent being his emblem. Until he became king, his glory would be less. |
| DONORUM DEI DISPENSATIO FIDELIS | A faithful dispensation of the gifts of God. Harrow Sch., founded 1571 by John Lyon, yeoman of Preston parish of Harrow, under royal charter. |
| DORESEAVANT | Henceforward. Edward Stafford, 3rd Duke of Buckingham, executed 1521 owing to machinations of Cardinal Wolsey; it was alleged that motto was allusion to an intention to seize the Crown. |
| DOUCEMENT | Softly. Ross, Bts. |
| DOV'E GRAN FUOCO, E GRAN FUMO | Where there is great fire, there is great smoke. Odet de Foix, Seigneur de Lautrec, Marshal of France, 1485–1528. His vanity prompted this motto, meaning that his merits equalled his pride. |
| DREAD GOD | Carnegie, Bts., Carnegy, Gordon of Earlston, Bts., Hay, Hodgson, Monro, Bts., Platt of Rushholme, Bts., Ross, Earls of Southesk (Carnegie). |
| DREAD SHAME | Leighton, Bts., Leighton of Medonsley, Lord Leighton (NEP). |
| DRE WERES AGAN DEW NY | By the help of our God. Glynn. |
| DROGO NOMEN, ET VIRTUS ARMA DEDIT | Drogo is my name, and valour gave me arms. Drewe of Castle Drogo. According to Victorian account, Drew descended from the family of Drogo, but there is no sign of this in B.L.G. 1952 article, where pedigree begins in 1744. |
| DROIT ET AVANT | Just and forward. Viscount Dawson of Penn (NEP), Ramsden, Viscount Sydney (Townshend) (NEP), Lords Trent (Boot) (NEP). |
| DROIT ET LOYAL | Just and loyal. Dudley, Earl of Leicester temp. Elizabeth I, Lords Huntingfield (Vanneck). |
| DROP AS RAIN, DISTILL AS DEW | Distillers' Co., inc. 1638. |
| DUBIA FORTUNA | Doubtful fortune. King James I of Aragon, 1213–76. |
| DUCANT ASTRA | Let the stars be your guide. RAF station, Calshot, Hants. |
| DUCAT AMOR DEI | Let the love of God lead. Trevor-Battye (formerly of Little Hampden). |

| | |
|---|---|
| DUCENTE DEO | With God leading. Lepper. |
| (DUCENTI SEDECIM) CCXVI DONA FERENS | 216 bearing gifts. 216 Sq., RAF. |
| DUCIMUS CETERI SECUNTER | We lead others follow (third word = sequuntur). 635 Sq., RAF (dropping flares for target identification). |
| DUCIT AMOR PATRIAE | Patriotism leads me. Blades, Foley-Philipps, Bt., Lord Kylsant (Philipps) (NEP), Lechmere, Lloyd-Philipps, Lords Milford (Philipps), Philipps of Dale Castle, Viscount St Davids (Philipps). |
| DUCIT QUI CONDUCIT | He leads who collects. Inst. of Works Managers, 1962. |
| DUCTUS PER SCIENTIAM | Led through science. S.W. Essex Tech. Coll. |
| DULCE DECORUM EST PRO CHRISTI ET PATRIA MORI | Sweet and lovely it is to die for Christ and our country (adapted from Horace, Odes III. ii. 13). John Louis, Count of Nassau, d. 1653. |
| DULCE MEUM TERRA TEGIT | The earth covers my sweet one. Mary Queen of Scots, d. 1587 (referring to death of her first husband, Francis II, King of France). |
| DULCE PERICULUM | Danger is sweet. McCall, Macauley, Bishop McCauley of Silversprings, Maryland, USA (instance of arms grant (of which motto is part) from the Chief Herald of the Republic of Ireland to an American citizen). |
| DULCE PRO PATRIA PERICULUM | Danger is sweet for one's country. Ker, Seymer. |
| DULCE QUOD UTILE | That is agreeable which is useful. Strange, Stronge, Bts. |
| DULCIS AMOR PATRIAE | The love of one's country is sweet. Clifford, co. Gloucs., Fitswygram, Bts., Robinson, Wigram, Bts., Lords Wigram. |
| DULCIUS ASPERIS | The sweeter being gained from hardships. Ferguson, Bts. (crest is a bee on a thistle). |
| DULCIS PRO PATRIA LABOR | Labour for one's country is sweet. McKerrell. |
| DUM CRESCO SPERO | While I grow I hope. Bromley (Kent). Bor. of. |
| DUM DEFLUAT AMNIS | While the river flows. Stourport (Worcs.) UDC, 1962, Walton and Weybridge (Surrey) UDC, 1946. |
| DUM DEO PLACUERIT | While it shall please God. Treffry. |
| DUM MEMOR IPSE MEI | While I am mindful of myself. Irvine, co. Fermanagh. |
| DUM SISTO VIGILO | Whilst I stand still I watch. Gordon of Newtimber, Gordon of Letterfaurie, Bts. |
| DUM SPIRO COELESTIA SPERO | While I have breath I hope heavenly things. Booth-Jones, Jones. |
| DUM SPIRO DIMICABO | While I breathe I will fight. Milnes-Coates, Bts. |
| DUM SPIRO SERVO | While I breathe I serve. Chitty, Viscount Leathers. |
| DUM SPIRO SPERO | While I breath I hope. Aschmaty, Asscotti, Auchmuty, Bainbridge, Baker, Bannatyne of Newhall, Bloxham, Brooke, Bushell, Carlton, Casement, Collet of St Clere, Bt. Colquhon, Compton, Corbet, Bts., Coryton of Pentillic Castle, Cornwall, Cotter, Bts., Davies, Dearden, Viscount Dillon, Dillon, Bts., Doran, Drummond, Elrick, Glazebrook, Going, Gordon, |

Gracey, Gurney, Harding, Harrison of Eaglescliffe, Bts., Hoare, Bts., Hoare, Holmes, Holt, Hunter, Jackson of Putney Hill, Jackson of Wandsworth, Bt., Jeffcoat, Learmouth, Lee-Dillon, Manser, Milburn, Bts., Monk-Mason, Moore, Morice, Morris, Oldfield, O'Reilly, Partridge, Pearson, Lords Playfair *(NEP)*, Price, Ripley, Bts., Roberts, Rodwell, Rylands, Sandford, Sharp, Smith, Stanton, Stretton, Spearman, Bts., Spry, Symonds, Tatlock, Thompson, Bts., Thompson, co. Durham, Walker, Westerman.

| | |
|---|---|
| DUM TEMPUS HABEMUS OPEREMUR BONUM | While we have time let us do good. Queen Elizabeth's Hosp., Clifton, Bristol, founded 1586 by John Carr, a Bristol merchant. Motto taken from Pauline injunction. |
| DUM VIGILO TUTUS | While I am vigilant I am safe. Gordon of Cairnfield, Gordon-Canning of Hartbury, co. Glos. |
| DUM VIVIMUS VIVAMUS | While we live let us live. Cory-Wright, Bts., Doddridge, Hewitt, Vyvyan. |
| DUM VIVO SPERO | While I live I hope. Latta, Monteath, Stuart-Menteith, Bts., Thom, Whiteway. |
| DUM VIVO VIREO | While I live I flourish. Latta, Bt. |
| DURA FRANGO PATIENTIA | I break hard things with patience. Lords Langford (Rowley-Conwy). |
| DURA VIRUM NUTRIX | A hard nurse of men. Sedbergh Sch., Cumberland, founded 1525 by Dr Roger Lupton, Provost of Eton. |
| DURABO | I will endure. Cardinal Innocent Cybo, son of Francesco Cybo, King John II of Aragon, 1458–79. |
| DURATE | Endure. Evelyn, Bts., Cardinal (Antonio Perenoto) de Granveld, d. 1586. Minister of Charles V and Philip II and governor of Spanish Netherlands. Of middle-class origin. Motto implies that his fame would outlast that of the nobles. A by no means flattering account of the Cardinal is in J. L. Motley, *Rise of the Dutch Republic*, Part 2. |
| DURIS NON FRANGOR | I am not disheartened by difficulties. Moore, Muir, Muir, Bts., Mure. |
| DURUM PATIENTIA FRANGO | By patience I break a hard thing. Kennedy-Craufurd-Stuart. |
| DURUM SED CERTISSIMUM | Hard but most sure. Gillanders. |
| DUTY | Birchenough, Brouncher, Goldsworthy, King, Ursuline Convent High Sch., Brentwood, Essex, 1964. |
| DUW A DDARPAR Y'R BRAIN | God provides for the crows. Hughes of Plas Coch, Williams of Treffus. |
| DUW A DIGON | God is enough. Denbighshire CC, Nicholl, Prytherch, Vaughan of Courtfield. |
| DUW AR FY RHAN | God for my portion. Bruce of Blaen-y-cwm, co. Glam. |
| DUW AU BENDITHIS | God with us. Pryse, Bts. |
| DUW AUFENDITH YW FY NGWENWTH (NGHYNNYDD) | God's blessing is my increase. Riall. |

| | |
|---|---|
| DUW DY RAS | God thy grace. Kemeys-Jenkin, Kemeys-Tynte, Kemmis. |
| DUW EIN HYMDDIFFYNFA | God is our refuge. Thomas of Ynyshir, Bts. |
| DUW FO FY RHAN | God be my support. Lewis, Lord Llewellin *(NEP)*. |
| DUW GADWO BRAIN | God supports the ravens. Evans of Lovesgrove, Evans of Nantymoch. |
| DUWIOLLDEB DIWYRDWYDD | (archaic) Port Talbot, Bor. of, 1953. |
| DUX FEMINA FACTI | A woman leader of what has to be done (Virgil). Westfield Coll., London Univ., 1882. |
| DUX VITAE RATIO | Reason is the guide of life. Alston-Roberts-West, Boulton, Fanshawe, Leigh-Bennett, West. |
| DYSGU I EHEDDEG | Teaching to fly. No. 5 Flying Training Sch., RAF. |
| DYWYSYGNETH BA GWYRYONETH | Perseverance and sincerity (Cornish). Trevarthew. |

# E

**E DUOBUS UNUM** — One out of two. Corinthian Casuals Football Club, Welding Inst., 1968.

**E FLAMMIS ATQUE RUINIS SALUS** — Safety from the flames and ruins. RAF Sch. of Fire Fighting and Rescue.

**E FLUCTIBUS OPES** — Strength from the waves. Shaw of Wolverhampton, Bt.

**E GLANDE QUERCUS** — The oak from an acorn. Dorking and Horley (Surrey) RDC, Wokingham (Berks.) Bor. of, 1953.

**E LABORE DULCEDO** — Pleasure arises out of labour. Boyle, Innes of Fordoun, MacInnes.

**E LABORE LIBERTAS** — Liberty from work. Freeman, Bts.

**E LABORE STABILITAS** — Stability from labour. Vestey, Bts., Lords Vestey.

**E MARE ET INDUSTRIA** — From the sea and from industry. West Hartlepool Bor. of.

**E MINIMIS MAXIMA** — The most from the smallest. UK Atomic Energy Authority, 1955. This motto, along with the Authority's very elaborate and striking coat of arms, is one of the most outstanding examples of the adaptability of heraldry to express the most modern institutions (full description and illustration in Pine, *Teach Yourself Heraldry and Genealogy*, 1957, p. 133).

**E MULCIBERE GARAE** — From Vulcan? East Midlands Gas Bd.

**E NATURA INGENIOQUE COPIA** — Plenty from nature and intellect. National Coll. of Agricultural Engineering.

**E NOCENTIBUS INNOCENTIA** — Out of harmful things, harmless things. 5131 Bomb Disposal Sq., RAF.

**E NUBIBUS** — From the clouds. No. 28 Maintenance Unit, RAF.

**E NUCE NUCLEUM** — From the nut (get) the kernel. Baker-Cresswell, Cresswell.

**E PARVIS MAXIMA** — Out of small things very great things. Strike Cmd. Armament Sch. (original name Bomber Cmd. Armament Sch.), RAF.

**E PLURIBUS UNUM** — One out of many. Motto from arms of USA since 1782.

**E PUR SI MUOVE** — And yet it does move. These words, traditionally ascribed to Galileo Galilei after his recantation, referring to the earth moving round the sun and not vice versa, have been used as motto for series of scientific works in England.

**E RUPE ERUMPET AQUA** — Water shall break forth from the rock. Grimsby, Cleethorpes & District Water Bd. (probably ref. to Moses' action in striking the rock to bring forth water).

| | |
|---|---|
| E SABULO AD SIDERA | From the sand to the stars. No. 4 Flying Training Sch., RAF. Unit was formed in Egypt in 1921, hence motto and badge of palm trees in front of a pyramid. |
| E SINGULIS COMMUNITAS | A community out of separate individuals. RAF station, Lichfield, Staffs. |
| E SPINIS | From among thorns. Delap, Dunlop. |
| E TENEBRIS LUX | Light out of darkness, National Coal Bd. |
| E TERRA DIVITIAE | Riches from the earth. Swadlincote UDC, 1947. |
| E TERRA MARIQUE VIS | Strength from land and sea. West Midlands Gas Bd., 1967. |
| E TRIBUS UNUM | One out of three. Norfolk Joint Police Authority (recent formation by amalgamation). |
| E VENTIS VIRES | Strength from the winds. Seaford (Sussex) UDC, 1953. |
| EACH DAY A SERVICE | Farr. |
| EACH FOR ALL, ALL FOR GOD | Wakefield Girls' High Sch., 1963. |
| EASTWARD | RAF HQ, Far East. |
| ECCE AGNUS DEI QUI TOLLIT PECCATA MUNDI | Behold the Lamb of God, which taketh away the sins of the world (John 1:29). Tallow Chandlers' Co., 1461. |
| ECCE EGO, MITTE ME | Here am I, send me (Isaiah 6:8). Holy Island (Northumb.) Parish Council. |
| ECCLESIAE FILII | Sons of the Church. St Edmund's Sch., Canterbury, 1749. |
| EDRYCG I FYNU | Powell. |
| EDURAT RE BILSTONIA | Bilston lasts in affair(s). Bilston (Staffs.) UDC. |
| EENDRAGT MAAKT MAGT | Unity is strength. Province of Transvaal, 1955. |
| EFFICIENCY | No. 94 Maintenance Unit, RAF. |
| EFFICIUNT CLARUM STUDIA | Studies make him illustrious. Lords Milne. |
| EFFLORESCO | I bloom greatly. Earls Cairns, Cairnes. |
| EGYPT, JAVA, AVA, NIAGARA, SEVASTOPOL | 89th Foot (2nd Bn. Princess Victoria's Royal Irish Fusiliers). |
| EHED A'I EDYN EI HUN | He flies on his own wings. Jones of Pentower. |
| EI BRI EIN BRANT | Her fame is our privilege. Brecknockshire Agricultural Soc. |
| E'EN DO AND SPAIR NOCHT | Lees, MacGregor of MacGregor, Bts. |
| E'IN DO AND SPARE NOT | Greg, Gregorson, Macgregor, Bts., McGrigor, MacPeter. |
| EINE FESTE BURG | A firm fortress. RAF station, Laarbruck. |
| EINE WAHRHEIT, EIN GOTT, EIN RECHT | One truth, one God, one right. Order of Duke Peter of Oldenburg. |
| EIRINN GO BRATH | Ireland for ever. Carlow Rifles Militia. |
| EL HUMAYA ESSADIQA | Protect well. Air Force Middle East and HQ British Forces, Aden. |
| EL HOMBRE PROPONE, DIOS DISPONE | Man proposes, God disposes. Davy. |

| | |
|---|---|
| ELOQUENTIA SAGITTA | Eloquence is my arrow. Bland. |
| ELOQUENTIA VIRTUS EVOCANT | Virtue by eloquence – these call out. Lords Silsoe (Trustram-Eve). |
| EMENDATUS AD UNGUEM | Flawless to the last degree. No. 4 Ground Radio Servicing Sq., RAF. |
| EMPIRE AND LIBERTY | 3rd King Edward's Horse (1914–15). |
| EN AVANT | Forward. Chad, D'Eyncourt, Lucy, Tennyson D'Eyncourt, Bts., Tritton, Bts. |
| EN BON ESPOIR | In good hope. Cokayne, Bt., De Lisle, Nicholas, Willoughby. |
| EN BOY FOY | In good faith. Bagwell-Purefoy, Chadwick, Sacheverell. |
| EN BONHEURE PUISSE | In good time one can. March. |
| EN DIEU AFFIE | Trust in God. Malet. |
| EN DIEU EST MA FOI | In God is my faith. Cheevers, Legh, Mauleverer, Lords Newton (Legh), Staunton, co. Warwick. |
| EN DIEU EST MON ESPÉRANCE | In God is my hope. Gerard, Lords Gerard, Jarrett, Walmsley. |
| EN DIEU EST TOUT | In God is everything. Lords Alington (NEP), Chambers, Chambre, Conolly, Davies, Malton (N.R. Yorks.) UDC, Ryland, Vernon-Wentworth, Watson, Watson-Wentworth, Wentworth, co. York. |
| EN GARDE | Be on your guard. 88 Sq., RAF (badge serpent = badge of 88 Sq., French Air Force 1914–18, adopted on account of comradeship of the two sqs.). |
| EN LA ROSE JE FLEURIE | I flourish in the rose. Edwards-Moss, Bts., Lennox, Dukes of Richmond and Gordon (Gordon-Lennox) (in the arms of Lennox are roses to which motto refers). |
| EN ROUTE | RAF station, Gan Indian Ocean (famous staging-post). |
| EN SUIVANT LA VERITÉ | By following truth. Earls of Portsmouth (Wallop), Wallop, Williams, co. Mon. |
| EN TOUT TEMPS DU BLÉ | In every season of wheat (play on name of Burgundian family of Blé). |
| ENDEAVOUR | Hendon, London Bor. of, Lord McFadzean. |
| ENDURANCE | 120 Sq., RAF. |
| ENDURE FORT | Endure boldly. Earls of Crawford and Balcarres (Lindsay), Lindsay. |
| ENSIS EST ET NON AURUM | It is the sword and not gold. De Montfort. |
| ENTALENTÉ À PARLER D'ARMES | Equipped to speak of arms. The Heraldry Soc., 1957. |
| ENTERPRISE IN THE SKIES | Eagle Aviation Ltd. |
| ENTERPRISE WITH PRUDENCE | London Chamber of Commerce. |
| ENTIRELY ENGLISH | Queen Anne's coronation medal, and the sentiment expressed at her first opening of Parliament. |
| EODEM SIGNO CONJUNCTI | Joined by the same sign. Washington Development Corp., co. Durham. |

| | |
|---|---|
| EOTHEN | Out of the East. 127 Sq., RAF (motto forms title of Kinglake's classic travel book). |
| EQUANIMITAS MAGNANIMITAS | Equanimity is magnanimity. Viscount Buckmaster. |
| EQUITES NOSTRE ARMA SUMUNT | Our knights take up arms. RAF station, Ta Kali, Malta. |
| ERECTA FERAR AT NON CONNIVEBO | I will be erect and not blink. Joseph, Comte de Montmajeur, d. 1570, from his emblem of an eagle looking directly at the sun, one of the fanciful ideas of that age being to credit the bird with that power. |
| ERECTUS NON ELATUS | Exalted but not elated. Beaumont, Bts. Beaumont of Barrow, Clark, Phillips. |
| ERIMUS | We shall be. Middlesbrough (N.R. Yorks.), Bor. of. |
| ERIN GO BRAG | Carlow Rifles (Mil.) |
| ERIPIMUS JOVI FULMEN | We grasp the thunder from Jove. HMS *Thunderer* had a badge with a hand grasping thunderbolts. |
| ERIT ALTERA MERCES | One (or other) will be the reward. Marc Antonio Colonna, *c*.1522. |
| ERIT HAEC QUOQUE COGNITA MONSTRIS | This will be made known to (both) monsters. Louis XIII of France. The monsters were heresy and rebellion; *haec* was used with the king's device, a club, or two clubs of Hercules. |
| ESCORT | RAF Queen's Colour Sq. |
| ESPÉRANCE | Hope. Ducs de Bourbon, Moncrieff of Culfargie, Percies, Wallace of Hartford House, Bt. |
| ESPÉRANCE EN DIEU | Hope in God. Durand Bts., Dukes of Northumberland (Percy), Persse. |
| ESPÉRANT FIDELEMENT | They hope faithfully. Moncrieff of Kinmonth. |
| ESPÈRE ET PERSEVERE | Hope and persevere. Paget, Bts. |
| ESSAYEZ | Try. Lords Allerton (Lawles Jackson), Dundas of Arniston, Bts., Dundas of Beechwood, Bts., Dundas of Dundas, Dundas of Richmond, Bt., Jackson, Marquesses of Zetland (Dundas). |
| ESSE POTIUS QUAM VIDERI | Rather to be than to seem. 77 Sq., RAF. |
| ESSE QUAM VIDERI | To be rather than to seem. Addenbrooke, Ashville Coll., Harrogate, Yorks., Ashford Sch., Kent, Beadon, Bedford Coll., London Univ., 1849, Bonham, Bonham, Bt., British Standards Inst., Earls Brownlow (Cust) *(NEP)*, Lords Brownlow (Cust), Bunbury, Bts., Burton, Charles, Churchill, co. Dorset, Collett, Cook, Bts., Couts, Croft, Bts., of Cowling Hall, Croft, Bts., of Croft Castle, Lords Croft, Crawley-Boevey, Bts., Cust, Bt., Deline, Eykyn, Flinn, Lords Franks, General Dental Council, Grattan, Hammerton, Heaton, Hill, Hood, Hopkins of St Pancras, Bt., Hulse, Bts., Lane, Longley, Lords Lurgan (Brownlow), Maitland, Maris, Mathil, Norman, co. Kent, Oakes, Pollard, Raphael, Bt., Renshaw, Bts., Round, Lord Robins *(NEP)*, St Paul, St Paul, Bts., Savory, Bts., Sheriff, Swire, Thurston, Truro School, 1879, Turner, Turnour, Williams of Llanrumney Hall, Earls Winterton (Turnour), Woodcock. |

| | |
|---|---|
| ESSE QUOD ESSE VIDERIS | To be what you seem to be. Barber of Cullum, Bt. |
| ESSENTIAL SUPPORT | No. 131 Maintenance Unit, RAF. |
| EST CONCORDIA FRATRUM | Harmony becomes brothers. Brown, Bts., Brown of Brandon, Pigott-Brown, Bts. |
| EST EN FORGEANT | Practice makes perfect. 287 Sq., RAF. |
| EST ET SILENTIO MERCES | There is also reward for silence. Findlay, Bts. |
| EST MERUISSE SATIS | It is sufficient to have deserved. Massingberd, Montgomery-Massingberd. |
| EST MIHI CAUDA DECUS | My tail is my glory. Amadeus I of Savoy, Count of Maurienne, c.1050, in allusion to his magnificent train of attendants and his device of a peacock. |
| EST MODUS IN REBUS | There is a measure in things. Roy. Inst. of Chartered Surveyors. |
| EST NEC ASTU | Neither is it the city (used of Athens only in classical Latin). Brooke of Almondbury, Bts., Brooke, co. York. |
| EST VOLUNTAS DEI | It is the will of God. Baldwin, Cliffe, Coates of Eyton House, Leominster. |
| ESTADOS UNIDOS DO BRASIL 15 DE NOVEMBRO DE 1889 | The United States of Brazil, 15 November 1889. Brazil, from arms assumed when Braganza family ceased to rule as Emperors of Brazil and country became a republic. |
| ESTE HIC DOMINI | Remain here (as) lords. Este (famous Italian family, supposed to be derived from the first word of the motto as spoken by a kingly benefactor). |
| ESTO CIVIS FIDELIS | Be a faithful citizen. Freeman. |
| ESTO FIDELIS | Be faithful. Aubertin, Fry of Woodburn, Bts., Sykes of Kingsknowes, Bts., Whitter. |
| ESTO MEMOR | Be mindful. Keates. |
| ESTO PERNOX | Be (ready) all night. Fowler. |
| ESTO PERPETUA | Be perpetual. Amicable Life Insurance Soc., Norwich Union Fire Insurance Soc. Ltd., Scaramanga. |
| ESTO QUOD ES | Be what thou art. Bossom, Bts., Lord Bossom (NEP). |
| ESTO QUOD ESSE VIDERIS | Be what you seem to be. Aufrere, Barkworth, Buzzard, Bts., Cole, Darling, Hooke, Legge, co. Fife, Milles, Mills, Earls Sondes (Milles-Lade), Watson of Chadwick Manor, Watson of Sulhamstead, Bts. |
| ESTO SEMPER FIDELIS | Be ever faithful. Duffield, George, Unthank, Yea, Bts. |
| ESTO SOL TESTIS | Let the sun be witness. Jones. |
| ESTO VIGILANS | Be vigilant. Huntsman, Lloyd of Dolobran, Lords Lloyd, Lloyds Bank Ltd., Okeover, Walker-Okeover, Bts. |
| ET ANGLIAE GLORIA | And the glory of England. Elizabeth I (who used also Video, I see; Taceo, I am silent; Vivat prudentia regnum, let the kingdom live by prudence; Sola phoenix omnis mundi, the only phoenix of the whole world; Non sine sole iris, no rainbow without the sun). |

| | |
|---|---|
| ET AUGEBITUR SCIENTIA | And knowledge shall be increased. Leeds Univ., 1905 (these words from Daniel 12:4 appear on an open book in coat of arms). |
| ET BELLO ET PACE | In war and in peace. Hanbury-Tenison. |
| ET CUSTOS ET PUGNAX | Both a preserver and a champion. Majoribanks. |
| ET DATO GAUDETIS | And you rejoice at what is given. South London Hosp. for Women and Children, 1947. |
| ET DECUS ET PRETIUM RECTI | Both the honour and the reward of rectitude. Viscount Daventry (FitzRoy), Disney, Fitz Roy, Dukes of Grafton (Fitzroy), Lords Southampton (Fitzroy). |
| ET DIEU MON APPUI | And God my support. Heathcote, Bts., Hungerford. |
| ET FACIO ET REFICIO | I both make and repair. No. 4 Maintenance Unit, RAF. |
| ET FIDE ET VIRTUTE | By both faith and virtue. Porter of Belle Isle. |
| ET FLORES ET FRUCTUS | Both flowers and fruit. Flower. |
| ET MEA MESSIS ERIT | My harvest will also arrive. Judd, co. Essex. |
| ET NOVA ET VETERA | Both new and old. Bryanston Sch., Blandford, Dorset, 1928. |
| ET PATRIBUS POSTERITATI | And to our fathers and to posterity. Hitchen (Herts.) UDC. |
| ET PLUI SUPER UNAM CIVITATEM | And I cause it to rain upon one city (Amos 4:7). Metropolitan Water Bd. |
| ET PUGNANT QUI DISCUNT | They also fight who learn. No. 8 Sch. of Tech. Training, RAF. |
| ET STERILES PLATANT MALA GESSERE VALENTES | The barren plane trees have produced good fruit. Italian Academy of Trasformati of Milan. |
| ET SUBSIDIUM ET PRAESIDIUM | Both a resource and a defence. No. 40 Group HQ, RAF. |
| ET VI ET VIRTUTE | By strength and virtue. Baird, Bt., Burrows of London, Bt., Stannus. |
| ET VIRTUTEM ET MUSAS | (I cultivate) virtue and the muses. Mill Hill Sch., London. |
| ETERNAL VIGILANCE | 155 Sq., RAF. |
| EVER ALERT | Air Control Centre, RAF. |
| EVER BETTER | No. 71 Maintenance Unit, RAF. |
| EVER FORWARD | Weston-Super-Mare (Somerset), Bor. of, 1960. |
| EVER LOOKING FORWARD | East Down (co. Down) RDC. |
| EVER LOYAL | Pickering (Yorks.) UDC. |
| EVER READY | Lord Armistead (NEP), Bryson, Burn, Burns-Hartop, Lords Inverclyde (Burns) (NEP). |
| EVER TO THE FORE | No. 125 Wing HQ, RAF. |
| EVER VIGILANT | Poultry Assn. of Great Britain (SPBA) Ltd., 1948. |
| EVER WATCHFUL | White of Bristol, Bts., No. 19 Group HQ, RAF (retitled) HQ Southern Maritime Air Region. |
| EVERY OUNCE COUNTS | No. 151 Wing, RAF (badge a Snow Leopard or Ounce to represent the unit having been only combatant RAF unit in Russia during World War II). |

| | |
|---|---|
| EVERYWHERE | Fighter Cmd. Communications Sq., RAF. |
| EWCH YN UWCH | Go higher. Radnorshire CC, 1950. |
| EWNDER GANS TREGERETH | Justice with mercy (Cornish). Trewyn. |
| EX AERE SALUS | Safety from the air. 293 Sq., RAF formed at Blida, Algeria, 1943. |
| EX AETERNA VIGILANTIA VIRES | From everlasting watchfulness comes strength. RAF station, Exeter, Devon. |
| EX ARMIS LIBER | Free by means of arms. Murray of Folla. |
| EX BELLO QUIES | Peace arises out of war. Murray of Ochtertyre, Murray-Buchanan of Leny, co. Perth. |
| EX CAELIS SCIENTIA | From the skies comes knowledge. Central Photographic Establishment, RAF. |
| EX CAELO AUXILIUM | Aid from the skies. 295 Sq., RAF (supplying weapons to resistance in occupied territories). |
| EX CLARA MENTE LUX | From a clear mind comes light. Admin. Apprentice Training Sch., RAF. |
| EX CORDE CARITAS | Charity from the heart. George Watson's Coll., Edinburgh (founded by George Watson, d. 1723). |
| EX CRUCE FLORES | Flowers from the Cross. Cross of Bolton-le-Moors, Bt. |
| EX CULTU ROBUR | Strength from culture. Cranleigh Sch., Surrey, 1863. |
| EX FIDE FORTIS | Strong from faith. Hillsborough (co. Down) RDC. |
| EX FIDE VIRTUS | Virtue from faith. Lord Godber. |
| EX GLANDE QUERCUS | From acorn to oak. Southgate, London Bor. of. |
| EX HERBIS REMEDIA | A remedy from herbs. Nat. Inst. of Medical Herbalists Ltd. |
| EX IGNE RESURGAM | I shall rise again from fire. Lisburn (Co. Antrim), Bor. of. |
| EX IGNI PULCHRITUDO | Beauty out of fire. W. T. Copeland & Sons Ltd. (makers of china), 1967. |
| EX MARE AD REFERIENDUM | From out of the sea to strike again. 278 Sq., RAF. |
| EX MARI SERVAMUS | We save from the sea. No. 207 Air Sea Rescue Unit, RAF. |
| EX MEA MESSIS ERIT | The harvest will be from my resources. Judd of Rickling. |
| EX OPERA ET INDUSTRIA | From work and industry, Allen. |
| EX OPERE OPERATO | From the work having been done. Davis, Bts. (theological phrase usually applied to the objective workings of the Sacraments). |
| EX ORIENTE SALUS | Salvation out of the East. Eastbourne Coll., Sussex. |
| EX RADIIS SALUTAS | Safety out of rays. Faculty of Radiologists, 1961. |
| EX SCIENTIA VIRES | Strength from knowledge. No. 10 Operational Training Unit, RAF. |
| EX SPINIS UVAS | (Gather) grapes from thorns. Bristol Gram. Sch., founded 1532 by merchant Robert Thorne and others. |
| EX TENEBRIS | Through (i.e. out of) darkness. 190 Sq., RAF. |

| | |
|---|---|
| EX TENEBRIS AD LUCEM | From darkness to light. RAF station, Leconfield. |
| EX TENEBRIS LUX | Out of darkness, light. HMS *Glow-worm*, which in 1940 rammed the German heavy cruiser *Admiral Hipper*, tearing away 130 feet of the latter's armoured belt, before blowing up. |
| EX TERRA COPIAM E MARI SALUTEM | From the land fullness and from the sea health. Worthing (Sussex), Bor. of. |
| EX TERRA LUCEM | Light out of the earth. St Helens (Lancs.), Co. Bor. of. |
| EX TERRA OPES | Wealth from the earth. Coalville (Leics.) UDC. |
| EX TERRA VIGEMUS | We flourish from the earth. Sedgefield (Durham) RDC, 1954. |
| EX TERRA VIRES | Power from the earth. Alfreton (Derbys.) UDC. |
| EX TERRENIS AD AETHERIA | From earthly things to heavenly. No. 3 Signals Sch., RAF (badge is the head of Mercury, messenger of the gods, as appropriate for a signals sch.). |
| EX UMBRIS ERUDITIO MDCCCCXX | Instruction out of the shades 1920. Soc. of Radiographers. |
| EX URGUE LEONEM | By his claws one knows the lion. 263 Sq., RAF operated in 1940 from a frozen lake in Norway (badge is lion holding in forepaws a cross from flag of Norway). |
| EX UNITATE VIRES | Strength from unity. Pembrokeshire CC, Union of South Africa, 1910, when arms were assigned. |
| EXALTABIT HONORE | I will exalt with honour. Smith of Duneske, Smythe of Greybrook, Smythe of Drumcree. |
| EXALTUM CORNU IN DEO | The horn is exalted in God. Truro, City of. |
| EXCELLERE CONTENDE | Strive to excel. 17 Fighter Sq., RAF. |
| EXCEPT THE LORD KEEP THE CITY | Halifax (Yorks.), Co. Bor. of. |
| EXCUDENDI GLORIA NOBIS | It is our glory to fashion. No. 21 Elementary Flying Training Sch., RAF. |
| EXEGI | I have accomplished it. Lees, Bts. |
| EXEMPLA SUORUM | Examples of our own. Innes. |
| EXEMPLO SINT VIRTUTIS | Let them be for an example of virtue, St Albans (Herts.) RDC. |
| EXEMPLUM ADEST IPSE HOMO | The man himself is present as an example. Franklin family (USA), includes Benjamin Franklin (1706–90). |
| EXEMPLUM DOCET | Example teaches. Shiplake Coll., Henley-on-Thames, 1959. |
| EXERCENDO RESURGAM | Recovery by exercises. RAF Medical Rehabilitation Unit, Collaton Cross. |
| EXERCET SUB SOLE LABOREM | It does its work under the sun. Barberini. This family used bees as their device. (Former Barberini Palace in Rome was used by Benito Mussolini as his office, the small balcony for his orations.) |
| EXERCITATIS NIL INVIUM | To the trained man nothing is impossible. RAF station, Cark. |

| | |
|---|---|
| EXIIT HINC LUMEN | From here went forth the light. RAF station, Drem, E. Lothian. |
| EXILIT QUOD DELITUIT | What was hidden leaps out. Italian Literary Academy of the Occulti. |
| EXITARI NON HEBESCERE | To be spirited, not inactive. De Grey, Lords Walsingham (De Grey). |
| EXITUS ACTA PROBAT | The result tests the act (*or* The end proves the deed). Biset, Lords Glendyne (Nivison), Nisbet, Nivison, Stanhope, Washington. |
| EXPECTA DOMINUM | Wait for the Lord. St Bees Sch., Cumberland (founded by Archbishop Grindal, 1583). |
| EXPECTES ET SUSTINEAS | Thou mayest hope and endure. Gwyn. |
| EXPEDITE | No. 431 Maintenance Unit, RAF. |
| EXPERIENDO | By experimenting. S. Wales Electricity Bd, 1949. |
| EXPERIENTIA DOCET | Experience teaches. No. 6 Elementary Flying Training Sch., RAF. |
| EXPERIENTIA EXPERIMUR | By practice we validate. Strike Cmd. Air-to-Air Missile Establishment. |
| EXPERTUS FIDELEM | Having found him faithful. Latham, co. Cheshire; Lewis of Harpton Court, Bts. |
| EXPLORAMUS | We seek out. 239 Sq., RAF. |
| EXPUGNAVI | I have taken by storm. Crawfurd-Pollok, Bt. |
| EXTANT RECTE FACTIS PRAEMIA | The rewards of good deeds endure. Coffin, Bt., Holden of Oakworth House, Bts., Lords Holden (*NEP*). |
| EYES OF DEFENCE | No. 966 Signals Unit, RAF. |

# F

| | |
|---|---|
| FABER FABRUM ADJUVET | Let the smith help the smith. Iron and Steel Inst. |
| FABER MEAE FORTUNAE | Smith of my fortune. Earls of Birkenhead (Smith). Chosen by 1st Earl as indicative of his self-made career and in play on his name. |
| FABULA SED VERA | A story but a true one. Story. |
| FACET SPERA | Do and hope. Askew, Ayscough, Caldwell, Lords Campbell of Eskan, Lords Colgrain (Campbell), Crommelin, Delacherois, Donald, Dunnell, Bt., Fea, Lords Glenarthur (Arthur), Heathcote, Hyatt, Ledsam, M'Gee, Macknight, Matterson, Matherson, Bts., Mynors, Lord Robson *(NEP)*, Scepter. |
| FAC PRO VIRIBUS | Do for your manhood. Bourne of Symondsbury House, Dorset. |
| FAC RECTE | Do rightly. Crawley. |
| FAC RECTE ET NIL TIME | Do right and fear nought. Thomas of Garreclwyd, Bts. |
| FAC RECTE ET SPERA | Do right and hope. Hovell. |
| FACE THE DAWN | Kingswood (Glos.) UDC. |
| FACIAM HERCLE SEDULO | By Hercules I will do it zealously. Jardine of Nottingham, Bt. |
| FACIE TENUS | Even to the face. Wheeler of Dublin, Wheler, Bts. |
| FACTA NON VERBA | Deeds, not words. Viscount Bearsted, Lords Blackford, Constantine Tech. Coll., Middlesbrough, Dawson of Edwarebury, Bts., De Renzey, De Rinzey, Eager, Lord Ennisdale (Lyons) *(NEP)*, Harwood, Hoyle, co. Yorks., Huntingdon of the Clock House, Bt., Joel, Knott, Bts., Lord Marshall of Chipstead *(NEP)*, Wells of Sporle, co. Norfolk, Wilson of Beckenham, 20 Sq., RAF. |
| FACTIS NON VERBIS | By deeds not by words. Money, Rimington-Wilson. |
| FACTA PROBANT | Facts prove. Cowell-Stepney, Bt., Stepney. |
| FAIR OAKS | No. 18 Elementary Flying Training Sch., RAF (badge an oak sapling and motto comes from fact of training at Fair Oaks). |
| FAIRE DEVOIR EN BONNE ESPÉRANCE | Do your duty in good hope. Holland, Bts. |
| FAIR MON DEVOIR | To do my duty. Fortrey-Heap, I'anson, Jocelyn, Joslin, Earls of Roden (Jocelyn). |
| FAIRE RIPAILLE | To behave as at Ripaille. Amadeus VIII, 1st Duke of Savoy, 1383–1451, retired from world with friends and lived like Hellfire 'monks' in eighteenth-century England; elected as anti-pope Felix V, but later persuaded to be content to be a cardinal. |

| | |
|---|---|
| FAIRE SANS DIRE | Do without speaking (i.e. Deeds not words). Lords Bridges, Fielder, Fox, Heyes, Earls of Ilchester (Fox-Strangways), Jeune, Kerrich-Walker, Kingsford, Parr, Lord St Helier (Jeune) *(NEP)*, Symons-Jeune, Todd, Warr of Grappenhall. |
| FAIS CEQUE BOIS ADVIENNE QUE POUSSA | Do what you may come what may. Viscount Chandos (Lyttelton). |
| FAIS CE QUE DOIS | Do what you ought. Ansell. |
| FAIS QUI DOIT ARRIVE QUI POURRA | Do your duty let what may happen. Capel Cure of Blake Hall, Ongar, Essex. |
| FAIT BIEN FAIT TOT | Do well do quickly. Beit, Bts. |
| FAITES MOY RAISON | Do me reason. Charles of Durazzo, d. 1386. |
| FAITH AND FREEDOM | RAF station, Waddington (badge, tower of Lincoln Cathedral, well-known landmark for pilots). |
| FAITH AND INDUSTRY | Abingdon (Berks.), Bor. of. |
| FAITH IN OUR TASK | RAF station, St Eval, Cornwall (badge is church of St Eval, a landmark for pilots). |
| FAITH IN SERVICE | Didcot (Berks.) Parish Council. |
| FAITH, UNITY AND INDUSTRY | Beeston and Stapleford (Notts.) UDC. |
| FAITH, WORK, SERVICE | Calne (Wilts.), Bor. of. |
| FAITHFUL ALLY | 152 Sq., RAF, presented by HEH the Nizam of Hyderabad, known by words of the motto. His personal headdress of a dastar is sq. badge. |
| FAITHFUL AND FIRM | Pyman. |
| FAITZ PROVEROUNT | Deeds will tell. Grimston. |
| FAL Y GALLO | As I can. Greenly of Titley Court. |
| FALCE MARIQUE POTENS | Powerful by sickle and sea. Larne (co. Antrim), Bor. of. |
| FAMA CANDIDA ROSA DULCIOR | Fame is sweeter than the white rose. Ames, Taylor. |
| FAMA SEMPER VIVET | Fame lives for ever. Gason, Swithinbank. |
| FAMA SEMPER VIVIT | Our renown shall live for ever. Gason, Liddell, Lord Ravensworth (Liddell) *(NEP)*. |
| FAMAM EXTENDERE FACTIS | To spread fame by deeds. Carolus Linnaeus (1707–78), Swedish botanist, whose system of naming plants and animals by genus, species, etc., forms basis of modern classification. Ennobled in 1767 as Carl von Linné. |
| FAMAM EXTENDERE FACTIS | To extend fame by deeds. All Hallows Sch., nr. Lyme Regis, Dorset (believed founded in sixteenth century), East Retford (Notts.) RDC, Viscount Galway (Monkton-Arundell), Viscount Monkton, Lords Monkton (Monkton-Arundell) *(NEP)*. |
| FAMILIAS FIRMAT PIETAS | Piety strengthens families. Ramsey, Wardlaw. |
| FARE FAC | Speak, do (Say it and do it). Lords Fairfax, Fairfax of Acomb House, Feacham. |
| FARI QUAE SENTIAT | To speak what he may think. Barkas, Earls of Orford (Walpole) *(NEP)*, Randolph, Walpole. |

| | |
|---|---|
| FARLO BENE | Do well. King-Farlow. |
| FAS DUCIT | Right leads. Rasch, Bts. |
| FAS | Right. Liddell. |
| FAS EST ET AB HOSTE DOCERI | It is lawful to learn even from an enemy. Black of Louth Park, Bt., Hoste, Bts. |
| FAST | Gray of Cartyne. |
| FAST WITHOUT FRAUDE | Brooke of Norton Priory, Bts. |
| FATA VIAM INVENIENT | The fates will find the way. Queen Christina of Sweden, 1626–89 (abdicated 1634, received into Roman Church), Spange, Vansittart. |
| FAUGH A BALLAGH | Clear the way. Gough, Viscount Gough. |
| FAUT UN FINIR | We must see it through. 248 Sq., RAF. |
| FAVEAT FORTUNA | Let fortune favour. Newton of Beckenham, Bts., Newton of the Wood, Bts. |
| FAVENTE DEO | God favouring. Fisher, Fisher-Rowe, Pawson, Reynolds, Templer, Wilkie, William III and Mary II (on their seal for Scotland). |
| FAVENTE NUMINE | By the favour of providence. Micklethwait, Bt., Peckham. |
| FAVENTE NUMINE REGINA SERVATUR | With God's favour the Queen is served. Micklethwait, Bt. (motto refers to service rendered to Queen Victoria and the Duchess of Kent at St Leonards, Sussex, for which Sir Sotherton Branthwayt Peckham-Micklethwait was cr. Bt., 1853). |
| FAX MENTIS HONESTAE GLORIA | Glory is the light of a noble mind. Lander, Molleson, Nova Scotia, Bts., Stuart-Forbes, Bts. (motto was favourite of Henry, Prince of Wales, eldest son of James I, who predeceased his father; adopted by the Nova Scotia Bts.). |
| FAX MENTIS INCENDIUM GLORIAE | The touch of glory inflames the mind. Brunton, Bts., Forbes, Earls of Granard (Forbes). |
| FAYTH HATHE NO FEAR | Rycroft, Bts. |
| FE DAL AM DARO | He will pay for attacking *or* striking. Jenkins of New South Wales. |
| FEAR GOD AND DREAD NOUGHT | Lords Fisher. |
| FEAR GOD AND HONOUR THE KING | Bromley Davenport, Haileybury Imperial Service Coll., Hertford, 1862 (the *and* in motto omitted), Porter of Merrion Square, Bts., Wrexham (Denbigh), Bor. of. |
| FEAR GOD AND SPARE NOUGHT | Brisbane, Bt. |
| FEAR GOD, FEAR NO MAN | Durtnell. |
| FEAR GOD IN LIFE | Somervell, Somerville. |
| FEAR HIM WHO FEARS NOT DEATH | Anderson. |
| FEAR NAUGHT IN UNITY | 353 Sq., RAF formed at Dum-Dum, nr. Calcutta, 1942. |

| | |
|---|---|
| FEAR NO MAN | 74 Sq., RAF. |
| FEAR NONE | HMS *Amphion*. |
| FEAR NOT HOLD FAST | Lords Ironside. |
| FEAR ONE | Lords Cozens-Hardy. |
| FEAR TO TRANSGRESS | Earls of Clonmell (Scott) *(NEP)*, Scott. |
| FEARLESS I DIRECT MY FLIGHT | 182 Sq., RAF. |
| FEDELE ALL'AMICE | Faithful to a friend. 224 Sq., RAF (formed at Otranto, 1918). |
| FEIGHT | Lords Sinclair (St Clair). |
| FEL Y GALLO | So far as he can (*or* So far as it is possible). Lords Brecon (Lewis). |
| FELICIOR QUO CERTIOR | Luckier as it is surer. Ormiston. |
| FELICITER SERVIMUS | Happily we serve. East Midlands Electricity Bd. |
| FELIS DEMULCTA MITIS | A stroked cat is gentle. Lords Brocket (Nall-Cain), Cain, Bts., Kane, Keane, Bts., Keane. |
| FELIX ET STABILIS | Happy and stable. Harman. |
| FELIX MERENDO | Happy in deserving. Lord Chalmers *(NEP)*. |
| FELIX QUI POTUIT | Happy who can. Sir William Carew, Kt., of Devon. |
| FELIX QUI PRUDENS | He is happy who is prudent. Lords Ashcombe (Cubitt), Cubitt (formerly of Eden Hall, Kent). |
| FELIX QUIA FORTIS | Happy because strong. St Felix Sch., Southwold, Suffolk. |
| FELLOWSHIP IS LIFE | Walthamstow Forest, London Bor. of, 1965. |
| FEOR MAGH EANAGH | Grass of the plain of watery places. Fermanagh CC (play on name of county). |
| FERAR UNUS ET IDEM | I will fear one and the same. Lord Collingwood, Collingwood of Lilburn Tower, Michell. |
| FERENDO ET FERIENDO | By fearing and by striking. Harrison of Copford Hall, Suffolk (hatchment in Thorpe Morieux church). |
| FERENDUM ET SPERANDUM | We must endure and hope. Mackenzie of Kincraig. |
| FERET AD ASTRA VIRTUS | Virtue will bear us to the skies. Kellet, Bts. |
| FERIENS TEGO | Striking I defend. 25 Sq., RAF. |
| FERIO FERRENDO | I fight by carrying. Transport Cmd., RAF (title changed to Air Support Control, 1967). |
| FERIO TEGO | I strike, I cover (*or* defend). Lords Alport, Hawdon, Herklott, Howden, M'Call, Sims, Syme. |
| FERIUNT SUMMOS FULMINA MONTES | Thunderbolts strike the mountain tops. Francesco Borgia, Duke of Gandia, illegitimate son of Pope Alexander VI. His dead body was found in the Tiber in 1497, his brother Cesare being suspected of the murder. |
| FERME EN ADVERSITÉ | Firm in adversity. Cordes. |
| FERME EN FOY | Firm in faith. Chichester, Chichester-Constable. |

| | |
|---|---|
| FEROS FERIOR | Fierce I strike. Chisholm of Chisholm, co. Roxburgh. The Chisholm anciently of great renown, as shown by the old saying, 'The Pope, the King, and the Chisholm.' |
| FERRÉ VA FERME | The shod horse goes surely. Farrer. Lords Farrer (NEP), Farrow. |
| FERRO COMITE | My sword my companion. Mordaunt, Bts., Tolson. |
| FERRO CONSULTO | I argue with the sword. Tregon. |
| FERRO MEA RECUPERO | I will recover my goods by iron. Bryan, co. Wexford. |
| FERRO NON GLADIO | By iron, not by the sword. Guest, Bts., Viscount Wimborne (Fox-Strangways-Guest). |
| FERRUM | Iron. Ferrier of Hemsby. |
| FERTE MANUS CERTAS | Bear sure hands. 427 Sq., RCAF. |
| FERVET OPUS | The work burns. Evesham (Worcs.) RDC, No. 15 Maintenance Unit, RAF (the work goes on with spirit). |
| FESTINA LENTE | Be quick without impetuosity. Adams, Allsopp, Audenshaw (Lancs.) UDC, Barnard, Blaauw, British Oak Insurance Co. Ltd., Brookes, Campbell, Colquhon, Everett, Festing, Earls of Fingall (Plunkett), Fletcher of Saltoun, Lords Dunsany (Plunkett), Lords Hindlip (Allsopp), Hughes-Onslow, Lords Louth (Plunkett), Lowth, Mewburn, Mewburn-Watson, Onslow, Bts., Earls of Onslow, Lords Plunkett, Lord Rathmore (Plunkett) (NEP), Rawlingson, Bts., Rigge, Rothery, Swifte, Trotter, Wall Morris, Westcombe, Whittaker. |
| FESTINA PRUDENTER | Hasten prudently. Bagshot (Surrey) RDC, Newnes, Bts. (1st Bt., Sir George Newnes, founded Putney Library on which the motto appears as *festina lente*). |
| FEU DE FER | Fire from iron. 34 Sq., RAF Regt. |
| FFYDDLON HYD ANGAU | Faithful unto death. David of Fairwater, Lords Ogmore. |
| FFYDDLAWN A PHASOD | Faithful and ready. Rees-Williams, Royal Flint Rifles Militia. |
| FI KULL MAKAN | In all places. No. 33 Wing, RAF Regt. |
| FIAT DEI VOLUNTAS | Let the will of God be done. Meredyth of Carlandstown, Bts. |
| FIAT JUSTITIA | Let justice be done. Bryce, Cassel, Bts., Coker, co. Oxford, Lord Nuffield (Morris) (NEP), South Molton (Devon), Bor. of, RAF Police. |
| FIAT JUSTITIA RUAT COELUM | Let justice be done, let the heaven fall (old English legal maxim). Spokes. |
| FIAT LUX | Let there be light. Moorfields Eye Hosp. |
| FIAT SECUNDUM VERBUM TUUM | Let it be done according to Thy word. St Marylebone, London Bor. of. |
| FIAT VOLUNTAS DEI | The will of God be done. Salwey. |
| FIDE | By faith. Hall of Melyniog. |
| FIDE CARITATE MINISTERIO | By faith, charity, service. Lord Inman. |
| FIDE CONSTANTIA | Constancy by faith. Felixstowe Coll., Suffolk. |

| | |
|---|---|
| FIDE DEO ET IPSO | Trust in God and yourself. Gibbons, Bt. |
| FIDE ET AMORE | By fidelity and love. Carden of Molesey, Bts., Carden of Templemore, Bts., Carden of Tipperary, Chadwick, Conway, Dicey, Gardiner, Heart, Marquesses of Hertford (Seymour), Sadler, Tonson-Rye. |
| FIDE ET ARMIS | By faith and arms. Imlay. |
| FIDE ET CONSTANTER | By faith and constantly. Inst. of Hosp. Administrators. |
| FIDE ET CONSTANTIA | By faith and constancy. Dixon, Lords Glentoran (Dixon), James, co. Kent, Lee. |
| FIDE ET DILIGENTIA | By faith and diligence. Crawford, co. Perth, Woking (Surrey) UDC, 1930. |
| FIDE ET FIDUCIA | By fidelity and confidence. Blackman, Chafy, co. Dorset, Gilchrist, Golborne (Lancs.) UDC, Harnage, Bts., Lords Magheramorne (McGarel-Hogg) (NEP), McGarel, Norwich Union Fire Insurance Soc. Ltd., Primrose, Bts., Earls Roseberry (Primrose), Thorlby, Watt. |
| FIDE ET FORTITUDINE | With faith and fortitude. Aubert, Barton, Bt., Barton, Braintree (Essex) RDC, Brickdale, Capel, Cox, Bt., Dixon, Earls of Essex (Capell), Farquharson, Hickson, Higgs, Kadar Research Flying Unit, RAF, Lawrence of Llanelweth, Lloyd of Coedmore, M'Farquhar, Madan, Lord Lugard (NEP), Noble, Penrith (Cumb.) UDC, 1952, Shaw-Mackenzie. |
| FIDE ET FORTUNA | By faith and fortune. Gillett, Lort-Phillips. |
| FIDE ET INDUSTRIA | By faith and industry. Anderson. Kirkby (Lancs.) UDC, Royston (Yorks.) UDC, Whittingham. |
| FIDE ET INTEGRITATE | By faith and integrity. Reliance Fire and Accident Insurance Corp. Ltd., 1952. |
| FIDE ET LABORE | By faith and labour. Allanby of Balblair, Allen, Viscount Allenby, Allcroft, Forster, Bt., Jenner, Bts., Harpenden (Herts.) UDC, Walsingham (Norfolk) RDC, Williams of Park, Bt. |
| FIDE ET LITERIS | In faith and scholarship. St Paul's Sch., founded 1509 by Dean Colet. |
| FIDE ET SPE | By faith and hope. Borthwick, Bowden, Bts. |
| FIDE ET TACITURNITATE | By faith and silence. Huyshe. |
| FIDE ET VIGILANTIA | By faith and vigilance. Pound, Bts., Stepney, Bts. |
| FIDE ET VIRTUTE | By faith and valour. Ackland, Brandling, Collins, co. Lanark, Davies-Evans, Evans of Wightwick, Bts., Gladstone, Bts., Gladstone of Capenoch, Viscount Gladstone (NEP), Lord Gladstone of Hawarden (NEP), Gledstanes, Gooch, Bts., Goodwin, Ramsbottom, Rochead. |
| FIDE LABORO | I labour with faith. Borrer. |
| FIDE NON FRAUDE | By faith not fraud. Philipson-Stow, Bts. |
| FIDE PARTA FIDE AUCTA | By faith obtained, by faith increased. Mackenzie of Fairburn, Mackenzie of Kilroy, Bts. |
| FIDE QUAM FORTUNA | By faith rather than by fortune. Lords Elton. |

| | |
|---|---|
| FIDE SED CUI VIDE | Trust, but be careful in whom. Viscount Allendale (Beaumont), Astley, Bts., Chetwynd-Stapylton, Hulme Gram. Sch., Oldham, 1611, Kerrison, Langley, co. Tipperary, Lees, Studdy, Watts, William Hulme's Gram. Sch., Manchester, 1887. |
| FIDE SED VIDE | Trust but take care. Petrie, Bts., Reynolds. |
| FIDE SEMPER DEO | Always with faith in God. Kershaw. |
| FIDEI COMMISSA TENEO | I hold things committed to faith. Lords Stamp. |
| FIDEI CONSTANS | Constant in faith. Manby-Colegrave. |
| FIDEI COTICULA CRUX | The Cross is the test of truth. Chevallier, Earls of Clarendon (Hyde Villiers), Earls of Jersey (Child-Villiers), Sherston Baker, Bts., Whatton. |
| FIDEI ET MERITO | For faith and merit. Order of St Ferdinand and of Merit (Naples). |
| FIDEI TENAX | Tenacious of faith. Lord Glyn (NEP), Lords Wolverton (Glyn). |
| FIDELE | Faithfully. Nicol of Ballogie, Roupell, Roussell. |
| FIDELI CERTE MERCES | To the faithful man there is assuredly a reward. Earls of Morley (Parker), Parker of Melford Hall, Bts. Saul. |
| FIDELI QUID OBSTAT? | What hinders the faithful? Firebrace. |
| FIDELI TUTA MERCES | Safe harvest for the faithful man. Thornton of Birkin. |
| FIDELIS | Faithful. Crichton, Hill, co. Oxon., Leadbitter, Milvain, Shepherd, Waldy, Wishere. |
| FIDELIS AD FINEM | Faithful to the end. Hall, co. Antrim. |
| FIDELIS AD URNAM | Faithful to the tomb. Malone. |
| FIDELIS ATQUE FORTIS | Faithful and strong. Newtownards (co. Down), Bor. of. |
| FIDELIS ET CONSTANS | Faithful and constant. Banon, Bragge, Castle, co. Suffolk. |
| FIDELIS EXSULATAE | Of the faithful banished. De Manbey. |
| FIDELIS IN ADVERSIS | Faithful in adverse things. Hamilton of Barns. |
| FIDELIS MORTE TAM VITAE | Faithful in death as in life. Allen of South Africa. |
| FIDELITAS | Fidelity. Order of Loyalty (Baden), Lords Pentland (Sinclair), Scott of Edinburgh, Purdie, Sinclair of Dunbeath, Bts. |
| FIDELITAS ET VERITAS | Fidelity and truth. Parsons-Peters. |
| FIDELITAS URBIS SALUS REGIS | The fidelity of the city is the safety of the king. Bridgnorth (Salop), Bor. of. |
| FIDELITAS VINCIT | Fidelity conquers. Cotton, Bt., Dunscombe. |
| FIDELITATE ET CLAMORE | By faithfulness and outcry. Johnston Stewart. |
| FIDELITATE ET INDUSTRIA STAT BILSTONIA | Bilston stands by faith and industry. Bilston (Staffs.), Bor. of. |
| FIDELITÉ EST DE DIEU | Fidelity is of God. Mellor, Viscount Powerscourt (Wingfield), Wingfield. |

| | |
|---|---|
| FIDELITER | Faithfully. Lords Cunliffe, Cunliffe, Bts., Deane, Hamilton, Havelock, Bts., Henry, Montgomery, Bts., Muckleston, Ogilvy, Ralph, Simonds-Gooding, Symonds, Teale. |
| FIDELITER AMO | I love faithfully. Scott of Glenaros. |
| FIDELITER ET CONSTANTER | Faithfully and constantly. Order of Saxe-Ernestine. |
| FIDELITER ET DILIGENTER | Faithfully and diligently. Graham of Kirkpalk, Bt. |
| FIDELITER ET HONESTE | Faithfully and honestly. Emerson. |
| FIDELITER, FORTITER, FELICITER | Faithfully, strongly, happily. Davies-Scourfield, Edgbaston High Sch., Birmingham, Scourfield, Bts. |
| FIDEM MEAM OBSERVABO | I will keep my faith. Shedden. |
| FIDEM PARTIT INTEGRITAS | Integrity begets faith. Bridgford, Kay. |
| FIDEM SERVABO | I will keep my faith. Bignold, Blackden, Kroyer-Kielberg. |
| FIDEM TENE | Keep faith. Hornyold. |
| FIDEM VITA FATERI | One's life to confess one's faith. St Mary's Coll., Merseyside, 1919. |
| FIDENS DEO CONFIDENS | Confident if trusting in God. Skeels. |
| FIDENS ET FIDELIS | Confiding and faithful. Marquesses of Cambridge (Cambridge). |
| FIDENS NON CONFIDENS | Faithful not confiding. Langley of Broseley. |
| FIDENTER AGO | I act faithfully. Guthrie, Bts. |
| FIDENTIA | Confidence. Lloyd's, Corp. of London. |
| FIDEO | I trust. Molesworth. |
| FIDES ATQUE INTEGRITAS | Faith and integrity. Soc. of Inc. Accountants & Auditors. |
| FIDES ET AMOR | Faith and love. Willink, Bts. |
| FIDES ET FORTITUDO | Faith and fortitude. Ropner, Bts. |
| FIDES ET JUSTITIA | Faith and justice. Farnborough (Hants.) UDC, Webster, Bts., Westbrook-Pratt. |
| FIDES INVICTA TRIUMPHAT | Unconquered faith triumphs. Gloucester, City and Co. Bor. of. |
| FIDES NON TIMET | Faith fears not. Harvey, Lee, Lords Monteagle (Rice), Rice. |
| FIDES NOSTRA VICTORIA | Faith is our victory. St John's Coll., Durham, 1957. |
| FIDES NUDAQUE VERITAS | Truth and naked faith. Lushington. |
| FIDES PRAESTANTIOR AURO | Faith is more estimable than gold. Clapperton, Gibb. |
| FIDES PROBATA CORONAT | Tried, faith crowns. Campbell, Roch, Laidlaw, Laidlay. |
| FIDES SEMPER FIRMA | Faith always firm. Smith-Carington. |
| FIDES SERVAND EST | Faith is kept. Leigh, Bts., Rothband, Bt. |
| FIDES SUFFICIT | Faith is enough. Halkett (formerly Wedderburn Bts.). |
| FIDES VISQUE MULTUM CONFICIT | Faith and force finish much. Letts. |

| | |
|---|---|
| FIDUCIA ET FIDES | Confidence and faith. British Bank of the Middle East. |
| FIDUCIA ET VI | By confidence and strength. Slough (Bucks.), Bor. of. |
| FIDUS AD EXTREMUM | Faithful to the last. Ivey, Leith. |
| FIDUS AMICIS | Faithful to his friends. Campbell of Islay. |
| FIDUS ET AUDAX | Faithful and bold. Callaghan, Garnett of Wyreside, Gillow, Leyland, Viscount Lismore (O'Callaghan) *(NEP)*, Naylor-Leyland, Bts., Slade, Bts. |
| FIDUS ET FESTINUS | Staunch and fast. No. 202 Maintenance Unit, RAF. |
| FIDUS ET FORTIS | Faithful and strong. Scott of Connaught Place, Bt. |
| FIDUS UT OLIM | Faithful as formerly. Lafone. |
| FIEL PERO DESDICHADO | Faithful though unfortunate. Dukes of Marlborough (Spencer-Churchill), Earls of Thanet (Tufton), Tufton (Desdichado was the famous motto, accompanied by an eradicated oak tree, of Ivanhoe, the disinherited knight in Scott's romance of that name). |
| FIER ET FORT | Proud and strong. Shelton. |
| FIER SANS TACHE | Proud, without blemish. Goff. |
| FIGHT | Ashe. Earls of Orkney (Hamilton), Earls of Rosslyn (St Clair-Erskine), St Clair, Lords Sinclair. |
| FIGHT THE GOOD FIGHT | Lords Robertson of Oakridge. |
| FILIA REGIS | The king's daughter. Queen Margaret's Sch., Escrick, Yorks., 1962. |
| FILEY ET FELICITAS | Filey and happiness. Filey (Yorks.) UDC. |
| FIND AND FOREWARN | 241 Sq., RAF. |
| FIND AND GUIDE | No. 360 Co. of Warwick Fighter Control Unit, RAAF. |
| FINDENDO FINGERE DISCO | I learn to make by separating. Inst. of Chemical Engineers. |
| FINDIMUS CAELUM | We cleave the sky. 197 Sq., RAF. |
| FINEM RESPICE | Consider the end. Bazley, Bts., Bligh, Brooke, Brooks, Bt., Collis, Earls of Darnley (Bligh), Lords Crawshaw (Brooks), Hall of Grappenhall, Hoskyns, Longmore, Pattenson. |
| FINIS CORONAT OPUS | The end crowns the work. Baker, Bt., Croham Hurst Sch., Croydon, Finnis, Leach, Wigston (Leics.) UDC, 1953. |
| FIRM | Dalrimple, Dalrymple, Dalrymple-Hay, Bts., Johnson-Walsh, Laing of Kindertis, Meason, Reid, Bts., Earls of Stair (Dalrymple), Walsh, Bts., Wall of Wortley Park, No. 3 Air Gunners' Sch., RAF, 36th Foot (2nd Bn. the Worcestershire Regt.), Worcestershire Volunteer Regt., 1914. |
| FIRM AND FAITHFUL | Lord Hinton of Bankside. |
| FIRM AND FAST | Earls of Lincoln (Laceys), referring to their device of a knot. |
| FIRM EN FOI | Firm in faith. Chichester, Bts. |
| FIRM IN FAITH | Straker-Smith. |

| | |
|---|---|
| FIRM TO MY TRUST | Glyn, Bts. |
| FIRM, VIGILANT, ACTIVE | Lords Muncaster (Pennington) *(NEP)*. |
| FIRMA DURANT | Strong things last. Airey, Lesly of Finrassie. |
| FIRMA ET ARDUA | Solid and lofty objects. Mackenzie of Rosehaugh, Earls of Wharncliffe (Stuart-Wortley-Mackenzie). |
| FIRMA ET STABILIS | Firm and stable. Kirleham (Lancs.) UDC. |
| FIRME | Resolutely. Dalrymple of Newhailes, Bts., Elphinstone-Dalrymple, Bts. (dormant), Hamilton-Dalrymple, Bts. |
| FIRMES VOLAMOS | Firmly we fly (Spanish). 164 Sq., RAF (subscribed by British community in Argentina). |
| FIRMIOR | Stronger. Brentford and Chiswick, London Bor. of. |
| FIRMIOR QUO PARATIOR | The more prepared the stronger. Hope-Dunbar, Bts., Prince-Smith, Bts., Earls Selkirk (Douglas-Hamilton). |
| FIRMITAS IN COELO | Stability in heaven. Maher, St George. |
| FIRMITATE CAELI FLOREAT ARBOR | By the strength of climate let the tree flourish. Flannery, Bts. |
| FIRMUM IN VITA NIHIL | Nothing in life is permanent. Bunbury, Bts., Dolphin, Richardson. |
| FIRMUS ET INTREPIDUS | Firm and intrepid. Auden, co. Westmorland. |
| FIRMUS IN FIRMIS | Firm among the firm. Kilpin. |
| FIRMUS MANEO | Firm I remain. Bourne, co. Leics., Breek, Lindsay of Dowhill, Bts., Sturdee, Bts. |
| FIRST | No. 203 Advanced Flying Sch., RAF. |
| FIRST FROM THE EYRIES | 71 Sq., RAF (first of the three Eagle Sqs.; badge of American eagle, as sqs. composed of American volunteers). |
| FIRST IN THE FIELD | RAF Station, Bawdsey, Suffolk. |
| FIRST THINGS FIRST | RAF station, Hornchurch, Essex. |
| FISCUM SERVA FIDELITER | Keep money faithfully. Inst. of Municipal Treasurers & Accountants. |
| FIT VIA VI | A way is made by labour (*or* force). Campbell of Invernaill, Kearley, Way, Bt., 500 Light Airfield Construction Sq., RAF. |
| FLAMMA FUMO EST PROXIMA | Flame is nearest to smoke. Southern Gas Bd. |
| FLECTA NON RESILIET | Bent but shall not spring back. Birmingham Gen. Hosp. |
| FLECTI NON FRANGI | To be bent, not to be broken. Houldsworth, Viscount Palmerston, Phillips. |
| FLECTIMUR NEC FRANGIMUR UNDIS | We are bent, not broken, by the waves. Colonna family of Rome. |
| FLECTIMUS NUNQUAM | We never bend. Anderton of Spaynes Hall, Essex. |
| FLECTITUR NON FRANGITUR | He is bent but not broken. Fane de Salis. |
| FLEGHESS PASK | Easter children (Cornish). Pascoe. |

| | |
|---|---|
| FLEISSIG UND TREU | Diligent and faithful (German). No. 3 Maintenance Unit Unit, RAF, formed 1948 at Hesedorf, Germany. |
| FLIUGA VAKTA OK GOSTA | To fly, to watch, to strike (Norse). 254 Sq., RAF worked over northern waters, hence motto and badge of a raven, symbol of the Vikings. |
| FLOREANT CONCILIA SALOPIAE | May Shropshire councils flourish. Whitchurch Parish Council. |
| FLOREANT SEPTEM QUERCUS | May seven oaks flourish. Sevenoaks (Kent) UDC, 1964. |
| FLOREAT ACTONA | Let Acton flourish, Acton, London Bor. of. |
| FLOREAT AILESBURIA | Let Aylesbury flourish. Aylesbury (Bucks.), Bor. of. |
| FLOREAT BATHON | Let Bath flourish. Bath, City of. |
| FLOREAT CASTELLUM ET OPPIDUM | May castle and town flourish. Workington (Cumb.), Bor. of. |
| FLOREAT ECCLESIA ANGLICANA | Let the Church of England flourish. Glastonbury (Somerset), Bor. of. |
| FLOREAT ETONA | May Eton flourish. Eton Coll. (the Coll. of the Blessed Mary of Eton, founded by Henry VI in 1440), Eton (Bucks.) UDC. |
| FLOREAT HOVA | May Hove flourish. Hove (Sussex), Bor. of. |
| FLOREAT IMPERII PORTUS | Let the port of Empire flourish. Port of London Authority. |
| FLOREAT INDUSTRIA | Let industry flourish. Batley (W.R. Yorks.), Bor. of., Darlington, Bor. of. |
| FLOREAT KEW | Let Kew flourish. The Kew Guild. |
| FLOREAT LINDUM | May Lincoln flourish. Lincoln, City of. |
| FLOREAT MAJESTAS | Let majesty flourish. Broun, Bts., McKerrell-Brown. |
| FLOREAT QUI LABORAT | Let him flourish who works. Lewis. |
| FLOREAT RUGBEIA | Let Rugby flourish. Rugby (Warwicks.), Bor. of. |
| FLOREAT SALOPIA | Let Shropshire flourish. Shrewsbury, Bor. of, Shropshire CC. |
| FLOREAT SCHOLA BEDFORDIENSIS | May Bedford School flourish. Bedford School, Bedford, probably pre-Conquest in origin. |
| FLOREAT SEMPER FIDELIS CIVITAS | Let the faithful city ever flourish. Worcester, City of. |
| FLOREAT SWANSEA | Let Swansea flourish. Swansea, City and Co. Bor. of. |
| FLOREO IN UNGUE LEONIS | I bloom in the lion's claw. King-King. Crest of this family shows a lion holding in his claws a rose. |
| FLORES CURAT DEUS | God careth for the flowers. Lord Battersea (Flower) (NEP), Flowers. |
| FLORES FRUCTUSQUE PERENNES | Perennial flowers and fruit. Academy Florimontana of Annecy, France, 1606. |
| FLORES VIRTUTE CAPESSO | In courage I am at the highest. RAF station, Waterbeach, Cambs. |
| FLORESCIT | It will flourish. Mewburn-Watson. |

| | |
|---|---|
| FLORET QUI LABORAT | He prospers who labours. Moseley (Warwicks.), Bor. of, Rawtenstall (Lancs.), Bor. of. |
| FLORET VIRTUS VULNERATA | Manhood wounded flourishes. Floyer, co. Dorset. |
| FLORUIT FLOREAT | It flourished, may it flourish. Newbury (Berks.), Bor. of. |
| FLOWER DEW | Lowson, Bts. |
| FLUCTUAT NEC MERGITUR | It undulates but is not submerged. City of Paris. |
| FLY TO ASSIST | RAF station, Thorney Island. |
| FOI, ROI, DROIT | Faith, king, right. Lines, Lynes. |
| FOLIUM NON DEFLUET | A leaf does not flow away. Noble of Ardkinglas, Bts. |
| FOLLOW LIGHT | Leeson. |
| FOLLOW ME | Breadalbane, Earls of (Campbell) *(NEP)*, Campbell, Bts., Gurwood. |
| FOLLOW THE GLEAM | Sunny Hill Sch., Bruton, 1960. |
| FONS ET ORIGO | Fount and source. La Fontaine Bts. |
| FONS VITAE SAPIENTIA | The fountain of life is wisdom. Trent Coll., Notts., 1866. |
| FOR COMMONWEAL AND LIBERTY | Mactaggart, Bts. |
| FOR EXCELLENCE WE STRIVE | Savoy Hotel Ltd., 1966. |
| FOR FREEDOM | 138 Sq., RAF, 408 Sq., RCAF. |
| FOR GOD AND CROWN | Northallerton (Yorks.) UDC. |
| FOR GOD AND THE EMPIRE | Order of the British Empire. This Order was created in 1917 by King George V in order to reward the large number of people who had distinguished themselves in World War I. |
| FOR KING, LAW AND PEOPLE | West Suffolk CC, 1959. |
| FOR KIRK AND KING | Kirk, co. Durham. |
| FOR KONGE, FEDRELAND OG FLAGGETS HEDER | For King, country and the honour of the flag. 333 Sq., RAF (Norwegian), 1943. |
| FOR LIBERTY | 121 Sq., RAF (badge an Indian warrior's head, indicative of American association of the second Eagle Sq. to be formed in RAF). |
| FOR LOVE OF GOD AND HOME | Mothers' Union. |
| FOR MY DUCHAS | Grant of Rothiemurchus. |
| FOR NORGE | For Norway. 331 Sq., RAF (Norwegian), 1941. |
| FOR RIGHT | Graham of Rednock. |
| FOR RIGHT AND REASON | Graham of Ardoch. |
| FOR TRUE LIBERTY | Renwick, Bts. |
| FOR'ARD FOR'ARD | Leicestershire CC. |
| FORCE AVEC VERTU | Strength with virtue. Leigh, Leigh-Mallory, Leigh-White. |
| FOREMOST IN ATTACK | 126 Sq., RAF. Formed in Malta, 1941, badge granted 1944 (Maltese Cross with laurel wreath), served in Malta for two years and destroyed 200 aircraft. |

| | |
|---|---|
| FORESIGHT | 140 Sq., RAF. |
| FORGED TO FIGHT | No. 17 Operational Training Unit, RAF. |
| FORGET NOT | Campbell of Auchinbreck, Bts., Campbell-Orde, Bts. |
| FORMA FLOS, FAMA FLATUS | Beauty is a flower, fame a breath. Bagshawe. |
| FORMOSA QUAE HONESTA | As beautiful as honest. Turton, Bts. |
| FORRARD | East Riding Yeomanry (Lancers). |
| FORT ET LOYAL | Bold and loyal. Selby, Selby-Bigge, Bts. |
| FORT ET VRAI | Strong and true. Mohun, Moore. |
| FORTE ET FIDÈLE | Brave and faithful. Lords Talbot de Malahide (Talbot); Bravely and faithfully, 48 Sq., RAF. |
| FORTE (I) ET FIDELI NIHIL DIFFICILE | To the brave and faithful man nothing is difficult. Deane, M'Carthy, Bt., Lords Muskerry (Deane), O'Keefe. |
| FORTE NIHIL DIFFICILE | Strongly nothing is difficult. Disraeli, Mills of Ebbw Vale, Bts. |
| FORTE SCUTUM SALUS DUCUM | A strong shield is the safety of leaders. Lord Carlingford (Parkinson-Fortescue) (NEP), Lords Clermont, Fortescue, Earls Fortesque. Family of Norman origin traceable from early twelfth century; allusion is to myth that first of the family covered William the Conqueror with his shield at Hastings. |
| FORTEM FORS JUVAT | Fortune favours the bold. Menzies. |
| FORTEM POSCE ANIMUM | Wish for a strong mind. Crampton, Bts., Fynney, Heriot, Lords Phillimore, Lords Saye and Sele (Twisleton-Wykeham-Fiennes), Twisleton-Wykeham-Fiennes, Bts. |
| FORTES CREANTUR FORTIBUS | The brave come from the brave. Law of Rosnaree, Van Straubenzee. |
| FORTES FORTUNA JUVAT | Fortune helps the brave. Blennerhassett, Bts., Lords Bloomfield, Dickson of Blackbeck, Doller, Donner, Bts., Lords Islington (Dickson, later Dickson-Poynder) (NEP), Murray, Troyte. |
| FORTHRIGHT | Bowser. |
| FORTI NIHIL DIFFICILE | Nothing is difficult to the strong. Southend High Sch., Essex. |
| FORTI NON IGNAVO | To the brave man, not to the dastard. Lords Lyell, Lyell of Kinnards, Bt., Lyle. |
| FORTIA FACERE ET PATI ROMANUM EST | To act bravely and to endure befits a Roman. Muzio Colonna, c.1516. |
| FORTIBUS ARDUA CEDUNT | Difficulties yield to gallant men. Southampton Univ. Air Sq., RAFVR. |
| FORTIBUS NON DESERUNT | They will not be wanting to the brave. Andrea di Capua, Duke of Termole; allusion to his device of a sheaf of javelins. |
| FORTIOR EX ARDUIS | Stronger from difficulties. Shaw-Mackenzie. |
| FORTIOR QUI SE VINCIT | He is stronger who conquers himself. Madden, Madden, Bts., Poley. |

| | |
|---|---|
| FORTIOR QUO PARATIOR | The better prepared the stronger. Hornsey, London Bor. of. |
| FORTIS AB JURE FORTIS | Strong and strong from the law. Stockenstrong, Bts. |
| FORTIS CADERE, CEDERE NON POTEST | The brave man may fall, but cannot yield. Earls of Drogheda (Moore), Moore. |
| FORTIS CEU LEO FIDUS | Strong as the lion is faithful. Macbrayne. |
| FORTIS EST VERITAS | Strong is the truth. Ángus of Ravenstone, Barton, co. Norfolk, Hutchon, Oxford, City and Co. Bor. of, 1st Oxfordshire Light Horse, Oxfordshire Militia, Oxfordshire Volunteer Regt., 1914. |
| FORTIS ET BENIGNUS | Brave and kindly. Denny of Dumbarton, Bts. |
| FORTIS ET CONSTANS | Brave and constant. Kiggell. |
| FORTIS ET FIDELIS | Brave and faithful. Beton, Bryan, Close, Douglas, Dunbar, Findlay, Finlay, Fitzgerald, Fletcher, Hind, Judkin-Fitzgerald, Bts., King's Coll., Taunton (refounded by Canon Woodward, 1879), Lalor, Lawlor, co. Kerry, May, Middleton, Orme, Uniake, 233 Sq., RAF. |
| FORTIS ET FIDUS | Brave and trusty. Flint, Loughnan, Maclachlan, Maclaughlin. |
| FORTIS ET HOSPITALIS | Brave and hospitable. Murphy of Altadore, Bt., O'Morchoe. |
| FORTIS ET PATIENS | Brave and patient. Barham of Wadhurst, Sussex. |
| FORTIS ET VELOX | Strong and swift. Fry, Waldron. |
| FORTIS IN ARDUIS | Brave under difficulties. Armit, Ashman, Bt., Beaton, Bethune, Findlay, Findlay-Hamilton, Lord, M'Dougall, M'Dowall, Middleton, Bor. of, Platt, Thompson. |
| FORTIS IN ARMIS | Strong in arms. Armstrong, Watson-Armstrong (a punning motto). |
| FORTIS IN PROELIIS | Valiant in battle. 105 Sq., RAF. |
| FORTIS QUI PRUDENS | He is brave who is prudent. Ball of Framewood, Bt., Ormsby, Prudential Assurance Co. Ltd., 1904, Whitworth, Bt. |
| FORTIS NOCTE | Strong by night. 149 Sq., RAF. |
| FORTIS QUI SE VINCIT | Strong is he who conquers himself. Princess Helena Coll., Hitchin, Herts., 1928. |
| FORTIS SI JURE FORTIS | Strong if strong is right. Lord Glanely (Tatem) (NEP). |
| FORTIS SUB FORTE FATISCET | The brave shall grow weary beneath the brave. De Robeck. |
| FORTITER | Bravely. Boswell, Clark, Clipsham, Cuthbert of Berthier, Inverness (family who became seigneurs of Berthier, Canada), Elliot of Harwood. Longbottom. M'Alister, M'Cray, M'Lachlan, Warrand, Wright. |
| FORTITER AC FIRMITER | Bravely and firmly. Lord Twining (NEP). |
| FORTITER ALTIOREM FIERI | Bravely to make higher (position). Morris of Cavendish Square, Bt. |

| | |
|---|---|
| FORTITER DEFENDIT TRIUMPHANS | It bravely defends and triumphs. Newcastle-upon-Tyne, City of. |
| FORTITER ET APERTE | Boldly and openly. Yatman. |
| FORTITER ET FIDELITER | Boldly and faithfully. Armitage, Briggs, Browne, Browne-Clayton, Cox, Fallous, Fulwood (Lancs.) UDC, Guildford (Surrey) RDC, Leahy, Melvin, Bt., Norrie-Miller, Bts., Norton, O'Fallon, Pangbourne Coll., Reading, Pennyman, Peperrell, Lords Oranmore & Browne, Wilson of Knowle Hall. |
| FORTITER ET HONESTE | Boldly and honourably. Abney. |
| FORTITER ET HUMANITER | Bravely and humanely. Portadown Coll., co. Armagh. |
| FORTITER ET RECTE | Boldly and rightly, Anderson, Allott, Bts., Craven-Smith-Milnes, Drake, Dyson, Eliott of Stobe Bts., London Master Builders' Assn., Lord Rank, Rankin, Wallis, Wardell. |
| FORTITER ET SINCERE | Bravely and sincerely. Dixon-Johnson. |
| FORTITER ET SUAVITER | Boldly and mildly. Bland of Debden, co. Essex, Lord Courtauld-Thomson (NEP), Muntz, Bts., Ogilvie of Milltown. |
| FORTITER FAC ET FIDENTER | Do bravely and confidently. Johnson. |
| FORTITER FIDELITER FELICITER | Boldly, faithfully, successfully. Auctioneers and Landed Property Agents, Inc. Soc. of, Hutchinson, Grovely Manor Sch. Ltd., Jackson, Mather-Jackson, Bts., Viscount Monck, Earls Rathdowne (Monck), Treves, Bt. |
| FORTITER GERIT CRUCEM | He bravely bears the cross. Chaine-Nickson, Earls of Donoughmore (Hely-Hutchinson), Fox-Hutchinson, Havelock-Allan, Bts., Hutchinson, Bts., Tritton. |
| FORTITER IN RE | Bravely in action (or Boldly in deed). Nunn, Lord Ramsden (NEP), HMS Sussex, 42 Sq., RAF. |
| FORTITER OCCUPA PORTUM | Bravely occupy the gate. Kelly Coll., Tavistock, Devon. |
| FORTITER PROSPICERE GLORIARI PRAETERITIS | Bravely to look forward, to glory in the past. Queen Elizabeth's Free Gram. Sch., Gainsborough, co. Lincoln. |
| FORTITER SI FORSITAN | Bravely if perhaps. Godfrey-Fausset. |
| FORTITER SUAVITER | Boldly, mildly. Curteis of Windmill Hill, Sussex. |
| FORTITUDINE | With fortitude. Barry, Bruen, Carter, co. Staffs., Duerry-House, D'Warris, Erskine, Bts., Fairlie-Cuninghame, Bts., Hall, Hobson, Hoste, Bts., Macrae of Ballimore, M'Cray, Mowbray, Order of Maria Theresa (Austria), Veale. |
| FORTITUDINE DEO | By fortitude with God. Hobson. |
| FORTITUDINE ET CONATU | By fortitude and attempt. Vincent, Bts. |
| FORTITUDINE ET FIDELITATE | By fortune and fidelity. Bartlett, Bts., Brown, Stuckey. |
| FORTITUDINE ET LABORE | By fortitude and labour. Reid of Springburn, Bts. |
| FORTITUDINE ET PRUDENTIA | By fortitude and prudence. Carson, co. Monaghan, Hacket, Hargreaves, Herbert, Lighton, Bts., Minchin, O'Reilly of Knock Abbey, Earls Powis (Herbert), Smithwick, Younge. |

| | |
|---|---|
| FORTITUDINE VINCIMUS | We conquer by fortitude. Lord Shackleton. |
| FORTITUDINE VINCIT | He conquers by fortitude. Conan Doyle, Doyle, Bts. |
| FORTITUDINE VIRTUTE DABITUR | It will be given by fortitude and virtue. Earls of Woolton (Marquis). |
| FORTITUDO EJUS RHODIUM TENUIT | His courage held Rhodes. Amadeus VI, Count of Savoy (called 'the Green'), d. 1383. Motto alluded to defence of Rhodes against Turks; called 'the Green' from colour of his apparel at a tournament. |
| FORTITUDO ET LENITUDO | Fortitude and mildness. Ledlie. |
| FORTITUDO ET SPES | Endurance and hope. Stockton-on-Tees, Bor. of. |
| FORTITUDO MEA DEUS | God is my fortitude. Lord Channing *(NEP)*. |
| FORTUNA ET LABORE | By good fortune and exertion. Latham, Bts., Sym. |
| FORTUNA FAVENTE | With fortune in my favour. Falkiner, Bts., Falkiner, co. Dublin, Pudsey. |
| FORTUNA FAVET FORTIBUS | Fortune favours the brave. Judd of Stewkley Grange, Pryce-Jenkin. |
| FORTUNA FORTIOR FORTITUDO | Fortitude is stronger than fortune. Ford, Bts. |
| FORTUNA FUGACIOR UNDIS | Fortune is more transient than the waves. Fortune. |
| FORTUNA MEA IN BELLO CAMPO | My fortune in a fair field. Earls Beauchamp (Lygon). Interesting case of play on title held by the Lygons; note that the Anglicized pronunciation of Beauchamp gave the familiar surname Beecham. |
| FORTUNA MELIORES SEQUITUR | Fortune follows the better (person). Westminster Chamber of Commerce, 1958. |
| FORTUNA SEQUATUR | Let fortune attend. Marquesses of Aberdeen (Gordon), Warren. |
| FORTUNAE NIHIL | Nothing to fortune. 429 Sq., RAF. |
| FORTUNE AMIE | Fortune my friend. Sir Thomas Gresham, founder of Royal Exchange, *temp.* Elizabeth I. |
| FORTUNE DE GUERRE | Fortune of war. Chute, Bt., Chute of the Vyne. |
| FORTUNE FAVOURS THE BOLD | RAF station, East Fortune, East Lothian. |
| FORTUNE, INFORTUNE, FORTE UNE | In fortune or bad fortune, one strong woman. Somewhat cabbalistic saying of Margaret of Austria, Duchess of Savoy, one-time ruler of Spanish Netherlands (to be distinguished from her great-niece, Margaret of Parma; see J. L. Motley, *Rise of the Dutch Republic*, 'Administration of the Duchess Margaret'). |
| FORTUNE LE VEUT | Fortune so wills it. Chator, Bts., Chaytor, co. York. |
| FORWARD | Lord Austin *(NEP)*, Balfour, co. Essex, Birmingham, City of, Campbell, Carrel, Earls of Castle Stewart (Stuart), Churchill Coll. Trust, Cambridge, Douglas, Hillingdon, London Bor. of, Howales, Ker, Macalister-Hall, Morland, Ogilvie, Ogilvy, Bts., Marquesses of Queensbury (Douglas), Richmond-Watson, Sandby, Speir, Stewart of Athenry, Bts., Stirling, Bts., Strachan, Ward, Earls Wemyss. |

| | |
|---|---|
| FORWARD AND ALOFT | Lord Douglas of Kirtleside *(NEP)*. |
| FORWARD IN THE NAME OF GOD | Kerr. |
| FORWARD OURS | Seton. |
| FORWARD TOGETHER | Brent, London Bor. of. |
| FORWARD TOWARDS THE LIGHT | Viscount Weir. |
| FORWARD WITHOUT FEAR | Gordon of Embo, Bts. |
| FOUNDATIONS FOR THE FUTURE | No. 15 Elementary Flying Training Sch., RAF. |
| FOURSQUARE TO ALL WINDS | Alford (Lincs.) UDC. |
| FOVET ET DISCUTIT | It nourishes and dissipates. François de France, Duke of Anjou, youngest son of King Henry II of France, ardent suitor of Queen Elizabeth I. Motto refers to his visit to the Netherlands with device of a sun dispersing clouds. Of his sottish behaviour there is a true account in Baroness Orczy's novel, *Flower of the Lily*. |
| FOY EN TOUT | Faith in everything. Sutcliffe, Yelverton. |
| FOY EST TOUT | Faith is all. Babington, co. Leics. Earls of Ripon (Robinson) *(NEP)*. |
| FOY POUR DEVOIR | Faith for duty. Lord Alcester (Seymour) *(NEP)*, Culme-Seymour, Bts., Seymour of the Army, Bts., Seymour, co. Galway, Dukes of Somerset (Seymour). |
| FOYALL LOYAL | Loyal faith. Fitzroy-Newdigate. |
| FRANC ET SANS DOL | Frank and without guile. Cartier, Bt. |
| FRANGAS NON FLECTAS | You may break but may not bend. 5th Army Co-op. Sq., RAF, Marquis Wielopolski (Gonzaga) Myszkowaki of Poland. |
| FRANGAS NON FLECTES | You may break but shall not bend. Barnes, Cassidi, Collins, Clifford, co. Glos., Lords Gorell (Barnes), Gower, Earls Granville (Leveson-Gower), Jones, Jourdain, Kimber, Bts., Leveson-Gower, Owen, Lords Rathcreedan (Norton), Dukes of Sutherland (Leveson-Gower), Earls Temple of Stowe, Wentworth Stanley. |
| FRANGIT INACCESSA | He breaks the inaccessible. Francois de Bonne, Duc de Lesdiguières, Constable of France and general of Henry IV. |
| FRAOCH BILEAN | Heather Island. Lords Macdonald (there are many islands so named, including one in Loch Arne). |
| FRAPPER JUSTE | Strike sure. No. 104 Wing HQ, RAF. |
| FRAPPES FORT | Strike hard. Kaulback, Earls of Kimberley (Wodehouse). |
| FREE FOR A BLAST | Clark of Cavendish Square, Bts., Clark of Courie Castle, Clark of Dunlambert, Bts., Clerk, Bts., Pennycock, Ratray of that Ilk. |
| FREELY WE SERVE | Amersham (Bucks.) RDC. |

| | |
|---|---|
| FRENA VEL AUREA NOLO | I do not wish for bridles albeit of gold. Hole of Caunton. |
| FRENAVIMUS MARE | We have tamed the sea. HMS *Castor*. |
| FRÈRE AYME FRÈRE | Frere love thy brother. Frere. |
| FRESH COURAGE TAKE | Newport Pagnell (Bucks.) RDC. |
| FRETA CUSTODIMUS ALTAQUE VERRIMUS | We guard the straits and scour the high seas. HQ, RAF, Gibraltar. |
| FRIENDSHIP | 341 Sq., RAF (French), transferred to French Army Air Force, 1945. |
| FROM DEFENCE TO ATTACK | 50 Sq., RAF (badge a sword severing a mantle). Sq. was formed at Dover, where St Martin dividing cloak is in the arms. The allusion to St Martin is from the incident in his life when as a Roman officer he gave half his cloak to a beggar. |
| FROM DUSK TILL DAWN | 219 Sq., RAF. |
| FROM GREAT THINGS TO GREATER | Tower Hamlets, London Bor. of. |
| FROM SEA TO SEA | 221 Sq., RAF. |
| FROM THE DEEP | 284 Sq., RAF. |
| FRONTI NULLA FIDES | There is no trusting a countenance (*or* appearances). Cripps, Horne, Bts., Lords Parmoor (Cripps). |
| FRUCTO NON FOLIIS | By fruit not by leaves. Bushby, co. Herts. |
| FRUCTUS VIRTUTIS | The fruit of virtue. Kekewich. |
| FRUGES ECCE PALUDIS | Lo, the fruits of the swamp. Mirfield (W.R. Yorks.) UDC (play on the name, Mire-field). |
| FRUSTRA | In vain. Italian Literary Academy of the Ostinati. |
| FUGIT | It flees. Lords Borwick. |
| FUGO NON FUGIO | I put to flight, I do not flee. 245 Sq., RAF. |
| FUIMUS | We have been. Lords Aberdare (Bruce), Marquesses of Ailesbury (Brudenell-Bruce), Bruce of Blaen-y-Cwm, co. Glam., Bruce of Downhill, Bts., Bruce of Miltown Castle, co. Cork, Earls of Elgin & Kincardine (Bruce), Kennedy, co. Ayr, The Lady Kinloss (Freeman-Grenville), Lords Thurlow (Cumming-Bruce). |
| FUIMUS ET SUB DEO ERIMUS | We have been, and we shall be, under God. Coham, Holland. |
| FUIMUS ET SUMUS | We were and we are. Whitby (Yorks.) UDC, 1935. |
| FULMEN ALATUM TENEMUS | We hold in readiness the winged thunderbolts. No. 42 Group HQ, RAF. |
| FULMINA EX IGNE POLITIORA | Thunderbolts (become) more polished (*or* perfected) out of fire. No. 81 Group HQ, RAF. |
| FULMINA REGIT JUSTA | The king's lightnings are just. 44 Sq., RAF (badge an elephant, based on seal of Lo Bengula, Chief of the Matabele at their conquest). |
| FULMINA SERVAMUS | We store thunderbolts. No. 21 Maintenance Unit, RAF. |
| FULMINIS INSTAR | Like the thunderbolt. 128 Sq., RAF. |

| | |
|---|---|
| FUNDAMENTA EJUS SUPER MONTIBUS SANCTIS | Her foundations are above the holy hills. Univ. of Durham (very appropriate, as university, is on the heights with the great cathedral). |
| FUNDAMENTO SEMPER STABILI | Always in a sound foundation. Structural Engineers, Inst. of. |
| FÜR BADENS EHRE | For Baden's honour. Military Order of Carl Friedrich (Baden). |
| FÜR EUR UND WAHRHEIT | For honour and truth. Order of the Zahringen Lion (Baden). |
| FÜR VERDIENST UND TREUE | For merit and truth. Order of Merit (Saxony). |
| FÜRCHTLOS UND TREW | Fearless and true. Order of the Crown (Württemberg). |
| FUROR ARMA MINISTRAT | Rage furnishes arms (Virgil, *Aeneid* i. 150). Baynes, Bts. |
| FURTACHD IS FOIR | Relief and aid. Fraser of Tain, Bts. |
| FURTH FORTUNE AND FILL THE FETTERS | Dukes of Atholl (Murray), Murray. Motto is supposed to refer to some words of a Scottish king to one of his nobles (a Murray) going out to catch a robber: 'Go forth, good fortune go with you and fill the fetters with your prisoner.' |
| FUTURUM CIVITATEM INQUIRIMUS | We seek for the coming citizenship. Prescot Gram. Sch., Lancs., 1933. |

# G

| | |
|---|---|
| GAIR DUW GOREW | God's word is best. St David's Coll., Lampeter, Wales. |
| GANG FORWARD | Keir, Stirling. |
| GANG WARILY | Algie, Earls of Perth (Drummond). |
| GARDE BIEN | Keep well. Carrick, Earls of Eglinton and Winton (Montgomerie), Montgomery. |
| GARDE BIEN LA FOY | Keep well the faith. Leeming, co. Lancs. |
| GARDE LA FOI or GARDE TA FOY | Keep the faith. Felsted Sch., Essex (founded 1564 by Richard, Lord Riche, Lord Chancellor of England), Lords Kensington (Edwardes), Rich, Bts. |
| GARDE GARDE | Guard, guard. Montgomerie. |
| GARDE LA CROIX | Guard the Cross. Ward of Stramshall. |
| GARDE LA LOI | Keep the law. Slator. |
| GARDE LE ROY | Defend the king. Lane of King's Bromley. A member of this family, Col. John Lane, was instrumental in saving Charles II after the Battle of Worcester. He sheltered the king at his house at Bentley, Staffs. Thence, by the agency of Col. Lane's brother and his sister Jane, King Charles was taken in disguise to Mrs Norton's at Abbot's Leigh nr. Bristol and thence to Col. Wyndham's at Trent, Somerset. A special augmentation of honour was granted to the family, namely the Royal arms of England, three lions passant, on a canton; also a crest of a strawberry roan horse holding between his forelegs the Royal crown (*B.L.G.*, 1952). See also Sir Arthur Bryant, *King Charles II*, 1949, p. 23: 'For the next week she [Jane Lane] carried the Crown of England in her hands, and never was trust more bravely or delicately performed.' |
| GARDE L'HONNEUR | Guard your honour. Hawksley. |
| GARDE TA BIEN-AIMÉE | Guard thy wellbeloved. Ashworth of Birtenshaw, Lancs., Maze. |
| GARDE TA FOY | Keep your faith. Sir Thomas Rich's Sch., Glos. |
| GARDEZ | Beware. Lords Braye (Cave), Cave-Browne-Cave, Bts., in allusion to the surname (Latin *cave* = beware). |
| GARDEZ BIEN | Watch well. Earls of Eglinton (Montgomerie), Livere, Montgomery. |
| GARDEZ LA FOY | Keep the faith. A'Deane, Dymocke (*temp.* Henry VIII), Earl Poulett. |
| GARDE L'HONNEUR | Preserve honour. Broadley, Bts., Hanmer, Bts., Pomfret. |
| GARE LA QUEUE DES ALLEMANDS | Beware the stem (or stock) of the Allemands. These formed a closely-knit group of families in region of the Isère in SW France. |

| | |
|---|---|
| GAUDEAT AGER | Let the field rejoice. Fylde (Lancs.) RDC. |
| GAUDEO | I rejoice. Brown, Browne, Joicey. |
| GAUDET TENTAMINE VIRTUS | Virtue exults in the trial. Earls of Dartmouth (Legge), Fry, Legge-Bourke. |
| GENERATIM DISCITE CULTUS | Generally learn of cultivation. Bath Univ. of Technology. |
| GENEROSITATE | By generosity. Nicolson of Glenbervie, Bts. |
| GENTES DIVERSI MENTE CONCORDES | Races diverse, agreed in mind. Sino-British Fellowship Trust. |
| GERECHTIGKEIT IST MACHT | Right is might. Order of Berthold I (Baden). |
| GIN YE DAUR | If ye dare. 603 City of Edinburgh Sq., RAAF. |
| GIVE INVENTION LIGHT | Bradford Univ. |
| GIVE THANKS TO GOD | Girdlers' Co., inc. 1449. |
| GIVE THE THANKS THAT ARE DUE | Ward of Northwood Park, IOW. |
| GIVE US OUR DAILY BREAD | Farmers' Co. (in 1952 approved as a livery company by Court of Aldermen, City of London). |
| GLADIO ET ARCU | With sword and bow. Stubber. |
| GLADIO STILOQUE FERAX | Brave with sword and pen. Lord Stamfordham (Bigge) *(NEP)*. |
| GLADIOS IN VOMERES | Swords into ploughshares. No. 8302 (Air Disarmament) Wing, RAF. |
| GLORIA DEO | Glory to God. Challen, Henn. |
| GLORIA EX DURIS | Glory from hardships. Erik, Duke of Brunswick, d. 1584. |
| GLORIA FILIORUM PATRES | Fathers are the glory of sons. Eltham Coll., Kent. |
| GLORIA FINIS | Glory is the end. Viscount Alanbrooke (Brooke), Grove, Sergison-Brooke, 43 Sq., RAF. |
| GLORIA IN EXCELSIS DEO | Glory to God in the highest (opening words of great hymn with which Holy Communion service ends in the Book of Common Prayer, 1662, transferred by Archbishop Cranmer from beginning of the Mass to end of the present service). Trinity Coll. of Music. |
| GLORIA PATRI | Glory to the Father (beginning of doxology). Dewar. |
| GLORIA PRISCA NOVATUR | The ancient glory renewed. Carrickfergus (co. Antrim), Bor. of. |
| GLORIA RURIS DIVINA | The divine glory of the country. Gower (Glam.) RDC. |
| GLORIA SAT DEUS UNUS | It is enough glory God being one. Weston. |
| GLORIA SOLI DEO | Glory to God alone. Penruddocke. |
| GLORIA VIRTUTIS UMBRA | Glory is the shadow of virtue. Earls of Longford (Pakenham), Pakenham. |
| GO AND DO THOU LIKEWISE | Colston, Lords Roundway (Colston) *(NEP)*, adopted in ref. to great Bristol philanthropist, Edward Colston, whose name is commemorated in the Colston Hall, Bristol. |
| GO FORWARD | Walton, Bt. |

| | |
|---|---|
| GO THROUGH | Brenton, Bt. |
| GOBAITH YABANNHA LAFUR | . . . Hope . . . work (trans. beyond two words shown considered doubtful). Probyn-Jones, Bts. |
| GOD CAN RAISE TO ABRAHAM CHILDREN OF STONES | Paviors' Co. (organized body since 1479, never inc.). Motto comes from St John the Baptist's words to the Pharisees (St Matthew 3:9). |
| GOD CARETH FOR US | Mitford, Lords Redesdale (Freeman-Mitford). |
| GOD FOR US | Douglas of Tilquhillie. |
| GOD FRIED (GOTT FRIEDE) | The peace of God. Godfrey, Bts. |
| GOD GIVES INCREASE | Balfour of Denmilne, Bt. |
| GOD GIVETH THE INCREASE | Allen. |
| GOD GRANT GRACE | Grocers' Co. (inc. by Royal charter 1428, the company being second only to the Mercers among the great Twelve; in shield of the arms are nine cloves, and the camel in the crest bears two bags of pepper, ref. to ancient Guild of Pepperers first mentioned 1180), Oundle Sch. (founded by Grocers' Co.). |
| GOD GRANT UNITY | Wheelwrights' Co., charter 1669. |
| GOD GUARD US | Brigg. |
| GOD IS OUR GUIDE | Masons' Co., inc. 1677. |
| GOD IS OUR STRENGTH | Ironmongers' Co., inc. 1463. |
| GOD SEND GRACE | Brocklebank, Marquesses of Bute (Crichton-Stuart), Crichton, Dalrymple, Earls of Erne (Crichton). |
| GOD SEND ME WEL TO KEPE | Anne of Cleves, 4th wife of Henry VIII. |
| GOD THE ONLY FOUNDER | Founders' Co., concerned with stirrups, buckles, spurs, candlesticks, lavers and pots; inc. 1614, when charter required all brass weights in the City and 3 miles' compass to be brought to Founders' Hall to be sized and marked. |
| GOD US AYDE | Farewell. |
| GOD WITH MY RIGHT | Bryson, Buchanan of Drumakill, Leith-Buchanan, Bts. |
| GOD WITH US | Dursley (Glos.) RDC, Gordon of Abergeldie, Moodie. |
| GOD'S PROVIDENCE IS MY INHERITANCE | Boyle, Bts., Earls of Cork & Orrery (Boyle). |
| GODAF I GEISIO | I rise to search. 614 Co. of Glamorgan Sq., AAF. |
| GOFAL DYN DUW AI GWERID | God will release man from care. Parry. |
| GOFALU | Taking care. No. 277 Maintenance Unit, RAF. |
| GOLUD GWLAD RHYDDID | The riches of a country is freedom. Cardiganshire CC. |
| GOING DOWN | 438 Sq., RCAF. |
| GOOJERAT | Viscount Gough. Sir Hugh Gough, Bt., was cr. a Baron, 1845, and a Viscount 1848–9. Goojerat was his last and greatest victory in which he shattered the Sikh army and concluded the Second Sikh War. |
| GORAU MOES GWASANAETH | The best virtue (or service). Aberystwyth (Card.), Bor. of. |

| | |
|---|---|
| GORAU NAWDD, NAWDD DUW | The best patronage, God's patronage. Hawarden (Flints.) RDC. |
| GORAU TARIAN CYFLAWDER | Justice is the best shield. Flintshire CC. |
| GOREU AWEN GWIRIONED | The best muse is truth. Univ. of Wales – inscribed on book forming part of crest, 1910. |
| GOREU BONEDD RHINWEDD | The highest nobility is virtue. Lords Davies. |
| GOREU CAMP CADW | The best art, protection. Gwynedd Police Authority, 1967. |
| GOREU OLUD IECHYD | The best riches, health. Royal Gwent Hosp. |
| GOTT EHRE VATERLAND | God, honour, fatherland. Order of Ludwig (Hesse). |
| GOTT UND MEIN RECHT | God and my right. Order of Friedrich (Württemberg). |
| GOULD BYDETH EVER BRIGHT | Baring-Gould. |
| GRACE ME GUIDE | Lords Forbes, Pownall of Hounslow. |
| GRACE SERRA LE BIEN VENU | Grace will be welcome. Lord Zouche, *temp.* Henry VIII. |
| GRADATIM | Gradually. Anderson (formerly Wood), Hopwood, Kilgour, Mitchell, co. Staffs. |
| GRADATIM VINCIMUS | We conquer by degrees. Browne, Curtis of Cullands Grove, Bts., Duke, Bts., Lords Merrivale (Duke). |
| GRADU DIVERSO VIA UNA | The same by different steps. Anstruther-Gough-Calthorpe, Bts., The Lords Calthorpe. |
| GRANDESCUNT AUCTA LABORE | The requirements of industry render illustrious. A Court, Lords Heytesbury (Holmes A Court). |
| GRATA MANU | With a grateful hand. Call, Bt. |
| GRATIA GRATIAM CAPIT | Grace takes grace. St Cuthbert's Soc., Durham, 1957. |
| GRATA SUME MANU | Take with a grateful hand. Briscoe, Bts., Winnington, Bts. |
| GRATIA VINCI | I have conquered by grace. Lawrence. |
| GRATIAS AGO | I give thanks. Lord Colwyn (Smith). |
| GRATIOR EST A REGE PIO | It is more pleasing from a pious king. Gibbons, Bts. |
| GRAVIS DUM SUAVIS | Grave but gentle. Graves, Greaves. |
| GRAVITER | Gravely. Anderson, Bts. |
| GRIANDACHT TAREIS NEILL | Sunshine after clouds (an Irish scholar writes that this is the correct form, instead of 'Spiandacht', etc., which is given in some reference works for the family). Lord Moynihan. |
| GRIP FAST | Arbuthnot-Leslie, Leslie, Leslie-Ellis, Earls of Rothes (Leslie). Attributed to a Leslie's rescue of Queen Margaret, wife of William of Scotland, when nearly drowned at a river crossing, and she was saved by hanging on to the Leslie's girdle. |
| GRIPE GRIFFIN HOLD FAST | De Trafford, Bts., Trafford of Trafford Park. |
| GROW AS A GROVE | Troyte-Bullock. |
| GUARD AND GUIDE | RAF station, Bishop's Court. |

| | |
|---|---|
| GUARD, SEEK AND STRIKE | RAF station, Berka. |
| GUARD THE FLIGHT | HQ Military Air Traffic Operations, RAF. |
| GUARD TO THE GATEWAY | RAF station, Gibraltar. |
| GUBERNAT NAVEM DEUS | God navigates the ship. Leckie, Lecky. |
| GUIDANCE | No. 23 Group HQ, RAF. |
| GUIDE TO ATTACK | RAF station, North Coates. |
| GUIDED STEEL | RAF station, Lindholme, nr. Doncaster, W.R. Yorks. Badge shows head and shoulders of a Roman centurion aiming with his dexter hand a steel tipped shaft, hence motto. Station adopted badge because Roman IX legion was located in vicinity of Lindholme. |
| GUN EAGAL | Without fear. Macnab, Bt. |
| GWAITH GYDA GOBAITH | Work with hope. Lawrence of Chelsea, Bts. |
| GWARY TEK | Fair play (Cornish). Polwyn. |
| GWASANAETHAEF | I serve. Lord Arwyn (Life Baron). |
| GWELL ANGAU NA GWARTH | Better death than dishonour. 2nd Bn. Pontymoel VRC Territorials, Monmouthshire Regt. |
| GWEDD CREFFT HEB EI DAWN | Art without inspiration is a widow. Swansea, Univ. Coll. of. |
| GWELL ANGAU NA CHYWILYDD | Better death than shame. Basset, Llewellyn of Raglan, Bts., Lloyd of Ferney Hall, Mackworth, Bts., 1st Brecknockshire Rifle Volunteers, 41st Foot, the Welsh Regt. |
| GWELL DYSG NA GOLUD | Better learning than riches. Llandovery Coll. (Coleg Llanymddyfri). (Carm.). |
| GWELLA BRAINT HEB GOLLI BRO | To improve privileges without losing locality. Vaynor and Penderyn (Brecknock) RDC, 1955. |
| GWIR YN ERBYN Y BYD | Truth against the world (Cornish). Gay, Truscott, Bts. |
| GWNA A DDYLIT DOED A DDEL | Do what you should, come what may. Lords Merthyr (Lewis). |
| GWRA PERTHY AN GWYR | Sustain the truth (Cornish). Penberthy. |
| GWYLIO'R GOROOEWIN O'R AWYR | To watch the west from the air. RAF station, Pembroke Dock, S. Wales. |

# H

| | |
|---|---|
| HA PERSA LA FIDE, HA PERSO L'HONORE | If I have lost faith, I have lost honour. Du Pré, Lewis of St Pierre. |
| HABENDA RATIO VALETUDINIS | A reason for health must be held. Pharmaceutical Soc. of Gt. Britain. |
| HABEO NON HABEOR | I hold but am not held. Gilbert. |
| HABERE ET DISPERTIRE | To have and to share. No. 92 Maintenance Unit, RAF. |
| HABITARE RURI DELECTATIONES COLERE | To dwell in the country to preserve its delights. Hailsham (E. Sussex) RDC. |
| HAEC FRUCTUS VIRTUTIS | These are the fruits of virtue. Waller, Bts. |
| HAEC GENERI INCREMENTA FIDES | Fidelity gave these honours to our race. Townshend. |
| HAEC MANUS INIMICA TYRANNIS | This hand is hostile to tyrants. Burrell, Hemsworth. |
| HAEC MANUS OB PATRIAM | This hand for my country. Mactier, Shuckburgh, Bts. |
| HAEC OMNIA TRANSEUNT | All these things pass away. Bourne, co. Staffs. |
| HAEC OTIA STUDIA FOVENT | These times of leisure favour studies. Univ. of Liverpool. |
| HAEC PORTA MOENIA VIRI | This is the gate, the walls are men. No. 7 Sch. of Recruit Training, RAF. |
| HAEC SUNT NOSTRA ROBORA | These are our strengths. Oakengates (Salop) UDC. |
| HALLELUJAH | Aylmer. |
| HANFOD TREF TREFN | The essence of a town. Ammanford (Carm.) UDC. |
| HAPPINESS THROUGH SERVICE | Lord Donovan *(NEP).* |
| HARAPLAH SA-LAGI BERNAFAS | (Malay words, put in Arabic characters in *B.L.G.* 1952). Brooke. Sir James Brooke became Rajah of Sarawak *c.*1838, suppressed piracy and head-hunting. Succeeded by his nephew Sir Charles Johnson-Brooke in 1868 (*B.L.G.* 1952). |
| HARDD HAFAN HEDD | Beautiful hermitage of peace. Llandudno (Caerns.) UDC. |
| HARASS | 450 Sq., R. Aust. A.F., founded 1941 in Australia. |
| HAUD IMMEMOR | Not unmindful. Lords Stanmore (Hamilton-Gordon) *(NEP).* |
| HAUD MUTO FACTUM | Not done by muteness. Broughton, Bts. |
| HAUD SICUT VULGUS | Not as the vulgar. Minoprio. |
| HAUD ULLIS LABANTIA VENTIS | Yielding under no winds. Irvine, Irving, Irwin. |
| HAULT EMPRISE | High enterprise. Haltemprice (E.R. Yorks.) UDC. |
| HAUT ET BON | High and good. Viscount Doneraile (St Leger), St Leger. |

| | |
|---|---|
| HAUT ON ASPIRE | Aspire highly. Horton. |
| HAVE COURAGE | Leigh Wood. |
| HAVE MYNDE | Hippisley-Cox. |
| HAVE NO FEAR | Lord Ismay *(NEP)*. |
| HAY, HAY, THE WHITE SWAN, BY GOD'S SOUL, I AM THY MAN | Motto used by Edward III with device of the white swan at a tournament, an exercise in which he delighted to participate, often in disguise. |
| HAYA INGIA NAPIGANA | Get in and fight (Swahili). 259 Sq., RAF, formed 1943 at Kitrevu, East Africa. |
| HAZARD YET FORWARD | Earls of Eglinton and Winton (Montgomerie), Seton. |
| HE HABITEN RONTERHOS | 431 Sq., RCAF (badge is head of Red Indian brave). |
| HEAL, TEACH, LEARN | United Birmingham Hosps. Bd., 1953. |
| HEALTH AND A DAY | Lords Horder (1st Lord Horder was a famous physician). |
| HEALTH AND HAPPINESS | Hornsea (E.R. Yorks.) UDC. |
| HEALTH IS A CROWN ON THE HEADS OF THE FIT THAT IS SEEN BY NONE BUT THE SICK | (Motto is in Arabic). RAF Hosp., Aden Protectorate Levies. |
| HEART AND HAND | Matheson, Bt. |
| HEART STAND FAST | Acton. |
| HEAVEN'S LIGHT OUR GUIDE | Order of the Star of India (inst. in 1861, no appointment made since 1947 when India became independent), Portsmouth, City of. |
| HEB DDUW HEB DDIM, DUW A DIGON | Without God, without anything, God is enough. Jones of Ystrad. |
| HEB DHU, HEB DHIM, DHU A DIGON | Without God, without anything, God is enough. Davies, Edwards, co. Wicklow, Hopkins, Gambier-Parry, Hughes, Jennings, Lloyd of Dan-y-alt, Meridith, Bts., Meyrick, Morgan, Lords Mostyn, Tapps-Gervis-Meyrick, Bts., Williams. |
| HEB DUW HEB DDIM | Without God we have nothing. Hughes-Morgan, Bts., Price. |
| HEB ELYNION, HEB GYMMERIAD | Without enemies, without repute. Gwynne-Evans, Bts. |
| HEB LAFUR HEB LWYDD | Without labour, without success. Jones. |
| HEB NEVOL NERTH NID SICR SAETH | Without help from above, the arrow flies in vain. Jones of Hartsheath, Jones of Chester, Jones-Mortimer. |
| HELD IN RESERVE | No. 33 Maintenance Unit, RAF. |
| HELDHAFTIG, VASTBERADEN, BARMHARTIG | Heroic, resolute, merciful. From the arms of the City of Amsterdam. |
| HELP | Foundling Hosp., London. |
| HEREWARD | 11 Sq., RAF. Name 'Hereward' means 'Guardian of the Army'. Badge of the sq., adopted 1931, is a Wake Knot, this being badge of Wake family. Hereward the Wake was last Englishman to hold out against Norman Conqueror. See Charles Kingsley, *Hereward the Wake*, |

also *De Gestis Herewardi Saxonis*, 1895, transcribed by S. H. Miller, trans. W. D. Sweeting. For a very able account of pedigree of the Wake Bts. from Hereward see *B.P.* 1970.

HERI DOCENDUM HODIE IMPLENDUM

Yesterday it had to be taught, today it has to be carried out. RAF station, Acklington.

HIC BENE DOCTI UBIQUE VOLANT

Having been taught well here, they fly everywhere. No. 242 Operational Conversion Unit, RAF.

HIC ERAM IN DIERUM SECULIS

Here I was in ages of days. Gatacre, Gataker.

HIC ET ALIUBI

Here and everywhere. Pigott, Bts.

HIC ET UBIQUE

Here and everywhere. 201 Sq., RAF.

HIC FRUCTUS VIRTUTIS

This is the fruit of valour. Craig-Waller, Waller, Bts. Motto refers to an exploit at Agincourt, 1415, in which Sir Richard Waller of Groomsbridge, Kent, captured Charles, Duke of Orleans. A considerable ransom was demanded by Sir Richard and while it was being collected, Orleans remained (for twenty-five years) in England. He mastered English sufficiently to produce verse which has retained a place in English medieval lyrics. Motto is supposed to refer to Sir Richard's profit from the ransom. On the Waller crest of a walnut-tree is depicted, hanging from a bough, a shield charged with three fleurs-de-lis, again an allusion to the capture of Orleans. It is impossible to give precise details because the church of St Mary the Virgin at Speldhurst in Kent was destroyed in 1791 with the Waller memorials. The 1st Bt., Sir Jonathan Waller, put mural tablet in rebuilt church on which were recorded names of twenty of his ancestors back to 1183 (Waller of Braywick Lodge, *B.P.* 1970 and personal investigation by the author).

HIC HAEC HOC TACEATIS

May you keep silence in this, that and the other (i.e. in everything). Edmund of Langley, 1st Duke of York and 5th son of Edward III, supposed to have some allusion to the Yorkist cause espoused by his grandson.

HIC HAUD

I hold it (Flemish words, allusion to playing dice). Jean sans Peur, Duke of Burgundy, *c.*1419.

HIGH ENDEAVOUR

No. 54 Maintenance Unit, RAF.

HIGHER

Galloway of Blervie.

HINC GARBAE NOSTRAE

Hence our sheaves. Cummin, Cuninghame.

HINC LUCEM ET POCULA SACRA

Hence light and sacred cups. Cambridge Univ.

HINC NOSTRAE CREVERE ROSAE

Hence have grown our roses. Charles I when at Holyrood in 1633 had device of a thistle with this motto, signifying right to English Crown through Scotland's royal line.

HINC ODOR ET FRUCTUS

Hence fragrance and fruit. Italian Literary Academy, the Accesi.

HINC ORIOR

Hence I rise. Paterson, Bts., Stewart.

HINC SPES EFFULGET *or* AFFULGET

Hence hope shines forth. Aberdour., Innholders' Co., 1514.

| | |
|---|---|
| HINC VIGILO | Hence I watch. Philip II of Spain on marriage with Mary I (Bloody Mary) of England, implying his watch on heresy in England. |
| HINC VULNUS, SALUS ET UMBRA | Hence wound, healing and shade. Don Ferdinando Carefa, Count of Soriano. |
| HIRBARHAD | Diligence. Lords Merthyr (Lewis). |
| HIS MODIS AD VICTORIAM | By this means to victory. 154 Sq., RAF. |
| HIS TRUTH SHALL BE THY SHIELD | Lord Hannen (NEP). |
| HISTORY WILL TELL | No. 1 Initial Training Sch., RAF (Air Crew Officer Training Sch.). Motto refers to hope of Sch. staff that pupils would be a credit to sch. in the future. |
| HITHERTO | Bull, Bts. |
| HLABEZULU (MATABELE) | The stabber of the sky. 266 Sq., RAF, Rhodesia. |
| HOC AGE | Do this. Bradford Gram. Sch. (known to have existed in 1548), Levett, Paul, co. Suffolk. |
| HOC EST SIGNUM DEI | This is the sign of God. Manfred, d. 1266, usurper of Naples, alluding to fall of his crest from his helmet. |
| HOC FONTE DERIVATA COPIA IN PATRIAM POPULUMQUE FLUIT | Wealth, drawn from this spring, flows forth unto our country and our people. Wells (Som.), City of, 1951. |
| HOC IN LOCO DEUS RUPES | In this place God is a rock. Hockin. |
| HOC MAJORUM OPUS | This is the work of our ancestors. Eliott. |
| HOC OPUS EST | This is the work. Pedro I ('the Cruel'), King of Castile and Leon 1350–69, restored to his throne by the Black Prince at the Battle of Navaretta, 1367. |
| HOC PRETIUM CIVE SERVATO TULIT | He bears this reward for having saved a citizen. Roy. Humane Soc. On the medal which bears this inscription is a representation of a civic wreath, alluding to the coveted Roman award of a crown of oak leaves for saving the life of a Roman citizen; award was won by Julius Caesar at siege of Rhodes. |
| HOC SECURIOR | Safer by this. Collison, Lord Fairfield (Greer) (NEP), Grier, Grierson, Bts., Grieve, Lockhart. |
| HOC SIGNO VINCES | Thou shalt conquer in this sign. Moore of Mayes Park. |
| HOC VIRTUTIS OPUS | This is the work of virtue. Bulwer-Lytton, Bts., Earls of Lytton. |
| HODIE DISCO CRAS VINCO | Today I learn, tomorrow I conquer. No. 3 Sch. of General Reconnaissance, RAF. |
| HODIE FELIX CRAS TER | Happy today, thrice tomorrow. Craster of Craster Tower, Alnwick, Northumb., family which has held Craster (hence its surname and pun in motto) since 1166. |
| HODIE NON CRAS | Today, not tomorrow, Bowyer-Vaux, Hague, Mostyn, Sykes, Lords Vaux of Harrowden (Gilbey). |
| HOEG FY MWALL | Whet my axe! Bransby-Williams (one of his ancestors was called Whetter of the Battleaxe). |

| | |
|---|---|
| HOLD FAST | Ancram, Downie, Frome, Lesly, Macleod, Marshall of Rachan, Stilwell. |
| HOLD FAST, SIT SURE | Saddlers' Co., charter 1363. |
| HOLD ON | Willans. |
| HOLD TO THE TRUTH | Braintree and Bocking (Essex) UDC. |
| HOLDE FASTE | Rivett. |
| HOLD THE RIGHT | Rawnsley. |
| HOMINEM ET ESSE MEMENTO | Remember that thou art a man. Wybergh. Famous saying used when a Roman general rode in triumph in his chariot through Rome; a slave who held the crown of laurel over his head whispered these words in his ear. |
| HOMME D'ÉTAT | Man of state. Mann, Bts. |
| HOMO HOMINI LUPUS | Man is a wolf to man. Wolseley (crest is a wolf's head). |
| HOMO PLANTAT, HOMO IRRIGAT, SED DEUS DAT INCREMENTUM | Man plants, man waters, but God gives the increase. Merchant Taylors' Sch. (1561, Master & Wardens of Merchant Taylors' Co.) Motto derived from St Paul's phraseology in I Corinthians 3:6 and Galatians. |
| HOMO PROPONIT, DEUS DISPONIT | Man proposes, God disposes. Barber-Starkey, Starkey. |
| HOMO SUM | I am a man (part of the familiar verse of Terence). Homan, Bts., Mann, Manns. In the Latin, pun on name of Homan. |
| HOMO SUM; HUMANI NIHIL A ME ALIENUM PUTO | I am a man; I think nothing human alien to myself (Terence, *Heauton Timorumenos* I. i. 25). The London Hosp., founded 1740. |
| HONESTA QUAM MAGNA | How great are honourable things. Milson, Walker. |
| HONESTA QUAM SPLENDIDA | Honour rather than splendour. Askwith. Viscount Barrington, Dickens, Hine. |
| HONESTAS OPTIMA POLITIA | Honesty is the best policy. Cunliffe-Owen, Bts., Davis-Goff, Bts., Goff, Granger, Howard Thompson, Owen, Bts., Sparrow of Redhill. |
| HONESTE AUDAX | Honourably bold. Edingtown, Lawrence of Minstead, Parkyns, Wolley. |
| HONESTE CONABO | Honestly I will try. Haggard. |
| HONESTE PROGREDIEMUR CONANDO | We progress honestly in trying. Selsdon (Surrey) RDC, 1952. |
| HONESTE VIVE (*or* VIVO) | Live honestly (*or* I live honestly). Halkett (formerly Wedderburn, Bts.). |
| HONESTUM PRAEFERRE UTILI | To prefer the honest to the profitable. Raikes of Treberfydd. |
| HONESTUM PRO PATRIA | What is honourable for my country. Hamilton of Craighlaw. |
| HONESTY IS THE BEST POLICY | Thomas of Yapton, Bts., Marquesses of Willingdon (Freeman-Thomas). |
| HONESTY WITHOUT FEAR | Lord Kelvin (Thomson) *(NEP)*. |

| | |
|---|---|
| HONI SOIT QUI MAL Y PENSE | Evil be to him who evil thinks. Order of the Garter, founded by Edward III of England, 1348 (official date, despite mentions of earlier foundation; 1948 was sescentenary when Princess Elizabeth (now Elizabeth II) and Duke of Edinburgh were installed as Lady and Knight of the Garter). Popular story of motto's origin – that Edward retrieved a lady's garter that had dropped off at a court festival – can be neither proved nor disproved. |
| HONNEUR AULX DIGNES | Honour to the worthy. Roedean Sch., Sussex. |
| HONNEUR ET PATRIE | Honour and my country. Order of Legion of Honour (France). |
| HONNEUR SANS REPROCHE | Honour without reproach. Keeling. |
| HONNEUR SAUF SOUCI NUL | No honour without care. D'Avigdor-Goldsmid, Bts. |
| HONOR ALIT ARTES | Honour fosters the arts. Burton-on-Text (Staffs.), Co. Bor. of, Chichester Coll. of Further Educ. |
| HONOR DEO | Honour to God. Mercers' Co., inc. 1393 (the first among the great twelve City Companies of London). |
| HONOR ET HONESTAS | Honour and honesty. Rotheram, Tremayne. |
| HONOR ET INDUSTRIA | Honour and industry. Bacup (Lancs.), Bor. of. |
| HONOR ET VERITAS | Honor and truth. Kind, Waller of Newport, Bts. |
| HONOR ET VIRTUS | Honor and virtue. Atkins, Grogan, Morgan, Lords Muskerry (Deane). |
| HONOR FIDELITATIS PROEMIUM | Honour is the reward of fidelity. Lords Boston (Irby), Irby, Victoria Coll., Belfast, 1951. |
| HONOR PROBATAQUE VIRTUS | Honour and approved valour. Fitzgerald of Turlough, MacDermott. |
| HONOR VIRTUTIS | The honour of virtue. Burdon, De Butts. |
| HONOR VIRTUTIS CALCAR | Honour is the spur of virtue. Barnston of Crewe Hill, Bt. |
| HONOR VIRTUTIS PRAEMIUM | Honour is the reward of virtue (or valour). Arnold Sch., Blackpool, Bell, Blood, Boyle, Dickie, Earl Ferrers (Shirley), Fielding, Goldney, Bts., Hawtin, Hawtyn, Hayter-Hames, Hole of Park Hickie, Jennings of Gelli-Deg, Jervois, Lee-Norman, Palmer, Shirley. |
| HONOR VIRTUTIS SATELLES | Honour is the attendant of virtue. Baker of Lismacue. |
| HONORABILE ET FORTITER | Honourably and bravely. Lloyd of Rhu, Bts. |
| HONORANTES ME HONORABO | I will honour those who honour me (motto comes from 1 Samuel 2:30; verse concludes: 'and they that despise me shall be lightly esteemed'). Atthill, Maunsell. |
| HONORATE, DILIGITE, TIMETE | Honour, love, fear. Moseley, co. Staffs. |
| HONORE ET AMORE | With honour and love. Algar, Grantham, Hammersley, Richards, Solosborough. |
| HONORE ET LABORE | By honour and labour. Levy, Roan Sch., 1927. |
| HONORE ET VIRTUTE | With honour and virtue. Gilbey, Bts., Gillbanks, MacDermot of Coolavin. |
| HONOREM CUSTODE | Keep your honour. Wilkinson, Bts. |

| | |
|---|---|
| HONOS INDUSTRIAE PRAEMIUM | Honour is the reward of industry. Lord Duveen *(NEP)*, King, Bts. |
| HONOUR BEFORE HONOURS | Skinners' Co. Sch. for Girls, N. London, founded 1890. |
| HONOUR GOD | Carpenters' Co., inc. 1477. |
| HONOUR THROUGH DEEDS | 288 Sq., RAF. |
| HONOUR WISDOM | Queen's Sch., Chester, 1936. |
| HOPE | Dickson of Aldie, Lambe, Rhode Island, USA. |
| HOPE ME ENCOURAGITHE | Bush (formerly of Eastington Park, co. Glocs.). |
| HORA E SEMPRE | Now and always. Denys, Bts., Farmer, Bts., Lords Hesketh, Earls Pomfret. |
| HORA VENIT | The hour comes. Viscount Templewood (Hoare) *(NEP)*. |
| HORRENT COMMOTA MOVERI | Things which are moved hate to be moved. Somewhat enigmatic motto of the great Orsini family of Rome, whose device was a bear, from a play on their surname (Latin *ursus* = a bear). |
| HORS CEST AVEL, POINT N'AY AMOUR | Not to love outside this ring. St Louis IX, King of France 1214–70; reference to his love for his wife, Margaret de Provence. |
| HOS GLORIA REDDIT HONORES | Glory confers these honours. Williams-Drummond, Bts. |
| HOSTEM A COELO EXPELLERE | To expel the enemy from the sky. 40 Sq., RAF. Has broom for badge because Major Mannock served with it and used to tell his pilots: 'You must sweep the . . . Huns from the air.' |
| HOSTES NUNC AMICI | Enemies now friends. Abergavenny (Mon.), Bor. of. |
| HOSTIBUS OBVIAM | Against the foe. 902 Co. of London Sq., AAF. |
| HOSTIS HONORI INVIDIA | Envy is an enemy to honour. Dickens, Harborough, Market Harborough (Leics.) UDC, Pattison, Lords Sherard, Sherrard, Wegg. |
| HOUMONT | Cornwall, Duchy of. See ICH DIEN. |
| HOWEVER WIND BLOWS | 251 Sq., RAF. |
| HUIC GENERI INCREMENTA FIDES | Faithfulness caused the increase of this family. Duncan, Townshend. |
| HUIC HABEO NON TIBI | I hold it for him not for thee. Burroughs, Ellis, Bt., Newton. |
| HUJUS STAT FOEDERE MUNDUS | The world stands by the union of this. Bell (formerly of Pendell Court, Surrey) having figure of Justice as crest. |
| HUMANI NIHIL A ME ALIENUM PUTO | Nothing human I think alien from me (Terence). The London Hospital. |
| HUMANI NIHIL ALIENUM | Nothing that relates to man is indifferent to me (part of quotation from Terence). Bradford of South Audley Street, Bts., Maconchy, Talbot, Young. |
| HUMANI NIL ALIENUM | Nothing human is alien. Lord Pearce, Talbot of Belfast, Bts. |
| HUMBLE AND REVERENCE | Elizabeth of York, queen of Henry VII and dau. of Edward IV. |

| | |
|---|---|
| HUMBLE ET LOIALE | Humble and loyal. Margaret of Anjou, queen of Henry VI of England; dau. of René, Duke of Anjou, and (titular only) King of Sicily, Naples and Jerusalem. This brave, talented but most unhappy woman d. 1482 having survived husband, son and Lancastrian cause. |
| HUMILITATE | With humility. Carlisle. |
| HUNA TAMWEEN | Here is supply. No. 114 Maintenance Unit, RAF, Aden. |
| HUNT AND DESTROY | 169 Sq., RAF. |
| HWY CLOD NA GOLUD | Better fame than riches. Rhondda (Glam.), Bor. of, 1955. |
| HWY PERY CLOD NA GOLUD | Fame lasts longer than riches. Lloyd of Aston. |
| HYEME VIRESCO | I flourish in winter. Strode. |

# I

| | |
|---|---|
| I AM READY | Fairley, Fraser of Tornaveen, Hall-Maxwell, Maxwell, Bts., Scot of Hundilshope, Stirling-Maxwell, Bts. (dormant). |
| I BEND BUT NOT BREAK | Moore of Kyleburn, Bts. |
| I BRING THE BREATH OF LIFE | No. 279 Maintenance Unit, RAF (unit supplies oxygen). |
| I BYDE MY TYME | Campbell of Auchmannock, Crawfurd of Newfield, Dale, Bt., Pennefather, Simpson of Bowerswood. |
| I DARE | Adair, Earls of Carnwath (Dalzell) *(NEP)*, Dalsiel, Dalyell, Dalziell. |
| I DIE FOR THOSE I LOVE | Patterson, Stacpole, Stewart. |
| I DISTRIBUTE CHEARFULLIE | George Heriot's Sch., Edinburgh, founded 1628 by George Heriot, goldsmith and banker to James VI and I. |
| I DREAD GOD | Munro. |
| I DDUW BO'R DIOLCH | To God be thanks. Evan-Thomas, Lloyd of Bronwydd, Thomas of Welfield. |
| I GROW AND I REJOICE | Crawley (Sussex) UDC. |
| I GUIDE THE HUNTER | 3608 North Riding Fighter Control Unit, RAAF (badge is a pointer). |
| I HAVE LIVED TODAY | Hooper, Bts. |
| I HOLD MY AIM | Central Gunnery Sch., RAF. |
| I HOPE | Gordon of Pitlurg, Joynt, Straloch. |
| I HOPE IN GOD | Macnaghten, M'Naughten. |
| I HOPE TO SPEED | Earls Cathcart (Cathcart). |
| I HOPE TO SHARE | Nisbet, Riddell of Riddell, Bts. |
| I'LL STAND SURE | Grant of Corrimony. |
| I LIKE MY CHOICE | Earls of Halifax (Wood). |
| I LIVE AND DY IN LOYALTYE | Goodacre. |
| I MAK SICKER (I MAKE SURE) | Famous saying by friend of King Robert Bruce when the latter said he thought he had killed the Red Comyn, whereupon the friend went into church to the Comyn and made sure. Escotts, Johnston, Kirkpatrick. |
| I MEAN WELL | Callender, Shaw, Bts., Shaw-Stewart, Bts., Stewart, Sutcliffe. |
| I PEDE FAUSTO | Go with fortunate foot. Oadby (Leics.) UDC. |
| I PERSEVERE | Madge, Bts. |
| I PRESERVE | No. 10 Maintenance Unit, RAF. |
| I RIPEN AND DIE YET LIVE | Seely, Lord Sherwood (Seely) *(NEP)*. |

| | |
|---|---|
| I SPREAD MY WINGS AND KEEP MY PROMISE (IN ARABIC) | 14 Sq., RAF (location near burial place of St George; Cross of St George on badge). Motto (from the Koran) suggested by Emir Abdullah. |
| I SUPPLY YOUR NEEDS | No. 107 Maintenance Unit, RAF. |
| I THINK IN TIME | Lords Erskine of Rerrick. |
| I TO THE HILLS | Lords Amulree (Mackenzie). |
| I WILL DEFEND THE RIGHT | 129 Sq., RAF, Mysore (the Gunda Bherunda, mythical bird of Mysore, forms badge to commemorate generosity of donors). |
| I WILL MAINTAIN | Brixham (Devon) UDC. Motto of William III (of Orange), seal of Brixham represents William landing on the shore. On scroll above design is inscription: 'Landing of the Prince of Orange, 1688' (Scott-Giles, *Civic Heraldry*, p. 291). |
| I WILL MAKE GOOD | No. 32 Maintenance Unit, RAF. |
| I WILL NEVER QUIT | Boulton, Bts. |
| ICARUS RENATUS | Icarus reborn. RAF station, Digby. |
| ICH DIEN | I serve. Used by Prince of Wales along with ostrich feathers ever since time of Edward the Black Prince, who d. 1376 before his father, Edward III. Legend says both feathers and motto derived from blind King of Bohemia who fell in 1346 at Crecy, the great battle won by the Black Prince. Considerable doubt about this story; some historians consider that ostrich feathers and motto came from the Prince's mother's family of Hainault. Use of another motto, 'Houmont', by the Prince would seem to strengthen this view. For discussion in full see L. G. Pine, *Princes of Wales*. The King's Colonials, Imperial Yeomanry, formed 1901, in four sqs. representing the senior members of the Empire, 6th Carmarthenshire Rifle Volunteer Corps., 87th Foot, Royal Irish Fusiliers. ('Ich dien' appears on a label in arms of Norfolk CC.) |
| ICH KANN NICHT ANDERS | I can no other (Luther's famous remark when asked to recant at the Diet of Worms). Lords Beaumont of Whitley. |
| IDDOW BORDIOLCH | To God be thanks. Lloyd of Bronwydd, Bts. |
| IECHYD AC ADDYSG | Health and learning. Ebbw Vale (Mon.) UDC. |
| IECHYD, HARDDWCH, HEDDWCH | Health, beauty, peace. Colwyn Bay (Denbighs.), Bor. of. |
| IGNAVUS NUNQUAM | Never idle. Jenyns. |
| IGNE ET FERRO | By fire and iron. Hickman, Bts. |
| IGNE NON FRANGOR | I am not broken by fire. Refractories Assn. of Gt. Britain, 1958. |
| IGNEM MORTEMQUE DESPUIMUS | We spit fire and death. 234 Sq., RAF (sq. originally equipped with Spitfires and has dragon-fire-belcher as badge). |
| IGNI RENATUS | Born again by fire. 198 Sq., RAF. Motto alludes to badge of Phoenix rising from the ashes, a piece of ancient fabulous natural history; see Clemens Romanus, *1st Epistle to Corinthians*. |

| | |
|---|---|
| I'LL BE WARY | Finlay. |
| I'LL DEFEND | Furness of Tunstall Grange, Bts., Viscount Furness. |
| IL ME PLAIT LA TROUBLE | Troubled (waters) please me. Allusion to idea that a camel muddies water before drinking; used by Virginio Orsini, Prince of Bracciano, c.1497, for taking pay of French king Charles VIII. |
| IL PIÚ BEL FIOR NE COGLIE | The best flour does not gather (or collect). Accademia della Crusca (i.e. bran), name of institution designed to cultivate the Italian language on lines of the French Academy, was originally derived from Platonic Academy founded in Florence by Cosimo de Medici. Full details of the latter in P. Villari, Life of Savonarola, 1888, p. 55 et seq. |
| IL TEMPO PASSA | Time flies. Boynton, Bts. |
| ILFRACOMBE POTENS SALUBRITATE | Ilfracombe powerful by healthiness. Ilfracombe (Devon) UDC. |
| ILLAESO LUMINE SOLEM | To behold the sun with sight unhurt (allusion to ancient belief that eagle could look at the sun without blinking). Earls of Rosslyn (St Clair-Erskine), Wedderburn. |
| ILLINGWORTH REMEMBERS | Illingworth. |
| ILLUSTRANS COMMODA VITAE | Illustrating the conveniences of life. Roy. Inst. of Gt. Britain. |
| IMITARE QUAM INVIDERE | To imitate rather than to envy. Child, Bts., Child of Newfield Hall, Jellett, Pleydell. |
| IMMER BEREIT | Always ready. RAF station, Wildenrath. |
| IMMER WACHSAM | Always alert. No. 26 Signals Unit, RAF. |
| IMMERSABILIS EST VERA VIRTUS | True virtue cannot be overwhelmed. Coddrington. |
| IMMOTA FIDES | Immovable faith. Order of Henry the Lion of Brunswick. |
| IMPAVIDO PECTORE | With dauntless breast (ref. appears to be to Gray's Elegy – 'some village Hampden that with dauntless breast'). Murchison, Bt. |
| IMPAVIDUM FERIENT RUINAE | Ruin will strike the fearless. Horace, Odes, iii. 3 and 7. Michel de l'Hopital, d. 1573, Chancellor of France, resigned after massacre of St Bartholmew, d. in honourable poverty. Dangers shall strike me unappalled (example of the two-way rendering in Latin). Mundell, Perring, Bts. |
| IMPELLE OBSTANTIA | Thrust aside obstacles. Arthur. |
| IMPERATRICUS AUSPICIIS | Imperial in its auspices. Order of the Indian Empire, 1866. |
| IMPERIO REGIT UNUS AEQUO | One rules with unbiased sway. Gunning, Bts. |
| IMPERIUM IN IMPERIO | Authority within authority (saying often used, though not here, of power improperly exercised). Wetherby (Yorks.) RDC 1938. |
| IMPETUM DEDUCIMUS | We launch the spearhead, 570 Sq., RAF. |
| IMPI VENKOSI NE SIHIANGU SE NBOLO | Helge Fosseus, Swedish Bishop of the Evangelical Lutheran Church in Southern Africa. |

| | |
|---|---|
| IMPIGER ET ACER | Energetic and keen. 29 Sq., RAF (fighter). |
| IMPRIMATUR | Let it be printed. Inst. of Printing Ltd., 1965. No more appropriate motto could be adopted; still used in Roman Church to signify that no theological objection has been found to a book. |
| IMPROVE | Bomber Command Development Unit, RAF. |
| IN ACCORD AND CONCORD | Carbutt, Bt. |
| IN ACTION FAITHFUL AND IN HONOUR CLEAR | Order of the Companions of Honour, cr. 1917. |
| IN ADVERSIS PERFUGIUM | Refuge in adversity. RAF station, Valley, Anglesey. |
| IN AETERNUM NON COMMOVELITUR | It shall not be moved in eternity. Cosimo de Migliorati, Archbishop of Ravenna and Cardinal priest of Holy Cross, Pope Innocent VII, 1404–6. |
| IN ALTA TENDE | Strive for the heights. Lord Ashfield (Stanley) *(NEP)*, Webb, co. Wilts. |
| IN ALTAM | Toward heaven. Alston. |
| IN AQUILA STELLA SECURITAS | Security in the eagle star. Eagle Star Insurance Co. Ltd. |
| IN ARDUA | On high. Hoare. |
| IN ARDUA TENDIT | He reaches towards things difficult of attainment. M'Allum, M'Callem. Malcolm. |
| IN ARDUA VIRTUS | Virtue against difficulties. Leathes, Wolstenholme. |
| IN ARDUIS AUDAX | Bold in difficulties. Oppenheimer, Bts. |
| IN ARDUIS FIDELIS | Faithful in difficulties. Lords Riverdale (Balfour), 3rd London Volunteer Infantry. |
| IN ARDUIS FORTIOR | Stronger in difficulties. Lilley. |
| IN ARDUIS FORTIS | Strong in adversity. Fordyce. |
| IN ARDUIS FORTITUDO | Fortitude in adversity. Burnett of Croydon, Bts., Hamilton. |
| IN ARDUIS VIGET VIRTUS | Virtue flourished in adversity. Lords Cranworth (Gurdon), Dorien, Dorman, Gurdon, Gurdon-Rebow, Magens. |
| IN BELLO AUT IN PACE | In war or in peace. Knapp. |
| IN BELLO INVICTUS, IN AMORE PROBUS | In war unconquered, in love honest. Steele (Steele-Graves), Bts. |
| IN BELLO QUIES | There is peace in war (i.e. Peace is obtained by war; *or* Cool in action). Lords Birdwood, Murray of Óchtertyre, Bts. |
| IN BENEFICIUM AMBORUM | To the benefit of both. Inst. of Business Agents Ltd. |
| IN BONO VINCE | Conquer in the good. St Lawrence Coll., Ramsgate, 1879. |
| IN CAELO QUIES | There is rest in heaven. Bewicke, Boscawen, Viscount Chaplin, Coldham, Dolphin, Gundry, Horlock, Yale. |
| IN CAELO SUSTINEO | I support the sky. No. XIV Maintenance Unit, RAF, formed at Carlisle. Roman numerals used referring to occupation of Carlisle by XIV Roman legion. |

| | |
|---|---|
| IN CAELUM VOLANTEM IN MARE TONANTEM | Flying into the sky, thundering into the sea. RAF station, Gosport, Hants. |
| IN CALIGINE LUCET | It shines in darkness. Baillie, Bts. (crest an estoile out of a cloud). |
| IN CANDORE DECUS | There is honour in sincerity. Burton-Chadwick, Bts. |
| IN CANOPO UT AD CANOPUM | (On board) the *Canopus* (a ship of war) as at Canopus (Aboukir), the Canopic mouth of the Nile. Louis, Bts. Both 1st and 2nd Bts. were RN Admirals: Sir Thomas Louis, 1st Bt., d. on board *Canopus* off Egyptian shore, 1807. |
| IN CHRISTO FRATRES | Brothers in Christ. Skinners' Co., charter 1327. |
| IN CHRISTO SALUS | Salvation in Christ. Scott of Rotherfield, Bts. |
| IN CHRISTO SPERAVI | I have hoped in Christ. Lord Peckover *(NEP)*. |
| IN COELO SALUS | Salvation in heaven. Seale, Bts. |
| IN COMMON ENDEAVOUR | Harlow (Essex) UDC. |
| IN CONCILIO CONSILIUM | Council in council *or* In council is wisdom. Armagh, City of, Lancashire CC. |
| IN CONSILIO SAPIENTIA | In counsel is wisdom. Tewkesbury (Glocs.), Bor. of. |
| IN COPIA CAUTUS | Careful amid plenty. Dod. |
| IN COUNSEL IS STABILITY | Windsor (Berks.) RDC, 1962. |
| IN CRUCE ET LACHRYMIS SPES EST | There is hope in the Cross and in tears. Hincks of Breckenbrough. |
| IN CRUCE FIDES | Faith in the Cross. Glendening, Rudge. |
| IN CRUCE SALUS | In the Cross is safety. Abercromby, Adams, Bourke, Brigham, Chetwood-Aiken, Langholme, Lawrence, Marr, Mountem, Tailour, Tailyour. |
| IN CRUCE SPERO | I hope in the Cross. Allardice, Barclay, Ewart of Glenmachan, Bts. |
| IN CRUCE VICTORIA | Victory is in the Cross. Fanshawe. |
| IN CRUCE VINCO | Through the Cross I conquer. Copley, Lords Cromwell (Copley). |
| IN CRUCIFIXA GLORIA MEA | My glory is in the Crucifix. Lords Brabourne (Knatchbull), Knatchbull. |
| IN DANGER READY | 1st Gloucestershire (City of Bristol) Rifle Volunteer Corps. |
| IN DEFENCE | Allardyce, Williamson. |
| IN DEO | In God. Hambro of the Hyde. |
| IN DEO CONFIDE RECTE AGE | Trust in God and do well. Lord Gardiner (Life Baron). |
| IN DEO CONFIDO | I trust in God. Jekyll, Jessop of Doory, Kirkman Lawford, Moore, Lord Toovey, Tovy. |
| IN DEO FIDEMUS | We shall have faith in God. Brighton (Sussex), Co. Bor. of. |
| IN DEO FIDES | My trust is in God. Chapple, Hall of Burton Park, Bts., Lords Maclay, Lords Meston, Viscount Muirshiel (Maclay). |

| | |
|---|---|
| IN DEO NOSTRA SPES EST | In God is our hope. Rocke. |
| IN DEO SOLO SALUS EST | Salvation is in God alone. Sparrow. |
| IN DEO SOLO SPES MEA | My hope is in God alone. Kay, Key, Spicer, Bts. |
| IN DEO SOLUM ROBUR | In God alone is strength. Harris of Westcote. |
| IN DEO SPERAVI | In God have I trusted. Clark of Edinburgh, Bts. |
| IN DEO SPERO | I place my hope in God. Lords Mottistone (Seeley), Lords De Saumarez. |
| IN DEO SPES | In God hope. Barber, Bts., Mitchell, Bts., Pearson of St Dunstan's, Bts. |
| IN DEO SPES MEA | In God is my hope. Bonython, Conran, co. Devon. |
| IN DEO TUTAMEN | Protection in God. Oldfield. |
| IN DOMINO CONFIDO | I trust in the Lord. Cardinal Henry Beaufort, d. 1447, bastard son of John of Gaunt by Katherine Swinford (who became Gaunt's 3rd wife), Cahill, Elmhirst, Inman, Key, Bts., Knyfton, Makgill, Bts., Shuttleworth, Whyte-Venables, Willyams. |
| IN DOMINO ET NON IN ARCU MEO SPERABO | I will rest my hope on the Lord, and not in my bow. Molony. |
| IN DUBIIS RECTUS | Right in doubtful matters. Lees, co. Lancs. |
| IN DURIS SERVATA FIDES | Faith kept in hard things. Barwick, Bts. |
| IN FIDE ET IN BELLO FORTIS | Strong both in faith and war. Bagwell, Carroll, O'Carroll. |
| IN FIDE FIDUCIA | Confidence with faith. Leys Sch., Cambridge, 1878. |
| IN FIDE OFFICIOQUE FORTIS | Strong in faith and duty. J. R. Carroll of Toledo, Ohio, from arms grant given to an American by Chief Herald of the Republic of Ireland. |
| IN FIDE SALUS | Safety in faith. Order of the Star of Rumania. |
| IN FINEM PERSEVERANS | Persevering to the end. Viscount Maugham. |
| IN FUTURUM VIDERE | Look into the future. 4 Army Co-op. Sq., RAF. |
| IN GOD IS ALL | Fraser, Frazer, Lords Saltoun (Fraser). |
| IN GOD IS ALL MY TRUST | Grant of Rothiemurchus, Pewterers' Co., inc. 1473. |
| IN GOD IS ALL OUR TRUST | Aldenham Sch., Herts., founded 1597 by Richard Platt, Brewer of London. Brewers' Co., inc. 1437. |
| IN GOD IS ALL OUR TRUST, LET US NEVER BE CONFOUNDED | Tylers' & Bricklayers' Co., inc. 1568, Plumbers' Co. |
| IN GOD IS MY TRUST | Lawrence. |
| IN GOTT ALLEIN | In God alone. Schuster, Bts. |
| IN HOC SAXO TEMPLUM AEDIFICABO | On this stone I will build a temple (allusion to Jacob's words at Bethel, in Genesis 28: 22). De Costobadie. |
| IN HOC SIGNO | Under this sign. Woodhouse, co. Staffs. |
| IN HOC SIGNO SPES MEA | In this sign is my hope. D'Urban, Gleed, Viscount Taaffe (NEP). |

| | |
|---|---|
| IN HOC SIGNO VINCES | In this sign thou shalt conquer. Words come from vision of Roman Emperor Constantine I, before the Battle of the Milvian Bridge, after which he made a standard with the Cross and words on his standard called the Labarum. He won the battle in 312 and became the first Christian Emperor. The families who use this motto have crosses in their arms. Earls of Arran (Gore), Braithwaite, Bt., Burke of Glinsk, Bt., Campbell of Bleaton Hallett, co. Perth, Earls of Chesterfield (Stanhope) *(NEP)*, Chisenhale-Marsh, Colvill, Gore-Booth, Bt., Lords Harlech (Ormsby-Gore), Knox-Gore Bts., Leeming, O'Donnell, Seagrim, Taaffe, Earls Temple of Stowe, Watson-Taylor. |
| IN HOC VINCE | Conquer in this. Barclay, co. Surrey (formerly of Urie). |
| IN HONOUR BOUND | Earl Mountbatten of Burma, Marquesses of Milford Haven (Mountbatten), RAF station, Mount Batten. A tower still stands at Mount Batten in Devon erected by a member of Batten family during the Civil War, from which the placename is thought to have been derived. |
| IN LABORE CREDO | I believe in labour. Eckstein, Bts. |
| IN LABORE QUIES | In labour is rest. Helyer, Sewell. |
| IN LEARNING IS OUR STRENGTH | Aberdeen Univ. Air Sq., RAFVR. |
| IN LIBERTATE CONSILIUM | Counsel in liberty. Gas Council. |
| IN LUMINE SAPIENTIAE | On the threshold of wisdom. York Univ. Trust Fund, 1962. |
| IN LOCO DELICIOSO | In a pleasant place. Cricklade (Wilts.) Parish Council. |
| IN LOCO PARENTIS | In place of a parent (well-known phrase much used in legal language). Cheadle Hulme Sch., Cheshire, 1855. We act as guardians. 200 Sq., RAF. |
| IN LUMINE LUCE | By light in light. Artindale, Makins, Bts., Lords Sherfield (Makins), Thompson of Rathnally. |
| IN MEDIAS RES | Into the middle of things. 258 Sq., RAF. |
| IN MEDIO TUTISSIMUS | In the middle path safest. Smith of Lydiate, Lord Sydenham of Combe (Clarke) *(NEP)*. |
| IN MEMORIAM MAJORUM | In remembrance of our ancestors. Farquharson |
| IN MODO SUAVITER FORTITER IN RE | Suavely in manner, boldly in fact. Longsdon. |
| IN MONTES UNDE AUXILIUM | Unto the hills, whence cometh my help (Psalm 121:1), Wardlaw of Gogarmount. |
| IN MUTATIS IDEM | The same in changed circumstances. Galloway of Auchendrane. |
| IN MY END IS MY BEGINNING | (from T. S. Eliot, *East Coker*). Far Bletchley Training Coll. |
| IN NEMINEM PERFIDUS | Perfidy to none. Lord Mais (Life Baron). |
| IN NOBIS VINCULUM | We form a chain. No. 84 Group Communication Sq., RAF. |
| IN NOCTE CONSILIUM | Counsel in the night. Birkbeck Coll. (original purpose of Birkbeck was to give evening lectures and tuition). |

| | |
|---|---|
| IN NOMINE DEI NOSTRI MAGNIFICABIMUR | In the name of our God we shall be greatly esteemed. Roy. Holloway Coll., London Univ., 1883. |
| IN OFFICIO IMPAVIDUS | In duty fearless. Falsham, Bt. |
| IN OMNIA PARATI | Ready for anything. 24 Communications Sq., RAF. |
| IN OMNIA PARATUS | Ready for all things. Lords Dunalley (Prittie), Furnell, Ray. |
| IN OMNIBUS PRINCEPS | Chief in all things. No. 1 Fighter Sq., RAF. |
| IN OMNIA FIDELIS | Faithful in all things. Verdin. |
| IN OMNIA PROMPTUS | Ready for everything. Rae, Rea. |
| IN OMNIBUS CARITAS | Charity in all things. Austin Friars Sch., Carlisle, 1951. |
| IN OMNIBUS REQUIEM QUAESIVI | I have sought peace in all things. Blundell of Crosby Hall. |
| IN PARVIS POTESTAS | Power in small things. British Tugowners' Assn. |
| IN PATIENTIA SUAVITAS | In patience, tact. Charles of Anjou. King of Naples, d. 1309. |
| IN PECTORE ROBUR | Strength in the breast. Forest Sch., London, E.17, 1834. |
| IN PERICULIS AUDAX | Bold in danger. Maher, Mott, Bts. |
| IN PORTU QUIES | There is rest in port. Baker Wilbraham, Bts., Earls of Lathom (Bootle-Wilbraham) *(NEP)*, Port and Harbour Commissioners of Londonderry, Lords Skelmersdale (Bootle-Wilbraham), Wilbraham of Delamere. |
| IN PRETIUM PERSEVERO | I persevere for my reward. Jenner, Jenour. |
| IN PRINCIPIO ERAT VERBUM ET VERBUM ERAT APUD DEUM | In the beginning was the Word and the Word was with God. Oxford Univ. Main charge in the arms is an open book on which the above – the opening words of St John's Gospel – is inscribed. This appears to have been so when the arms were recorded at Heralds' Visitation of 1574. |
| IN PRINCIPIO ET SEMPER | In the beginning and always. RAF station, Upavon, Wilts. |
| IN PROMPTU | In readiness. Dunbar of Mochrum, Bts., Trotter. |
| IN PROSPERIS TIME, IN ADVERSA SPERA | In prosperity fear, in adversity hope. Gabriel, Bt. |
| IN QUADRIVIO PARATUS | Ready at the crossroads. RAF station, Nicosia, Cyprus. |
| IN QUASCUMQUE FORMAS | In whatever forms. Italian Academy of the Infocati. |
| IN RECTE FIDES | Faith in (acting) rightly. Linthorne. |
| IN REGEM CIVEMQUE JUSTITIA | Justice to king and citizen. Inst. of Taxation, 1945. |
| IN RELIQUIAM LABORAMUS | We work towards the future. Rayleigh (Essex) UDC, 1962. |
| IN ROBORE DECUS | Decoration in strength. Aiken. |
| IN RUPE AEDIFICABIMUS | We will build on the rock (ref. to end of Sermon on the Mount, St Matthew 8:24). S.E. Gas Bd., 1950. |
| IN SALE SALUS | Safety in salt. Anderdon (name changed from Salt), Salt of Weeping Cross, Bts. |

IN SANGUINE FOEDUS — A covenant by blood. Order of St Januarius of Naples (at annual festival of the saint, his blood (a relic) is believed to liquefy; see Cardinal Newman, *Apologia pro Vita Sua*, appendix), Order of the Two Sicilies.

IN SANGUINE VITA — Life in the blood. Cobbe. Crest is a pelican vulning (wounding) itself; the old belief being that the pelican nourished its young on its own blood. Hence the pelican often seen in church windows and religious pictures as a type of Christ. Also refers to the Pentateuch where blood was held to be the life of any creature.

IN SCIENTIA VERITAS, IN ARTE HONESTAS — In knowledge truth, in art honesty. Wells, Bts.

IN SE TERES — Polished in himself. Lords St Levan (St Aubyn), Trevenen.

IN SEIPSO TOTUS TERES — Fully furnished in himself. Lords Dudley (Smith), Smith.

IN SILENCE WE SERVE — Balloon Unit, RAF.

IN SILENTIO FORTITUDO — Courage in silence. Hardress, Thoresby, Thursby.

IN SINU JESU — In the bosom of Jesus. Cardinal Carlo Carmelo de Vasconcell, Archbishop of Sao Paulo, Brazil.

IN SOLE LABORATE — Work in the sun. RAF station, Bahrein.

IN SOLIDO DEUS — God (being with us) we are in safety. Wheler.

IN SOLO DEO SALUS — Salvation is in God alone. Earls of Harewood (Lascelles).

IN SOMNO SECURITAS — Security in sleep. Assn. of Anaesthetists of Gt. Britain & Ireland.

IN SPE SPERO — I hope in hope. Tharp.

IN SPE SPIRO — In hope I breathe. Oulton.

IN STELLA TUTUS — Safe in one's star. Lord Cherwell (Lindemann) *(NEP)*.

IN TE DOMINE CONFIDO — In Thee, O Lord, do I trust (part of last verse of Te Deum). Abbs, Baddeley, Bts., Greenhill, Haire, Lyon of Auldabar, Prestwick, Rouse, Vale, Wayne.

IN TE DOMINE SPERAVI — In thee O Lord have I put my trust. (Psalm 31:1), Lyons of Oldpark, Prestige, Prickett, Earls of Strathmore and Kinghorne (Bowes-Lyon).

IN TE DOMINE SPERO — In Thee, O Lord, I hope. Marquesses of Carisbrooke (Mountbatten).

IN TE SPERO DOMINE — In Thee, I hope, O Lord. Exshaw.

IN TEMPESTATE FLORESCO — In a tempest I begin to flourish. Pine-Coffin, Pyne.

IN TENEBRIS LUCIDIOR — The brighter in darkness. Inglis.

IN TENEBRIS LUX — Light in darkness. Lords Howard De Walden, Scott.

IN TERRA DIVITIAE — Riches in the earth. Blaby RDC.

IN THE SWEAT OF THY BROWS SHALT THOU EAT THY BREAD — Motto from Genesis 3:19. Gardeners' Co., inc. 1605. Shield shows a man clad in a skin, delving into the ground with a spade, i.e. Adam.

| | |
|---|---|
| IN TIME | Houston-Boswell, Bts., Houston of Houston, Bts., 218 Sq., RAF (badge an hour-glass to symbolize late formation of sq. in 1918). |
| IN TRINITATE ROBUR | Strength in the Trinity (from the arms of Otto von Bismarck (1815–98), Prussian prince). Motto must surely have been inherited; one would hardly suspect the man of blood and iron of deep religious conviction. |
| IN TUNE | Blakiston-Houston, Houston of West Toxteth, Bt. |
| IN TURRE SECURITAS | Security in a tower. Im Thurn. |
| IN UNITATE CUM NATURA | In unity with nature. Unigate Ltd., 1962. |
| IN UNITY PROGRESS | Ilford (Essex), Bor. of, Redbridge, London Bor. of. |
| IN UTRAQUE FORTUNA PARATUS | Prepared for either good or bad fortune. Viscount Combermere (Stapleton-Cotton). |
| IN UTROQUE FIDELIS | Faithful in either case. Carey, Viscount Falkland (Carey), Nash. |
| IN UTROQUE PARATUS | Prepared in either case. Akroyd, Blome, Deacon, Elphinston, Viscount Knollys, Muir Mackenzie of Delvine, Bts., Murray of Clarendon, Truscott, Bts. |
| IN UTRUMQUE PARATUS | Prepared for either event. Univ. of Glasgow & Strathclyde Air Sq., RAFVR. |
| IN VARIETATE CONSTANS | Constant through changes. RAF station, Eastchurch, Kent. |
| IN VERITATE | In truth. Inst. of Quantity Surveyors, 1955. |
| IN VERITATE ATQUE FORTITUDINE | In truth and fortitude. Lord Carron (NEP). |
| IN VERITATE RELIGIONIS CONFIDES | You confide in the truth of religion. 25th Foot, KOSB. |
| IN VERITATE TRIUMPHO | I triumph in the truth. Biddulph, Clegg, Greaves, Myddleton. |
| IN VERITATE VICTORIA | Victory is in truth. Abney, Aykroyd, Ecroyd, Hastings, Bts., Earls of Huntingdon (Hastings), Huntingdon of Bonawe House, Ingham, Loughborough (Leics.), Bor. of, Sharp of Maidstone, Bts. |
| IN VERITATE VIS | Strength in truth. Adkins. |
| IN VIA HONORIS | In the way of honour. Kent. |
| IN VIA VIRTUTI NULLA EST VIA | No way is barred to valour. Highly appropriate motto of Henry IV of France, who united Navarre with France and brought peace to the kingdom; was murdered. |
| IN VIRTUTE ET FORTUNA | In valour and fortune. Gardner. |
| IN VIRTUTE ET HONORE SENESCE | Grow old in virtue and honour. Senecey (Burgundy). |
| IN VIRUM PERFECTUM | In to the perfect man. Kingham Hill Sch., Oxford, 1886. |
| IN WELL BEWARE | Wombwell, Bts. |
| INCEPTA PERFICIAM | I finish (what I) begin. Joseph, Bts. |
| INCONCUSSA VIRTUS | Unshaken virtue. Benson, Delamer, Lane. |
| INCORRUPTA FIDES | Uncorrupted faith. Page, Whitmore. |

| | |
|---|---|
| INCORRUPTA FIDES, NUDAQUE VERITAS | Uncorrupted faith and the naked truth. Forde, Myers, Waskett. |
| INDE QUERCUS | Thence the oak. Mallinson, Bts. Crest an arm grasping stock of a tree eradicated. |
| INDE SPES | Thence hope. Scott-Moncrieff of Fossaway. |
| INDIA–ARABIA | 67th Foot (2nd Bn. the Hampshire Regt.). |
| INDIGNANTE INVIDIA FLOREBIT JUSTUS | The just man will flourish despite envy. Crosbie. |
| INDOCILIS PAUPERIEM PATI | Untaught to suffer poverty. Merchant Adventurers of City of Bristol. |
| INDUSTRIA | By industry. Calrow, Crierie, Fettes, Bt., Fettes Coll., Edinburgh, Fiddes, Gentle, Keltie, M'Crire, Ogilvy, Earls Peel, Peel, Bt. |
| INDUSTRIA CONSTANTIA SAPIENTIA | Industry, constancy, wisdom. Derby Sch., Bury, Lancs. |
| INDUSTRIA DITAT | Industry enriches. Chepping Wycombe, Bor. of, High Wycombe (Bucks.), Bor. of, Knottingley (Yorks.) UDC, Paxton Bt., Radcliffe, Lancs., Bor. of, Reath, Vanderplant, Wauchope, Waugh, Widnes (Lancs.), Bor. of. |
| INDUSTRIA ET FORTITUDINE | By industry and fortitude. Twiston Davies. |
| INDUSTRIA ET PERSEVERANTIA | By industry and perseverance. Lords Broadbridge, Cowper. |
| INDUSTRIA ET SPE | By industry and hope. Barge, Claxton, Fenouillet, Horrocks, Lord Molson (Life Baron), Sage, Skipton Bldg. Soc., 1965, Skipton (Yorks.) UDC, 1951. |
| INDUSTRIA ET VIRTUTE | By industry and virtue. Beaver (formerly of Glynn Garth), Bolton, Bts. |
| INDUSTRIA EVENHIT | Industry bears out. Lords Bruntisfield (Warrender). |
| INDUSTRIA OMNIA VINCIT | Industry overcomes all things. Morley (W.R. Yorks.), Bor. of. |
| INDUSTRIA VIRTUS ET FORTITUDO | Industry, valour and fortitude. Derby, Co. Bor. of, Smellie, co. Sussex, Smiley, Bts. |
| INDUSTRIA VIRTUTE ET LABORE | By industry virtue and labour. Yeovil (Somerset), Bor. of. |
| INDUSTRIAE PRAEMIUM | The reward of industry. Heath. |
| INDUSTRY AND LIBERALITY | Jejeebhoy, Bts. |
| INDUSTRY AND PRUDENCE CONQUER | Accrington (Lancs.), Bor. of. |
| INDUSTRY ENRICHES | Spenborough (W.R. Yorks.), Bor. of, 1949. |
| INÉBRANLABLE | Unshakeable. Acland. |
| INEST SUA GRATIA PARVIS | In his own grace to the small. Mackeson, Bts. |
| INFENSA VIRTUTI INVIDIA | Envy is the foe of virtue. 165 Sq., RAF. |
| INFESTOS FERIMUS | We strike the troublesome. RAF station, Habbaniya. |
| INGENIO ET CONSILIO | By intellect and counsel. Irlam (Lancs.) UDC. |

| | |
|---|---|
| INGENIO ET LABORE | By mind and labour. Gibson Watt. |
| INGENIO EXPERIOR FUNERA DIGNA MEO | I suffer a death worthy of my mind. Prospero Colonna, *c.*1523, Lord of Paliano. |
| INGENIO FLOREMUS | We flourish by intellect. Witney (Oxon.) UDC, 1955. |
| INGENIUM INDUSTRIA ALITUR | Intellect is nourished by industry. Ripley (Derbys.) UDC. |
| INGREDERE UT PROFICIAS | So walk that you may progress. Abingdon Sch., Oxon. Foundation of school may be assigned to pre-Norman days. School re-endowed in 1563 by John Roysse of Mercers' Co., after dissolution of the abbey. |
| INGREDERE UT PROFICIAS SUPER ANTIQUAS VIAS | So walk that you may progress (stand) above the ancient ways. St Peter's Sch., York (founded in sixth century; first headmaster St Wilfred, Archbishop of York). |
| INIMICUS INIMICO | An enemy to the enemy. 411 Sq., RCAF. |
| INITIUM SAPIENTIAE EST TIMOR DOMINI | The fear of the Lord is the beginning of wisdom (Psalm 110:10; Proverbs 1:7). Martin of Long Melford, Bts. |
| INNE DEFEATE FEARE ME MOSTE | Chamberlayne. |
| INNOCENT AND TRUE | Arbuthnot, Bts. |
| INNOCENTIA INFANTIS, SAPIENTA SERPENTIS | The innocence of the infant, the wisdom of the serpent. Vaughan, co. Leics. |
| INNOCENTIAE SECURUS | Secure in innocence. Jackson of Fork Hill, Bts. |
| INNOCUE AC PROVIDE | Harmlessly and providently. Bowdler. |
| IRRETIMUS HOSTES | We entrap the enemy. No. 4 Balloon Centre, RAF. (First word of motto is from Latin verb *irretio* (= to entangle in a net) hence familiar *retiarius*, the gladiator with a net with which he sought to entangle his armed opponent.) |
| INSERVA DEO ET LAETARE | Serve God and rejoice. Howard of Bushy Park, Bt., Earls of Wicklow (Howard). |
| INSIDIANTIBUS INSIDIAMUR | We ambush the ambushers. 172 Sq., RAF. |
| INSIDIAS CAVENTO | Let them beware the ambush. 945 City of Glasgow Balloon Sq., RAF. |
| INSPERATA FLORUIT | It has flourished unexpectedly. Inglefield-Watson, Bts., Watson. |
| INSPERATO | Unexpectedly. 62 Sq., RAF. |
| INSTATE | Press on. No. 25 Group HQ, RAF. |
| INSTRUENDO, PRAESTANDO, EXPERIENDO | By setting up, by affording, and by finding out. Inst. of Plant Engineers, 1959. |
| INSTRUMENTA FUNDAMENTA | Supplies are the foundation. No. 16 Maintenance Unit, RAF. |
| INSULA DEFENSOR | The island fortress. Malta Sector, RAF. |
| INTEGER VITAE | Sound in life (part of well-known Horatian line, (*Odes* I. xxii. 1), which continues *scelerisque purus*). Christie of Glyndbourne. |
| INTEGRITAS ET INDUSTRIA | Integrity and industry. Newson-Smith, Bts. |
| INTEGRITAS ET SCIENTIA | Integrity and science. Inst. of Motor Industry, inc. 1955. |

| | |
|---|---|
| INTEGRITAS ET VIGILANTIA | Integrity and vigilance. London Investment Building Soc. |
| INTEGRITATE ET FIDELITATE | By integrity and fidelity. Kingerlee. |
| INTEGRITATE ET MERITO | By integrity and merit. Order of Leopold of Austria. |
| INTEGRITY | Dukinfield (Ches.), Bor. of, Freake of Cromwell House, Bts. |
| INTEGRITY AND ENTERPRISE | Inst. of Directors. |
| INTEGRITY AND INDUSTRY | Salford (Lancs.), City of. |
| INTEGRITY AND UNDERSTANDING | Lords Martonmere (Robinson). |
| INTELLECTU ET INNOCENTIA | By intellect and innocence. Headlam, Bt. |
| INTENTO ANIMO | With intent mind. Rotherham (W.R. Yorks.) RDC, 1955. |
| INTER CRUCES TRIUMPHANS IN CRUCE | Amongst crosses, triumphing in the Cross. Dalton. |
| INTER FERA SALUS | In midst of ferocity, healing. RAF Hosp., Wegberg, Germany. |
| INTER MARE ET CAELUM | Between sea and sky. RAF station, Hal Far. |
| INTER MONTES ET LACUS | Between mountains and lakes. Lakes (Westmorland) UDC. |
| INTER OMNES | Among all. Cardinal Ippolito de Medici, d. 1535, nephew of Pope Leo X. Choice of motto determined by his love for the beautiful Giulia de Gonzago; part of line from Horace: *micat inter omnes Julius sidus.* |
| INTER SILVAS QUAERERE VERUM | Seek truth among the woods. Brockenhurst Gram. Sch., Hants (a clump of trees forms the crest, with a badger, his dexter forepaw resting on an open book). |
| INTER SYLVAS ET FLUMINA HABITANS | Dwelling twixt woods and rivers. Morpeth (Northumb.), Bor. of. |
| INTER UTRUMQUE TENE | Keep between the two. Harford, Jemmett. |
| INTERCIPERE ET DELERE | To intercept and to blot out. 3505 Fighter Control Unit, RAAF. |
| INTERNA PRAESTANT | Internal things are best. Carnegy-Arbuthnott. |
| INTO THE REMOTE PLACES | RAF station, Khorramshahr, Iran. |
| INTUS ET RECTE, NE LABORA | Right within, toil not. Shrewsbury Sch., founded 1552 by Edward VI. |
| INTUTA QUAE INDECORA | Things indecent are unsafe. Butler of Ewart Park, co. Northumberland. |
| INUTILE UTILE EX ARTE | That which is useless is made useful through skill. Ossett (W.R. Yorks.), Bor. of. |
| INVENI PORTUM | I have found a harbour. Salvesen. |
| INVENIAM AUT FACIAM | I will find or I will make. Delmege. |
| INVENIAM VIAM AUT FACIAM | I will find a way or I will make one. Percival-Humphries. |
| INVICTA | Unconquered. Bexley (Kent) UDC, Duke of Connaught's Own Royal East Kent Yeo. (Mounted |

|                              | Rifles), East Kent Militia, Kent Artillery Volunteers, Kent CC, Kent Volunteer Fencibles, Queen's Own (Royal West Kent Regt.), Sidcup (Kent) UDC, 131 Sq., RAF, County of Kent. |
|------------------------------|---|
| INVICTA FIDES | Unconquered faith. Jalland. |
| INVICTAE FIDELITATIS PRAEMIUM | The reward of faithfulness unconquered. Hereford, City of. |
| INVICTUM | Unconquered. Kittoe. |
| INVICTUS MANEO | I remain unconquered. Armstrong. |
| INVIDIAE FINES VIRTUTE RELIQUIT | He left the bounds of envy by valour. Jules Mazarin, Cardinal, 1602–61 (Italian in service of Cardinal Richelieu who succeeded him in 1642 as chief minister of France). |
| INVISUS VIDENS | Seeing though unseen. 684 Sq., RAF (badge of a mask indicative with motto of function of photographic reconnaissance). |
| INVITA FORTUNA | Though fortune be unwilling. Lords Knightley of Fawsley (NEP). |
| INVITUM SEQUITUR HONOR | Honour follows one who desires it not. Chichester, Marquesses of Donegall (Chichester), Lords Rathcavan (O'Neill), Scott of Beauclerc, Bts., Lords Templemore (Chichester). |
| IPSE ALIMENTA SIBI | He provided his own nourishment. Flavio Orsini, c.1698, alluding to absurd idea that a bear nourishes itself by sucking its paws; his device as an Orsini was a bear (reference is to his extensive culture as drawn from internal resources). |
| IRAE EMISSARII | Emissaries of wrath. 178 Sq., RAF. |
| IRE IN ADVERSUM | To go against adversity. Stokes. |
| IRRESISTIBLE | No. 33 Base, RAF. |
| IRREVOCABILE | Irrevocable. Bennett, Bruce of Balcaskie, Bt. |
| IRRITATUS LACESSIT CRABIO | The hornet attacks when roused. 213 Sq., RAF. |
| IRRUIMUS VASTATUM | We rush in to destroy. 181 Sq., RAF. |
| ISÄNMAAN HYVAKSI | For the good of the Fatherland. Order of the White Rose of Finland. |
| ISÄNMAAN PUOLESTA | For the Fatherland. Order of the Cross of Liberty (Finland). |
| ISLIP OR I SLIP | A play on the name of John Islip, Abbot of Westminster, as can be seen in chapel which he designed as a chantry to be used for masses for his soul. He was much concerned with erection of Henry VII's Chapel. |
| ISTO VELOCIOR VITA | Thither is life swifter. Shuttleworth of Old Warden. |
| IT SHALL BE DONE | 117 Sq., RAF. |
| ITER TUTISSIMUM | The safest journey. Cesare Gambia, member of Italian Academy of the Insensati of Perugia. |
| ITO TU ET FAC SIMILITER | Go, and do thou likewise (from Parable of Good Samaritan, St Luke 10:37). Oliver. |

# J

| | |
|---|---|
| J'AI AINSI MON NOM | Thus I have my name. Viscount Simon. |
| J'AI BIEN SERVI | I have served well. Prevost. |
| J'AIME LA LIBERTÉ | I love liberty. Mussenden, Ribton, Bts. |
| J'AIME LE MEILLEUR | I love the better. Viscount Thurso (Sinclair). |
| J'AY BONNE CAUSE | I have good reason. Marquesses of Bath (Thynne), Thynne. |
| J'AY FALU, FAUX ET FAUDRAY | I have Falu, etc. Seigneurs de Faudray, who possessed these properties. |
| J'AYME À JAMAIS | I love for ever. James, Lords Northbourne (James). |
| J'AYME PORTER SECOURS | I love to bring help. Horsbrugh-Porter, Bts. |
| J'AVANCE | I advance. Bartram, East, Ker of Abbot Rule, Viscount Mersey (Bigham). |
| J'EN SUIS CONTENTE | I am content with it. Anne, dau. Duke of Burgundy, 1st wife of John, Duke of Bedford, *d.* 1432. |
| J'ESPÈRE | I hope. Hamilton, Swinton of that Ilk. |
| J'ESPÈRE BIEN | I hope well. Carew. |
| J'Y SUIS | I am here. Lord Crowther (Life Baron). |
| J'Y SUIS J'Y RESTE | Here I am and here I stay. RAF station, Lübeck, Germany. |
| JACTA EST ALEA | The die is cast. Mathias. Words uttered by Julius Caesar as he led his army across the Rubicon, the small stream which was boundary of Roman Republic. By this unauthorized crossing he declared war on the Republic. |
| JACULAMUR HUMI | We strike them to the ground. 235 Sq., RAF. |
| JAGA MUTU PEDANG | 478 Sq., RAAF. |
| JAM FELICITER OMNIA | Now all is well. Isabella of Valois, d. 1568, who became 2nd wife of Philip II of Spain, as part of Peace of Cambrai with France. |
| JAMAIS ARRIÈRE | Never behind. Douglas, Fryer, Dukes of Hamilton (Douglas-Hamilton), Earls of Selkirk (Douglas-Hamilton). |
| JAMAIS SANS ESPÉRANCE | Never without hope. Duckworth-King, Bts. |
| JANUA MARIS | The doors of the sea. Southampton Harbour Bd., 1954. |
| JANUA SECURITAS | Security is a gate. Temperance Bldg. Soc., 1954. |
| JATA DHARMA STATA JAYA | Lords Sinha. |
| JE AYME | I love. Earls of Lindsay (Lindesay-Bethune). |

| | |
|---|---|
| JE AVANCE | I advance. Bertram, co. Lanark. |
| JE DIS LA VERITÉ | I tell the truth. Pedder. |
| JE GARDERAY | I will be careful. Lords Fitzwalter (Plumptre), Lord Fitzwalter (Bridges) *(NEP)*, Earls of Sussex (Ratcliffe) (extinct 1641). |
| JE L'AY EMPRIS | I have undertaken it. Charles the Bold *or* the Rash, Duke of Burgundy, k. 1475 in combat with the Swiss. |
| JE LE TIENDRAI | I will hold it. Airey. |
| JE LE TIENS | I hold it. Lords Audley (peerage passing through the female line, being a barony by writ; now (1979) Lord Sudley is 25th holder), Touchet, one of the surnames of holders of above barony. |
| JE MAINTIENDRAI | I will maintain. Earls of Malmesbury (Harris), Nisbitt, Order of Golden Lion of Nassau, Order of the Oak Crown, Order of Oranje-Nassau, William III (of Orange) and Mary II. |
| JE MAINTIENDRAI QUE JE GAGNERAI | I will maintain what I gain. Thomas of the Poolfold. |
| JE MAINTIENDRAY CHALON | I will maintain Chalons. René of Orange-Chalon, Prince of Orange, d. 1542, having bequeathed his Principality of Orange (in Provence) to his cousin William of Nassau (i.e. William the Silent); see *The House of Orange* by Marion E. Grew. |
| JE MAINTIENDREY | I will maintain. Most commonly used motto of William of Orange (William the Silent), murdered 1584; founder of the Seven Provinces of United Netherlands. |
| JE ME FIE EN DIEU | I trust in God. Blois, Bts., Sir Thomas Brooke, 8th Baron Cobham, *c*.1514 (dormant title, *NEP*), Earls of Plymouth (Windsor-Clive), Windsor. |
| JE ME MAINTIENDRAY CROY | I will myself uphold Croy. Charles Philippe de Croy, Duc d'Arschot, Prince de Chimay, *c*.1612. |
| JE ME TOURNE VERS L'OCCIDENT | I turn towards the west. Westropp. |
| JE M'Y OBLIGE | I bind myself. Eyton. |
| JE MEURS OU JE M'ARRACHE | I die or I attach myself. Lewis of Portland Place, Bts. |
| JE MEURS POUR CEUX QUE J'AIME | I die for those I love. Paterson of Castle Huntley. |
| JE NE CHANGE QU'EN MOURANT | I change but in death. Salvin, Salvin-Bowlby. |
| JE NE CHERCHE QUE UNE | I seek but one. Compton, Marquesses of Northampton (Compton). |
| JE N'OUBLIERAY JAMAIS | I will never forget. Hervey, Marquesses of Bristol (Hervey). |
| JE PARLE BIEN | I speak well. Sayer. |
| JE PENSE | I think. Swinton of that Ilk, Weymiss, Wemyss. |
| JE PENSE EN BIEN | I think well. Pinsent, Bts. |
| JE PENSE PLUS | I think the more. Earls of Mar and Kellie (Erskine). |

| | |
|---|---|
| JE REÇOIS POUR DONNER | I receive to distribute. Mitchell-Innes. |
| JE RESPONDERAY | I will reply. Sir William Finch, *temp.* Henry VIII (see *B.P.*, Earls of Winchilsea and Nottingham). |
| JE SERA JE SERVIRAI | I shall be, I shall serve. Barling, Bt. |
| JE SUIS GROLÉE | I am Grolée. An ultra-aristocratic motto, for Grolée family. |
| JE SUIS LOYAL | I am loyal. Le Mesurier. |
| JE SUIS LE RUSSELAY | I am the Russell. John Russell, Bishop of Rochester, 1476, Lord High Chancellor of Richard III. |
| JE SUIS PREST | I am ready. Fraser, Lords Lovat (Fraser). |
| JE SUIS PRÊT | I am ready. Lords Farnham (Somerset Maxwell), Earl of Farnham (Maxwell) *(NEP)*, Perceval-Maxwell, Simpson. |
| JE SUIS VEILLANT | I am watching. Saunderson. |
| JE TE PLUMERAI | I will pluck thee. 425 Sq., RCAF. |
| JE TIENDRAI | I will hold. Armitage-Smith. |
| JE TIENS FIRME | I hold firm. Gosling. |
| JE VAIS DROIT | I go rightly. Jervis. |
| JE VEUX DE BONNE GUERRE | I wish for fair play. Lord Knaresborough (Meysey-Thompson), Lawley, Meysey-Thompson, Bts., Thompson, Bts., Lords Wenlock (Lawley) *(NEP)*. |
| JE VEUX LE DROIT | I wish what is right. Duckett, Bts. |
| JE VIS EN ESPOIR | I live in hope. Stephens of Church House. |
| JE VIVE EN ESPÉRANCE | I live in hope. Akers. |
| JE VIVE EN ESPOIR | I live in hope. Rous, Stephens, Earls of Stradbroke (Rous). |
| JE VOLE A TOUS VENTS | I fly whatever the wind. RAF station, Kirton in Lindsey, Lincs. |
| JEDEN JESTRAH MNOHO VRAN ROZHANI (CZECH) | One hawk scatters many crows. 313 Sq., RAF (Czech). |
| JEHOVAH | Boddam-Whetham. |
| JEHOVAH JIREH | The Lord will provide (from Genesis 22:14 and refers to Abraham's sacrifice of a ram in place of his son Isaac). Grant of Monymusk, Bts. |
| JERUSALEM | Esmonde, Bts. |
| JEWEL OF THE THAMES | Maidenhead (Berks.), Bor. of. |
| JOIN LOYALTY AND (*or* WITH) LIBERTY | Joiners' Co., inc. 1571. |
| JOIR EN BIEN | To joy in good. Beckwith. |
| JOUR DE MA VIE | Day of my life. Said to have been assumed by Roger de la Warre on account of his taking part in capture of King John of France at Poitiers, 1356. Perhaps the best comment on these stories occurs in Conan Doyle's *White Company*, where John is in some danger from the number of his captors. Earls De La Warr (Sackville), Lords Sackville (Sackville-West), West. |

| | |
|---|---|
| JOVI CONFIDO | I confide in Jove. Gairdner. |
| JOVIS OMNIA PLENA | All things are full of Jove (Virgil, *Eclogues*, iii. 60). Goodden, Waldie-Griffith, Bts., Westby. |
| JOYE SANS FIN | Joy without end. Widdrington. |
| JUBILATE | Rejoice. Chapel Royal of St Peter ad Vincula, Tower of London (Choral Foundation) (arms granted 1969). |
| JUDGE BY OUR LABOUR | Hammersmith, London Bor. of. |
| JUDGE NOCHT | Judge not. Earls of Buchan (Erskine). |
| JUBILEE | Stamer, Bts. |
| JUDICIUM PARIUM AUT LEX TERRAE | The judgment of our peers or the law of the land (in another version *lex* is given in the plural, *leges*). Marquesses of Camden (Pratt), Raines. |
| JUNCTA JUVANT | Joined things help. Lord McGowan. |
| JUNCTI PROGREDIAMUR | Let us advance together. Hounslow, London Bor. of. |
| JUNCTI VALEMUS | Being joined we are powerful. Walker of Mount St John. |
| JURE ET DIGNITATE GLADII | By the law and the dignity of the sword. Cheshire CC. |
| JUS TENE NIL TIME | Keep to the law, fear nothing. Parker of High Wycombe. |
| JUSSA DOMINI DEI | The commands of the Lord God. Humbert the Whitehanded, d. *c.*1047–50, founder of dynasty of Savoy, formerly kings of Italy. |
| JUST IN TIME | Milligan. |
| JUSTE ET DROIT | Just and frank. Stancliffe. Whichcote, Bts. |
| JUSTE NEC TIMIDE | Justly not timidly. Farnworth (Lancs.), Bor. of. |
| JUSTIS CREATOR FAVET | The Creator favours the just. Graaf, Bts. |
| JUSTITIA AEQUITAS FIDES | Justice, equity and faith. Lords Bradbury. |
| JUSTITIA ET PAX | Justice and peace. Plumbers' Co., inc. 1611. |
| JUSTITIA ET VERITAS | Justice and truth. Charles I, Charles II and James II. |
| JUSTITIA ET VIRTUS | Justice and virtue. Charlesworth. |
| JUSTITIA, MERITUM, FIDELITAS | Justice, merit, fidelity. General Accountants' Assn. |
| JUSTITIA PROPOSITQUE TENAX | Justice is tenacious of its purpose. Courthope-Munroe. |
| JUSTITIA TURRIS NOSTRA | Justice is our tower. Hackney, London Bor. of, 10th Co. of London Bn. (Hackney) Territorials. |
| JUSTITIA VIRTUTUM REGINA | Justice is queen of the virtues. Goldsmiths' Co. (original charter 1327). |
| JUSTITIAE PROPOSITI TENAX | Tenacious of his word for the sake of justice. Stuart of Oxford, Bts. |
| JUSTITIAE SOROR FIDES | Faith is the sister of justice. Lords Thurlow (Cumming-Bruce). |
| JUSTITIAE TENAX | Tenacious of justice. Astley, Lords Hastings (Astley), Bangor Gram. Sch., co. Down. |
| JUSTORUM SEMITA LUX SPLENDENS | The narrow path of the just is a shining light. Blonham Sch., Banbury, Oxon. |

| | |
|---|---|
| JUSTUM AC (*or* ET) TENACEM | Just and firm of purpose. Bowen-Colthurst, Colthurst, Bts., Lord Dovercourt (Holmes) *(NEP)*, Macknight, M'Knight, Parish. |
| JUSTUM PERFICITO NIHIL TIMETO | Act justly and fear nothing. Foster of Hornby Castle, Rogers. |
| JUSTUS AC TENAX PROPOSITI | Just and tenacious of what is laid down. Jones of Gungrog. |
| JUSTUS ESTO ET NON METUE | Be just and fear not. Charley, Langman, Robson. |
| JUSTUS ET PROPOSITI TENAX | Just and firm of purpose. Chedworth, How, Penrice. |
| JUSTUS ET TENAX | Just and firm. Hunt-Grubbe. |
| JUSTUS PROPOSITI TENAX | The just is firm of purpose. Ferrand. |
| JUVANT ASPERA FORTES | Difficulties help the brave. Seton-Stewart, Bts. |
| JUVANT ASPERA PROBUM | Difficulties assist the honest man. Denham, Bts., Steuart of Coltness, Bts. |
| JUVANTE DEO | By God's assistance. Layard. |
| JUVAT IMPIGROS DEUS | God aids the diligent. Huddersfield Bldg. Soc., Huddersfield, Co. Bor. of. |
| JUVAT IPSE LABOR | Labour itself helps. Lords Netherthorpe (Turner). |
| JUVAT ME SERVIRE | It helps me to serve. Johnson of Abbots Lea. |
| JUVENTUTEM FORMAMUS | We form youth. RAF, Uxbridge (well known as birthplace and cradle of Air Force). |

# K

| | |
|---|---|
| KADIMAH | Eastward (Hebrew). Seven-branched candlestick as badge. 38th, 39th, 40th and 42nd Bns. the Royal Fusiliers (1914–18). |
| KAMI MELINDONGI SEMUA | We shelter many. RAF station, Changi, Singapore. |
| K'AN SHOU | Vigilant. No. 117 Signals Unit, RAF. |
| KAMI MENGAWAL | We guard. Air HQ, RAF, Malaya. |
| KAR DEW (D) RES PUB TIA | The love of God over all things (Cornish). Harris. |
| KARANZA WHEELAS KARANZA | Love worketh love (Cornish). Polwhele. Also as Karenza wheelas karenza (Cornish). By Pol, Tre and Pen you may know the Cornish men. |
| KEEP FAITH | Crewkerne (Som.) UDC. |
| KEEP STRAIGHT ON | Collett, Bts. |
| KEEP TRAIST | Buchan-Hepburn, Bts. |
| KEEP TRYST | Belches, Lord Hailes (Buchan-Hepburn), Hepburn, Lords Sempill (Forbes-Sempill). |
| KEEP WITH THE PACK | No. 14 Operational Training Unit, RAF. |
| KEEPERS OF THE PEACE | Second Tactical Air Force, RAF (retitled Royal Air Force Germany, 1973). |
| KEIN HINDERNIS ZU HOCH | No obstacle too high. No. 646 Signals Unit, RAF. |
| KELAT or KHELAT | Willshire, Bts. Sir Thomas Willshire, 1st Bt., served with distinction in Afghanistan campaign and captured Kelat in 1839. |
| KENSAL TRA TONKEYN OUNA DEW MATERN YN | Before all, Tonkyn, fear God and the King (Cornish). Tonkyn. |
| KERNOW KEXSA | Cornwall first (Cornish). Curnow. |
| KHOTSO KE KE VALA | British colony of Basutoland, 1951–66. |
| KIND HEART | Gordon-Duff. |
| KITA CHARI JAUH (MALAYAN) | We search far. 230 Sq., RAF (badge is Malayan tiger in front of a palm tree, sq. having served in Malaya). |
| KITA KAWAK DARI UDARA | We protect from the skies. RAF station, Kuala Lumpur, Malaya. |
| KITA SOKONG SINGA | We support the lion. Air HQ, RAF, Singapore. |
| KNOWLEDGE AND PROGRESS | Inst. of Management Consultants. |
| KNOWLEDGE DISPELS FEAR | No. 1 Parachute Training Sch., RAF. |
| KNOWLEDGE FORTIFIES THE KINGDOM | Air Armament Sch., RAF (motto changed to Knowledge fortifies the empire). |

KNOWLEDGE IS POWER — Hibbert of Chorley, Bt., Sch. of Aeronautical Engineering, RAF, Sch. of Oriental Studies, Univ. of London, founded 1916. Lord Riddell *(NEP)*.

KNOWLEDGE SUSTAINS — No. 4 Sch. of Tech. Training, RAF.

KNOWN BY THEIR FRUITS — Sittingbourne (Kent) UDC.

KWA HARAKA NA SAWA — With speed and accuracy (Swahili). RAF Signals Centre, Eastleigh, Hants. (unit was stationed in E. Africa).

KYND KYNN KNAWNE KEPE — Keep your own kin-kind. Lister-Kaye, Bts., Lords Shuttleworth.

# L

| | |
|---|---|
| L'AMOUR ET L'AMITIÉ | Love and friendship. Ivimey. |
| L'ASSOTTIGLIAI LA PIÙ MEGLIO ANCHE FORA | The more it is sharpened, it will be even better. Italian Academy of Lesina. |
| L'ESPÉRANCE ME CONFORT | Hope comforts me. Berry of Tayfield, co. Fife, Lords Nairn of St. Ford, Nairne. |
| L'HOMME VRAI AIME SON PAYS | The true man loves his country (a play on name of Homfray). Homfray, co. Staffs. |
| L'UNION FAIT LA FORCE | Union makes strength. King Leopold of the Belgians. |
| LA CROIX MA COURONNE | The Cross my crown. Julian. |
| LA FORTUNE PASSE PAR TOUT | The vicissitudes of fortune are common to all. Lewis, Lords Rollo. |
| LA FOY QUE J'AY | The faith which I have. Françoise de Luxembourg, d. 1557, wife of John, Count Egmont. This motto is inscribed on her tomb with 32 quarterings of coats of arms, 16 for her and 16 for the Count. Whether the faith mentioned referred to this continental armigerous achievement or to a higher source is unclear. |
| LA LIBERTÉ | Liberty. Ackers of Huntley Manor, Glos. |
| LA MAIN À L'OEUVRE | Set your hand to the task. Lords De Villiers. |
| LA MAINTIENDRAY | I will maintain it. Lords Hastings, c.1520. |
| LA MORT N'Y MORT | Death is not here. Clément Marot, 1493–1544, French poet who greatly influenced French poetry. |
| LA PAIX | Peace. Lendrum. |
| LA VI DURANTE | During life. Legh. |
| LA VIE DURANTE | During life. Amyard (Later Cornewall), Bt., Cornwall, co. Salop, Leigh, co. Cheshire. |
| LA VOLANTÉ DE DIEU ME SUFFIT | The will of God suffices me. Mary Tudor, 1498–1533, 3rd dau. of Henry VII of England, m. Louis XII of France and after his death, Charles Brandon, Duke of Suffolk (*B. Ext. P.*, 1883), grandmother of Lady Jane Grey, the Nine Days' Queen. |
| LABES PEJOR MORTE | A stain is worse than death. Durrant, Bts. |
| LABOR ARMA MINISTRAT | Labour supplies the arms. RAF station, Henlow, Beds. |
| LABOR ET VERITAS | Labour and truth. Elliot of Penshaw, Bts., Vassar-Smith, Bts. |
| LABOR IPSE VOLUPTAS | Toil itself is pleasure. Groves, King of Croydon, Earls of Lovelace (King), Nichols of Lawford Hall (in the case of John Nichols, FSA, no motto could have been more appropriate, as for 40 years he edited the *Gentleman's Magazine* and was author of *History of Leicestershire* and other erudite works), Paget of Harewood Place, Bts. |

| | |
|---|---|
| LABOR MAGNA RE | Labour is a great matter. Easthope of Firgrove, Bts. |
| LABOR NOBILITAT | Labour ennobles. Lords Nathan. |
| LABOR OMNIA SUPERAT | Labour conquers all things. Laing. Turner, co. Leics. |
| LABOR OMNIA VINCIT | Labour conquers all things. Attlee (the 1st Earl Attlee was Labour Prime Minister, 1945), Ashton-under-Lyne (Lancs.), Bor. of, Bradford (W.R. Yorks.), City and Co. Bor. of, Brown, Burbidge, Bts., Burder, Lords Calverly (Muff), Chadderton (Lancs.) UDC, Chaplin, Cheltenham Coll., 1841, Cramsie, Daniel, Eddington, Green, Ilkeston (Derbys.), Bor. of, Lipton, Bt., Marr, Bts., Lords Lucas of Chilworth, M'Nair, Prattinan, Royal Marsden Hosp., Strathallan Sch., Perth, 1912, Lords Terrington (Woodhouse), Lord Uvedale, Vere Hunt, Waterlow of London, Bts. |
| LABOR OMNIA VINCIT IMPROBUS | Relentless labour conquers all things. Tech. Training Sch., RAF, formed 1946 (Belgian). |
| LABOR PARIT OPES | Labour begets wealth. Bradford & Bingley Bldg. Soc. |
| LABOR PROBUS OMNIA VINCIT | Virtuous labour overcomes all things. Wenger. |
| LABOR VINCIT | Labour conquers. Richmond, Bts. |
| LABOR VINCIT OMNIA | Labour conquers all things. Butler Longmore, Colman of Reigate, Bt., Hasell, Ffarington, Richardson. |
| LABOR VIRIS CONVENIT | Labour becomes men. Richard I of England (Coeur-de-Lion). Also used *Christo duce* (With Christ as leader) in ref. to his exploits as Crusader. |
| LABORA | Labour. Mackie, McKie. |
| LABORA SI VIS TONDERE | Work if you wish to make smooth, Whiston (Lancs.) RDC, 1975. |
| LABORA SICUT BONUS MILES | Work as a good soldier. Miles, Bts., Miles of King's Weston. |
| LABORA UT IN AETERNUM VIVAS | Strive that you may live for ever. Apreece, Bt. |
| LABORANTE NUMEN ADEST | God is with him that endeavours. Macfarlane, McFerran. |
| LABORARE EST ORARE | To labour is to pray. Lord Arnold *(NEP)*, great Benedictine Order, Lords Dowding, Gloucestershire Training Coll., Lords Renwick, Shaddon, Bt., Viscount Watkinson, Willesden, London Bor. of. |
| LABORE | By labour. Abbot, Pulley, Bt., Lords Tenterden (Abbott), Walmesley. |
| LABORE AGRICOLAE FLOREAT | May it flourish by the labour of the farmer. Nat. Farmers' Union. |
| LABORE EST ORARE | With labour is to pray. Arnold. |
| LABORE ET CONSILIO | By labour and counsel. Lord Rendel *(NEP)*. |
| LABORE ET HONORE | By industry and honour. Bowden, Lords Greenway, Horsfall, Bts., Johnson, co. Leics., Newman of Newmarket, Bts., Pemberton, Lords Rendlesham (Thelluson), Thelluson, Viner. |

| | |
|---|---|
| LABORE ET INTEGRITATE | By labour and integrity. Manchester & Salford Police Authority. |
| LABORE ET ORA | With labour and pray. Asher. |
| LABORE ET PERSEVERANTIA | By labour and perseverance. Campbell of Succoth, Bts., White-Todd, Bt., Woods. |
| LABORE ET PRUDENTIA | By labour and prudence. Brighouse (W.R. Yorks.) |
| LABORE ET SCIENTIA | By industry and science. Horlick, Bts., Ince, Jarrow (Durham), Bor. of, Wylie, Bt. |
| LABORE ET VIRTUTE | By industry and virtue. Bates, Bts., Bruce-Gardner, Bts., Gardner, Lords Ilkeston (Foster) (NEP), Pigott. |
| LABORE IPSE MERCES | From labour the reward itself. Parts of Holland (Lincs.) CC. |
| LABORE OMNIA FLORENT | All things flourish by industry. Eccles (Lancs.), Bor. of, No. 34 Maintenance Unit, RAF (By labour all things prosper). |
| LABORE OMNIA VINCIT | He conquers all things by labour. Lord Adams (NEP), Rowland, Bts. |
| LABORE TERRESTRI CAELESTIS VICTORIA | Victory in the air by dint of work on the ground. Tech. Training Cmd., RAF. |
| LABORE VINCES | You will overcome by toil. Lewis of Banstead, Lords St Leonards (Sugden), Sugden. |
| LABORES PROSINT CETERIS | May our labours assist the rest. Lydney (Glos.) Parish Council. |
| LABORO FIDE | I work in faith. Lord Kaberay, Readhead, Bts. |
| LABOUR OVERCOMES ALL THINGS | Erith (Kent) UDC. |
| LAETITIA ET SPE IMMORTALITATIS | With joy and hope of immortality. Ffooks, Fooks, Lyte, Shaw. |
| LAETUS SORTE MEA | Happy in my lot. Adams, Batchelor of Combe Flory, co. Som., Dawson, Bts., of Appleton Roebuck. |
| LAETUS SORTE VIVES SAPIENTER | Glad of your lot you will live wisely. Kelk, Bts. |
| LAIMH NAH SARIS | An Irish expert stated: 'It appears to be so corrupt that I can make no suggestion as to a more acceptable form or as to a meaning.' O'Hara. |
| LAIRNIN FILES THE FETTERS | Lord Murray of Newhaven (Life Baron). |
| LAMH DERG EIRIN | The red hand of Ireland. O'Neill, Lords O'Neill, Earls of Tyrone (O'Neill, extinct). The Red Hand, usually called 'of Ulster', now badge of Order of Baronets, is by legend ascribed to an invader of Ulster who cut off his own hand and threw it on shore to claim the land. |
| LAMH FOISDINEACH AN UACHTAR | What we gain by conquest we secure by clemency. Sullivan, Bts. |
| LAMH LAIDIR AN NACHTAR | The strong hand uppermost. Lords Inchiquin (O'Brien), Macdermott, O'Brien, Bts. |
| LAMPADA FERENS | Bearing torches. Hull Univ. (arms grant 1927 to Hull Univ. Coll., recertified on change of status. Ref. to a torch in the arms). |

| | |
|---|---|
| LANA SPES NOSTRA | Wool is our hope. Woolmens' Co. (no charter, but a 'mystery' of woolmongers existed in 1328). |
| LAPIS REPROBATUS CAPUT ANGULI | The rejected stone is the head of the corner. (Psalm 118:22: 'The stone which the builders refused is become the head stone of the corner.' Saying attributed by Christ to himself and repeatedly used in NT by Him and His apostles.) Grand Lodge of Mark Master Masons. |
| LAQUEATOS INTERCIPIMUS | We intercept those who have been ensnared. 3508 Co. of Northumberland Fighter Control Unit, RAAF. |
| LASAIR ROMHAINN ABU | The torch that leads to victory. Mahony. |
| LATEAT SCINTILULLA FORSAN | Perhaps a little spark may lie hid. Roy. Humane Soc., 1774. |
| LAUDA FINEM | Praise the end. Nottingham High Sch. |
| LAUDARI A LAUDATO | To be praised by (one who) has been praised. Hammick, Bts. |
| LAUREAM QUI MERUIT FERAT | Let him who deserves bear the laurel. Council for Nat. Academic Awards. |
| LAURO SCUTOQUE RESURGO | I rise again with laurel and shield. Loraine, Bts. |
| LAUS DEO | Praise to God. Andrus, co. Kent, Viscount Arbuthnott, Lush, Bt. |
| LAUS VIRTUTIS ACTIO | Action is the praise of virtue. Rawson. |
| LAUSANA CIVITAS EQUESTRIS | Lausanne chivalric city. Lausanne, City of. |
| LAW AND LOYALTY | Viscount Greenwood. |
| LE BON TEMPS VIENDRA | The good time will come. Farrington, Bts., Griffith of Llwynduris, Harcourt, Wrey, Bt. |
| LE CAMP VAUX MIEX QUE L'OR | The camp is of more value than gold. Champion. |
| LE CRIDHE'S LE CLIU | With heart and . . . (motto thus rendered by Gaelic scholar who found rest unintelligible). Lords Strathcarron (Macpherson). |
| LE DIEU LE FORT L'ETERNEL PARLERAY | God, the strong, the eternal will speak. Scott of Yews, Bts. |
| LE DROIT LE DESMONTRE | The right shows it. Ingelby of Ripley, co. Yorks. |
| LE FIN COURONNE LES OEUVRES | The end crowns the works. Dunn-Yarker. |
| LE FROID ME CHASSE | The cold chases me. Marie de Rabutin-Chantal, Marquise de Sévigné, 1626–96, famous for her letters; ref. is to device of swallow flying to warmer climes. |
| LE JOUR VIENDRA | The day will come. Earls of Durham (Lambton), Lambton. |
| LE LIERRELIE LONGS LIENS | The fastening has long bands. Leir. |
| LE MAITRE VIENT | The Master comes. Peek, Bts. |
| LE MONDE EST MON PRÉ | The world is my meadow. Dupree, Bts. |
| LE ROY ET L'ESTAT | The king and the state. Earls of Ashburnham *(NEP)*. |
| LE ROY, LA LOY | The king, the law. Larcom, Bts. |

| | |
|---|---|
| LE TEMPS VENDRA | The time will come. Jean de France, Duc de Berry, d. 1416, 3rd son of King John of France, beside whom he stood, aged only nine at Battle of Poitiers, 1356. He hoped to become King of France but, perforce, on his tomb described himself as son, brother and uncle of Kings of France. |
| LE TRONC EST VERT ET LES FEUILLES SONT ARCES | The trunk is green and the leaves are burnt. Arces. |
| LEAD AND GUIDE | RAF station, Stornoway, Lewis. |
| LEAD ON | Lords Hotham. |
| LEADS THE FIELD | 12 Bomber Sq., RAF (originally equipped with Fox aircraft – badge a fox's mask). |
| LEAL AND TRUE | Coutts-Duffus. |
| LEARN AND LEAD | No. 3 Air Navigation Sch., RAF. |
| LEARN BY DEGREES | Univ. of London Air Sq., RAFVR. |
| LEARN TO BE FREE | Normanton Gram. Sch., W.R. Yorks. |
| LEARN TO SERVE | No. 10 Sch. of Tech. Training, RAF. |
| LEARN TO TEST, TEST TO LEARN | Empire Test Pilots' Sch. |
| LEGE ET LUCE | By law and light. Walker-Smith, Bts. |
| LEGES ARMA TENENT SANCTAS COMMERCIA LEGES | Arms keep laws sacred (both) commerce and laws. Benson. |
| LEGES CIVITATEMQUE SERVAMUS | We serve the laws and the state. Soc. of Town Clerks, 1962. |
| LEGES JURAQUE COGNOSCAMUS | Let us know the laws and rights. Coll. of Law. |
| LEGES JURAQUE SERVA | Observe the laws and ordinances. Grant of Kilgraston, Impey-Lovibond, Leigh of Belmont. |
| LEGES JURAQUE SERVAMUS | Let us keep the laws and rights. Incorp. Law Society. |
| LEGI REGI FIDES | Faith to the law and king. Lords Rosmead (Robinson) (NEP). |
| LEGI REGI FIDUS | Faithful to law and king. Lynch Robinson, Bts. |
| LEGIS PLENITUDO CARITAS | Charity is the fullness of the law. Ratcliffe Coll., Leics., 1844. |
| LEN YN GWYR | Faithful in truth (Cornish). Searle. |
| LENTE SED CORTE | Slowly but with the bark. Ansbacher. |
| LEO INIMICIS AMICIS COLUMBA | A lion to his enemies, a dove to his friends. Dilkie, Bts., Fetherston-Dilke. |
| LESSIS DIRE (or LESSES DIRE) | Let speak. Middleton, Bts. |
| LET BROTHERLY LOVE CONTINUE | Plasterers' Co., inc. 1500, Pipemakers' Co. |
| LET CURZON HOLD WHAT CURZON HELD | Curzon. Marquess Curzon of Kedleston (NEP), Earls Howe (Curzon), Viscount Scarsdale (Curzon). This family has been seated at the same property, Kedleston, Derbys., since end of the eleventh century. Name Curzon is Norman, brought from Courson in Normandy. |

| | |
|---|---|
| LET PEACE FOLLOW MY LABOUR | Lord Forster of Harraby. |
| LET THE DEED SHAW | Addison, Fleming, Mowbray. |
| LET THE LOSSE LIGHTE EASILLIE | United Reinsurers Ltd., 1956. |
| LET TYRANTS TREMBLE | 199 Sq., RAF. |
| LET US GROW IN SERVICE | Louth (Lincs.) RDC. |
| LET US LOVE ONE ANOTHER | Basketmakers' Co., inc. 1569. |
| LET US TO THE BATTLE | 133 Sq., RAF (manned by Americans). |
| LEUM A BALLA FAR IS IOSHLE | Leap the dyke at its lowest. Maclean of Ardgour. |
| LEVAVI OCULOS | I have lifted up my eyes (from Psalm 121:1: I will lift up mine eyes unto the hills). Lord Schuster *(NEP)*. |
| LEVAVI OCULOS MEOS IN MONTES | I have lifted up mine eyes to the hills (Psalm 121:1). Malvern (Worcs.) UDC, Workington (Camb.), Bor. of (also has on patent of arms: *Floreat oppidum laborans*, Let the working town flourish). |
| LEVE ET RELUIS | Rise and shine. Lawson of Brough Hall, Bts. |
| LEVIUS FIT PATIENTIA | It is rendered lighter by patience. Burgess, Gloster, Lamb, Vardon. |
| LEX ET JUSTITIA | Law and justice. Law of Glanconway. |
| LEX LIBERTATIS ORIGO | Law is the origin of liberty. Solicitors' Co., formed on pattern of ancient guild as City of London Solicitors' Co., 1909, and in 1944 received grant of livery from Court of Aldermen. |
| LEX MEA LUX | The law my light. Lords Birkett (very appropriate wording for one of the greatest advocates of the twentieth century; the 1st Baron). |
| LEX TUA MEDITATIO MEA | Thy law is my meditation. Lord, Coleraine (Law). |
| LIBERA DEINDE FIDELIS | Free therefore faithful. Godalming (Surrey), Bor. of. |
| LIBERAMUS PER CAERULA | We liberate through tropical skies. 355 Sq., RAF. |
| LIBERATE | Liberate. 161 Sq., RAF. |
| LIBERTAS | Liberty. Bailey, Birch, Bts., Lords Carbery, Chatteris, Evans, Lords Glanusk (Bailey), Gregory, Lewis, Lords Mountevans (Evans), Stewart-Liberty, Worthington-Evans, Bts. |
| LIBERTAS ET NATALE SOLUM | Liberty and my native soil. Adams, Freeman, Hawkins-Whitshed, Bts., Sanderson. |
| LIBERTAS IN LEGIBUS | Liberty in the law. Best, Lords Wynford (Best). |
| LIBERTAS SUB REGE PIO | Liberty under a pious king. Addington, Packe, Viscount Sidmouth (Addington). |
| LIBERTÉ, ÉGALITÉ, FRATERNITÉ | Liberty, equality, fraternity. Motto of the French Republic, established during the French Revolution, 1789–93. Then usually accompanied by the threat *'ou la mort'*, which was frequently carried out. |
| LIBERTÉ TOUT ENTIÈRE | Liberty unfettered. Butler-Danvers, Lane, Bts., Earls of Lanesborough (Butler). |
| LIBERTY | Havering, London Bor. of, Kippen. |

| | |
|---|---|
| LICET ESSE BEATIS | It is permitted to be with the happy. Warde of Barham Court, Bt. |
| LIFE IN HOPE | Ardley. |
| LIFE IN OUR HANDS | Inst. of Hosp. Engineering. |
| LIGHT AND LIBERTY | Kirk. |
| LIGHT, LOVE, LIFE | Southlands Coll. of Education, 1968. |
| LIGHT ON | Leighton. |
| LIGNUM CRUCIS ARBOR SCIENTIAE | The wood of the Cross is the tree of knowledge. Denstone Coll., Staffs., 1868. |
| LIKE AS THE OAK | Uckfield (Sussex) RDC, 1948. |
| LINK AND GUIDE | No. 26 Group HQ, RAF. |
| LINK PEN AND SWORD | Southern Communications Sq., RAF. |
| LIVE AND LET LIVE | Methuen, Bts. |
| LIVE BUT DREID | Earls of Lindsay (Lindesay-Bethune), Lindsay. |
| LIVE TO LIVE | Charlton (formerly Bate), Dundas, Huntington-Whiteley, Bts., Sutton, Whiteley, Whitley, Witeley. |
| LLAFUR ORFU BOBPETH | Labour overcomes all. Llantrissant and Llantwitfardre (Carm.) RDC, Rhys Williams, Bts. |
| LLIFA'R DWR LLEWYRCHA'R BOBL | The water flows, the people flourish. Brecknock RDC. |
| LLWYDDIANT O DDIWYDIANT | Success from industry. Connah's Quay (Flints.) UDC. |
| LOCO ET TEMPORE | By time and place. Alfonso d'Este (Duke of Ferrara, c.1534; great artillerist, helped French by this means to win Battle of Ravenna; motto given to him by poet Ariosto), King Edward of Portugal, 1433–8). |
| LOOK AHEAD | Butcher, Bts. |
| LOOK FORWARD | Lords Colyton (Hopkinson), Hopkinson. |
| LOCK SICKER | Be sure. Douglas of Carr, Bts., Megget, Earls of Morton (Douglas). |
| LOI ET LOYAUTÉ | Law and loyalty. Viscount Sumner (Hamilton) (NEP). |
| LOIALTÉ MAINTIENT AMOR | Loyalty upholds love. Sir William Skeffington, temp. Henry VIII. |
| LOISGIM AGUS SOILLEIRGHIM | I will burn and enlighten. Macleod of Cadboll. |
| LONDINI DEFENDI TUOS DEUS OPTIME CIVES | O God, the best, defend Thy citizens of London. Guild of Freemen of the City of London. |
| LOOK BEYOND | Lord Perry (NEP). |
| LOOK FORWARD | Coll. of Air Training, RAF. |
| LOOKING AHEAD | Central Servicing Development Establishment, RAF. |
| LOOKING BACKWARD, LOOKING FORWARD | Twickenham (Middx.), Bor. of. |
| LOS EN CROISANT | Praise in growth. Order of Croissant d'Or, instituted by René of Anjou. |

| | |
|---|---|
| LOVE ALL MEN, FEAR NO MAN | Cropper of Ellergreen, Kendal, Westmorland. |
| LOVE AND DREAD | Baker, co. Yorks., Tower. |
| LOVE AND LOYALTY | Crompton, Bts., Crompton-Stansfield, Inglefield. |
| LOVE AS BRETHREN | Coopers' Co., inc. 1501. |
| LOVE BUT DREAD | Lindesay. |
| LOVE, SERVE | Ashley, Ashley-Cooper, Cooper, Earls of Shaftesbury (Ashley-Cooper). |
| LOYAL | Clutterbuck of Rowington. |
| LOYAL À MORT | Loyal to death. Adair, Chatterton, Bt., Marquesses of Ely (Loftus), Hepworth of Pontefract, Laforey, Bt., Loftus. |
| LOYAL AND FREE | Bennett, co. Lincoln. |
| LOYAL AND INDUSTRIOUS | Rowley Regis (Staffs.), Bor. of. |
| LOYAL AND TRUE | Chatham (Kent), Bor. of. |
| LOYAL AU MORT | Loyal to the death. Adair, Loftus, Lord Rowton (Lowry-Corry), Lord Waveney (Adair) (NEP). |
| LOYAL DEVOIR | Loyal duty. De Carteret, Grenfell, Malet de Carteret, Lords St Just (Grenfell). |
| LOYAL EN TOUT | Loyal in everything. Brown, Earls of Kenmare (Browne) (NEP), Puxley, Wilson of Eshton Hall, Bts., Wood of Hetton. |
| LOYAL ET S'APPROVARA | Loyal and I will prove it. Sir William Fitzwilliam, K.G., cr. Earl of Southampton, 1537 (B.Ext.P.). |
| LOYAL JE SERAI DURANT MA VIE | I will be loyal as long as I live. Lords Mowbray, Segrave & Stourton (Stourton), Stourton. |
| LOYAL JUSQU' À LA MORT | Loyal to the death. Ellerman, Bts. |
| LOYAL, SECRET | Loyal, confidential. Lawson of Knavesmire, Bts. (adopted by Sir George Lawson, temp. Henry VIII, on being appointed Gov. of Berwick-on-Tweed), Lawson-Tancred. |
| LOYAL SUIS JE | Loyal am I. Shirley. |
| LOYAL UNTIL DEATH | White of Walling Wells, Bts. |
| LOYAL YET FREE | Stracey-Clitherow. |
| LOYALLE SUYS | I am loyal. Sir Walter Devereux, K.G., great-grandfather of Elizabeth I's favourite, the Earl of Essex. |
| LOYALMENT JE SERS | I serve loyally. Jephson, Jephson-Norreys of Mallow Castle, Bts. |
| LOYALTY | 33 Sq. (bomber), RAF (badge a hart's head – sq. orig. equipped with Hart aircraft). |
| LOYALTY | Thompson of Walton-on-the-Hill, Bts. |
| LOYALTY AND SERVICE | Master Mariners' Co., inc. 1930; designation of Honourable Co. given by George V, June 1928. |
| LOYALTY BINDS ME | RAF station, Coningsby. |

| | |
|---|---|
| LOYAUTÉ ME LIE | Loyalty binds me. Viscount Margesson, Richard III (1483–5). |
| LOYAUTÉ ME OBLIGE | Loyalty binds me. Earls of Ancaster (Heathcote-Drummond-Willoughby), Lords Willoughby de Eresby, Joint Hereditary Lords Great Chamberlain. |
| LOYAUTÉ M'OBLIGE | Loyalty binds me. Bertie, Earls Lindsey & Abingdon (Bertie). |
| LOYAULTÉ MON HERITAGE | Loyalty is my heritage. Chavasse. |
| LOYAUTÉ SANS TACHE | Loyalty without defect. Dare. |
| LOYOUE AS THOU FYNDS | Greenly, Tempest. |
| LUCE MAGISTRA | With light as mistress. Queen Ethelburga's Sch., Harrogate, 1962. |
| LUCE SCIENTIAE VINCES | Thou shalt conquer by the light of science. S. Wales & Monmouth Sch. of Mines. |
| LUCE SCRIBIMUS | We write by light. RAF Sch. of Photography. |
| LUCEM FERAT ET SERENITATEM – φῶς φεροι ἤδη γαλήνην | Let light bring peace. Catherine de Medici, 1519–89, dau. of Lorenzo de Medici; queen of Henry II, mother of three French kings, organizer of Massacre of St Bartholomew. Used rainbow or iris, hence motto used by her in both Latin and Greek. |
| LUCEM FERO | I bear the light. Davies of Plas Llangoedmore. |
| LUCEM SPERO | I hope for light. Kemp, Viscount Rochdale (Kemp). |
| LUCEM SPERO CLARIOREM | I hope for clearer light. Preston, Bts. |
| LUCEM TUAM DA NOBIS DEUS | Give us thy light, O Lord. Glaziers' Co., inc. 1637, but in existence under name of 'verrers' at least three centuries earlier. 'The Co.'s control of the trade had largely ceased by the 18th century but the Co. of Glaziers is still an active force in fostering the art. Many of its members are prominent artists; prizes are awarded for notable work; gifts of windows are from time to time made; and a close association is maintained with the British Society of Master Glass Painters', John Bromley and Heather Child, *Armorial Bearings of the Guilds of London*, 1960, p.115. |
| LUCEO NON URO | I shine but do not burn. Earls of Cromartie (Mackenzie), Fraser-Mackenzie, Mackenzie of Scatwell, Bts., M'Leod of Colbeck, Lord Seaforth (Stewart-Mackenzie) *(NEP)*, Smith. |
| LUCK TO LOYNE | Lancaster, City and Bor. of (Loyne is a form of Lune, the river whence Lancaster takes its name). |
| LUCKNOW | Havelock (see *Fortiter gerit crucem*). |
| LUCTOR ET EMERGO | I struggle and emerge. Province of Zealand, whose arms are a lion rising out of the sea. |
| LUDOVICUS MAG. INSTIT 1693 | Louis the Great instituted 1693. Order of St Louis, France. |
| LUDUS SUPRA PRAEMIUM | The game above reward. Wolverhampton Girls' High Sch., 1962. |

| | |
|---|---|
| LUMEN ACCIPE ET IMPERTI | Receive the light and communicate it. Jones of Brecon, Hollingsworth. |
| LUMEN MONSTRO PRO SALUTE | Show a light for safety. Burnham-on-Sea (Som.) UDC. |
| LUMEN RECTIS | A light to the upright (ref. to column of fire which guided Israelites by night on journey from Egypt to Promised Land). Francis II (1544–60) of France, 1st husband (probably nominal) of Mary Queen of Scots. |
| LUMEN SEVIMUS ANTIQUE | We sowed light of old. Redwood, Bts. |
| LUPUS VULT LUPUS VOLAT | The wolf wills, the wolf flies. 34 Sq., RAF. |
| LUTTER À MA PUISSANCE | Fight for my power. Lutterworth (Leics.) RDC. |
| LUX ANGLIS CRUX FRANCIS | Light for the English, a cross for the French. Rooper. |
| LUX ET HUMANITAS | Light and humanity. Blackwell RDC. |
| LUX ET VERITAS | Light and truth. Yale Univ., USA. |
| LUX, LEX, LIBERTAS | Light, law, liberty. Colfox, Bts. |
| LUX EX TENEBRIS | Light from darkness. Viscount Davidson, Wigan & District Mining & Tech. Coll., 1948. |
| LUX IN LITTERIS | Light in letters. Henniker Heaton, Bts. |
| LUX IN TENEBRIS | Light in darkness. Andrews, co. Bucks., Lord Uthwatt (NEP), Services Kinema Corp., 1969, Fullerton, Henry the Young, Duke of Brunswick, d. 1568. |
| LUX INDEFICIENS | Light never failing. City of Casal of Montserrat, Sardinia. |
| LUX SALUBRITAS ET FELICITAS | Light, health and happiness. Clacton-on-Sea, Essex. |
| LUX TUA VIA MEA | Thy light is my way. Blount, Kent Coll., Canterbury, 1885. |
| LUX VITA CARITAS | Light, life, charity. Wesley House, Cambridge, 1926. |
| LUX VITAE | The light of life. Burton (formerly of Bakewell). |
| LY BORDIS | Miller of Myres. |
| LYRAE NERVOS APTAVI | I tuned the strings of my lyre. Sirr. |

# M

| | |
|---|---|
| MA FORCE D'EN HAUT | My strength is from above. Landon, Malet, Bts., Mallet. |
| MACTE | Go forward. Smith of Jordanhill. |
| MACTE VIRTUTE | Well done (well-known Latin sentence used by, e.g., Cicero and Livy; can be rendered 'Good luck go with thee'). Lord Dunedin (Murray) (NEP), Hollins, Bts., Murray-Graham. |
| MACTE VIRTUTE ESTO | Well done. Lowndes. |
| MAGÍS AMICA VERITAS | Rather friendly truth. Jackson. |
| MAGISTRATUS INDICAT VIRUM | The magistracy shows the man. Brabazon-Lowther, Earls of Lonsdale (Lowther), Lowther, Bts., Viscount Ullswater (Lowther). |
| MAGNA CIVITAS, MAGNA SOLITUDO. LITERARIUM RADICES AMARAE, FRUCTUS DULCES | A great commonwealth, great solitude. The roots of knowledge are bitter, the fruits sweet (?a reminiscence of St Jerome when learning Hebrew). Birkbeck Coll., London Univ. 1823. |
| MAGNA EST VERITAS | Great is truth (part of verse in Apocrypha (I Esdras 4:35): Great is the truth and stronger than all things). Magnay, Bts. |
| MAGNA VIS FIDELITATUS | The force of fidelity is great. Newman. |
| MAGNANIMITER CRUCEM SUSTINE | Sustain the Cross with magnanimity. Kenyon, Marston, Whitney. |
| MAGNI CONSILIUM PRETII | Counsel of great price. Highworth (Wilts.) RDC. |
| MAGNOS VEHIMUS | We carry the great. AHQ (1) Communication Sq., RAF. |
| MAILLE A MAILLE SE FAIT L'AUBERGEON | Ring on ring makes the habergeon (harness). Aubergeon. |
| MAIN ROAD OF AFRICA | (original in Arabic script). RAF station, Khartoum. |
| MAINTIEN LE DROIT | Uphold the right. Bridges, Brydges, Bt., Hodsoll, Keynsham (Som.) UDC, Leatham. |
| MAIUS OPUS | A greater work. Cardinal Guido Bentivoglio, d. 1644. |
| MAJOR AB ADVERSIS | Greater through adversity. Bewes. |
| MAJOR OPIMA FERAT | Let the more worthy carry off the honours (probably an oblique reference to spolia opima, the Roman custom when a leader slew the opponents' leader). Moir, More. |
| MAJOR PROVIDENTIA FATO | Providence is greater than fate. Sturt. |
| MAJOR VIRTUS QUAM SPLENDOR | Virtue is preferable to splendour. Auld, Baillie of Jerviswood, Earls of Haddington (Baillie-Hamilton). |
| MAJORA CEDUNT | The greater yield. John I, King of Castile, 1379–90. |
| MAJORA TENTO | I aim at greater things. Officer Cadet Training Unit, RAF. |

MAJORA, UBERIORA, PULCHRIORA | Greater, richer, more beautiful. Hemel Hempstead Development Corp., Herts.

MAK SICCAR | Make things sure. No. 66 (Scottish) Group HQ, RAF.

MAKE ALL SURE | Armourers' and Braziers' Co. *See also* We are one.

MAKE YOURSELF NECESSARY | Lords Melchett (Mond).

MALA PRAEVISA PEREUNT | Evils foreseen perish. Hodges, Twisden, Bts.

MALGRÉ LE TORT | Despite the wrong. Davis, De Houghton, Bts., James.

MALIS MEDERI NEMINI NOCERE | To cure the bad, to harm none. Lord Cohen of Birkenhead (a doctor).

MALLEM MORI QUAM MUTARE | I would rather die than change. Gilbert.

MALO MORI QUAM FOEDARI | I would rather die than be disgraced. Allen, co. Antrim, Anne de Bretagne, *c.*1513 (queen of (1) Charles VIII and (2) of his cousin, Louis XII of France), Earls of Athlone (extinct), Barnewall, Bts., Beale, Booth, Boucher, Carson, Casley, Chetham Strode, Daeg, De Freyne, Esmonde, Bts., Ffrench, Frankland-Payne-Gallwey, Bts., French, Gingle, Ginkell, Gore-Hickman, Harty, Bts., Higginson, Jackson, Viscount Kingsland, Lister, Mulloy, Murray, O'Mulley, Payne, Peck, Poe, Rigby, Bts., Ryan, Strode, Surtees, Tenison, Lords Trimelstowne (Barnewall).

MALOREM VICTOR | I would rather be winner. Aldous.

MANCHESTER | The Manchester Regt., which carries shield and crest and supporters of City of Manchester.

MANE PRAEDAM VESPERE SPOLIUM | Game in the morning, and a feast at night. Hurt.

MANENT OPTIMA COELO | The best things await us in heaven. Christie-Miller, Lords Inchyra (Millar), Miller.

MANEO, NON FUGIO | I stand firm and do not fly. Gordon, Wartnaby.

MANET ULTIMA COELO | The last remains with heaven. Henry III of France, 1551–89, 3rd son of Catherine de Medici, eventually assassinated; had homosexual tendencies, married but no heir.

MANGEUR MANGÉ | The eater eaten. Mirrlees.

MANIBUS PEDIBUSQUE | By hand and feet. Ashdown.

MANIBUS VICTORIA DEXTRIS | Victory by our right hands. Adair, Bt.

MANNERS MAKYTH MAN | Hood, co. Lancs., Wickham, Winchester Coll. (founded by William of Wykeham, Bishop of Winchester and lord Chancellor, 1382), Wykeham.

MANU FORTE | With a strong hand. Earls of Inchcape (Mackay), M'Cay, M'Casker, Mackay, Lords Reay (Mackay), Lords Shaughnessy.

MANU SCIENTE | With a knowing hand. Plastic Surgeons, British Assn. of.

MANUS ARTIFICIS AQUILAS ALUNT | The hands of the craftsman feed the eagles. No. 109 Maintenance Unit, RAF.

| MANUS HAEC INIMICA TYRANNIS | This hand is hostile to tyrants. Earls of Carysfort (Proby), Dossey, Hemsworth, co. Norfolk, Manley, Proby, Bts., Probyn, Lords Riversdale (Tonson), Tonson. |
|---|---|
| MANUS JUSTA NARDUS | A just hand is a precious ointment. Maynard. |
| MANUS NOSTRAE ALAS SUSTINENT | Our hands uphold the wings. No. 30 Maintenance Unit, RAF. |
| MANY MINDS, ONE HEART | Chelmsford (Essex), Bor. of. |
| MARE DIDAT FLORES DECORAT | The sea enriches, the flowers decorate. Exmouth (Devon) UDC. |
| MARE DITAT PINUSQUE DECORAT | The sea enriches, the pinetree decorates. Sheringham (Norfolk) UDC. |
| MARE ET FERRO | By sea and steel. Redcar (N.R. Yorks.), Bor. of. |
| MARE TRANSEO INTERNUM | I travel across the inland sea. Malta Communications and Target Towing Sq., RAF. |
| MARIA TURI DOCEMUS ALUMNOS | We teach the young fledglings to guard the seas. No. 4 Operational Training Unit, RAF. |
| MARMORA MESSALAE FINDIT CAPRIFICUS | The wild fig tree splits Messala's marble. Cola Conte di Campo Basso, a captain of mercenaries. Motto comes from Martial, *Epigrams* X.2, in allusion to Campo Basso's part in final defeat of Charles the Bold of Burgundy. |
| MARS DENTALIA TUTATUR | Mars guards the ploughshares. Marsden. |
| MARTE ET ARTE | By valour and skill. Drummond of Megginch Castle, Lawrence-Jones of Cranmer Hall, Bts. (Lt. Gen. Sir John Thomas Jones, K.C.B., was cr. Bt. 1831 for distinguished services in the Peninsula War. The word Netherlands is inscribed in the arms above a castle. Sir John is now represented by Sir Christopher Lawrence-Jones, 6th Bt.), Lord Strange (Drummond). |
| MARTE ET INGENIO | By war and wit. Hamilton-Spencer-Smith, Bts. |
| MARTE SUO TUTUS | Safe in his own resources. Byers. |
| MARTELEZ TOUJOURS DROIT | Labour always for the right. Martel. |
| MARTEM INTER NUBES PARO | I prepare war among the clouds. No. 31 Bombing and Gunnery Sch., RAF. |
| MARIS NON CUPIDINIS | Of Mars not Cupid. Aubrey-Fletcher, Bts., Lord Winster (Fletcher) *(NEP)*. |
| MARTYRII MEMORES | Mindful of martyrs. Ridley Hall (theological coll.), Cambridge, 1952. |
| MATIA TOY GATOY | Eyes of a cat. No. 280 Signals Unit, RAF, Cyprus. |
| MATURE | Hasten (*or* Maturely). Ashmead-Bartlett, Barttelot, Bts., Pope Paul III, Alessandro Farnese (reigned 1534–49, having been forty years a Cardinal and having sons and daus. – Von Ranke, *History of the Popes*; John Farrow *Pageant of the Popes*, 1950). |
| MAXIMA PAULATIM | The greatest things, little by little. Elwin. |
| MAXIMUS NE METUIT | The greatest did not fear. 87 Sq., RAF. |
| MAY DUNMOW PROSPER | Great Dunmow (Essex) Parish Council, 1956. |

| | |
|---|---|
| MAYA | Cameron of Fassifern, Bt. (second motto borne under the arms in allusion to pass forced by Col. John Cameron in 1813; see Arriverette). |
| ME EXACTAVIT IN PETRA | It has driven me onto a rock. Stanton of Snelston Hall. |
| ME JUVAT IRE PER ALTUM | It helps me to go through the deep. Waller-Bridge. |
| ME MINERVA LUCET | Minerva enlightens me. Le Marchant, Bts. |
| MEA CULPA FIDES | Faith is my guilt. Lawlor. |
| MEA DOS VIRTUS | Virtue is my dower. Meadows, co. Suffolk. |
| MEA GLORIA FIDES | Faith is my glory. Gilchrist, Lords Manton (Watson), Watson of Ballingarrane. |
| MEA SPES EST IN DEO | My hope is in God. Church, Bts., Miller, Smith-Gordon, Bts. |
| MEA TELA NOCENT | My weapons do harm. No. 11 Maintenance Unit, RAF. |
| MEA VIRTUTE ME INVOLVO | I wrap myself in my virtue. Williams (Hamlyn-Williams, Bts.). |
| MEDIA NOX MERIDIES NOSTER | The middle night is as our midday. 409 Sq., RCAF. |
| MEDIIS TRANQUILLUS IN UNDIS | Tranquil in the midst of waters. Smyth, co. Perth. |
| MEDIO TUTISSIMUS IBIS | The middle path is safest. Busfield, Langrishe, Bts., Senior. |
| MEDIOCRIA FIRMA | Mediocrity is safe. Bacon, Bts. (Sir Francis Bacon, Lord Verulam & Viscount St Albans (*never* as in many legal treatises 'Lord Bacon'), had this motto over the door of his house at Gorhambury), Lord Grimston of Westbury, Lawder, Lowndes-Stone, Earls of Verulam (Grimston), St Albans Sch., Herts., founded sixteenth century, though existing in 1100. Charters with endowments from wine licences from Elizabeth I and James I. |
| MEDIOCRIA MAXIMA | Middle things are the greatest. Monins. |
| MEDITARE | Meditate. Fairlie. |
| MEEN SUCKER REAGUE | (Irish scholar writes: 'More usually found, I think, as *Min, sicker reag*. If indeed it is Irish, it is corrupt. It may have been *Min, soceir reidh* – Gentle, calm, ready. Each of the three words can mean *smooth*'). Conner. |
| MEET THE SUN HALFWAY | Lord Balerno, Life Peer (Buchanan-Smith), Buchanan-Smith. |
| MELIOR | Better. Mellor, Bts. |
| MELIOR FORTUNA NOTABIT | Better fortune will mark (it). Ludovico, Cardinal of Aragon, related through illegitimate line to Kings of Naples (early sixteenth century). Motto refers to ancient Roman custom of stones used to mark good or bad fortune. |
| MELIORA LATENT | The better things are concealed. Italian Academy of Intronati of Siena. |
| MELIORA SEQUAMUR | May we follow better things. Blackpool Boys' Gram. Sch., Brighton Gram. Sch., Eastbourne, Co. Bor. of. |
| MELIORA SPERANS | Hoping for better things. Tees Conservancy Commissioners. |

| | |
|---|---|
| MELIORA SPERO | I hope for better things. Hobhouse, Walsh. |
| MELIORE FIDE QUAM FORTUNA | With better fidelity than fortune. Gresley, Bts. |
| MEMBERS OF ONE ANOTHER | Harlow Development Corp., Essex. |
| MEMBRA SUMAS CORPORIS MAGNI | Mayst thou take the members of a great body. Bootham Sch., York. |
| MÊME NON ROI | Even my king. Sellar. |
| MEMENTO CREATORIS TUI | Remember thy Creator (motto from Ecclesiastes xii:1, Remember how thy Creator in the days of thy youth). Grenville Coll., Bideford, Devon, 1954. |
| MEMENTO MEI | Remember me. L'Estrange. |
| MEMOR | Mindful. James, co. Glos., Watts-Russell. |
| MEMOR ESTO | Be mindful. Campbell, Graham of Killern, Graham of Larchfield, Greer, Hutchinson of Hardiston, Bts., Lord Hutchison of Montrose (NEP), Hutchison of Rockend, M'Fell, M'Phail. |
| MEMOR ET FIDELIS | Mindful and faithful. Peachy, Reed of the Cragg. |
| MEMOR ET GRATUS | Mindful and pleasing. Gooch. |
| MEMOR RURIS DISCIPLINAE CUSTOS | Mindful of the country, guardian of discipline. Macclesfield (Ches.) RDC. |
| MEMORARE NOVISSIMA TUA | To remember thy latest moments. Handford. |
| MEMORES POLLICITI NOSTRI | Mindful of our promise. Savings and Loan Soc. Ltd., 1956. |
| MEMORIA PII AETERNA | The memory of the pious man is eternal. Lords Sudeley (Hanbury-Tracy), Tracy. |
| MENCHARI DENDAN SUNYI | Silently we seek (Malayan). Southern Sector Operations Centre, RAF, Singapore. |
| MENGAMIL DAN MELATEH | Recruit and train (Malayan). Malaya Training Centre, RAF. |
| MENS AEQUA IN ARDUIS | A mind equal in difficulties. François de Bassompierre, Marshal of France, d. 1646. |
| MENS AEQUA REBUS IN ARDUIS | A mind equal in arduous matters. Viscount Hardinge. |
| MENS AGITAT MOLEM | Mind moves matter. Lords Conesford (Strauss), Rossall Sch. Lancs., 1844, Warwick Univ., 101 Sq., RAF (Mind over matter). |
| MENS CONSCIA RECTI | A mind conscious of right (from Virgil, Aeneid i. 604). Viscount Ashbrook (Flower), Collis, Gooke-Collis, Iredell, Jary. |
| MENS CUJUSQUE IS EST QUISQUE | As the mind of each, so is the man (Cicero, De Republica vi. 26). Earls of Cottenham (Pepys), Howard of the Moat, Leslie, co. Surrey, Lords Milverton (Richards), Pepys, Bts. |
| MENS FLECTI NESCIA | The mind which cannot be bent. Hulton, Bts. |
| MENS OMNIBUS AEQUA | A mind equal to all. Walker of Warden Court. |
| MENS PRISTINA MANSIT | The original mind hath remained. Popham. |

| | |
|---|---|
| MENS SANA IN CORPORE SANO | A sound mind in a sound body (Juvenal, *Satires* x. 356 – one of the most famous of proverbial Latin sayings). Burlton, co. Hereford, Chelsea Coll. of Physical Education, Eastbourne, Summer Fields Sch., Oxford, 1963. |
| MENS SIBI CONSCIA RECTI | A mind conscious in itself of right. Champion de Crespigny, Bt., Eshton Hall Sch., Wright, Bts. |
| MENS STELLA CEREBRI | The mind is the star of the brain. Lords Brain (a punning motto). |
| MENTE ET LABORE | By mind and labour. Lawrence of Ealing Park, Bts. |
| MENTE ET MANU | By mind and hand. 4th (Queen's Own) Hussars. |
| MENTE MANUQUE | With heart and hand. Benshaw, Borthwick of Stow, Farquhar. |
| MENTIS HONESTAE GLORIA | The glory of an honest mind. Grey. |
| MEOR RAS THA DEW | Gracious is thy God (Cornish). Williams. |
| MERCATORUM SALUS | The safety of merchants. London Assurance. |
| MERCES HAEC CERTA LABORUM | This is the sure reward of industry. Seton of Pitmedden, Bts. |
| MERCIE (MERCY) IS MY DESIRE | Abercromby, Bts., Laing, Lang, Wishart. |
| MERE FIDE ET DILIGENTIA | By plain faith and diligence. Williams of Trewylan. |
| MEREBIMUR | We will deserve. 15th (The King's) Hussars. |
| MERENTI | For the deserving. Order of Military Merit (Bavaria). |
| MERET QUI LABORAT | He deserves who works. Cornwall, Bt., Peel of Tyershall, Bt. |
| MERITE | Rightly. Cameron of Garth, Shetland, Currier. |
| MERITIS AUGENTUR HONORES | Honours are increased by merit. Lacy. |
| MERITO | Deservedly. Delap, Delop, Dunlop. |
| MERITUM, OPPORTUNITAS, OFFICIUM | Merit, opportunity, service. Assn. of Certified & Corporate Accountants. |
| MERITUS QUI LABORAT | He has deserved who works. Inst. of Industrial Supervisors. |
| MERSES PROFUNDO PULCHRIOR EVENIT | Sink him in the sea, he comes out fairer. Davison, co. Northumb., Viscount Slim. |
| MERUI | I have deserved. Paterson of Castle Huntley. |
| MES AN MEN-MA OW THASOU A'VE TREGHYS | From this rock were my fathers hewn (Cornish). Thomas. |
| MESSIS AB ALTIS | Harvest from the deeps. Tynemouth (Northumb.), Bor. of. |
| METUE NUNQUAM | Never fear. Stewart of Balgownie, Bts. |
| METUENDA COROLLA DRACONIS | The dragon's crest is to be feared. Marquesses of Londonderry (Vane-Tempest-Stewart), Stewart. |
| METUS IN SECUNDIS | Fear in prosperity. Lord Hodson (Life Baron). Mid dalle gelli gwell Williams of Gwyndwr, Bts. |
| MIEUX SERA | It shall be better. Baroness Beaumont (Fitzalan-Howard). |

| | |
|---|---|
| MIGHT AND MAIN | 209 Sq., RAF. (Badge an eagle falling, as sq. claimed to have brought down German Ace of World War I, Baron Von Richthofen.) |
| MIHI CURA FUTURI | My care is for the future. Ascroft, Acton Tech. Coll., W. London, Ongley, No. 93 Group HQ, RAF. |
| MIHI ET MEA | To me and mine. Anne Boleyn, 2nd wife of Henry VIII. |
| MIHI GRAVATO DEUS | God is with me though troubled. Ridgeway. |
| MIHI PARTA TUERL | To defend the things acquired by me. Le Strange, North. |
| MIHI RES NON ME REBUS | Things for me, not me for things. Lords O'Hagan (Towneley-Strachey). |
| MIHI RES SUBJUNGERE CONOR | I try to join matters for myself. Crackanthorpe, co. Westmorland. |
| MIHI SOLICITUDO FUTURI | I have a care for the future. Thackwell. |
| MIN AL-FARR ILA AL-SAMA | From the land to the sky. RAF station, Sharjok. |
| MINISTRANDO DIGNITAS | Dignity with service. Leyton, London Bor. of. |
| MINISTRI FULMINIS | Suppliers of the thunderbolt. No. 128 Maintenance Unit, RAF (supplying ammunition to M.E. Air Force). |
| MISERICORDIA FIDELITAS JUS | Mercy, fidelity and law. Lords Craigmyle (Shaw). |
| MISERIS SUCCURRERE DISCO | I learn how to help the wretched. Alexander, Lords Cobham (Alexander) (dormant, *NEP*), Loder-Symonds, Lord Macmillan *(NEP)*, Middlesex Hosp., Ward of Blyth, Bt. |
| MITEM ANIMUM AGRESTI SUB TEGMINE SCABRO | A gentle mind under a rough rural covering. Charles d'Amboise of Chaumont, Marshal of France, d. 1510, nephew of Cardinal Amboise. |
| MITIS ET FORTIS | Gentle and brave. Campbell-Orde, Bts., Orde. |
| MITJAR QATL MIRBUK | An airfield never beaten. RAF station, Luqa, Malta. |
| MITTE PENSA DURA | Send hard and weighty matters. Lord Tucker (Life Baron). |
| MITTO QUO POSTULAT USUS | I send where her use demands. 5604 Fighter Control Unit, RAAF (badge a falcon on a gauntlet). |
| MODERATA DURANT | Moderate things endure. Irvine. |
| MODERATION IS MY GLORY | Fitzhugh. |
| MODICE AUGETUR MODICUM | A little is increased by degrees. Lords Forres (Williamson), Williamson of Hutchinfield. |
| MODUS ET ORDO | Method and order. Edward IV of England. |
| MOENIBUS CREDE LIQUEIS (LIT.) | Believe (*or* Trust) in watery ramparts. Motto is thus rendered in arms illustration in *B.L.G.*, 1952, but more correct form would appear to be *Moenibus crede ligneis*, 'Trust to wooden walls'. Clarke of Achareidh, Nairn. |
| MOLIRE MOLENDO | By moving to move. Millfield Sch. |
| MON DESIRE LOYALTÉ | My wish is loyalty. Middlemore, Bts. |
| MON DIEU EST MA ROCHE | My God is my rock. Lords Fermoy (Roche), Roch, Roche. |

| | |
|---|---|
| MON DIEU, MON ROI ET MA PATRIE | My God, my king and my country. Kirwan. |
| MON DROIT | My right. Ingilby. |
| MON MAM CYMRU | Mona, mother of Wales. Anglesey CC. Mona was the old name for Anglesey, the sacred island of the Britons which was captured by the Roman governor Suetonius and all the priests slain at their altars. Motto quoted by Giraldus Cambrensis in 1188 in *Itinerary through Wales*. |
| MON SANG TEINT LES BANNIÈRES DE FRANCE | My blood stains the banners of France. Chateaubriand (François-René de Chateaubriand (1768–1848), famous French writer). |
| MONE SALE | Advice with wit. Lords Emly (Monsell) *(NEP)*, Viscount Monsell. |
| MONEMUS ET MUNIMUS | Let us watch and ward. Monmouth, Bor. of. |
| MONENDO DEFENDO | Warn to defend. No. 3700 (Co. of Middlesex) Radar Reporting Unit, RAAF. |
| MONEO ET MUNIO | I advise and I defend. Lords Banbury of Southam, Dalrymple, Leigh of Thorpe Satchville. |
| MONERE ALACER MORERE ACER | Swift to warn, sharp to bite. 3620 Co. of Norfolk Fighter Control Unit, RAAF. |
| MONERE DUCERE ET FERIRE | To find, lead and strike. No. 926 Signals Unit, RAF. |
| MONITI MELIORA SEQUAMUR | Let us, being admonished, follow better things (from Virgil, *Aeneid* iii. 188). Mahon, Bt. |
| MONITUS MUNITUS | Forewarned, forearmed. Horn, Horne. |
| MONSTRANT REGIBUS ASTRA VIAM | The stars show the way to kings. King John II of France, 1319–64, a singularly inappropriate motto, since he was captured at Poitiers in 1356 by the Black Prince, and being unable to pay his ransom, returned to die in captivity in England. Ref. in motto is to the Three Kings or Wise Men en route to Bethlehem. John is treated by Edouard Perroy, *La Guerre de Cent Ans*, in an unintentionally humorous manner. 'His gaoler [i.e. Edward III] became fond of him.' |
| MONSTRARE VIAM | To show the way. No. 218 Maintenance Unit, RAF. |
| MONSTRAT ITER | It shows the way. Pedro I, King of Portugal, 1357–67. Allusion to Star of Bethlehem device. |
| MONTE ALTO | From a high hill. Moat, Nowat. |
| MONTES EXCELSI REFUGIO | The high hills for a refuge. North Cotswold (Glos.) RDC. |
| MONTES UNDE AUXILIUM MEUM | The hills whence cometh my help (Psalm 121:1). Keswick (Cumb.) UDC. |
| MONTIS INSIGNIA CALPE | The insignia of the Calpe mountain (Calpe, now Gibraltar, one of the two Pillars of Hercules, at western entrance to the Mediterranean, Abyla being the other on the African side). The Essex Regt., 12th Foot, the Suffolk Regt. (ref. to cap badge of Castle and Key, with scroll inscribed above, Gibraltar; Latin motto is on scroll beneath). 39th Foot, Dorsetshire Regt., 58th Foot, Northamptonshire Regt. (By War Office instruction, 30 |

January 1900, all regiments having a representation of the Castle of Gibraltar in their badges had to show the correct pattern of the Castle as having three turrets with the key suspended below the central gateway. This pattern was that shown on (Spanish) seal of Gibraltar granted in 1502 and subsequently on coinage of Gibraltar, 202 years before the British conquest.)

| | |
|---|---|
| MONTJOYE SAINT DENIS | The war-cry of the Kings of France (St Denis being the patron saint of France). |
| MOOSA ASWARJITA | 419 Sq., RCAF. Badge is a moose apparently attacking. |
| MORA TRAHIT PERICULUM | Delay brings danger. Suckling. |
| MORE LIGHT | Lords Russell of Liverpool. |
| MORE LIGHT, MORE POWER | Shoreditch, London Bor. of. |
| MORE MAJORUM | In the manner of our ancestors. Colyton Parish Council, Kirby. |
| MORE OPTIMO EXERCEMUR | We train in the best tradition. No. 8 Flying Training Sch., RAF. |
| MORES ANTE NOMEN | Manners before a name (i.e. fame). Lindsay-Hogg, Bts. |
| MORES COMPONUNT HOMINEM | Manners compose a man. Dixon of Astle, Bts. |
| MORES MELIORES METALLO | Manners are better than metal. Cusack-Smith, Bts. |
| MORIBUS ANTIQUIS | With ancient manners. Moore of Colchester, Bts., Throckmorton, Bts. |
| MORIBUS ANTIQUIS PAREAMUS | Let us obey ancient manners. Bungay (Suffolk) UDC. |
| MORIBUS CIVILIS | As a citizen in manners. Tynemouth Sch., 1961. |
| MORIBUS FORTUNA VINCITUR | Fortune is vanquished by manners. Llewellyn of Bwllfa, Bts. |
| MORIENDO VIVAM | By dying I live. Shakerley, Bts. |
| MORIENS CANO | Dying I sing. Cobbe. Ref. is to swans in the arms (cob is a male swan), which are supposed to sing only when dying, hence the expression, swan-song. |
| MORIENS SED INVICTUS | Dying but unconquered. Gamble, Gammell. |
| MORIER PRO MEIS | I might die for my own. Pulling. |
| MORS AEQUAT OMNIA | Death levels all things. Used in Rome in funerals of great personages. |
| MORS ANTE DEDECORA | Death before disgrace. Davie-Thornhill. |
| MORS AUT HONORABILIS VITA | Either death, or life with honour. Joyce. |
| MORS AUT VITA DECORA | Either death or honourable life. Dempster, Hall-Dempster. |
| MORS CELERRIMA HOSTIBUS | Very swift death to the enemy, 401 Sq., RCAF, formed 1937 in Canada. |
| MORS CHRISTI MORS MORTIS MIHI | Christ's death is to me the death of death. Boothby, Bts. |
| MORS GLORIA FORTI | Death is glory to the strong. Bradney, co. Monmouth. |

| | |
|---|---|
| MORS JANUA VITAE | Death is the gate of life. Brograve, Davenport, HMS *Valhalla* (these words appear on the doors through which coffins pass at Golders Green Crematorium, N. London). |
| MORS LEVIOR QUAM DEDECUS | Death is lighter than disgrace. Allpress. |
| MORS LUPI AGNIS VITA | The death of the wolf is the life of the lamb. Ouseley, Bts., Rendell. |
| MORS POTIOR MACULA | Death rather than infamy. Chamberlayne, Nutting, Bts. |
| MORS ULTIMA LINEA RERUM | Death is the last goal of things (from Horace). Norris of Hackney. |
| MORT EN DROIT | Death in the right. Plunkett-Ernle-Erle-Drax. |
| MORT VIE LIES | Death and life, bound together. Jean de Morvilliers, d. 1577, Chancellor of France. |
| MORTEM AUT TRIUMPHUM | Death or triumph. Clifton of Lytham, co. Lancs. |
| MORTEM HOSTIBUS | We bring death to the enemy. 357 Sq., RAF. |
| MORTEM NON DEDECUS | Death not disgrace. Oldnall. |
| MORTON SE RÉVEILLE | Morton awakes. Lord Morton of Henryton, Life Baron. |
| MOS LEGEM REGIT | Custom rules the law. Lord Anslow (Mosley) *(NEP)*, Mosley, Bts., Lords Ravensdale (Mosley). |
| MOULT ME TARDE | Much I long. Philip le Hardi, Duke of Burgundy, *c.*1404. |
| MOVEO ET PROFICIOR | I move and I succeed. Knox, Earls of Ranfurly (Knox), Wells. |
| MUI NOBRE E SEMPRE LEAL CIDADELE LISBOA | Very noble and always loyal city of Lisbon. Lisbon, City of. |
| MULLAC A BOO | Victory for the Duns (war-cry of the sept of O'Duinne). Doyne, Dunne. |
| MULLACHAR A BUADH | (Translation uncertain, but *Mullachar* might be a corruption of a place name.) Fitzgerald, Knight of Kerry, Bts. |
| MULTA TULI FECIQUE | I have endured and done much. Arkwright, co. Derbys. (family descended from Sir Richard Arkwright, inventor of the spinning frame). |
| MULTI PERTRANSIBUNT ET AUGEBITUR SCIENTIA | Many shall pass through and learning shall be increased (motto based on Daniel 12, and refers to Gray's and Lincoln's Inns). Holborn, London Bor. of. |
| MULTI SOCIETATE TUTIORES | Many are safer in the society. Alliance Assurance Co. Ltd. |
| MULTIS DOMUS | Home to many. RAF station, Innsworth. |
| MULTOS SUSTENTARE | To sustain many. RAF station, Innsworth. |
| MULTUM IN PARVO | Much in little. Rutland CC, 1950. |
| MUNDUS MEA PROVINCIA | The world is my province. Lord Rusholme (Palmer). |
| MURUS AENEUS CONSCIENTIA SANA | A sound conscience is a wall of brass. Lord Ashton (Williamson) *(NEP)*, Loder, Bts., Lumley, Maples, Earls of Scarborough (Lumley), Lords Wakehurst (Loder), Williamson. |

| | |
|---|---|
| MURUS AHENEUS ESTO | Be thou a wall of brass. Macleod, Reynell, Bts. |
| ʍUSARUM TEMPLA COLAMUS | We preserve the temples of the muses. Museums Assn. |
| MUSTER | No. 3 Co. of Devon Maritime Unit, RAAF. |
| MUTARE FIDEM NESCIO | I cannot break faith. Outram, Bts. |
| MUTARE NON EST MEUM | It is not mine (i.e. my nature) to change. Frewen. |
| MUTARE SPERNO | I scorn to change. Hobhouse, Lefroy (Lefroys were a Huguenot family who came to England *c.*1589 from Cambrai during Spanish persecution of religion. Motto therefore refers to refusal to change faith), Singleton. |
| MUTARE VEL TIMERE SPERNO | I scorn to change or fear. Barnes, Dukes of Beaufort (Fitzroy Somerset), Bolton Sch., Bolton, Bythesea, Lever, Viscount Leverhulme (Lever), Little Lever UDC, Lords Raglan (Somerset), Somerset. |
| MUTAS INGLORIUS ARTES | Not glorious (*or* ambitious) to the silent arts. Halford, formerly Vaughan, Bts. (motto comes from Virgil, *Aeneid* xii. 397, as 1st Bt., Sir Henry Vaughan, attained highest eminence in practice of medicine). |
| MUTUA CONTENTIO VINCIT | If we get together we can cure you. Medical Rehabilitation Unit, RAF, Headley Court. |
| MY HOPE IS CONSTANT IN THEE | Macdonald. The Macdonald chief was Lord of the Isles (title now borne by the Prince of Wales). Ref. is to King Robert Bruce's confidence in the Macdonald. Sir Walter Scott expressed it thus in his poem 'The Lord of the Isles', where Bruce says:<br>'Lord of the Isles, my trust in thee<br>Is firm as Ailsa rock.' |
| MY LIFE IS HIS WHO GAVE IT | Jehangir, Bts. |
| MY PRINCE AND MY COUNTRY | Lords Harris, Harris of Brackenburgh Tower. |
| MY TRUST IS IN GOD ALONE | Clothworkers' Co., inc. 1480, Sutton Valence Sch., Maidstone, Kent (founded 1576 by William Lambe, mem. of Clothworkers' Co.). |

# N

| | |
|---|---|
| N'Y DESSUZ N'Y DESSOUZ | Neither above nor below. Troyte-Bullock. |
| N'OUBLIEZ | Do not forget. Dukes of Montrose (Graham). |
| NA AHYSWAR NAG OWNEH | Neither rash nor fearful (Cornish). Dyer. |
| NA BEÁN D'ON CHAT GUN LAMHAINN | Touch not the cat but a glove. Macpherson of Pitmain. |
| NA MNOZOTVI NEHLEDTE | Never regard their numbers (Czech). 311 Sq., RAF (Czechoslovak). |
| NABBATH HIG HORDERN AC GOD HIC FETT | Hordern. |
| NATION SHALL SPEAK PEACE UNTO NATION | British Broadcasting Corporation. |
| NATURAE DISCERE MORES | To learn the habits of nature. Linnaean Soc. |
| NATURA POTENTIOR ARS | Nature is the more powerful art. Titian, *c.*1487–1576 (greatest Venetian Painter). |
| NATURAM AD USUM TRACTAMUS | We treat nature according to use. Northampton Coll. of Advanced Tech. (since 1966, The City University, London). |
| NAUTAE FIDA | Faithful to the sailor. Sirr. |
| NAUTIS NAVIBUSQUE | For sailors and ships. Milford Haven Conservancy Bd. |
| NAVEM MERCIBUS IMPLERE | Fill the ship with goods. Runcorn (Ches.) UDC, 1956. |
| NAY JE DROIT | Have I not right. Ralph, Lord Cromwell, Lord High Treasurer 1434–44 (see *B.P.* 1970). |
| NE A META OCULOS AVERTAM | I shall not take my eyes from the goal. Neame, co. Kent. |
| NE CEDE ARDUIS | Do not give in to difficulties. Troubridge, Bts., Wailes-Fairbairn, Welch, Bts. |
| NE CEDE MALIS | Do not yield to misfortunes. Earls of Albemarle (Keppel), Bowlby, Bts., Doig, Herne Bay (Kent) UDC, Keppel, Tregarthen. |
| NE CEDE MALIS, SED CONTRA | Yield not to misfortunes, on the contrary meet them with fortitude. Viscount Canning, Lords Garvagh (Canning), Lords Stratford. |
| NE CEDO MALO | I do not yield to evil. Adami. |
| NE INVITI OTIENTUR | Lest unwillingly they are idle. National Dock Labour Bd. |
| NE ME TOGUES IL PEUT | Do not touch me, he can. Philippa of Gueldres, wife of René II, Duke of Lorraine. |
| NE OBLIVISCARIS | Do not forget. Dukes of Argyll (Campbell), Campbell, Campbell Coll., Belfast, founded 1894. |
| NE OUBLIE(Z) | Do not forget. Barclay-Grahame of Morphie, Graham, Grehan, Dukes of Montrose (Graham). |

| | |
|---|---|
| NE PARCAS NE SPERNAS | Neither spare nor scorn. Lamont. |
| NE QUID FALSI | Nothing false. Wollaston. |
| NE QUID NIMIS | Not too much. Godwin-Austin (it was after a member of this family, Henry Haversham Godwin-Austin, that Peak K2, the second highest summit of the Himalayas, was named), Lords Glenavy (Campbell), Hubert (formerly Smith), Reynard, Sherbrooke, Threlfall. |
| NE QUIS IMPUNE PRAETERITO | They shall not pass with impunity. No. 18 Group HQ, RAF (retitled HQ., Northern Maritime Air Region). |
| NE SUPRA MODUM SAPERE | Be not wise overmuch. Newport, Bt. |
| NE TE QUAESIVERIS EXTRA | Seek nothing beyond your sphere. Hewett, Hewitt. |
| NE TENTA VEL PERFICE (or NE TENTA VEL PERFICITE) | Attempt not or accomplish. Hill, Bts. |
| NE TENTES AUT PERFICE | Attempt not or accomplish. Marquesses of Downshire (Hill), Electric Telegraph Co., Faudel-Phillips, Bts., Faunce, Fayrer, Bts., Hill, Morgan of Green Street, Bts., Tangye, Bts. |
| NE TIME CREDE TANTUM | Do not fear, believe so much. Kealy. |
| NE TOTUM IMPLEAT ORBEM | Lest it fill the whole world. Marc Antonio Colonna, d. 1584, commanded Papal soldiers at Lepanto in 1571 when Turkish fleet was beaten. |
| NE TRAVERSE PAS LE PONT | Do not cross the bridge. Briggs. Bt. |
| NE UNQUAM CESSERIS | Never cease. Foyle Coll., Londonderry. |
| NE VILE FANO | Bring nothing vile to the temple. Earls of Westmorland (Fane) (play on surname Fane). |
| NE VILE VELIS (or NE VILE) | Do not wish anything base (play on surname Neville, great medieval house now represented by the Marquesses of Abergavenny), (Neville)), Lords Braybrooke (Neville), Fetherstonhaugh, Earls of Halsbury (Giffard), Nevile, Neville, Usher, Ussher. |
| NEC ARROGO NEC DUBITO | I neither abrogate nor hesitate. Assheton. |
| NEC ASPERA TERRENT | Difficulties do not daunt. Bowater of Friston, Bts., Hardman of Clough Hall, Johnson of New York, Order of the Guelph, Honourable Artillery Co., Rice, Tyler, 3rd Foot (The Buffs–East Kent Regt.). 8th Foot (Liverpool Regt.), 14th Foot (W. Yorkshire Regt.), 25th Foot (KOSB), 27th Foot (Light Co. Royal Inniskilling Fusiliers), The King's (Liverpool Regt.), 3rd (King's Own) Light Dragoons, Royal Military Coll., Sandhurst, 1812. |
| NEC CITO NEC TARDE | Neither swiftly nor slowly. Marshall of Patterdale Hall. |
| NEC CUPIAS, NEC METUAS | Neither desire, nor fear. Earls of Hardwicke (Yorke), Yorke. |
| NEC CURO NEC CAREO | I neither care nor lack. Macrae of Ballimore. |
| NEC DEFICIT ALTER | Nor let another be wanting. Roddam. |
| NEC DEGENERO | I do not degenerate. Joynt. |
| NEC DESIT VIRTUS | Nor let valour be wanting. Furse. |

| | |
|---|---|
| NEC DIU NEC FRUSTRA | Not long nor in vain. Knowles. |
| NEC FLATA NEC DEJECTA | Neither overjoyed nor dejected. Northmore. |
| NEC FERRO NEC IGNE | Neither by sword nor by fire. Appleby (Westmorland), Bor. of. |
| NEC FLUCTU NEC FLATU | Neither by wave nor by wind. Burnet, Burnett-Stuart. |
| NEC FLUCTU NEC FLATU MOVETUR | Not moved by flood or wind. Parker. |
| NEC IN ARIDO DEFIT | Nor is he deficient in dry matters. Green-Emmott. |
| NEC INVIDEO | Nor do I envy. Gardner. |
| NEC MALE NOTUS EQUES | A knight not badly known. Southwell. |
| NEC MENS INFERIORA SORTI | Nor is my mind inferior to my lot. The Elector of Hanover before he became George I of Great Britain. |
| NEC METUAS, NEC OPTES | Neither fear nor desire. Coddington. |
| NEC OPPRIMERE NEC OPPRIMI | Neither to oppress nor to be oppressed. Kynnersley, Scott-Moncrieff of Basford Hall, Sneyd. |
| NEC PARVIS SISTO | I do not continue in small matters. Batho, Bts., De Bath, Bts., De Burgh of West Drayton. |
| NEC PLURIBUS IMPAR | Not unequal to many. Louis XIV of France (1638–1715) (Le Roi Soleil, the sun having been his emblem from birth, was conceived almost by accident; *Louis XIV*, by Vincent Cronin). |
| NEC PRECE, NEC PRETIO | Neither by entreaty nor by reward. Bateman, Lords Cottesloe (Freemantle), Hanbury. |
| NEC QUAERERE, NEC SPERNERE HONOREM | Neither to seek nor to despise honour. Viscount Bolingbroke (St John), Boughey, Bts., Fletcher, St John. |
| NEC REGE NEC POPULO SED UTRIUSQUE | Neither for king nor for people but for both. Rolle. |
| NEC SINIT ESSE FEROS | It (education) does not suffer then to be brutal (Ovid, *Tristia* II. ix. 47). Grazebrook, Langham, Bts. (crest of these families is a boar's head muzzled). |
| NEC SORTE NEC FATO | Neither by lot nor by fate. William III of Orange, Stadtholder of the Netherlands, 1672. |
| NEC SPE NEC METU | Neither by hope nor by fear. Konig. |
| NEC TE QUAESIVERIS EXTRA | Do not seek anything more. Carr-Ellison. |
| NEC TEMERE NEC TIMIDE | Neither rashly nor timidly. Abbot, Addenbrooke, Aldworth, Barnard Castle (Durham) UDC, Barne, Bent, Blair, Blosse, Booth, Earls of Bradford (Bridgeman), Bridgeman, Buckle, Buckeley, Bulley, Chinnery, Chinnery-Haldane, Cannock (Staffs.) UDC, Dukes of Cleveland (Powlett), Cotterel, Fletcher-Vane, Bts., Forbes, Graham, Guest, Heaton, Holden, Homer, Hyde, Bt., Joyce, Lords Inglewood (Fletcher-Vane), Ludlow, Mallet, Market Harborough (Leics.) UDC, Milward, Mitchell, Earls of Munster (Fitz-Clarence), Neale, Oswestry (Salop) RDC, Owen, Pemberton, Purvis, Richards, Sandford, Simeon, Bts., Travers, Vane, Wakeman, Walker, Lords Western (*B.Ext.P.*), Lords Barnard, Lynch-Blosse, Bt., Western, Bts., Williams-Bulkeley. |

| | |
|---|---|
| NEC TIMEO NEC SPERNO | I neither fear nor despise. Viscount Boyne (Hamilton-Russell), Glover, Greene of Kilkea Lodge, Pagen, Sheppard, Bts. (Cotton-Sheppard), Skinner, Bts., Smyth, Bts., 110 Sq., RAF (I neither fear nor spurn). |
| NEC TIMERE NE TEMERE | Neither timidly nor rashly. Rashleigh. |
| NEC TIMIDUS NEC TIMIDUS | Not timid, not timid. Guthrie of Craigie. |
| NEC TRISTE NEC TREPIDUM | Neither sad nor fearful. Trist. |
| NEC VI NEC ASTUTIA | Not by force nor by cunning. Waring. |
| NEC VIRTUS NEC COPIA DESUNT | Neither virtue nor plenty are lacking. Macclesfield (Ches.), Bor. of. |
| NEGLIGIT IMA | It disdains low things. Matteo di Capua, High Admiral of Naples. |
| NEMINEM METUE INNOCENS | Being innocent, fear no one. Eyre. |
| NEMINEM RECTE FACIENDO TIMEAS | You may fear no one while acting rightly. Wells of Kent. |
| NEMINEM TIMERE | Fear none. Gregory, Bt. |
| NEMO AD IMPOSSIBILE TENETUR | No one is held to impossibilities. Jean de Luxembourg, Comte de Ligny, d. 1482 (motto refers to his emblem of a camel sinking under its burden). |
| NEMO ME IMPUNE LACESSIT | No one provokes me with impunity. Irwin, Macgeough Bond, Nettles, Order of St Andrew of Scotland, Order of the Thistle, The Royal Scots (Lothian Regt.), 1st Volunteer Bn. The Black Watch, 2nd Royal Lanark Militia, 9th (Glasgow Highland) Bn. Territorials, 42nd Foot (1st Bn. The Black Watch-Royal Highlanders), 78th Lancashire (Manchester) Rifle Volunteer Corps, 79th Foot-Queens Own Cameron Highlanders, 91st Foot (1st Bn. Princess Louise's Argyll & Sutherland Highlanders). |
| NEMO NON PARATUS | No one unprepared. 78 Sq., RAF. |
| NEMO SIBI NASCITUR | No one is born for himself alone. Coles Patteson, Scott. |
| NERTH GWLAD EI GWYBODAU | A country's strength is her knowledge. Univ. Coll. of South Wales & Monmouthshire. |
| NESCIA FALLERE VITA | A life unable to make a slip. Conyngham Greene. |
| NESCIT OCCASUM | It knows not setting. Order of the North Star (Sweden). |
| NESCIT VOX MISSA REVERTI | When a word is once spoken it cannot be recalled. Halsey, Bts. |
| NEU COMES IRE RECUSO | And I do not refuse to go as a companion. Newcome (play on the surname). |
| NEVE FESTINES NEVE LANGUESCAS | Neither hasten nor dawdle. Lang of Toronto. |
| NEVER A BACKWARDS STEP | Lord Thompson of Fleet. |
| NEVER BEHIND | Crewe (Ches.), Bor. of. |
| NEVER DETERRED | Air Despatch Letter Service Sq., RAF. |

| | |
|---|---|
| NEVER FAILING | 98 Sq., RAF (badge is a Cerberus or three-headed dog, because sq. claimed to have barred the enemy's way, front and rear, during German retreat in 1918; motto commemorates message of congratulation received from GOC, 1918). |
| NEVER GIVE IN | Lawrence of Lucknow, Bts. |
| NEVER WONNE NE NEVER SHALL | Reigate (Surrey), Bor. of, 1951. |
| NEW ZEAL AND HONOUR | Freyberg (1st Baron Freyburg was Gov. Gen. of New Zealand). |
| NI UNDAS NI VIENTOS | Neither water nor winds (allusion to storm-beaten oak, badge of King Alfonso II of Portugal, 1248–78, who after much trouble with Castile succeeded in establishing Portuguese frontier at the Guadiana river). |
| NID BYD BYD WYBODAETH | A world without knowledge is no world. Univ. Coll. of Wales, Aberystwyth, 1928. |
| NID CADARN OND BRODYDDE | Fellowship alone is strong. Merthyr Tydfil (Glam.), Bor. of. |
| NID DA LLE GELLII GWELL | It is not good that can be better. Williams of Glyndwr, Bt. |
| NID GRYM HEB GREFFT | Craftsmanship is essential for might. No. 48 Maintenance Unit, RAF. |
| NIET PRATEN MAAR DOEN | Actions not words. 322 Sq., RAF (Dutch), 1943. |
| NIET ZONDER ARBYT | Nothing without labour. No. 3 Group HQ, RAF. Dutch motto adopted to commemorate the Group's flying over Holland on way to Germany and to help given to Allied aircrews who landed in Holland. |
| NIHIL AMANTI DURUM | Nothing is hard for a lover. Reid. |
| NIHIL CARITATE CLARUS | Nothing clear for charity. Aston Charities Trust Ltd. |
| NIHIL CELERIUS | Nothing swifter. No. 367 Signals Unit, RAF. |
| NIHIL FORTIUS | Nothing is stronger. 136 Sq., RAF. |
| NIHIL HUMANA MOROR | I do not delay at human things. Albright. |
| NIHIL IMPENETRABILE | Nothing impenetrable. 184 Sq., RAF. |
| NIHIL NOS EFFUGIT | Nought escapes us. 206 Sq., RAF. |
| NIHIL NOS LATET | Nothing escapes us. 683 Sq., RAF. |
| NIHIL SEMPER FLORET | Nothing flourishes for ever. Schilizzi. |
| NIHIL SINE DEO | Nothing without God. Dawes, Peterson. |
| NIHIL SINE DOCTRINA | Nothing without learning. No. 16 Operational Training Unit, RAF. |
| NIHIL SINE LABORE | Nothing without labour. Berry, Cator, D'Abreu, Eator, Templer, Thearle, Wakeley, Bts. |
| NIHIL SINE NUMINE | Nothing without Providence. Sleeman. |
| NIHIL TIMEO | I fear nothing. 502 Ulster (B) Sq., AAF (Red Hand of Ulster as badge). |
| NIHIL VOLENTI DURUM | Nothing hard to him who wishes. Jones. |

| | |
|---|---|
| NIHILO NISI CRUCE | Nothing but the Cross. Barbour. |
| NIL ACTUM CREDO SI QUID SUPERSIT AGENDUM | I think nothing done if anything remains undone. 345 Sq., RAF. |
| NIL ACTUM SI QUID AGENDUM | Nothing has been done if aught remains to be done. Clavering, Bt. |
| NIL ADMIRARI | Not to admire. Appach, Bolingbroke, Carew, Earls of Clare (Fitzgibbon) *(B.Ext.P.)*. |
| NIL AMPLIUS ORO | I pray for nothing more. Snead Cox. |
| NIL ARDUUM | Nothing is difficult. Brickwood, Bts., Gordon of Banff. |
| NIL CLARIUS ASTRIS | Nothing is brighter than the stars. Bailie, Baillie. |
| NIL CONSCIRE SIBI | To have a conscience free from guilt. Biss, Bullock, Carew, Bts., Collingwood, Finch, French, Gape, Lords Hillingdon (Mills), Michel, Rogers, Rothwell, Savile, Sibthorp, Walker, Webb, Earls of Winchelsea & Nottingham (Finch-Hatton). |
| NIL CONSCIRE SIBI PALLESCERE CULPA | To be conscious to oneself, to grow pale for no crime (Horace, *Ep.* i. 1. 60). Sanders. |
| NIL DESPERANDUM | Never despair. Adams, co. Staffs., Anson, Bts., Anson Bn., Royal Naval Div., Coddington, Bts., Eastwood, Forester-Walker, Bts., Gradwell, Grisewood, Hayes, Bts., Hedley-Dent, HMS *Dauntless*, Knill, Bts., Lee, Earls of Lichfield (Anson), McCalmont, Musgrove, Bt., Staveley, Stewart of Ramelton, Bts., Walker of Teignmouth, Williams of Tregullow, Bts. |
| NIL DESPERANDUM AUSPICE DEO | Never despair under the auspices of God. Jackson-Barstow, Sunderland (Durham), Co. Bor. of. |
| NIL DESPERANDUM CHRISTO DUCE | Never despair with Christ as leader. Hanbury. |
| NIL DESPERO ARDUA VINCO | I do not despair, I conquer difficulties. Lord Wade. |
| NIL DIMIDIUM EST | Nothing is half (done). Lord Heyworth. |
| NIL LYNCEA LATEBIT | Nothing shall be hidden from Lynceus. Central Interpretation Unit, RAF (title changed 1974 to Air Reconnaissance Intelligence Centre, function, examination of air photography with badge of lynx's face, hence motto). |
| NIL MAGNUM NISI BONUM | Nothing is great unless good. Cooper, Bts. |
| NIL MOROR ICTUS | I heed not blows. Money-Kyrle. |
| NIL MORTALIBUS ARDUUM | Nothing is hard for mortals (from Horace, *Odes* I. iii. 37). Kater. |
| NIL NISI CRUCE | Nothing unless by the Cross. Beresford, Beresford-Pierse, Bts., Lords Decies (De la Poer Beresford), De la Poer, Gully, Pack-Beresford, Marquesses of Waterford (De la Poer Beresford). |
| NIL NISI HONESTUM | Nothing unless honest. Philips of Weston, Bts. |
| NIL NISI JURANTIBUS | Nothing except to those who take oath. Hughes-Hallett. |
| NIL NISI QUOD HONESTUM | Nothing except honest. Leather. |

| | |
|---|---|
| NIL NISI VERITAS | Nothing but the truth. Inst. of Pathology and Tropical Medicine, RAF. |
| NIL NOBIS OBSTARE POTEST | Nothing can stop us. 79 Sq., RAF. |
| NIL NOS TREMEFACIT | Nothing makes us tremble. 55 Sq., RAF. |
| NIL OBSTARE POTEST | Nothing can withstand. 514 Sq., RAF. |
| NIL PENNA SED USUS | Not the quill but its use. Gilmer, Gilmour, Bts. |
| NIL SINE AQUA | Nothing without water. S. Staffs Waterworks Co. |
| NIL SINE DEO | Nothing without God. Awdry of Notton, Wilts., Reeves. |
| NIL SINE LABORE | Nothing without labour. Atkinson, Beecham, Bts., Dax, Edgar, Bt., Kleinwort, Bts. |
| NIL SINE LABORE VIRET | Nothing flourishes without labour. Abram. |
| NIL SINE NUMINE | Nothing without the Deity. Blundell, Harmood-Banner, Bts., Weld of Lulworth. |
| NIL SINE STUDIO | Nothing without study. Kleinwort, Benson Ltd., 1962. |
| NIL SISTERE CONTRA | Nothing to oppose us. Lords Carnock (Nicholson), Nicholson of Carnock, Stewart of Greenock. |
| NIL SOLIDUM | There is nothing unchangeable. Goldie, Williams of Dorset, Williams of Bridehead, Bts. |
| NIL SPERNO, MIROR, METUO | I spurn nothing, wonder at nothing, fear nothing. Daniell. |
| NIL TEMERE | Not rashly. Balfour, co. Perth, Lords Kinross (Balfour), Tennyson, Tennyson-D'Encourt. |
| NIL TEMERE, NEQUE TIMORE | Nothing rashly nor with fear. Berney, Bts. |
| NIL TIBI | Nought for thee. Campbell (formerly of Tullichewan, Dumbarton). |
| NIL TIME | Fear nothing. 501 Co. of Gloucester (E) Sq., AAF. |
| NIL TIMENDUM AUSPICIIS NOS | Nothing is to be feared with (favourable) auspices. Sunderland Building Soc., 1963. |
| NIL TIMERE NEC TEMERE | Neither to fear nor to be rash. Combe of Cobham Park, Surrey. |
| NILI NOMEN ROBORIS OMEN | The name of the Nile is an omen of strength. 47 Sq., RAF (served in both Russia and Sudan and badge is of demoiselle crane's head, bird found in both countries). |
| NISI ARDEAT | Unless it burns. Italian Literary Academy, Ardenti of Pisa. |
| NISI DOMINUS | Except the Lord (from Psalm 127:1). Compton, Hartbury. |
| NISI DOMINUS AEDIFICAVERIT | Unless the Lord shall have built. Rickmansworth (Herts.) UDC. |
| NISI DOMINUS CUSTODIERIT CIVITATEM | Unless the Lord shall guard the city. Halifax (W.R. Yorks.), Co. Bor. of. |
| NISI DOMINUS FRUSTRA | It is vain without the Lord. Canford Sch., Wimborne, Dorset, Chelsea, Royal Bor. of, Edinburgh, City of, Glenlola Collegiate Sch., Bangor, co. Down, Hinde, Inglis, Littleboy, Ripon, Wakefield & Bradford Diocesan |

|  | Training Coll., 1963, Roy. Alexandra & Albert Sch. Royal Wolverhampton Sch., Staffs., Wellington Sch., Som., 25th Foot (King's Own Scottish Borderers). |
|---|---|
| NISI DOMINUS PRO NOBIS | Except the Lord be on our side. RAF station, Kenley. |
| NITENDO | By trusting. Lords Kenilworth (Siddeley). |
| NITI FACERE EXPERIRI | To strive to do is to experience. Caldwell. |
| NITIMUR ET MUNITUR | We strive and it is fortified. Maconochie-Welwood. |
| NITOR DONEC SUPERO | I strive until I overcome. Russell of Charlton Park, Bts., Sharp of Heckondwike, Bts. |
| NITOR DONEC SUPERAVERO | I strive until I shall have overcome. No. 3 Sch. of Recruit Training, RAF. |
| NITOR IN ADVERSIS | I shine in adversity. Lewis, co. Glam., Raynsford, co. Lancs. |
| NITOR IN ADVERSUM | I contend against adversity. Gooding, Horner, Moore, Bts. |
| NO DEVIATION | Marine Craft Training Sch., RAF. |
| NO ODDS TOO GREAT | 67 Sq., RAF. |
| NO THORN, NO ROSE | Radcliffe. |
| NOBILIS EST IRA LEONIS | The wrath of the lion is noble. Broome, Buchanan-Jardine, Bts., Marquesses of Bute (Crighton-Stuart), Inglis, Piers, Bts. |
| NOBILIS IRA | Noble in anger. Creighton-Stuart, Stuart of Tillicoultry, Bts., Earls of Wharncliffe (Stuart-Wortley-Mackenzie). |
| NOBIS FLAMMA ACCENDENDA | We must kindle a flame. No. 51 Group HQ, RAF. |
| NOBIS HABITATIO FELIX | Our habitation is happy for us. Wilmslow (Ches.) UDC, 1951. |
| NOBIS OFFICIUM ALIIS USUS DEO GLORIA | A duty for us, a use for others, glory to God. Trustees for Methodist Church Purposes. |
| NOCET DIFFERE PARATIS | It harms to put off things prepared. Harris of Chepping Wycombe, Bts. |
| NOCTE VOLAMUS | We fly by night. Lords Deramore (De Yarburgh-Bateson). |
| NOCTES DIESQUE PRAESTO | I am ready by night and day. Murray. |
| NOCTIVIDUS | Seeing by night. 153 Sq., RAF. |
| NOCTOVAGA | Night wandering. 410 Sq., RCAF. |
| NOCTU DIUQUE VENAMUR | We may come by night or by day. 85 Sq., RAF. |
| NOCTURNA MORS | Death by night. 630 Sq., RAF. |
| NOCTURNI OBULAMBAMUS | We prowl by night. 96 Sq., RAF. |
| NODO FIRMO | With a firm knot. Harrington (the Harrington family of Harrington bore the heraldic device of a fret, termed their knot). |
| NOLENS NIHIL NOSSE | Not willing to have known nothing. Knowles. |
| NOLI ALTUM SAPERE SED TIME | Do not seek to know the height but fear. Hare of Docking Hall. |

| | |
|---|---|
| NOLI IRRITARE LEONEM | Irritate not the lion. Abbs, Underwood, Walsh. |
| NOLI IRRITARE LEONES | Do not exasperate the lions. Lyons, Penrice-Lyons. |
| NOLI JUDICARE | Do not judge. Lords Moyne (Guinness). |
| NOLI ME TANGERE | Touch me not. Graeme of Garvock, Wormald, 103 Sq., RAF. |
| NOLO SERVILE CAPISTRUM | I will not bear a servile halter. Marsh. |
| NOMEN EXTENDERE FACTIS | To promote one's name by deeds. Neeld. |
| NON ALIUNDE PENDERE | Not to depend on another direction. Coke, Coke-Steel. |
| NON ARTE SED MARTE | Not by art but by war. Naesmyth, Bts. |
| NON BOS IN LINGUA | No unfitness (*lit.* bull) in language. Sandars. |
| NON BUELVO SIN VENCER | I do not roar without conquering. Alessandro de Medici, 1st Duke (poisoned by another Medici). |
| NON CANTU SED ACTU | Not by singing but by acting. Gillman. |
| NON CATE SED CAUTE | Not cleverly but cautiously. Gatty. |
| NON CRAMBEM SED CARNEM | Not cabbage but meat. No. 13 Group HQ, RAF. Motto (with the words 'We want' implied) is intended to convey same idea as Russian Marshal Budenny's war-cry: 'We are not vegetarians.' |
| NON CRUX SED LUX | Not the Cross but its light. Black, Blair, Cramer, Griffiths. |
| NON DEERIT ALTER AUREUS | Another golden fruit shall not be wanting (Virgil, *Aeneid* vi. 143). Don-Wauchope, Bts., Gold. |
| NON DEFICIT ALTER | Another is not wanting. Algeo, Aljoy, Auldjo, Stainforth, Walwyn. |
| NON DEGENER | Not degenerated. Earls of Dundee (Scrymgeour-Wedderburn), Grindley, Kinlock of that Ilk, Bts., Kinglake of Saltmoor, Wedderburn. |
| NON DORMIT QUI CUSTODIT | The sentinel sleeps not. Coghill, Bts., Lords Glentanar (Coats), Gulliver, Louthian, M'Kellip, M'Killop, Myers, co. Essex, Shore of Norton Hall, Antonio Altoviti, Archbishop of Florence, d. 1573, James III, King of Scotland, Murdered after Battle of Sauchieburn, 1488. |
| NON DESERET ALTA | He will not leave the heights. Armand Jean Duplessis, Cardinal and Duc de Richelieu (1585–1642) (allusion to badge of an eagle looking down contemptuously on two serpents). |
| NON DUM | Not yet. Charles V, King of Spain and Holy Roman Emperor, 1500–58, referring to his youth (he was eighteen when he used this motto). |
| NON DUM IN AUGE | Not yet in zenith. Charles V, Holy Roman Emperor. |
| NON EST MORTALE QUOD OPTO | It is not mortal that I seek. Shiffner, Bts. |
| NON EST SIMILIS ILLI | None is like him. Eleanor of Austria, d. 1558, 2nd wife of Francis I and sister of Emperor Charles I (loved her husband but it was not reciprocated as marriage was of political convenience following Treaty of Cambrai). |

| | |
|---|---|
| NON EST VIVERE SED VALERE VITA | Life is not living, but health is life (Martial, *Epigrammata* VI. lxx). Royal Society of Medicine. |
| NON FALLENT PRAETEREUNTES | None shall pass unseen. No. 75 Wing HQ, RAF. |
| NON FALLO(R) | I am not deceived. Kennedy of Clowburn, Bt. |
| NON FECIMUS IPSI | We have not done these things ourselves. Duncombe, Pauncefort Duncombe, Bts. |
| NON GENERANT AQUILAE COLUMBAS | Eagles do not beget doves. Lempriere, Lords Rodney. |
| NON HAEC SINE NUMINE | These things are not without the Deity. Baker, Lords Dover (Agar-Ellis) *(NEP)*. |
| NON IGNOBILITER ANCILLARI | To serve not ignobly as a handmaid. Dental Training Establishment, RAF. |
| NON IN TENEBRIS | Not in the darkness. Martin, King of Aragon 1395–1410. |
| NON INFERIORA | Not inferior matters. Monro of Bearcroft, Bt. |
| NON INFERIORA SECUTUS | I have not followed inferior things. Bromley, Buchan, Buchan-Hepburn, Bts., Grant, Montford, Lords Tweedsmuir (Buchan), Marguerite de Valois (sister of Francis I, d. 1549 (m.(1) Duke of Alencon and (2) King of Navarre, grandmother of Henri IV, praised by Ronsard and other poets). |
| NON INTERIBUNT | They shall not perish. 275 Sq., RAF. |
| NON JURE DEFICIT | He is not wanting in right. Foulis, Bts. |
| NON LUMEN EFFUGIO | I shun not the light. Hewson. |
| NON MIHI NON TIBI SED NOBIS | Not for me, not for thee, but for us. Battersea, London Bor. of. |
| NON MIHI SED DEO ET REGI | Not for me but for God and the king. Crooke, Warren, Bts. |
| NON MIHI SED OMNIBUS | Not for me but for all. Warmington, Bts. |
| NON MIHI SED PATRIAE | Not for myself but for my country. Heycock, Hippisley, Loyd, Lord Overstone (Loyd) *(NEP)*, Spring, Springe. |
| NON MINIMA SED MAXIMA PETIMUS | We seek not the least but the greatest. Aycliffe Development Corp., co. Durham. |
| NON MINOR EST VIRTUS QUAM QUAERERE PARTA TUERI | To defend what you have gained is no less valour than to gain. Master. |
| NON MORITUR CUJUS FAMA VIVIT | He dies not whose fame lives. Congreve. |
| NON MULTI SED MULTA | Not many men but many deeds. 312 Sq., RAF (Czechoslovak). |
| NON NISI MALIS TERRORI | Not for terror except to the bad. King's Sch., Macclesfield. |
| NON NOBIS | Not unto us. Woodd. |
| NON NOBIS DOMINE | Not unto us, O Lord. Adopted by Henry V after victory of Agincourt, 1415. |
| NON NOBIS LABORAMUS | Not for ourselves do we labour. 517 Sq., RAF. |
| NON NOBIS SED OMNIBUS | Not for ourselves but for all. Ash, Ashe, North Walsham (Norfolk) UDC. |

| | |
|---|---|
| NON NOBIS SOLUM | Not for ourselves alone. Beckenham (Kent) UDC, Blayney, Eardley, Fardell, Fosbery, Jacob, Lawless, Lockett, Moss, Univ. Coll., Durham, Wilson, co. Westmorland, Worsley (Lancs.) UDC. |
| NON NOBIS SOLUM SED TOTI MUNDO NATI | Born not for ourselves alone, but for the whole world. Robinson. |
| NON NOBIS TANTUM NATI | Not so much born for ourselves (alone). Lee-Warner. |
| NON OBEST VIRTUTE SORS | Chance does not hinder virtue. Nisbet of Dean, Bts. |
| NON OMNIA SIBI HABEAT | Let him have not all things for himself. Bishop Grosseteste Coll., Lincoln. |
| NON OMNIS MORIAR | I shall not all die (Horace, *Odes* III. xxx. 6). Wimberley. |
| NON POUR HAINE | Not for hate. Alington, Anthony. |
| NON PRODIGUS NEQUE AVARUS | Neither prodigal nor mean. Levett-Prinsep. |
| NON PROGREDI EST REGREDI | Not to progress is to regress. Chigwell (Essex) UDC. |
| NON QUAE SUPER TERRAM | Not those things which are above earth. Cardinal François de Tournon, d. 1562 (had device of manna or heavenly bread, allusion to Christ as bread of life). |
| NON QUID SED QUO MODO | Not by whom but in what manner. Lords Howard De Walden, Lord Seaford, Earls of Suffolk (Howard), Thompson of Hartsbourne Manor, Bts. |
| NON RAPUI SED RECEPI | I have not taken by violence, but received. Cotterell, Bts. |
| NON RECUSO LABOREM | I do not refuse labour. Dover Coll., Kent. |
| NON REVERTAR INULTUS | I shall not return unavenged. Earls of Lisburne (Vaughan). |
| NON ROBORE SED SPE | Not by strength but by hope. Tippet, Vivian. |
| NON SANS DROIT | Not without right. Hart (formerly Shakespeare), William Shakespeare. It first appears in 1599 when Shakespeare obtained from Heralds' College a grant of arms in the name of his father, John Shakespeare, then still living. As motto, is not part of a grant of arms; possible that the poet chose it himself with his boast: 'Not marble or the brazen monuments of princes shall outlive this powerful rhyme.' All that we know is that motto appears on draft of the grant above a pen sketch of arms and crest. Draft is preserved in Heralds' College and we know that Shakespeare saw and approved it. There was some criticism in seventeenth century as to propriety of granting arms to players. Dethick, the Garter King of Arms, in his preamble to the grant, refers to honourable military service of the Shakespeares and it may be that he chose the motto in defence of his grant. If so, it is the most astonishing example of an unconscious prophecy. The motto is not used by the present Shakespeares who, like the poet, are of Warwickshire origin. For full details of grant, see Sir Sidney Lee's *Life of Shakespeare* and on origin of the name, 'a spearman', R. H. Reaney's *Dictionary of British Surnames*. |
| NON SCOLAE SED VITAE DISCIMUS | (saying of Cicero). We learn not from school but from life. Queen's Coll., Taunton, Devon. |

| | |
|---|---|
| NON SIBI | Not for himself. Warburton. RAF station, High Wycombe, Bucks. (Not for ourselves). |
| NON SIBI SED ALIIS | Not for himself but for others. White of Boulge Hall, Bts. |
| NON SIBI SED OMNIBUS | Not for oneself but for all. Ackworth Sch., Yorks., Royal Russell Sch., Croydon, 1853, Whitley Bay (Northumberland), Bor. of. |
| NON SIBI SED PATRIAE | Not for himself but for country. Baker, Evelegh, Field-Marsham, Fisher of Winton House, Freebridge Lynn RDC. Heppesley, Earls of Romney (Marsham), Thomlinson, 226 Sq., RAF (For country not for self). |
| NON SIBI SED PATRIAE NATUS | Born not for himself but for his country. Jodrell (formerly Lombe), Bts. |
| NON SIBI SED SUIS | Not for himself but for his own. Duppa De Uphaugh. |
| NON SIBI SED TOTI | Not for oneself but for all. Camden, London Bor. of, Hampstead, London Bor. of, Hampstead Volunteer Training Corps (later 7th Bn.), 1914, Inst. of Office Management, 1966, Stocker, Synge-Hutchinson, Bts., Wynne. |
| NON SINE CAUSA | Not without a cause. Dru Drury, Drury. |
| NON SINE FOENORE | Not without usury. Elena Lucrezia Corraro Piscopia of Venice, a profoundly learned lady who d. 1684 at age of 38. |
| NON SINE JURE | Not without right. Charter, Lord Jenkins (NEP), Leslie-Ellis. |
| NON SINE NUMINE | Not without the Deity. Lords Gifford, Green, Greene. |
| NON SINE PERICULO | Not without danger. Hodson-Mackenzie. |
| NON SINE PRAEDA | Not without booty. Echlin, Bts. |
| NON SINE PULVERE PALMA | A reward not without labour. Beresford-Peirse, Bts. |
| NON SOLUM INGENII VERUM ETIAM VIRTUTIS | Not only of intellect but also of virtue. Liverpool Coll. |
| NON SOLUM NOBIS | Not for ourselves only. Italian Literary Academy Amorevole of Verona, 81 Sq., RAF. |
| NON SUFFICIT ORBIS | The world is not enough. Bond, co. Dorset. |
| NON TEMERE | Not rashly. Balfour of Albury Lodge, Bt., Forbes of Edinglassie, Bt. |
| NON TEMERE CREDERE | Not to believe rashly. Lord Adrian, famous physicist. |
| NON TEMERE SED FORTITER | Not rashly but boldly. Bloxsome, Wallington. |
| NON TERRA SED AQUIS | Not by land but by waters. Bailey of Chaseley, co. Chester (has in the arms a lymphad or galley under full sail), Dunnet. |
| NON TIMEO SED CAVEO | I fear not but am cautious. Hewitson, Oakeley, Bts., Strachan, Symmonds. |
| NON TIMIDUS PRO PATRIA MEA | Not fearful for my country. Rawlins of Stoke Courcy. |
| NON TUA TE MOVEANT SED PUBLICA VOTA | Let not thine own, but the public wishes move thee. Alleyne, Bts. (sometimes moveant is omitted as in B.P. 1970). |

| | |
|---|---|
| NON VESTRA SED VOS | Not yours but you. St Chad's Coll., Durham, 1951. |
| NON VI SED ARTE | Not by force but by art. Earls Beatty. |
| NON VI, SED VIRTUTE | Not by violence but by virtue. Elphinstone of Logie, Bts., Ramsbottom, Viscount Soulbury (Ramsbotham). |
| NON VI VIRTUTE | Not by force but by virtue. Borrowes, Burrowes. |
| NON VIDERI, SED ESSE | Not to seem but to be. Hare, Bts. |
| NON VIS SED PRAEMIA VIRTUTIS | Not force but the rewards of virtue. Rayer. |
| NON VOX SED VOTUM | Not the voice but the wish. Magle, Nangle. |
| NONE SHALL ECLIPSE ME | HMS *Eclipse*, which had representation of an eclipse as her badge. |
| NONE SUCH | Epsom & Ewell (Surrey), Bor. of. |
| NONUM PREMATUR IN ANNUM | Let it be kept to the ninth year (part of Horace's advice to writers, in his *Ars Poetica* 388). Paynter, co. Cornwall. |
| NOS DIFFICULTATES NON TERRENT | Difficulties do not deter us. RAF station, Ballykelly. |
| NOS LABOREMUS UT SUPERENT ILLI | Let us work that they may triumph. No. 7 Sch. of Tech. Training, RAF. |
| NOS NOSTRAQUE DEO | We and ours to God. Lord Blachford (Rogers) *(NEP)*, Rogers. |
| NOS QUOQUE TELA SPARSIMUS | We also have scattered javelins. Claughton. |
| NOSCE ARMA TUA | Know thy weapons. No. 1 Air Observers' Sch., RAF. |
| NOSCE TE IPSUM | Know thyself. Ashfordby-Trenchard, Buck, Frazer, James, Lambert, Murray, Pendred, Pringle, Stanfield, Tindal, Tregonwell, Thompson of Nunwick Hall, Viscount Trenchard, Walford. |
| NOSTRO AUXILIO FERUINT | With our aid they strike. No. 719 Signals Unit, RAF. |
| NOSTRUM EST RURA TUERI | Ours it is to guard country matters. Clitheroe (Lancs.) RDC. |
| NOSTRUM VIRET ROBUR | Our strength is a green tree. Wood Green, London Bor. of. |
| NOT FOR KING OR COUNTRY BUT FOR BOTH | Roll, Bt. |
| NOT FOR OURSELVES ALONE | Barnes, London Bor. of. |
| NOT THE LAST | Smith-Ryland. |
| NOT WHY WE CAN'T BUT HOW WE CAN | The Baroness Swanborough (Isaacs) *(NEP)*. |
| NOTA BENE | Take careful note. Handling Sq., RAF. |
| NOTHING HAZARD, NOTHING HAVE | Grant Suttie, Bts. |
| NOTHING WITHOUT LABOUR | Haslingden (Lancs.), Bor. of. |
| NOURISSEZ L'ESPÉRANCE | Nourish hope. Grove-White. |
| NOUS MAINTIENDRONS | We will maintain. Howard-Bury, Earls of Suffolk & Berkshire (Howard). |

| | |
|---|---|
| NOUS TENONS LE DROIT | We hold the right. Studd. |
| NOUS TRAVAILLERONS EN ESPÉRANCE | We will labour in hope. Blackett, Blackett-Ord. |
| NOUS Y SERONS | We shall be there. 107 Sq., RAF. |
| NOUS Y SOMMES | Here we are. 342 Sq., RAF (French, formed 1941 in Syria). |
| NOVA ET VETERA | New and old. St Catherine's Coll., Oxford, 1963. |
| NOVAM QUAERERE SCIENTIAM LATIOREM PROSPECTUM | To seek new knowledge and horizons. Queen's Univ. Air Sq., RAFVR. |
| NOVOS AMICOS DUM PARAS VETERES COLES | While you prepare new friends, cherish the old. Barnard-Hankey. |
| NOW | 3504 Co. of Nottingham Fighter Control Unit, RAAF. |
| NOW THUS, NOW THUS | De Trafford, Milborne-Swinnerton-Pilkington, Bts., Pilkington. Trafford. Motto was in use before the sixteenth century; crest, of a thresher wielding his instrument, used by both Trafford and Pilkington. A legend relates both motto and crest to an incident in the Norman Conquest. Trafford was an Englishman who opposed the Normans. At length the latter crossed a river into Trafford's territory and came suddenly upon him. He disguised himself and went into his barn and acted as a thresher, exclaiming, 'Now thus, now thus', as if he were an ignorant rustic. A sympathetic account of the legend by W. H. B. Bird appears in *The Ancestor*, vol. ix, pp. 65–82, followed soon after by an adverse criticism by J. H. Round. |
| NUL NE S'Y FRÔLE | None rubs himself there. Antoine de Burgundy, natural son of Philip the Good, Duke of Burgundy, was styled even in manuscripts and generally as Le Grand Bâtard de Bourgogne (L. G. Pine, *American Origins*, 1960, p. 268). |
| NUL Q'UN | Only one (God). Cayley, Bts. (anciently used by Lords Digby). |
| NULLA NISI ARDUA VIRTUS | No virtue unless hard. Kemball. |
| NULLA PALLESCERE CULPA | To turn pale from no crime. Corbett-Winder, Forbes, Mitchell, Patten, Pulleine, Waynflete, Lord Winmarleigh (Patten, sometime Wilson Patten) *(NEP)*. |
| NULLA RETRORSUM | None backwards. Ferrers, Viscount Hewart *(NEP)*. |
| NULLA ROSA SINE SPINA | No rose without a thorn. Ilbert, 616 Sq., AAF. |
| NULLI SECUNDUS | Second to none. Lombard Banking Ltd. |
| NULLIUS IN VERBA | In no man's words (i.e. at no man's orders). Banks, Benson, Gabb, the Royal Society. |
| NULLIUS NON MATER DISCIPLINAE | Mother of all discipline. Leeds Gram. Sch. (W. R. Yorks.), 1552. |
| NULLUS TANTUS QUAESTUS, QUAM QUOD HABES PARCERE. NUM TIBI CUM FAUCES URIT SITIS, AUREA QUARIS POCULA? | No gain so great as what you have to spare. When your throat burns with thirst, you won't seek golden cups, will you? London School of Economics, 1894. |

| | |
|---|---|
| NUMEN LUMEN | Deity is light. Jayne. |
| NUNC AUT NUNQUAM | Now or never. Bennett, co. Somerset, Hampsom, Bts., Earls of Kilmorey (Needham), Needham. |
| NUNCIA PACIS OLIVA | The olive is the messenger of peace. Mayo of Cheshunt. |
| NUNQUAM AD ARMA NON PARATUS | Never unprepared for arms. Johnston of Warristoun. |
| NUNQUAM CONCEDENDAM | I shall never concede. Carl Alexander von Volborth. |
| NUNQUAM DEFUIMUS | We have never failed. RAF station, Kalafrana, Malta. |
| NUNQUAM DOMANDI | Never be tamed. 125 Sq., RAF, Newfoundland. |
| NUNQUAM DORMIO | I never sleep. 605 Co. of Warwick Sq., AAF (badge, the famous bear and ragged staff). |
| NUNQUAM IMMEMOR | I am never unmindful. Arnall-Thompson. |
| NUNQUAM INTERMITTERE CURSUM | Never to break their flight. No. 12 Maintenance Unit, RAF. |
| NUNQUAM MUTANS | Never changing. Bowring. |
| NUNQUAM NISI HONORIFICENTISSIME | Never unless most honourably. Freeling, Bts. |
| NUNQUAM NON PARATUS | Never unprepared. Betton, Carleton, Lords Derwent (Vanden-Bempde-Johnstone), English and American Insurance Co. Ltd., Gibbs, Johnson, Johnston, Johnstone, Keegan, Knight, Kerrick, Lords Luke (Johnston), Shaw of Shaw Place, Skinner, Stewart-Stevens, Stoney, Lord Webb-Johnson, 2 Sq., RAF Regt. |
| NUNQUAM OBLIVISCAR | I shall never forget. Iverach, McIver, Bt., Simpson of Sittingbourn. |
| NUNQUAM VICTUS | Never conquered. Buchanan, Bts. |
| NUSOOR FEE AID SADEEQUA | Eagles in a friendly land. RAF station, Salalak. |
| NUTRISCO ET EXTINGUE | I nourish and extinguish. Francis I of France, 1494–1547 (captured by Emperor Charles V at Battle of Pavia, 1525). Used as his badge a salamander (the absurd natural history of Pliny and subsequent writers described the creature as being able to live in flames and to put them out). Renowned patron of culture, including work of Leonardo da Vinci. |
| NY DESSUX NY DESSOUX | Neither above nor below, Grove, Bts. |

# O

| O LECTOR SALVE, COELI PATEANT TIBI, VALE | Hail O reader, may the heavens be open to thee, be strong. Haverfordwest (Pemb.), Bor. of. Arms grant to bor. and town of Haverford, alias Haverfordwest. |
| O NERTH I NERTH | From strength to strength. Lewis, co. Glam. |
| OB ARDUA DELEGATUS | Chosen on account of difficulties. Obbard (play on surname, apparent in Latin but lost in translation). |
| OBLIER NE DOY | You must not forget. Ottley. |
| OBSTANTIA DISCINDO | I cleave obstacles asunder. Wedgwood. |
| OBSTANTIA NUBILA SOLVET | It disperses opposing clouds. Pierre de Luxembourg, Comte de Saint-Pol, d. 1482. Motto was derived from emblem of sun surrounded by clouds meaning that he would extricate himself from difficulties which followed his father's death. |
| OCCIDENS ORIENSQUE | West and East. 203 Sq., RAF. |
| OCCIDO REDEOQUE | I kill and return. 118 Sq., RAF. |
| OCCULTA PETO | I seek hidden things. Litton. |
| OCCULTUS NON EXTINCTUS | Hidden not extinguished. Ker of Glasgow, Tytler. |
| OCIORES ACRIORESQUE | Swifter and sharper. 11 Sq., RAF. |
| OCULI EXERCITUS | The eyes of the army. 6 Sq., RAF. |
| OCULUS IN COELUM | An eye to the heaven. Eye (Suffolk), Bor. of. Arms of bor. granted in 1592 by Heralds' College; in grant the motto is mentioned. Significance is thus explained: 'Issuing from the Crown of the Imperial Sun . . . the Star of Innocence furnished with the all-seeing eye of Jehovah' (Scott Giles, *Civic Heraldry*, p. 202). |
| OCULUS OCCULTUS | The hidden eye. No. 59 Signals Unit, RAF. |
| ODHJA ZACH CU CABRAH | From God every help (expert view is that motto should read *O Dhia gach aon chabhair*). O'Conor Don. |
| ODI ET AMO | I hate and I love (Catullus, *Carmina* lxxxv). Viscount Norwich (Cooper). |
| ODI PROFANUM | I hate whatever is profane (Horace, *Odes* III. i. 1). Viscount Blakenham (Hare), Hare, Earls of Listowel (Hare), O'Hehir. |
| OF OLD I HOLD | Lords Burnham (Lawson), Viscount Burnham (Lawson), Levy-Lawson. |
| OFFENCE DEFENCE | Fighter Command, RAF. |
| OFFICIO EGERE NOLO | I do not need ceremony. Edge, Bts. |
| OFNA DOUW AR BRENIN | Fear God and the king. Traherne. |

OFNER NA OFNO ANGAU — Let him be feared who fears not death. Lords Aberdare (Bruce). Motto is supposed to be based on a reply made by Gwaethwood, Lord of Cibwyr, to Edgar the Peaceful, King of England, c.975.

OHNE RAST ZUM ZIEL — Without rest, to the goal. Abel, Bts.

OLD YET EVER NEW — New Forest (Hants.) RDC.

OLIM CRUORE NUNC CANDORE — Formerly with blood, now with candour. Sandeman.

OLIM MEMINISSE JUVABIT — It will help to remember former things (from Virgil's *Aeneid* I. 203). Lymm Gram. Sch.

OLIM PLENA — Formerly full. Pope Pius II, 1458–64 (Enea Silvio Piccolomini) and his nephew Pope Pius III, 1503, their badge being the crescent moon.

OMNE BONUM AB ALTO — All good from above. Lords Somerleyton (Crossley).

OMNE BONUM DEI DONUM — Every good is the gift of God. Bonsor, Bts., Boughton, Bts., Edwards of Pye Nest, Bts., Hill-Wood Bts., Powell, Bt., Wood of Hengrave, Bts.

OMNE BONUM DESUPER — Every good is from above. Burney, Honywood, Bts.

OMNE BONUM SUPERNE — All good is from above. Miller of Manderston, Bts.

OMNE SOLUM FORTI PATRIA — Every land is a brave man's country. Lords Balfour of Burleigh (Bruce), Bruges, D'Oyly, Bt., Lords Joicey, Townley-Balfour, co. Louth, Wiltshire.

OMNEMQUE PRETIOSUM LAPIDEM — (We gather) every valuable stone. Gemmological Assn. of Gt. Britain.

OMNI LIBER METU — Free from all fear. Birley, co. Lancs.

OMNI NUNC ARTE MAGISTRA — A mistress now in every art. Robert Gordon's Coll., Aberdeen (founded 1729 by Robert Gordon who had made fortune trading in the Baltic ports).

OMNIA ACTA BENE FACTA — All deeds well done. RAF station, Martlesham Heath.

OMNIA AD AEDIFICATIONEM — Let all things be done unto edifying. 5004 Airfield Construction Sq., RAF.

OMNIA AD DEI GLORIAM — All to the glory of God. Lee-Elliott.

OMNIA AGERE HONORIFICE — To do all things in an honourable way. Johnson of Dulwich.

OMNIA BENE EVENIENT — All things shall turn out well. Albu, Bts.

OMNIA BONA BONIS — All good things to the good. Harwich (Essex), Bor. of.

OMNIA DESUPER — All good things are from above. Broderers' Co., inc. 1561 (Broderie Anglaise had been renowned, however, from a very early period).

OMNIA FIRMAT — It makes all things firm. Campbell-Colquhoun.

OMNIA MEI DONA DEI — All my things are gifts of God. Stockdale, Bts.

OMNIA PASSIM — I endure all things. 437 Sq., RCAF.

OMNIA PRO BONO — All things for good. Manchester Port Health Authority, Murdoch.

OMNIA PRO CHRISTO — All for Christ. Cardinal Wiseman Sch., Coventry.

OMNIA PROBATE QUOD BONUM TENETE — Prove all things; hold fast that which is good (1 Thess. 5:21). Regent's Park Coll., 1958.

OMNIA SI PATIENTER — (I can bear) all things if patiently. Evans of Tubbendens, Bts.

OMNIA SUBJECISTI SUB PEDIBUS OVES ET BOVES — Thou hast put all things under his feet, (all) sheep and cattle (from Psalm 8:6–7). Butchers' Co., inc. 1605. Pole-axes appear in the shield between two bulls' heads, with a boar's head in chief.

OMNIA SUNT HOMINUM PENDENTIA FILIO — All human things hang by a thread. Textile Inst., 1951.

OMNIA VANITAS — All is vanity. Joanna the Mad (d. 1555), Queen of Castile, to which she succeeded in 1504 on death of her mother Isabella; after she became insane, her father Ferdinand continued as King of Castile.

OMNIA VIDEMUS — We see all things. 269 Sq., RAF.

OMNIA VINCE PERSEVERANDO — Conquer all things by persevering. Caterham Sch., Surrey, founded 1811 for sons of Congregational Ministers.

OMNIA VINCIT ASSIDUITAS — Diligence overcomes all things. Stevenson of Balladoole.

OMNIA VINCIT LABOR — Labour conquers all things. Bowater of Hill Crest, Bts., Cook.

OMNIA VINCIT VERITAS — Truth conquers all things. Lords Cheylesmore (Eaton), Munn, Nash.

OMNIBUS IDEM ARDOR — The same ardour for all. Italian Academy of the Unamini.

OMNIBUS REBUS CURA ET PROVIDE — Take care and provide in all things. Wolfson, Bts.

OMNIBUS TEMPESTATIBUS — In all weathers. HMS *Stormcloud* (a destroyer).

OMNIBUS UBIQUE SERVIMUS — We serve all, everywhere. No. 7 Maintenance Unit, RAF.

OMNIBUS UNGULIS — With all talons. 608 North Riding (F) Sq., AAF.

OMNINO ADJUVANDO — Helping in every way. Valuers' Inst., 1938.

OMNIS MIHI VITA SUB ARMIS — A life under arms is everything to me. Vicomte de Turenne (1611–75) great Marshal of France, main builder of Louis XIV's earlier supremacy in Europe.

OMNIUM RERUM VICISSITUDO — All things subject to change. Ford, Bts.

ON — Ball, Bts.

ON, ON — 272 Sq., RAF.

ON, STANLEY, ON — Stanley UDC, 1968. Motto is used in Sir Walter Scott's poem 'Marmion': 'On, Stanley, on were the last words of Marmion' (at Battle of Flodden, 9 September 1513, urging the Earl of Derby's forces).

ON WINGS OF FIRE — 426 Sq., RCAF.

ONCE AND ALWAYS — Hopkinson of Llanvihangel Court.

ONE AND ALL — Cornwall CC (motto also the name of very famous Cornish Masonic Lodge), Royal Cornwall Rangers Militia, 32nd L.I. (1st Bn. the Duke of Cornwall's Light Infantry).

| | |
|---|---|
| ONE HEART ONE WAY | Stourbridge (Worcs.), Bor. of. |
| ONE TIME ONE PURPOSE | 162 Sq., RAF. |
| ONI HEURIR NI FEDR | He who sows not reaps not. Carmarthen RDC. |
| ONUS SUB HONORE | There is a burthen to sustain under honour. Johnson of Arncliffe Hall. |
| ONWARD | Lord Atholstan (Graham) *(NEP)*, Boorman, co. Kent, Castle Ward (Northumb.) RDC, Fleetwood (Lancs.), Bor. of, Hyde (Ches.), Bor. of, Lorimer. |
| OPERA BONA EFFULGENT | Good works shine forth. Jacoby. |
| OPERA VICTRIX | Hard work is the conqueror. 5003 Airfield Construction Sq., RAF. |
| OPERAMUR ET MOBILITANTUR | We labour and they are kept moving. No. 99 Maintenance Unit, RAF. |
| OPERATA APERTA | Hidden things revealed. 16 Army Co-op. Sq., RAF. |
| OPES CONSILIUM PARIT | Counsel begets wealth. Bridgwater (Som.), Bor. of. |
| OPES INDUSTRIA PARIT | Industry begets wealth. Bingley (W.R. Yorks.) UDC. |
| OPIFERQUE PER ORBEM DICOR | I am called a bringer of help throughout the world. Apothecaries' Soc., inc. 6 December 1617 (one of the few companies which still carries on its original functions, i.e. to train men to be registered as medical practitioners or to serve as qualified dispensers; in the arms is shown Apollo, the inventor of physic; words are ascribed to Apollo in Ovid's *Metamorphoses*, Bk. I.), Kadie, Kadle, Keddie. |
| OPITULANTE DEO | By God's help. Breeton. |
| OPORTET NOS PROGREDI | It behoves us to progress. Crickhowell (Brecknock) RDC. |
| OPORTET VIVERE | It behoves us to live. Todd. |
| OPTIMA EST VERITAS | Truth is best. Thomson, co. Angus. |
| OPTIMA PETAMUS | Let us seek the best. Darlington (Durham) RDC. |
| OPTIMA QUAEQUE HONESTA | Whatever things are honest are best. Lambert of Banstead. |
| OPTIMO COGNOMINE CRESCIT | It grows with the best name. Larpent, Bts. |
| OPTIMO QUOD OPPORTUNE | What is opportune is best. Hamilton-Campbell co. Ayr. |
| OPTIMUM SUFFICIT | The best suffices. Ulverston (Lancs.) UDC, 1955. |
| OPUS NOSTRUM DIRIGE | Direct our work. E. Suffolk CC. |
| ORA ET ARA | Pray and plough. S. Kesteven (Lincs.) RDC, 1948. |
| ORA ET LABORA | Pray and labour. Earls of Dalhousie (Ramsay), Holburton, Jatia, Lichfield (Staffs.) RDC, Mure, Orlebar, Patrick, Ramsay, Sibbald, Taunton Sch., Som., 1847, Westhead, Women's Legion (formed in 1915 by Lady Londonderry at first to supply cooks for the new armies). |
| ORA, LABORA, LUDE | Pray, work, play. The Abbey Girls' Sch., Malvern Wells, Worcs. |

| ORANDO, LABORANDO | By praying, by working. Rugby Sch., Warwicks., founded 1567 by Lawrence Sheriff of Rugby, mem. of Grocers' Co. |
|---|---|
| ORNAT FORTEM PRUDENTIA | Prudence adorns the brave. Lancaster. |
| ORNATUR RADIX FRONDE | The root is adorned by the foliage. Innes, Rose-Innes. |
| OSTANDO NON OSTENTO | I show, not boast. Betts, Isham, Bts., Richie. |
| OTIUM CUM DIGNITATE | Repose with dignity. Kelso. |
| OÙ QUE JE SOYE, JE N'OUBLIEROY CROY | Wherever I may be I shall never forget Croy. Guillaume de Croy, Duc de Soria c.1521. |
| OUBLIER NE PUIS | I cannot forget. Lords Clydesmuir (Colville), Colvil, Colville, Fraser of Reelig. |
| OUR CANNON SPEAK OUR THOUGHTS | 157 Sq., RAF. |
| OUR WORD OUR BOND | Baltic Exchange, Inst. of Chartered Shipbrokers. |
| OURS TO HOLD | RAF station, Aldergrove. |
| OUT OF DARKNESS COMETH LIGHT | Wolverhampton (Staffs.), Bor. of, 1898. |
| OVER ALL OBSTACLES | No. 29 Operational Training Unit, RAF. |
| OVER FORK OVER | Marquesses Conyngham, Cunningham, Cunninghame, Cunynghame, Fairlie-Cunninghame. One of these legendary sayings, found in England as in Scotland, about a prince being saved by concealment under hay which a faithful (apparent) rustic is turning. |

# P

| | |
|---|---|
| PACE | In peace. Jaffrey, Bt. |
| PACE ET BELLO PARATUS | In peace and war prepared. Birkin, Bts., Flavelle, Bts., Frazer, No. 3 Maintenance Unit, RAF. |
| PACEM | Through peace. Goschen. |
| PACEM AMO | I love peace. Scott. |
| PACEM AMOR FOVET | Love cherishes peace. Foster, co. Essex. |
| PACIS AC LEGIS JURE | By right of peace and law. Tothill. |
| PACIS NUNCIA | A messenger of peace. Murray of Stanhope, Bts. (family crest was a dove with olive branch in its beak, ref. to Genesis 8:11). |
| PACTO FIDELIA | Confidence from agreement. Manchester Stock Exchange. |
| PACTUM SERVA | Keep faith (or your promise). Burra of Rye, Sussex, Inst. of Purchasing, 1959. Motto is part of inscription on tomb of Edward I (1272–1307) – *Edwardus Primus Scotorum malleus hic est, 1308, Pactum Serva.* Last two words are supposed to refer to promise which the dying Edward I exacted from his son, later Edward II. (Dean A. P. Stanley thought, however, that the words were simply a moral maxim; see, for full details, his *Historical Memorials of Westminster Abbey*, 1868, pp. 140 ff.). |
| PADROEIRA DE REINO | Patron of the kingdom. Order of Villa Vicosa (Portugal). |
| PAIX ET PEU | Peace and a little. Barlow, Maitland, Walrond. |
| PALMA NON SINE PULVERE | No palm without labour. Archibald of Rusland Hall, Lancs., Lamb, Palmer. |
| PALMA VIRTUTI | The palm to virtue. Earls of Selborne (Palmer), Palmer. |
| PALMAN PERSEVERANDO | (Obtain) the palm by persevering. Angas. |
| PALMAN QUI MERUIT FERAT | Let him bear the palm who has earned it. Laking, Bts., HMS *Nelson*, Lords Remnant. |
| PAMBILI BO (ZULU) | Go straight ahead. 222 Sq., RAF (Natal), formed 1918 at Thasos. |
| PANACHE ET PRECISION | Panache and precision. 237 Operational Control Unit, RAF. |
| PANDITE COELESTES PORTAE | Open, ye heavenly gates. Gibson, Gibson Watt, Gibsone. |
| PANIS ET PAX | Bread and peace. Lord Boyd Orr (*NEP*). This peer was greatly concerned with problem of world famine. |
| PANNUS MIHI PANIS | Wool is my bread. Kendal (Westmorland), Bor. of. |
| PANS PLUS (JE PENSE PLUS) | I think more. Earls of Mar (Erskine). |

| | |
|---|---|
| PANTANG TA SEDIA | Never unprepared. 487 Signals Unit, RAF. |
| PAR CE SIGNE À AGINCOURT | By this sign at Agincourt. Entwisle motto is supposed to derive from an ancestor having been at Agincourt (1415), but no sign of this in the *B.L.G.* 1952 Entwisle pedigree. |
| PAR FOY ET AMOUR | By faith and love. Greenham of Greenham Barton. |
| PAR NOBILE FRATRUM | A noble pair of brothers. No. 38 Group HQ, RAF (motto refers to the Group working with army airborne forces). |
| PAR NON LEONINA SOCIETAS | Society equal is not leonine. Orient Steam Navigation Co. Ltd. |
| PAR ONERI | Equal to the task. RAF station, Dishforth. |
| PAR SIT FORTUNA LABORI | Let the success be equal to the labour. Buchanan of Drumhead, Lowman, Palmer of Carlton, Bts., Palmer of Grinkle Park, Bts. |
| PAR TERNIS SUPPAR | A pair more than a match for three. Lords Northwick (Rushout), Rushout, Bts. (formerly Cockerell). |
| PAR TEVIJU | Order of the Three Stars (Latvia). |
| PAR VIRIBUS VIRTUS | Virtue equal to strength. Lord Hampton (Pakington). |
| PARAMUS | We are ready. No. 228 Op. Conversion Unit, RAF. |
| PARATIOR | More ready. Philip II, Duke of Savoy, d. 1496. Often changed sides to suit his interests. |
| PARATUS | Ready. Hall of Grafham, Bts., Laycock, Sword. |
| PARATUS ET FIDELIS | Ready and faithful. Carruthers, Hamond, Hamond-Graeme, Bts., Walford. |
| PARATUS SUM | I am prepared. Campbell of Barcaldine, Bts., Fairlie, Maclure. |
| PARCE QU'IL ME PLAÎT | Because it pleases me. Sprot. |
| PARCERE PROSTRATIS | To spare the fallen. Le Hunte. |
| PARCERE SUBJECTIS | To spare the conquered (part of a line from Virgil, *Aeneid* vi. 853). Longfield, Robertson-Glasgow. |
| PAREO NON SERVO | I am obedient, not servile. Jenkinson, Bts. |
| PARI ANIMO | With equal mind. Leake. |
| PARITUR PAX BELLO | Peace is obtained from war. Blane, Bt. |
| PARTA TUERI | Defend your acquisitions. Jacob of Bromley, Lords Lilford (Powys), Powys. |
| PARTAGEZ VOTRE BLAGUE | Take part in your hoax. Bragg, co. Nottingham. |
| PARTES PER EOAS | Through eastern parts. Chartered Bank of India, Australia and China (original motto was *Per mundum orientalem*, present motto being apparently taken with the arms granted 1950). |
| PARUM SUFFICIT | Little sufficeth. Barrow, Bts., Browne, Bts. |
| PARVA COMPONERE MAGIS | Rather to bring small things together. Oakham (Rutland) RDC. |
| PARVI ARMA SINE CONSILIO | Arms are worth little without counsel. Central Fighter Establishment, RAF. |

| | |
|---|---|
| PARVIS IMBUTUS TENTABIS GRANDIA TUTUS | Imbued with small things you will be safe in trying great ones. Barnard Castle Sch., co. Durham, founded thirteenth century by John de Balliol (founder, with his wife, of Balliol Coll., Oxford). |
| PAS À PAS | Step by step. René, Duke of Anjou, had the title to three realms, Naples, the two Sicilies and Jerusalem, retired to Provence. (Sir Walter Scott, *Anne of Geierstein*, and Shakespeare, *3 Henry VI*, have references to him and his dau., Margaret of Anjou, Queen of Henry VI of England.) |
| PASS FRIEND | Lords Rugby (Maffey). |
| PASSES BIEN DEVANT | Press on well before. Sir William Courtenay of Powerham Castle (a particular Courtenay motto (Earls of Devon)). |
| PASSEZ AVANT | Pass forward. Carter, Critchley-Salmonson, Earls Waldegrave. |
| PASSIM AD ASTRA | Everywhere to the stars. No. 11 Flying Training Sch., RAF. |
| PATET OMNIBUS VERITAS | Truth lies open to all. Lancaster Univ. |
| PATIENCE PASSE SCIENCE | Patience surpasses knowledge. Boscawen, Viscount Falmouth (Boscawen). |
| PATIENS PULVERIS ATQUE SOLIS | Patient of dust and sun. Floyd, Bts. |
| PATIENTIA CASUS EXUPERAT OMNES | Patience overcomes all chances. Askew of Ladykirk, co. Berwick. |
| PATIENTIA ET DILIGENTIA | By patience and diligence. Porritt. |
| PATIENTIA ET PERSEVERANTIA | With patience and perseverance. Dent, co. Yorks. |
| PATIENTIA ET PERSEVERANTIA CUM MAGNANIMITATE | Patience and perseverance with magnanimity. Lords Ailwyn (Fellowes), Lords De Ramsey (Fellows), Fellows, Frisby. |
| PATIENTIA ET SPE | With patience and hope. Duguid. |
| PATIENTIA VINCIT | Patience conquers. Cheyne, Bts., Gall, Lindesay of Warmiston, Nafleur, Napier of Tayock. |
| PATIENTIA VINCIT OMNIA | Patience conquers all. Scarisbrick, Bts. |
| PATIENTIA VICTRIX | Patience is victorious. Dalton of the Hutts, co. Yorks., Sugrue. |
| PATIOR UT POTIOR | I endure as I enjoy. Spottiswood. |
| PATITUR QUI VINCIT | He who suffers, conquers. Lords Kinnaird, Lee, co. Ches. |
| PATRI AC IN FELICE FIDELIS | Faithful to my country also in happiness. Waddington. |
| PATRI PATRIAEQUE | To his father and to his country. Frederick Henry of Nassau, Prince of Orange, Stadtholder of the Netherlands, d. 1647. |
| PATRIA CARA CARIOR FIDES | My country is dear, my faith dearer. Nicolas, Earls of Radnor (Pleydell-Bouverie), Thompson of Clements. |
| PATRIA CARA CARIOR LIBERTAS | My country is dear but liberty is dearer. Roberts of Ardmore. |

| | |
|---|---|
| PATRIAE FIDELIS | Faithful to my country. Tiffin, Wood of Hollin Hall. |
| PATRIAE FIDUS | Faithful to my country. Orr-Lewis, Bts. |
| PATRIAE INFELICI FIDELIS | Faithful to my unhappy country. Earls of Courtown (Stopford), Lyons-Montgomery, Molyneux, Stopford. |
| PATRIIS VIRTUTIBUS | By hereditary virtues. Clements, Earls of Leitrim (Clements). |
| PAUPER NON IN SPE | Not poor in hope. Poore, Bts. |
| PAX | Peace. Foulis, Hatfeild, Hatton. |
| PAX ALMA REDIT | The bright peace returns. Domville, Bts. |
| PAX AUT DEFENSIO | Peace or defence. Landale. |
| PAX COPIA SAPIENTIA | Peace, plenty and wisdom. Fleming, Le Fleming, West. |
| PAX ET ABUNDANTIA | Peace and plenty. Altringham UDC. |
| PAX ET AMOR | Peace and love. Hodson, Bts., Jessop. |
| PAX ET CONCORDIA | Peace and concord. Dalrierus (Swedish family). |
| PAX ET PLENITUDO | Peace and plenty. Childe. |
| PAX ET SPES | Peace and hope. Lords Daryngton (Pease), Lords Gainford (Pease), Pease, Lords Wardington (Pease). |
| PAX FIAT PER FLUMINIS AQUAS | Let peace be made through the waters of the river. Trent River Authority, 1967. |
| PAX IN BELLO | Peace in war. Godolphin, Dukes of Leeds (Osborne) *(NEP)*, Osborne, Bts. |
| PAX OMNIBUS | Peace to all. Walker of Fonthill Abbey. |
| PAX POTIOR BELLO | Peace is more powerful than war. Bastard of Kitley, Devon. |
| PAX PROFUNDIS | Peace in the depths. Pascoe. |
| PAX QUAERITUR BELLO | Peace is obtained by war. Cromwell of Cheshunt Park, Hume-Williams, Bts. |
| PAX TIBI MARCE, EVANGELISTA MEA | Peace to thee, O Mark, my evangelist. These words appear on representation of a book in arms of City of Venice, where the book is held by a golden lion, i.e. the lion of St Mark, author of the second gospel and patron of Venice. |
| PEACE AND HOLY QUIET | Lords Granchester (Taylor). |
| PEACE AND PLENTY | Barns, Barns-Graham. |
| PEACE BE WITH YOU | (in Arabic). RAF, Aden Protectorate Levies. |
| PEACE THROUGH TRAVEL | British Travel Assn. |
| PEACE THROUGH UNDERSTANDING | Eisenhower (President, USA). |
| PECTUS FIDELE ET APERTUM | A breast faithful and open. Cantrell. |
| PEGASUS MILITANS | Pegasus at war. 512 Sq., RAF (badge, horse's head with sword, symbolic of unit's dual functions of army air support and transport). |
| PEJUS LETHO FLAGITIUM | Disgrace is worse than death. Martin, Sampson. |

| | |
|---|---|
| PEN LYNNOW | Headland of pools (Cornish). Penaluna. |
| PEN Y MYNYDD I MI | The mountain top for me (*or* Head of the mountain for me). Wynne-Jones. |
| PENETRABIT | I will penetrate. Charles de Bourbon, 7th Duc de Bourbon 1490–1527, changed from French service to that of Emperor Charles V; his troops captured and sacked Rome 1527, when he was killed reputedly by a shot fired by Benvenuto Cellini. |
| PENNAE EXTENTAE | Widespread wings. RAF Air HQ, Iraq. |
| PENNAE MARINAE PULLULANT | Sea wings are sprouting. No. 24 Elementary Flying Training Sch., RAF (sch. originated to train naval pilots; hence motto, and badge of a kittiwake alighting). |
| PENNAS UBIQUE MONSTRAMUS | We show our wings everywhere. 135 Sq., RAF. |
| PENSE A POINTER | Think to point. Poynter, Bts. |
| PENSEZ FORT | Think firmly. Bromley, Bts., Paunceforte, Scarborough Coll. |
| PEPERI | I have brought forth. Peperell. |
| PER ACUTA BELLI | Through the sharpness of war (from Horace, *Odes*). Bengough, Carpenter, Earls of Tyrconnel (Talbot). |
| PER AEQUITATEM SAPIENTIAMQUE DUCIMUS | Through justice and wisdom we lead. Officers' Advanced Training Sch., RAF. |
| PER ANGUSTA AD AUGUSTA | Through difficulties to honours. Antrim CC, Christall, Viscount Massereene & Ferrard (Skeffington), Skiffington. |
| PER ARDUA | Through difficulties. Berry, Bts., Lords Black, Clarkson, Crookshank, Curtis of Gatcombe, Bt., Drake, Bts., Knocker, M'Entire, M'Intyre, McVeagh, Masterton, Oakes, Bts., RAF Regt., Stubbert, Tailour, Thornton-Berry, Wright. |
| PER ARDUA AD AETHERA TENDO | I tend to the heights through difficulties. 60 Sq., RAF. |
| PER ARDUA AD ALTA | Through straits to heights. Achany, Birmingham Univ., Cuddon, Hall, Hannan, Hannay, Bts., Thompson of Gatacre Park. |
| PER ARDUA AD ASTRA | Through the steeps to the stars. RAF motto introduced 1913 for RFC; registered for RAF, 1923. |
| PER ARDUA AD PALMAS | Through difficulties to the palms. Lord Quibell *(NEP)*. |
| PER ARDUA AD SUMMA | Through difficulties to the heights. Beddington & Wallington (Surrey), Bor. of. |
| PER ARDUA ALIS | To the heights by wings. RAF Museum. |
| PER ARDUA IN FIDE SERVITE DEO | Through difficulties serve God in faith. Sutton, London Bor. of. |
| PER ARDUA LIBERI | Free, through difficulties. Pitt. |
| PER ARDUA STABILIS | Firm in adversity. Henshaw, Lawrence, Bt., Mann, Lord Pethick-Lawrence *(NEP)*. |
| PER ARDUA STABILIS ESTO | Be firm through difficulties. Kemp of Toronto. |

| | |
|---|---|
| PER ARDUA SURGAM | I will rise through difficulties. Beetham. |
| PER ARDUA SURGO | I rise through difficulties. Fenton, Harding of Madingley, Mahon, 45 Sq., RAF (I rise through the heights). |
| PER ARDUA VOLABIMUS | We shall fly through all difficulties. 134 Sq., RAF. |
| PER ASPERA AD ASTRA | By hard ways to the stars. Fraser of Cromarty, Bts., Order of the Three Stars (Latvia), Order of the Wendish Crown (Latvia). |
| PER ASPERA AD DULCIA CRUCIS | Through hardships to the sweetness of the Cross. Bretherton (formerly of Runshaw, Lancs.). |
| PER ASPERA SURGO | I rise through difficulties. Bennet, co. Mon. |
| PER BELLUM PATRIA | Our country through war. Battle (Sussex) RDC. |
| PER CAELUM VIA NOSTRA | Our way through the heaven. Guild of Air Pilots & Navigators. |
| PER CALLEM COLLEM | By path (and) hill. Collins (formerly of Betterton). |
| PER CASTRA AD ASTRA | Through the camp to the stars. Nicholson, Shaw, co. Ches. |
| PER CRUCEM AD COELUM | By the Cross to heaven. Hartley of Silchester House. |
| PER CRUCEM AD CORONAM | By the Cross to a crown. De la Poer, Power, Bts. |
| PER CRUCEM AD PALMAM | By the Cross to the palm. Lords Palmer, Palmer of Reading, Bt. |
| PER CRUCEM AD STELLAS | By the Cross to heaven. Legard, Bts. |
| PER DAMNA PER CAEDES | Through losses through slaughter. Bosanquet, co. Mon., Boyton. |
| PER DEUM ET FERRUM OBTINUI | By God and my sword I have prevailed. Marquesses of Downshire (Hill), Hill. |
| PER DEUM ET INDUSTRIAM | Through God and industry. Banbridge (co. Down) UDC. |
| PER DEUM ET INDUSTRIAM OBTINUI | I have gained through God and industry. Tubbs, Bt. |
| PER DEUM MEUM TRANSILIO MURUM | By the help of my God I leap over the wall. Earls Baldwin of Bewdley (Miss Monica Baldwin, in *I Leap over the Wall*, 1950, p.7, wrote of the Baldwin motto: 'Nearly 400 years ago, my ancestor Thomas Baldwin of Diddlesbury leaped to freedom from behind the walls of the Tower of London . . . His name with an inscription and the date "July 1585" can still be seen where he carved it on the wall of his cell in the Beauchamp Tower'; later he added the motto to his arms and it has remained that of the Baldwins ever since), Childe of Kinlet, Bewdley, Salop. |
| PER DIEM PER NOCTEM | By day, by night. 7 Sq., RAF (bomber); badge Ursa Major). |
| PER DILIGENTIAM VINCIMUS | By diligence we conquer. No. 5 Glider Training Sch., RAF. |
| PER DOCTRINAM AD DIGNITATEM | Through doctrine to dignity. Inst. of Meat, 1947. |

| | |
|---|---|
| PER DOLUM CONFUNDIMUS | Confound the enemy (We confound by craft). 171 Sq., RAF. |
| PER FIDEM ET OFFICIUM | By faith and duty. Garton of Pylle. |
| PER FIDEM ROBUR | Strength through faith. Ackroyd, Bt. |
| PER FLUCTUS AD ORAM | Through waves to the shore. Burrell, Bts. |
| PER FRUGALITATEM DOMUS | A home through frugality. Leek & Westbourne Bldg. Soc. |
| PER IGNUM VINCIMUS | Through fire we conquer. 550 Sq., RAF. |
| PER IGNUM PER GLADIUM | By fire and sword. Welby, Bts. |
| PER IL SUO CONTRARIO | By its opposite. Marquesses of Anglesey (Paget), Lord Queenborough (Paget) *(NEP)*. |
| PER INCERTA CERTUS AMOR | Love certain through things uncertain. Romanis. |
| PER JUGA PER FLUVIOS | Through hills and rivers. Harland, Bts. |
| PER LABOREM AD HONOREM | By toil to honour. Bank Line Ltd., Lords Inverforth (Weir). |
| PER LABOREM AD SUMMA | Through toil to supremacy. Flying Training Cmd., RAF. |
| PER LABOREM PAX | Peace through labour. Benjamin, co. Sligo, Henry, Bt. |
| PER LABOREM SCIENTIAM ARTEM | Through labour, science, art. Maltby (W.R. Yorks.) UDC. |
| PER LUCEM AC TENEBRAS MEA SIDERA SANGUINE SURGENT | By light and darkness my stars rise in blood. Cayley, Bts. |
| PER MARE | By the sea. Anderson of Aberdeen, Anderson of Notgrove Manor, co. Glocs. |
| PER MARE PER AERA | Through the sea, through the airs. Commonwealth Telecommunications Bd. |
| PER MARE PER ECCLESIAM | Through the sea, through the Church. Southend-on-Sea (motto acknowledges Southend's debt to the sea and to the Church, most of the charges in the arms having religious significance). |
| PER MARE PER INDUSTRIAM | Through the sea, through industry. Coal Factors' Soc. |
| PER MARE PER TERRAM | By sea, by land. Royal Marines, RMLI. |
| PER MARE PER TERRAS | By sea, by lands. Alexander, Bosville Macdonald, Bts., Earls of Caledon (Alexander), Drummond, Lithgow, Bts., Macalester, M'Alister, Macdonald, Macdonell of Glengarry, Robertson-Shersby-Harvie. |
| PER MARE PER TERRAS PER ASTRA | By sea, by land, by the stars. Earls Alexander of Tunis (1st Earl was Supreme Allied Commander, Mediterranean, 1944–5; this command of all services may have led him to add the last two words to Alexander family motto). |
| PER MARE TERRAM AEREM | By sea, land and air. No. 1 Movement Unit, RAF. |
| PER MARE UBIQUE | Everywhere through the sea. Royal Mail Lines Ltd. |
| PER ME TUTUS | Safe through me. HMS *Telemachus* (destroyer; ship's badge a dolphin, all. to Telemachus having been saved by a dolphin from drowning). |

| | |
|---|---|
| PER MORTEM VINCO | I conquer through death. Waterlow of Harrow Weald, Bts. |
| PER MUTUA SERVIENDO TUTIORES | Safer in serving through mutual interest. National Employers' Life Assurance Co. Ltd. |
| PER NOCTEM VIGILANS | Watching through the night. Westlake. |
| PER NOCTEM VOLAMUS | We fly through the night. 9 Bomber Sq., RAF. |
| PER NOS VOLANT | Thanks to us they fly. No. 58 Maintenance Unit, RAF. |
| PER OBSCURA AD METAM | Through darkness to the goal. 3603 City of Edinburgh Fighter Control Unit, RAAF. |
| PER ORBEM | Through the world. Clay, Bts. |
| PER PERICULA AD DECUS IRE JUVAT | It helps to go through perils to glory. Scarborough (N.R. Yorks.), Bor. of. |
| PER PURUM TONANTES | Thundering from a clear sky. 61 Sq., RAF. |
| PER SALUBRITATEM OPES | Wealth through health. Ilkley (W.R. Yorks.) UDC. |
| PER SAPIENTIAM PROVENITE | Come forth through wisdom. Bristol Coll. of Tech. |
| PER SCIENTIAM PROGREDIAMUR | Let us progress through science. Kingston Coll. of Tech. |
| PER SCIENTIAM VIS | Strength through knowledge. Leyton. |
| PER SE CONFIDENS | Confident in himself. Nelson, Bts. |
| PER SE VALENS | Strong through himself. Percival. |
| PER SERVITIUM FELICITAS | Happiness through service. Lord Donovan. |
| PER SINUM CODANUM | Through the Codamus Gulf. Graves-Sawle, Bts. (not strictly speaking a motto, but forms part of crest of Graves-Sawle, i.e. an eagle displayed or, supporting in the dexter claw a staff erect ppr. thereon hoisted a pennant formed and flowing to the sinister with the inscription (as above) in letters of gold; according to *Burke's General Armory*, ref. is to the Baltic Sea but, although the 4th and last Bt. was Admiral RN, there is no explanation of this inscription and as the *General Armory* was published in 1884 words must refer to earlier achievement). |
| PER TENEBRAS TENAX | Dogged in the dark. No. 238 Operational Conversion Unit, RAF. |
| PER TERRAS PERQUE CAELUM | By land and sky. 657 Sq., RAF. |
| PER TERRAS UBIQUE | Everywhere through the earth. Guildhall Insurance Co. Ltd. |
| PER TOT DISCRIMINA RERUM | Through so many critical moments in affairs. Lord Hammond of Kirkella *(NEP)*, Tringham. |
| PER UNDAS | Through the waves. Smith of Crowmallie, Bts. |
| PER UNDAS PER AGROS | By water and by land. Cambridgeshire CC. |
| PER VARIOS CASUS | By various fortunes. Douglas, Drysdale, Hamilton, Lammie, L'Amy, Walker. |
| PER VIAS BONAS | Through good ways. Rhodes, Bts. |

| | |
|---|---|
| PER VIAS RECTAS | By right ways. Blackwood, Carling, Lords Dufferin, Marquesses of Dufferin & Ava (Blackwood), Pixley, Pride-Collins. |
| PER VIRES PAX | Peace through strength. RAF station, Butzweilerhof. |
| PERACTUS CONAMINE | Having acted thoroughly in an endeavour. Kersey. |
| PERAGIMUS QUOD COEPIT CONDITOR | We carry on what our founder began. P. Wigham-Richardson & Co. Ltd., 1964. |
| PERCUTIT INSIDIANS PARDUS | The watchful panther strikes. 146 Sq., RAF (badge granted 1945 of panther's head, unit having been stationed in Assam and Bengal, where black panther is found). |
| PEREANT HOSTES | Destruction to the enemy (lit. Let the enemy perish). 3609 West Riding Fighter Control Unit. |
| PEREGRINUS IN TERRA | A pilgrim in the land. Landon. |
| PERENNE SUB POLO NIHIL | There is nothing permanent under heaven. Perrins, Pont. |
| PERFERO | I endure. Cumberland CC, Hadwen, William II (Rufus) (supposed to indicate that he was not behind his father in ability, as he was certainly not in rapacity). |
| PERFICIOR | I am made perfect. Victor Amadeus I, 1587–1637, Duke of Savoy. |
| PERFICIS CURSUM | You finish your course. Isherwood, Bts. |
| PERGE QUO COEPISTI | Proceed where you have begun. Richardson of Weybridge. Bts. |
| PERGE SED CAUTE | Advance but cautiously. Jenkins, co. Salop, Lees. |
| PERICULUM EX ALIIS FACITO | Make danger out of others. Jones. |
| PERICULUM FORTITUDINE EVASI | I have escaped danger by fortitude. Harland, Mahon. |
| PERICULUM IN MORA | Peril in delay. Lords McNair. |
| PERIISSEM NI PER IISSEM | I had perished unless I had gone through it. Anstruther. Now used by Carmichael-Anstruther, Bts. (in note 12 to *Waverley*, Sir Walter Scott wrote: 'One of that ancient race, finding that an antagonist, with whom he had fixed a friendly meeting, was determined to take the opportunity of assassinating him, prevented the hazard by dashing out his brains with a battle-axe. Two sturdy arms brandishing such a weapon form the usual crest of the family with the above motto.'). |
| PERIISSEM NI STERILISSEM | I had perished unless I had (rendered him) sterile. Anstruther of Balcaskie, Bts. (usually varied as *periissem ni per-iisem* (q.v.)). |
| PERIMUS LICITIS | We die by things permitted. Lords Teignmouth (Shore). |
| PERIT UT VIVAT | It dies that it may live. Sir John Fenwick, *temp.* Henry V (all. to badge of phoenix, fabulous bird which rose again from its funeral pyre; Clement of Rome, *First Epistle*). |
| PERITIA POTIUS QUAM VI | By cleverness rather than by strength. Tower Hamlets Engineer Volunteers. |

| | |
|---|---|
| PERSEVERA | Persevere. Stroud (Glos.) UDC, 1960. |
| PERSEVERA ET VINCE | Persevere and win. Viscount Kemsley (Berry), Lords Killearn (Lampson), Lampson, Bts. |
| PERSEVERANCE | Burrard of Lymington, Bts., Crawshay of Cyfarthfa, co. Glam. (originally ironmasters, mentioned in the novel *Rape of the Fair Country* by Alexander Cordell), Lord Glantawe (Jenkins) *(NEP)*, Lords Strathcona and Mount Royal (Howard, originally Smith), Trueman, No. 4 Air Observers' Sch., RAF. |
| PERSEVERANCE CONQUERS ALL DIFFICULTIES | Cordiner. |
| PERSEVERANDO | By persevering. Brinkman, Bts., Brooks, Cammell, Cope, co. Leics., Lords Colchester (Abbot), Dawson, Dendy, Earls of Ducie (Moreton), Dugdale, Lord Crathorne (Dugdale), Edwards, Farnell, Flower, Frampton of Moreton, Gandell, Henley, Howell, Lord Ilford (Hutchinson), Larkworthy, MacGillivray, M'Kellar, Moreton, Morton, Reynolds, Bts., Roxby, Sheepshanks, Turnly, Wilson, co. Yorks., Wood of Barnsley, Bts. |
| PERSEVERANDO VINCIT | He conquers by persevering. Curtis of Denbury Manor. |
| PERSEVERANTI DABITUR | It shall be given to the persevering. Gilmour, Robertson, Simpson, Bts., Terry. |
| PERSEVERANTIA | Perseverance. Bell, Bts., Bell, co. Cork, Duckworth, Bts., Hansen, Bt., Morrison-Bell, Bts., Solihull Sch. (founded *c. temp.* Richard II). |
| PERSEVERANTIA ET CONSTANTIA | Perseverance and constancy. Jarrett. |
| PERSEVERANTIA ET JUSTITIA | Perseverance and justice. Judge. |
| PERSEVERANTIA ET LABORE | By perseverance and work. Nelson, co. Lancs., Pitcher. |
| PERSEVERANTIA ET SPES | Perseverance and hope. Branston of Branston, co. Lincs. |
| PERSEVERANTIA OMNIA VINCIT | Perseverance conquers all things. Cooper of Woollahra, Bts., Hill of Brynderi. |
| PERSEVERANTIA PALMAM OBTINEBIT | Perseverance will obtain the reward. Munro-Lucas-Tooth, Bts., Tooth, Wright of Swansea, Bts. |
| PERSEVERANTIA VICTOR | Victor by perseverance. Campbell of New Brunswick, Bt. |
| PERSEVERANTIA VINCIT | Perseverance conquers. Alexander-Sinclair, Hagart-Alexander of Ballochnyke, Bts., Nicholls, Bts., Parts of Kesteven CC. |
| PERSEVERE | Brandram, Burrard of Walhampton, Bt., Colville, co. Staffs., Congreve, Bts., Denton UDC, Farnall, Feardon, Fordyce, Gardiner, Gibbs, Greig, Guild, Harrison-Topham, Hett, Jeffcock, Jessel, London Coll. of Music, Oakes, Bts., Oates, co. Yorks., Phillips of Reigate, Romilly, Smythe, Whittall. |
| PERSEVERE RESOLUTELY | No. 22 Flying Training Sch., RAF. |
| PERSEVERO | I persevere. Cheney, Lords Pender. |

| | |
|---|---|
| PERSIST | RAF station, Ouston (badge is a lion rampant in front of a Roman helmet; latter refers to the Roman wall which runs parallel to camp boundary and also indicates that the RAF Regt. stationed there operates as infantry, as most Romans did; the lion is a charge in the arms of the Percy family). |
| PERSISTE | Persist. Humphrey of Horam Hall. |
| PERSTO ET PRAESTO | I persist and excel. Stowe Sch., co. Bucks., 1923. |
| PERTAMA DI MALAYA | First in Malaya (Malayan). 205 Sq., RAF. |
| PESTIS PATRIAE PIGRITIES | Sloth is the bane of a country. Dugdale of Merevale, Bts. |
| PETIT ALTA | He seeks high things. Abercromby, Bts. |
| PETIT ARDUA VIRTUS | Virtue seeks difficulties. Douglas, Errington, Bts. |
| PETRA IMMOBILIOR | Less movable than a rock. Tenison. |
| PIE REPONE TE | Repose with pious confidence. Earls Manvers (Pierrepont, previously Medows) (NEP), Mordey, Pierrepont. |
| PIETAS PARENTUM | Piety of parents. St Edward's Sch., Oxford. |
| PIETATE ET JUSTICIA | With piety and justice. Charles IX of France, 1550–74, who under influence of his mother, Catherine de Medici, gave order for St Bartholomew's Day massacre, 1572. |
| PIETATE FORTIOR | Stronger by piety. Stanier, Bts. |
| PIEUX QUOIQUE PREUX | Pious although chivalrous. Viscou:.t Long, Long of Hurts Hall. |
| PISCATORES HOMINUM | Fishers of men. National Soc. |
| PLACEAM DUM PEREAM | I will please though I perish. Murray of Melgund, Bts. |
| PLAISIR EN FAITES D'ARMES | Pleasure in feats of arms. Kemeys-Tynte. |
| PLUS EST EN VOUS | More is in you. Gordonstoun Sch., Elgin, Moray. |
| PLUS MELLIS QUAM FELLIS | More of honey than of gall. Adrien Amboise, Bishop of Treguier (d. 1616), badge being a swarm of bees. |
| PLUS OULTRE | More beyond. Burgundian motto of Charles V, Holy Roman Emperor, in connection with his device of the Pillars of Hercules, as his empire extended to the newly discovered America. |
| PLUS QU'ONQUE MES | More than ever mine. Cleves. |
| PLUTÔT MOURIR QUE CHANGER | Rather die than change. Quilter, Bts. |
| POB DAWN O DDVW | All gifts from God. Jeffreys. |
| POINCT FLECHIR | Not to flinch. Spears, Bt. |
| POINT DU JOUR | Break of day (turn out early). Lowestoft (Suffolk), Bor. of, HMS Lowestoft. |
| POLLET VIRTUS | Virtue excels. Carew-Pole, Bts., Lords Maryborough (Wellesly-Pole, ext.), Pole, Poole, Wilson of Currigrave, Bt., Wilson of Daramona. |
| POLUS DUM SIDERA PASCET | So long as the sky shall feed the stars. 692 Sq., RAF. |

| | |
|---|---|
| PONE NOS AD HOSTEM | Follow us to find the enemy. 63 Sq., RAF. |
| PONS HERI PONS HODIE | A bridge yesterday and a bridge today. RAF station, Gatow. |
| PONTIFICES AGITE ET VOS REGES DICITE JUSTA | Pontiffs do just things and you kings speak them. Georges Amboise, Cardinal and Bishop of Rouen, minister of Louis XII, d. 1510. |
| POPULO BENE SERVIRE | To serve the people well. Provincial Bldg. Soc. |
| POR DYSSERVER | To examine. Carr-Ellison. |
| POR LA RAZON O LA FUERZA | By reason or by force. From arms of Chile, 1834. |
| PORRO UNUM EST NECESSARIUM | Moreover one thing is needful. Earls Cowley (Wellesley), Wellesley. |
| PORTA MARIS PORTA SALUTIS | A gate of the sea and a haven of health. Margate (Kent), Bor. of. |
| PORTA VACAT CULPA | The gate is free from blame. Repton Sch., Derby, founded by Sir John Port, hence punning motto. |
| PORTA VAGAE | Port of the Vaga. Ross-on-Wye (Herefords.) UDC, 1953. |
| PORTAM CUSTODIMUS | We guard the gate. RAF station, West Malling, Kent. |
| PORTIO MEA DOMINE SIT IN TERRA VIVENTIUM | Be my portion in the land of the living, O Lord. Jean Grolier, d. 1565, Frenchman and collector of valuable books in Paris. |
| PORTIO MEA SIT IN TERRA VIVENTIUM | Let my portion be in the land of the living. Pope Martin IV, 1281–5, a Frenchman, Simon de Brion. |
| POSSIDE SAPIENTIAM | Possess wisdom. Farrington's Sch. |
| POSSUNT QUIA POSSE VIDENTUR | They are able because they seem to be. Attwood, Cahn Bts., Christ's Coll., Brecon (founded 1541 by Henry VIII), Fowler of Gastard House, Bts., Goodere, Keightley, Oakes, co. Derbys., Radford-Norcop, 19 Sq., RAF. |
| POST CURAM OTIUM | Relaxation after care. Soc. of Chiropodists, Ltd. |
| POST FUNERA VIRTUS | Virtue survives death. Massy-Westropp, Roberts of Glassenbury, Bts., Roberts, co. Cork, Robertson. |
| POST MORTEM PATRIS PRO FILIO | After the death of the father, held for the son. Pontefract (W.R. Yorks.), Bor. of. Pontefract Castle during the Civil War was held by the Royalists but destroyed by the Roundheads; garrison refused to surrender after execution of Charles I in 1649; motto adopted by the town after Restoration of Charles II in 1660. |
| POST MORTEM SPERO VITAM | I hope for life after death. Ley, Bts. |
| POST NUBES LUX | After clouds light. Coll. of Aeronautics, Blunstone. |
| POST NUBILA PHOEBUS | After clouds, sunshine. Ahrends, Cranworth, Jack, Jaffray, Bts., Jaffrey, Pinkerton, Purvis, Robinson, Rolfe, Shuldham, Tarleton, Talton. |
| POST PRAELIA PRAEMIA | After battle, honour. Ballymena, Bor. of, Fellows, M'Innes, Nicholson, Lords Rossmore (Westenra). |
| POST PROELIA CONCORDIA | Concord after strife. Market Bosworth RDC. |
| POST SALUM SALUS | After the sea health. Blyth Harbour Commission. |

| | |
|---|---|
| POST SPINAS PALMA | After thorns the palm. Godfrey, Paget, Scholfield. |
| POST TENEBRAS AURORA | After darkness dawn. Lord Woodbridge (Churchman). |
| POST TENEBRAS LUCEM | After darkness (we find) light. Bright, co. Herefords, Langdale, co. Yorks. |
| POST TENEBRAS LUX | After darkness light. Bovey, Hewatt, Langdale, Samuelson, Bts. |
| POST TENEBRAS SPERO LUCEM | After darkness I hope for light. Hutton (formerly of Gate Burton). |
| POST TOT NAUFRAGIA PORTUM | After so many shipwrecks, a haven. Hine, Earls of Sandwich (Montagu). |
| POSTERA CRESCAM LAUDE | Ever new, my after fame shall grow (Horace, *Odes* III. xxx). University of Melbourne, 1854. |
| POSTERA LAUDE RECENS | Ever fresh in the admiration of posterity. Hardinge, Bts. |
| POSUI DEUM ADJUTOREM MEUM | I have put God as my helper. One of the mottoes of Edward III of England, used on some of his coins, and by several of his successors. |
| POTESTATE, PROBITATE ET VIGILANTIA | By power, probity and vigilance. Inst. of Incorporated Clerks of Works of Gt. Britain. |
| POTIUS INGENIO QUAM VI | By brain rather than by force. Edgar, Richardson, co. Yorks. |
| POTIUS MORI QUAM FAEDARI | Better die than be disgraced. Hanbury-Tenison. |
| POUR BIEN DESIRER | For wishing well. Barrett Lennard, Bts., Bolden, Lord Brand, Lords Dacre (Brand), Viscount Hampden (Brand). |
| POUR ENTRE TENIR | To hold within. Sir Giles Capell of Stebbing, Essex, *temp.* Henry VIII, represented by Earls of Essex (*B.P.*, 1970). |
| POUR LA FOI | For the faith. Lawes, Bts. |
| POUR ME APRENDRE | For me to learn. Sir James de Debenham of Framlingham, Suffolk. |
| POUR PAR VENIR | To be able to come. Blount, Blunt. |
| POUR PARVENIR A BONNE FOY | To succeed with good faith. Cutlers' Co., inc. 1416. |
| POUR TROIS | For three. Latter. |
| POUR Y PARVENIR | To accomplish it. Viscount Canterbury (Manners-Sutton) *(NEP)*, Dukes of Rutland (Manners), Manners. |
| POUR Y PARVENIR À BON FOI | To arrive there at good faith. Inc. Co. of Cutlers in Hallamshire. |
| POWER IN TRUST | Central Electricity Generating Bd., Daventry (Northants.) RDC. |
| POWER TO THE HUNTER | RAF station, Kinloss. |
| POWYS PARADWYS CYMRU | Powys, paradise of Wales. Montgomeryshire CC. |
| PRAE SALUTEM NOTANDA | Things must be noted before safety. Preesall (Lancs.) UDC. |
| PRAECEDENTIBUS INSTA | Press hard upon those who go before. Earls of St Germans (Eliot). |

| | |
|---|---|
| PRAECEPTA NON HOMINES | Precepts not men. Newport Pagnell (Bucks.) UDC. |
| PRAECLARUM REGI ET REGNO SERVITIUM | Distinguished service to king and kingdom. Ogilvie of Barras, Bts. |
| PRAEDAM MARI QUAERO | I seek my prey at sea. 204 Sq., RAF (badge is a cormorant). |
| PRAEMIA VIRTUTIS HONORES | Honours are the rewards of virtue. Norwich Sch. (earliest mention 1256), Portsmouth Gram. Sch., 1732. |
| PRAEMIANDO INCITAT | It incites by rewarding. Order of St Stanislas (Russia). |
| PRAEMIUM VIRTUTIS GLORIA | Glory is the reward of virtue. Hodge, Bts. |
| PRAEMIUM VIRTUTIS HONOR | Honour is the reward of virtue. Cheere, Clarke of Borde Hill, Cox, co. Perth, Lovelace, Tetlow. |
| PRAEMONEMUS | We forewarn. 3617 Co. of Hampshire Fighter Control Unit, RAAF. |
| PRAEMONEO DE PERICULIS | I give advance warning against danger. No. 91 Signals Unit, RAF. |
| PRAEMONITUS PRAEMUNITUS | Forewarned is forearmed. Intelligence Sch., RAF Sch. founded in September 1942 at Highgate, N. London, in house of the late Sir Robert Waley-Cohen. |
| PRAEPAREMUS BELLUM | We prepare for war. Wing HQ, 3 RAF Regt. |
| PRAESIDIA NOSTRA EXERCEMUS | We exercise our defences. 286 Sq., RAF. |
| PRAESIDIUM BURGI DE DUMFRIES ALOREBURN | The guard of the town of Dumfries. Dumfries-shire Volunteer Regt., 1914. |
| PRAETER SESCENTOS | More than 600. 600 City of London Sq., AAF. Motto is intended to convey meaning of 'an immense number' and hence a redoubtable adversary. |
| PRAESTA IN OFFICIIS | Excel in duties. RAF station, Syerston. |
| PRAESTAT OPES SAPIENTIA | Wisdom affords wealth. Hampden Sch., Middx. (founded 1557 by Robert Hammond, a Hampton merchant), Upcher (Wisdom excels wealth). |
| PRAESTAT UNI PROBO QUAM MILLE IMPROBIS PLACERE | Better that I should please one good man than a thousand bad men. Frederick I 'Barbarossa', Holy Roman Emperor, drowned crossing a river in Asia Minor in Third Crusade, 1190. |
| PRAESTO ET PERSISTO | I undertake and preserve. Briscoe, Bts., Drake-Briscoe, Earls of Haddington (Baillie Hamilton), Winchester. |
| PRAESTO ET PERSTO | I am ready and go on. Earls of Haddington (Baillie Hamilton), Weeks. |
| PRAESTO UT PRAESTEM | I am forward that I may excel. Preston of Valleyfield, Bts. |
| PRAETIO PRUDENTIA PRAESTAT | Prudence supplies with a reward. Lords Margadale (Morrison), Morrison of Islay House. |
| PRAISE GOD | Kerr. |
| PRAISE GOD FOR ALL | Bakers' Co., inc. 1486 (three garbs (*or* corn sheaves) in shield). |
| PRATIS PRAESTO VIRENTIBUS | Distinguished by flowering meadows, East Grinstead (Sussex) UDC. |

| | |
|---|---|
| PRAVDA VITEZI | Order of the White Lion (Czechoslovakia). |
| PRAEVOLAMUS DESIGNANTES | We fly before marking. 582 Sq., RAF (unit dropping flares to mark targets). |
| PRECISION IN DEFENCE | 116 Sq., RAF. |
| PRELUDE TO PROFICIENCY | No. 56 Operational Training Unit, RAF. |
| PREMI NON OPPRIMI | To be pressed not oppressed. Viscount Bennett *(NEP)*, Bennit. |
| PREMO AD HONOREM | I press forward to honour. Walker of Pembroke House, Bts. |
| PREND MOI TEL QUE JE SUIS | Take me as I am. Bell, Marquesses of Ely (Tottenham), Loftus, Ricketts, Bts. |
| PRENEZ EN GRÉ | Take in good will. Ogle. |
| PRENEZ HALEINE, TIREZ FORT | Take breath, pull strongly. Giffard. (according to story recounted in Elvin's *Handbook of Mottoes*, motto relates to incident when Sir John Giffard of Chillington shot a panther which had escaped from his private zoo; the Giffards are one of the few Norman families in *B.L.G.*, and the Sir John in question attended Henry VIII at Field of Cloth of Gold, 1520), Smith-Dorrien-Smith. |
| PREPARE | No. 227 Operational Conversion Unit, RAF. |
| PREPARE AND HOLD | No. 22 Maintenance Unit, RAF. |
| PREPARED | No. 216 Maintenance Unit, RAF. |
| PREPARED FOR ALL THINGS | 296 Sq., RAF. Has scroll in badge signifying unit's role in dropping leaflets over enemy territory. |
| PREPARE FOR BATTLE | No. 12 Operational Training Unit, RAF. |
| PREPARED TO ATTACK | No. 231 Operations Conversion Unit, RAF. |
| PRESPICE ET PROSPICE | Press and look forward. Hoylake (Ches.) UDC. |
| PRESS FORWARD | Grissell, Mortimer. |
| PRESS ON REGARDLESS | 463 Sq., RAAF. |
| PRESS THROUGH | Borelands, Cockburn, Lords St Helens (Hughes-Young), Young. |
| PREST A FAIRE | Ready to do. Fareham (Hants.) UDC, Dyke, Bts., Sir John Pecke of Lullingstone, Kent, who accompanied Henry VIII to Field of Cloth of Gold, 1520, possibly 'breaking his back by laying manors on it'. |
| PREST D'ACCOMPLIR | Ready to accomplish. Heber, co. Yorks., Earls of Shrewsbury & Waterford (Chetwynd-Talbot), Talbot. |
| PREST MAIN | Have the hand ready. Priestman. |
| PREST POUR LE ROY | Ready for the king. De La Bere, Bts. |
| PREST POUR MON PAYS | Ready for my country. Monson. |
| PRESTANTE DOMINO | The Lord helping. Dundee High Sch., founded by monastery of Lindores thirteenth century. |
| PRESTS POUR NOSTRE PAYS | Ready for our country. Welton (Lincs.) RDC, 1955. |
| PRÊT À TRESSAILLIR | Ready to tremble. Horton-Smith-Hartley. |

| | |
|---|---|
| PRÊT D'ACCOMPLIR | Ready to accomplish. Aston, Nuneaton (Warwicks.), Bor. of (Aston family formerly owned much land in the bor.). |
| PRETIO PRUDENTIA PRAESTAT | Prudence is better than profit. Morison, Richardson, co. Glam. |
| PRETIOSUM QUOD UTILE | That is valuable which is useful. Affleck. |
| PRETIUMQUE ET CAUSA LABORIS | Both the prize and the motive of labour. Burnley (Lancs.), Co. Bor. of. |
| PREUX ET AUDACIEUX | Brave and audacious. 22 Sq., RAF (served in France, 1914–18). |
| PRIDE IN LOYALTY | No. 67 Group HQ, RAF. |
| PRIDE IN OUR PAST FAITH IN OUR FUTURE | Hertford, Bor. of. |
| PRIDE IN SERVICE | RAF station, Brampton. |
| PRIMI HASTATI | The first of the legion. 109 Sq., RAF (in earlier history of the Roman army, above term was used to describe the front ranks; meaning also men of full military age). |
| PRIMORDIA QUAERERE RERUM | Seek the beginnings of things. Lord Rutherford of Nelson. |
| PRIMUM AGMEN IN CAELO | The vanguard in the heavens. 237 Sq., RAF (Rhodesia) (originally unit of Southern Rhodesian Air Force). |
| PRIMUS ADMONERE PRIMUS FERIRE | First to warn, first to strike. No. 1 Signals Unit, RAF. |
| PRIMUS CIRCUMDEDISTI ME | You are the first to encompass me. Manuel I the Fortunate (also called the Great) 1495–1521; King of Portugal, under whom Portuguese discoverers made great voyages round Africa and in the Indian Ocean; the King's badge was the globe, to which of course the words applied. |
| PRIMUS IN INDIS | First in India. 39th Foot (Dorsetshire Regt.), motto reflects pride of the Regt. in being the first to serve in the Indian peninsula. |
| PRIMUS IN URBE | First in the City. 5th City of London Bn. (London Rifle Brigade) Territorials. |
| PRIMUS INTER PARES | First among equals. No. 20 Service Flying Training Sch., RAF. (This famous phrase is applied to the Pope by ecclesiastics who recognize his position as premier bishop of the Christian Church but do not accept him as Vicar of Christ and temporal head of the entire Church.) |
| PRIMUS VEL IN PRIMIS | First or among the first. Hatfield Coll., Durham Univ. |
| PRINCEPS ET PATRIA | Prince and country. Order of St Charles (Monaco). |
| PRINCIPIA NON HOMINES | Beginnings not men. Sandbach (Ches.) UDC, 1956. |
| PRINCIPIIS OBSTA | Meet the danger at its approach. Lord Badeley (NEP), Ffolkes, Bts. |
| PRISCA CONSTANTIA | Ancient constancy. Newcastle-under-Lyme (Staffs.), Bor. of. |
| PRISTINAE VIRTUTIS MEMOR | Mindful of the valour of our ancestors. RAF station, Bassingbourn, 2nd Foot – Royal West Surrey Regt. |

| | |
|---|---|
| PRIUS FRANGITUR QUAM FLECTITUR | He is sooner broken than bent. Ballantine Dykes. Pedigree in *B.L.G.*, 1952 records the history of Thomas Dykes of Wardhall, a devoted adherent of Charles I; imprisoned and fined heavily by Puritans and offered liberty if he would renounce his loyalty; his reply was in the above words, which were adopted as motto by his descendants. |
| PRO ALIIS VIVO | I live for others. Eley, Bt. |
| PRO ANGLIA VALENS | Valiant for England. RAF station, Honington. |
| PRO ARIS ET FOCIS | For our altars and our homes (motto is reminiscent of passage in Macaulay, *Lays of Ancient Rome*, Horatius). Alleyne, co. Cork, Blomfield, Campbell of Arduaine, co. Argyll, Campbell of Shirven, Viscount Cilcennin *(NEP)*, 1972, Lords Chatfield, Lords Kirkland, M'Naught, Phelips, Purdon, Snell, Wait, Wills, Woodford, RAF station, Upwood (For hearths and homes), 1st Chepstow VRC Territorials (Monmouth Regt.), 11th County of London Bn. (Finsbury Rifles) Territorials, Duke of Cambridge's Middlesex Yeomanry Hussars, Exeter Volunteer Regt., 1914, Fife Light Horse (1908, Fife and Forfar Yeomanry), Middlesex Imperial Yeomanry, North Somerset Yeomanry (Dragoons), Queen's Own Royal Staffordshire Yeomanry. |
| PRO BONO MALUM | Evil for good. Ludovico Ariosto, 1474–1533, Italian poet, author of *Orlando Furioso* and many other works; allusion to his treatment by Cardinal D'Este. |
| PRO BONO AMNIUM | For the good of all. Guinness Mahon Holdings Ltd. |
| PRO BONO OPPIDO | For the good town. Horbury UDC. |
| PRO CHRISTO ET PATRIA | For Christ and my country. Gilbert, Ker, Verner, Bts. |
| PRO CHRISTO ET PATRIA DULCE PERICULUM | For Christ and my country, danger is sweet. Carr, Dukes of Roxburghe (Innes-Ker). |
| PRO CIVITATE | For the citizens and the city. Fulham, London Bor. of. |
| PRO DEO ET CATHOLICA FIDE | For God and the Catholic faith. Altham of Timbercombe, Som. |
| PRO DEO ET ECCLESIA(E) | For God and the Church. Bishopp, Bt. |
| PRO DEO ET PATRIA | For God and country. Hughes of Denford, Bt., Innes, Lillingston, Maguire, Peart. |
| PRO DEO ET POPULO | For God and the people. Bishop's Stortford (Herts.) UDC. |
| PRO DEO ET REGE | For God and the king. Bickerton, Blacker, Golding, Hawkins, Bts., Masterton, Parsons, Bt., Richardson of Rossfad, Earls of Rosse (Parsons). |
| PRO DEO ET REGE, PRO PATRIA ET LEGE | For God and king, for country and law. De Stacpoole. |
| PRO DEO PATRIA ET REGE | For God, my country and my king. Beugo, Blades, James, Bts., Taylor of Dodworth. |
| PRO DEO PATRIA ET AMICIS | For God, country and friends. The Lady Kinloss (Freeman–Grenville). |

| | |
|---|---|
| PRO DEO PRODEO | I come forth for God. St Thomas of Canterbury R.C. Sch., Blackpool, 1967. |
| PRO DEO, REGE ET PATRIA | For God, my king and my country. Blaydes of Rawby, Lords Ebbisham (Blades), Fane de Salis, McDowall, Woodbridge Sch., Suffolk, 1577, refounded 1662. |
| PRO ECCLESIA | For the Church. Ecclesiastical Insurance Office Ltd. |
| PRO ECCLESIA DEI | For the Church of God. Swainson. |
| PRO FIDE ABLECTUS | Chosen for fidelity. Ablett. |
| PRO FIDE AC PATRIA | For faith and country. Longe, Wade. |
| PRO FIDE, REGE ET LEGE | For faith, king and law. Order of the White Eagle (Russia). |
| PRO FIDE, REGE, ET PATRIA PUGNO | I fight for faith, king and country. Lentaigne. |
| PRO JURE SEMPER | Always for the right. Pearce-Edgcumbe. |
| PRO JUSTITIA PRO REGE | For justice and the king. HMS *Southampton*. |
| PRO LEGE ET GREGE | For the law and the flock. Alfonso X 'the Wise', King of Castile and Leon 1252–84, renowned student of Ptolemaic astronomy, the study of which he preferred to being elected Holy Roman Emperor (see Bryce, *Holy Roman Empire*). |
| PRO LEGE ET LIMITE | For the law and the limit. Scott-Elliot. |
| PRO LEGE ET REGE | For the king and the law. Horton, Kidson, Mandit, Stewart of Fincastle. |
| PRO LEGE SENATUQUE REGE | For law, state and sovereign. Dodsworth, Bts. |
| PRO LEGIBUS AC REGIBUS | For laws and kings. Maryon-Wilson, Lords Nunburnholme (Wilson), Wilson of Sandbach. |
| PRO LIBERIS | For the free. Independent Schools Assn., Inc. |
| PRO LIBERTATE | For liberty. Wallace of that Ilk, 106 Sq., RAF (For freedom). |
| PRO LIBERTATE PATRIAE | For liberty of my country. Lords Clarina (Massey) *(NEP)*, Evans, Massy, Maysy. |
| PRO LUCE NOBILIS SUM | I am noble on behalf of the light. James Ensor, 1860–1949, Anglo–Belgian painter and lithographer, cr. Baron by King of the Belgians, 1949. |
| PRO MAGNA CHARTA | For Magna Carta. Dashwood of West Wycombe, Bts., Lords Le Despencer, Stapleton. |
| PRO MITRA CORONAM | A crown for a mitre. Sharp-Bethune, Sharpe. |
| PRO PATRIA | For my country. Adamson, Bannerman, Bts. (whose ancestors were hereditary banner-bearers to the Kings of Scotland), Betson, Bulman, Bonsall, Cameron, Bt., Carbery, Bts., Cooke, Douglas of Carnoustie, Bt., Groseth, Hastie, Hay, Bts., Higgins, Lords Hotham, James, Bts., Kane, Kay, Newlands, Newton of that Ilk, Ogilvie, Old Boys' Corps, 1914 (Inns of Court), Order of the Sword (Sweden), Provan, Rochead, Scott, Skipton, Sterling-Hamilton of Preston, Bts., Turner, Earls Wavell *(NEP)*, Warrington, Widdrington, Wood of Holm Hall, Woodley. |

| | |
|---|---|
| PRO PATRIA CONAMUR | For our country we try. 18th (Queen Mary's Own) Royal Hussars (also has Pro Rege, pro lege, pro patria conamur). |
| PRO PATRIA DIMICANS | Fighting for our country. Ellesmere Coll., Salop, 1884. |
| PRO PATRIA ET REGE | For country and king. Jones of Llanmiloe, Thomas. |
| PRO PATRIA INVICTUS | Unconquered for my country. Odell. |
| PRO PATRIA MORI | To die for my country. Wolfe. |
| PRO PATRIA NON TIMIDUS PERIRE | Not afraid to die for my country. Mostyn-Champney, Bts. |
| PRO PATRIA OMNIA | All things for one's country. Viscount Lee of Fareham (NEP). |
| PRO PATRIA POPULOQUE | For country and people. Blundell's Sch., Tiverton, Devon (founded under will of Peter Blundell, clothier of Tiverton, by his executor Lord Chief Justice Sir John Popham; was thus still fairly young when 'girt John Ridd' attended (Blackmore, Lorna Doone). |
| PRO PATRIA SEMPER | For my country ever. Power, Bts. |
| PRO PATRIA VIVERE ET MORI | To live and die for our country. Grattan. |
| PRO PELLE CUTEM | Hide for a hide. Hudson's Bay Co. |
| PRO PLURIMIS ADSTO | I stand ready on behalf of many. RAF station, Steamer Point. |
| PRO RECTO LABORA | Work for the right. Lord Citrine. |
| PRO REGE | For the king. Burnaby, Bt., Christie of Durie, co. Fife, Graham of Lymekilns, Charles Edgar Hires of Pennsylvania (granted by College of Arms), Macfie, Mackie, Macphie, Porcher, Sebright, Bts., Titterton. |
| PRO REGE AC FIDE AUDAX | Bold for king and faith. Bideford (Devon), Bor. of. |
| PRO REGE DIMICO | I fight for the king. Punning motto, since it belongs to the Dymoke family, refers to fact that since 1377 the head of the house of Dymoke has held the office of King's or Queen's Champion. Privilege derives from holding the manor of Scrivelsby; duty attached to the office was that the Champion should appear in full armour, mounted on a charger, at the Sovereign's Coronation Banquet in Westminster Hall, and should then challenge to mortal combat all who denied the Sovereign's title. The last time this ceremony was carried out was in 1821, when Sir Henry Dymoke rode a horse from Astley's Circus (which was trained to walk backwards) into Westminster Hall. In 1953 the present John Dymoke established his right as Champion before the Court of claims and as such had his place at the Coronation (see B.L.G., 1952 and (in fiction) Sir Walter Scott's Redgauntlet). |
| PRO REGE ET IMPERIO | For king and Empire. Norton-Griffiths, Bts. |
| PRO REGE ET LEGE | For king and the law. Horton, Kidston, Mandit, Leeds, City of, Leeds Volunteer Training Corps, Stewart. |

| | |
|---|---|
| PRO REGE ET PATRIA | For king and country. Aberherdour, Ainslie, Armistead, Bell, Cameron of Garth, Shetland, Cameron of Lochiel, Lords De Tabley *(NEP)*, Franklyn, Hamond, Lords Hardinge of Penshurst, Leicester, Leslie, Earls of Leven and Melville (Leslie-Melville), Lyon, MacCubbin, Nightingale, Pode, Rooke, Smith of Preston, Bts., Stewart of Wheatley. |
| PRO REGE ET POPULO | For king and people. Barrow, Bts., Basset, co. Cornwall. |
| PRO REGE ET RELIGIONE | For king and faith. Wight-Boycott (formerly of Rudge Hall, Salop), descended in female line from Silvanus Boycott and his brother Francis who were granted arms in 1663 for services to Charles I in providing grenades and shot; arms show grenades in shield and crest. |
| PRO REGE ET REPUBLICA | For king and state. Paul. |
| PRO REGE EXACUUNT | For the king they point their sting. Ferdinand de Medici, Cardinal and Grand Duke of Tuscany, d. 1609. |
| PRO REGE, LEGE, GREGE | For the king, the law and the people. Earls of Bessborough (Ponsonby), Lords Brougham and Vaux (Brougham), Lords Forteviot (Dewar), Lords De Mauley (Ponsonby), Ponsonby, Lords Sysonby (Ponsonby), Whither. |
| PRO REGE PATRIA ET DEO | For king, country and God. Benthall of Benthall, Salop. |
| PRO REGE SAEPE, PRO PATRIA SEMPER | For the king often, for my country always. Eyre, Lawrence, co. Galway, Redington. |
| PRO REGE SEMPER | Always for the king. Thoyts. |
| PRO REGI ET PATRIA PUGNANS | Fighting for my king and country. Pasley, Bts. |
| PRO REPUBLICA | For the state. Nicholson. |
| PRO RURE ET FOCIS | For the country and our hearths. Yeovil (Som.) RDC, 1953. |
| PRO RURE PRO PATRIA | For the country and for our country. Hertford RDC. |
| PRO SAEPE SALUTE, PRO SALUTEM SEMPER | For safety often, for health always. Bridlington (E.R. Yorks.), Bor. of. |
| PRO SALUTE | For safety. Legal and General Assurance Soc. Ltd. |
| PRO TANTO QUID RETRIBUAMUS | What shall we repay for so much. Belfast, City and Co. Bor. |
| PRO VIRTUTE | For virtue. Earl Loreburn (Reid) *(NEP)*, Reid. |
| PROBE PROBARE | To test properly. Aeroplane & Armament Experimental Est. |
| PROBITAS VERUS HONOS | Honesty is true honour. Bateson, Viscount Chetwynd, Dalby, co. Leics., Harvey, Lacon, Bts., Mardon, Newman of Mamhead, Bts., Vicary. |
| PROBITATE AC VIRTUTE | By probity and virtue. Rose of Rayners, Bts. |
| PROBITATE ET ARTE | By probity and art. Inc. Assn. of Architects & Surveyors. |
| PROBITATE ET LABORE | By honesty and toil. Baring Bts., Lord Cable *(NEP)*, Earls of Cromer (Baring), Gould, Lords Northbrook (Baring), Lords Revelstoke (Baring), RAF station, West Raynham. |

| | |
|---|---|
| PROBUM NON PAENITET | The honest man repents not. Leader, Lords Sandys (Hill), Sandys, co. Lancs. |
| PROBUS ET FIDELIS | Upright and faithful. Inst. of Bankers. |
| PROCEDAMUS IN PACE | Let us proceed in peace. Molineux-Montgomerie. |
| PROCESSUS PER SCIENTIAM | Advance through science. Nat. Coll. of Food Tech. |
| PROCURE, PREPARE, PROVIDE | No. 9 Mechanical Transport Base Depot, RAF. |
| PRODEANT VEXILLA | Let the standards go forward. Standard Bank Ltd., 1962. |
| PRODESSE | To serve. Hindley (Lancs.) UDC. |
| PRODESSE CIVIBUS | To benefit my fellow citizens. Beckett, co. Yorks, Denison, Lords Grimthorpe (Beckett). |
| PRODESSE QUAM CONSPICI | To be available rather than conspicuous. Buck of Agecroft, Chamberlayne, Cocks, Grote, Leigh, Lords Somers (Cocks), Rydal Sch., Colwyn Bay, 1885 (To be of benefit rather than to be seen). |
| PRODUCAT TERRA | The earth produces. Tobacco Pipe Makers & Tobacco Blenders Co. |
| PROELIUM REDINTEGRATUR | By repairing we fight again. No. 57 Maintenance Unit, RAF. |
| PROEMIUM VIRTUTIS GLORIA | Glory is the reward of virtue. Lords Wyfold (Hermon-Hodge). |
| PROFITAS ACCURATIO JUSTITIA | Profit, accuracy, justice. Inst. of Cost and Works Accnts. |
| PROGREDERE | Advance. Jarvis, Bts. |
| PROGREDERE NE REGREDERE | Advance, not recede. Honyman, Bts., White of Salle Park, Bts. |
| PROGREDI ET CONSERVARE | To progress and to conserve. Pershore (Worcs.) RDC, 1962. |
| PROGREDIAMUR | Let us progress. Eccles (Lancs.), Bor. of. |
| PROGREDIEMUR ET SURSUM | We progress and lift up. Bunting of West Hartlepool. |
| PROGREDIENS CONFIRMATUR ANIMUS | The spirit is confirmed while advancing. Bletchley (Bucks.) UDC. |
| PROGRESS | Blackpool (Lancs.), Co. Bor. of, Flying Coll., RAF, Inst. of Mechanical Engineers, Littlehampton (W. Sussex) UDC, RAF Coll. of Air Warfare. |
| PROGRESS BY ENDEAVOUR | Air Fighting Development Sq., RAF, Long Eaton (Derbys.) UDC. |
| PROGRESS IN UNITY | Teeside, Co. Bor. of. |
| PROGRESS THROUGH ENDEAVOUR | Spalding (Lincs.) RDC, 1954. |
| PROGRESS WITH HONOUR AND DIGNITY | Flaxton RDC. |
| PROGRESS WITH HUMANITY | Haringey, London Bor. of. |
| PROGRESS WITH INDUSTRY | Brooklands County Tech. Coll., Weybridge, Surrey. |
| PROGRESS WITH SAFETY | Assn. of Mining, Electrical & Mechanical Engineers. |
| PROGRESS WITH SECURITY | Wolverhampton & District Bldg. Soc., 1963. |

| | |
|---|---|
| PROGRESS WITH THE PEOPLE | Newham, London Bor. of. |
| PROGRESS WITH UNITY | Ealing, London Bor. of. |
| PROGRESSIO CUM POPULO | Progress with the people. East Ham, London Bor. of. |
| PROGRESSIO ET ALACRITAS | Progress and alacrity. Pennine Insurance Co. Ltd. |
| PROGRESSIO ET CONCORDIA | Progress and concord. Kettering (Northants.), Bor. of. |
| PROGRESSIVE | 654 Sq., RAF. |
| PROMISE AND FULFIL | RAF station, Odiham. |
| PROMISSO STO | Stand to what is promised. Wheeler, Bts. |
| PROMPTE ET CONSULTO | Quickly and advisedly. Lord Plender (NEP), Plenderleith. |
| PROMPTUS | Ready. Blair of Harrow Weald, Bt., Donaldson-Hudson, Russell of Aden, co. Aberdeen. |
| PROMPTUS AD VINDICTAM | Swift to avenge. 412 Sq., RCAF. |
| PROMPTUS ET FIDELIS | Ready and faithful. Carruthers, co. Dumfries, Crondace. |
| PROMPTUS ET FORTIS | Ready and strong. No. 64 Group HQ, RAF. |
| PROPERE ET PROVIDE | Hasten and foresee. Robinson of Toronto, Bts. |
| PROPOSITI TENAX | Firm of purpose. Lords Barnby, Lords Belper (Strutt), Bunny, Lords Chorley, Evans Lombe, Hubbersty, Lister, Piggott, co. Sussex, Smith, Strutt, Tomlinson, Bts., Yeatman. |
| PROPRIA TUEMUR | Let us guard our own. Southborough (Kent) UDC, 1953. |
| PRORSUM IN FUTURUM | Straight on to the future. Lords Rootes. |
| PRORSUM SEMPER | Always forward. Gloucestershire CC. |
| PRORSUM SEMPER HONESTE | Forward always honestly. Assn. of Secretaries. |
| PROSPERITY THROUGH FIDELITY | Beccles (Norfolk), Bor. of. |
| PROSUNT GENTIBUS ARTES | Arts benefit the people. Bermondsey, London Bor. of. |
| PROTECT | RAF station, West Drayton. |
| PROTECT THE POPULACE | Corps of Volunteers Artillery Regt., 1914. |
| PROTECTION | Bradford Permanent Bldg. Soc. |
| PROTEGIMUS | We protect. No. 47 Maintenance Unit, RAF. |
| PROUD TO SERVE | Perring, Bts. |
| PROUDLY | RAF station, Abingdon. |
| PROUDLY WE SERVE | Horsham (W. Sussex) UDC. |
| PROVE BY TEST | Central Trade Test Board, RAF. |
| PROVE TO IMPROVE | RAF station, Aberporth. |
| PROVIDA FUTURI | Foreseeing the future. No. 41 Group HQ, RAF. |
| PROVIDENCE WITH ADVENTURE | Hawkins. |
| PROVIDENTIA | Providence. Anderson, co. Antrim, Anderson, Bts. |
| PROVIDENTIA DEI | The providence of God. Nicholson. |

| | |
|---|---|
| PROVIDENTIA DEI STABILIUNTUR FAMILIAE | Families are established by the providence of God. Lamplugh. |
| PROVIDENTIA ET LABORE | By providence and labour. Wilson of Rigmaden. |
| PROVIDENTIA PROFICIEMUS | We shall make progress with Providence. Norton (E.R. Yorks.) UDC. |
| PROVIDENTIA SALUS | Safety from providence. Economic Insurance Co. Ltd. |
| PROVIDENTIA TUTAMUR | We are protected by Providence. James of Chevington, Kenyon, Norden. |
| PROVIDENTIAE ME COMMITTO | I commit myself to Providence. Lord Inverairn (Beardmore), Kyle, Park. |
| PROVIDUS ESTO | Be thou circumspect. Maxtone, Maxtone-Graham. |
| PROVYD(E) | Drummond-Stewart of Blair, Bts., Rutherford of Liverpool, Bt. |
| PROXIME ET CELERRIME | Most closely and swiftly. 146 Wing HQ, RAF. |
| PRUDENS FUTURI | Prudent of the future. Letchworth (Herts.) UDC. |
| PRUDENS QUI PATIENS | He is prudent who is patient. Coke, Earls of Leicester (Coke), Lushington. |
| PRUDENS SIMPLICITAS BEAT | Prudent simplicity blesses. Frederick, Bts. |
| PRUDENTER AMO | I love prudently. Scott of Gala. |
| PRUDENTER ET CONSTANTER | Prudently and constantly. Mount, Bts. |
| PRUDENTER QUI SEDULO | He does prudently who does industriously. Lees-Milne. |
| PRUDENTIA | Prudence, Young of Bailieborough, Bts. |
| PRUDENTIA ET CONSTANTIA | With prudence and constancy. Denman, Kingdom of Denmark. |
| PRUDENTIA ET VIRTUTE | By prudence and valour. Rankin, Bts. |
| PRUDENTIA IN ADVERSIS | Prudence in adversity. Pope Gregory XII, 1406–15, Cardinal Angelo Corrario. |
| PRUDENTIA PRAESTAT | Prudence excels. Morison, Morrison-Low, Bts. |
| PSALLAM SPIRITU ET MENTE | I will sing with the spirit and the mind. Roy. Sch. of Church Music, 1950. |
| PUERTO | A haven. Snell. |
| PUGNA PRO PATRIA | Fight for your country. Aldershot (Hants.), Bor. of, Doughty–Tichborne. |
| PUGNAMUS FINITUM | We fight to a finish. 420 Sq., RCAF. |
| PUGNIS ET CALCIBUS | With fists and heels. 249 Sq., RAF. |
| PULCHRA TERRA DEI DONUM | A beautiful land is the gift of God. Herefordshire CC. |
| PULCHRIOR EX ARDUIS | The brighter from difficulties. Mackenzie of Coul, Bts. |
| PULCHRITUDO ET SALUBRITAS | Beauty and health. Bournemouth (Hants.), Bor. of. |
| PUR FEL DUR | Pure as steel. Lords Trevethin and Oaksey (Lawrence). |
| PUREFOY MA JOYE | True faith is my delight. Purefoy. |
| PURITAS FONS HONORIS | Purity is the fountain of honour. Sykes (formerly of Brookfield). |

PUT ON THE WHOLE ARMOUR OF GOD — Inc. Assn. of Preparatory Schs., 1959 (St Paul's words in Ephesians 6:11).

PWY FEEDDIAN DEFFRO — Who dares wake us. Lloyd of Stockton Hall.

PYLKINGTON POLLEDOWN (or PILKYNGTON PAILEDOWN) — The master mows the meadows. Pilkington of Tore.

| | |
|---|---|
| QUA PANDITUR ORBIS | Which way the world extends. Campbell of Monzie. |
| QUA POTE LUCET | He shines whenever possible. Bowyer-Smyth, Bts., Smijth Wyndham of Waghen. |
| QUAE AMISSA SALVA | What has been lost is safe. Keith, Earls of Kintore (Keith). |
| QUAE JUNCTA FIRMA | Union is strength. Leslie of Kinivie, Reinsurance Corp. Ltd. |
| QUAE PROMISI EA PERFICIAM | What I have promised that I will perform. Musker. |
| QUAE PROSUNT OMNIBUS ARTES | Arts which are useful to all. Royal Coll. of Surgeons. |
| QUAE RECTA TENE | Hold what is right. Romsey (Hants.), Bor. of, 1959. |
| QUAE REGIS IN TERRIS NOSTRI NON PLENA LABORIS? | What part of the world is not full of our labours? Jean de Montluc, Bishop of Valence, Ambassador to Elizabeth I; quotation from Virgil refers to his diplomatic work. |
| QUAE RENDA QUAE SUPRA | What are returned are above. Peake. |
| QUAE SERATA SECURA | Things locked up are safe. Douglas of Barloch, Douglas of Mains. |
| QUAE SUPRA | Things which are above. Agar-Roberts, Roberts. |
| QUAE SURSUM SUNT QUAERITE | Seek those things which are above (part of apostolic injunction completed with 'where Christ sitteth at the right hand of God'). St John's Sch., Leatherhead, Surrey, 1851. |
| QUAE VERNANT CRESCUNT | Things which are green grow. Burnett of Kenway, co. Aberdeen. |
| QUAECUNQUE | Whatever. Lords Reith. |
| QUAERENDO SERVAMUS | We serve by seeking. 277 Sq., RAF. |
| QUAERERE VERUM | Seek what is true. Downing Coll., Camb., John Hart & Co., Liverpool, Royal Belfast Academical Inst., 1810. |
| QUAERIMUS ET PETIMUS | We search and strike (seek). 423 Sq., RCAF. |
| QUAERITE VERA | Seek true things. Salvage Assn. |
| QUAERO | I seek. 544 Sq., RAF. |
| QUALIS AB INCEPTO | The same as from the beginning. De Grey, Evans of Nantymoch, Hamilton, Lords Holm Patrick (Hamilton), Majendie, Mirehouse, Marquesses of Rippon (Robinson), Robb, Weddell. |
| QUALIS FIDES TALIS VITA | As is faith so is your life. Bishop's Coll., Cheshunt, Herts. |
| QUALIS VITA FINIS ITA | As is our life, so is our end. Lords Coleridge, Yonge. |

| | |
|---|---|
| QUAM BONUM IN UNUM HABITARE | How good it is to dwell in unity. Royal Bor. of Kensington and Chelsea (motto adopted with new arms grant, 1965, on union of the boroughs). |
| QUAM CELERRIME AD ASTRA | How swiftly to the stars. 27 (bomber) Sq., RAF. |
| QUAM NON TORRET HYEMS | Which winter does not nip with cold. Caunter, Kyd. |
| QUAM PLURIMIS PRODESSE | To do good to as many as you can. Worsley, Bts. |
| QUAND DIEU PLAYE | When God pleases. Aglionby (formerly of Nunnery, Cumb.). |
| QUAND MÊME | Even the same. Viscount D'Abernon (Vincent) *(NEP)* |
| QUANT JE PUIS | As much as I can. Stonyhurst Coll., Lancs. (founded 1593 at St Omer by Fr. Robert Parsons; at French Revolution came to England and Mr Weld of Lulworth in 1794 offered to his old masters his hall at Stonyhurst). |
| QUANTI EST SAPERE | Of how much worth it is to be wise. S.E. Derbyshire RDC, Sch. of Tech. Training, RAF (How important it is to be wise). |
| QUANTUM IN REBUS INANE | What emptiness in all things. Odell of Carriglea, Osborn, Bts. |
| QUANTUM SUFFICIT | As much as suffices. Lord Williamson (Life Baron). |
| QUASCUNQUE FINDIT | It divides whatever (things). Fernandes. |
| QUASI CURSORES | As the runners. Oakham Sch., Rutland, 1584. |
| QUASI MORIENTES ET ECCE VIVIMUS | Dying, behold we live (St Paul, 2 Corinthians 6:9). Archbishop Erling Eidem of Sweden, b. 1880. |
| QUE NUL NE S'Y FROTTE | That nothing vexes me. Crequy. |
| QUEM TE DEUS ESSE JUSSIT | What God commands thee to be. Earls of Sheffield (Holroyd). |
| QUERCUS | The oak. Wright, co. Lincs. |
| QUERCUS ROBUR SALUS PATRIAE | The strength of the oak is the safety of our country. Oakes. |
| QUHIDDER WILL ZIE | Stewart of Achnacone, Stewart of Ardpatrick, Stewart of Strathcarry, Bts. |
| QUI AMAT VIVAT | He who loves lives. Irvin. |
| QUI CAPIT CAPITUR | He who takes is taken. Smyth of Ashton Court, Bristol. |
| QUI CONDUCIT | Who leads. Borthwick of Borthwick, Lord Glenesk (Borthwick), Lord Whitburgh (Borthwick) *(NEP)*. |
| QUI CUSTODIT | Who guards. No. 399 Signals Unit, RAF. |
| QUI DOCET IN DOCTRINA | Who teaches in doctrine. Chester Diocesan Training Coll. |
| QUI FACILE VINCIT BENE INCIPIT | He begins well who conquers easily. Butler of Edgbaston, Bt. |
| QUI FACIT PER ALIUM FACIT PER SE | Who does something by means of another does it himself. Perse Sch., Cambridge, 1615. |
| QUI INVIDET MINOR EST | He who envies is inferior. Earls Cadogan, Pugh. |
| QUI LABOR ILLI GAUDIA | Who (has) labour has joys. Goodson, Bts. |

| | |
|---|---|
| QUI ME ALIT ME EXTINGUIT | Who nourishes me, extinguishes me. Jean de Poitiers, Seigneur de Saint-Vallier, captain of archers to Francis I of France; sentenced to execution for intrigues and saved on scaffold by intercession of his daughter Diane de Poitiers. |
| QUI NON DAT QUOD HABET NON ACCIPIT ILLE QUOD OPTAT | He who does not bestow what he has does not receive what he desires. Henry III, 1216–72. |
| QUI NON LABORAT NON MANDUCAT | He who does not work shall not eat. Philippe de Comines, 1447–1511, minister, first, of Charles the Bold of Burgundy, then of Louis XI of France, wrote celebrated *Mémoires*. |
| QUI NON PROFICIT DEFICIT | He who does not succeed fails. Barlow of Bradwall Hall, Bts., Channon of Kelvedon Hall, Essex. |
| QUI OPERIT CAELUM | Who covereth the heaven. RAF station, Topcliffe (badge is the Wakeman's Horn of Ripon used from early times to give alarm). |
| QUI PATITUR VINCIT | He who endures conquers. Kinnard. Kinnard Kinnaird, Wells, Bts. |
| QUI PENSE | Who thinks. Gaisford-St Lawrence, Earls of Howth (St Lawrence *(NEP)*, Lawrence, Walford. |
| QUI SERA SERA | What will be will be. Betterson, Edgell, Ffolkes, Bts., Wolferstan, co. Suffolk. |
| QUI STAT CAVEAT NE CADET | Let he that standeth take heed lest he fall (1 Corinthians 10:12). Domvile, Domville. |
| QUI UNUM TANGIT OMNES TANGIT | Who touches one touches all. London Retail Meat Traders' Assn. Inc., 1922. |
| QUI UTI SCIT EI BONA | Be wealth to him who knows how to use it. Lords Berwick (Noel-Hill), *(NEP)*. Hill. |
| QUI UTUNTUR NON UTANTUR | Those who use are not used. Queen's Coll., Birmingham. |
| QUI VIVE | Who goes there. RAF Northern Sector Operations Centre. |
| QUICQUID AGAS AGE | Whatever you are doing, do it. 28 Sq., RAF. |
| QUICQUID DIGNUM SAPIENTE BONQUE EST | Whatever is worthy is for wisdom and for good. Peach. |
| QUID CLARIUS ASTRIS? | What is brighter than the stars? Baillie of Hoperig, Lords Burton (Baillie), Lords Lamington (Cochrane-Baillie). |
| QUID NON | What not. Gilbert of Compton. |
| QUID NON DEO JUVANTE? | What can we not do with God's aid? Salt of Saltaire, Bts. |
| QUID NON PRO PATRIA? | What would one not do for his country? Campbell of Monzie Mathew. |
| QUID NOBIS ARDUI? | What is hard for us? 19th Bn. (Kensington), 1914, 13th Co. of London Bn. (Kensington) Territorials, Royal Bor. of Kensington. |
| QUID PRODEST? | What does it profit? Webb of Knocktoran. |

| | |
|---|---|
| QUID QUID AGIS AGE TOTO | Whatever you do, do it for the whole. Lord Upjohn (*NEP*). |
| QUID RETRIBUAM DOMINO? | What return shall I make to the Lord? King James' Gram. Sch., Knaresborough, Yorks. |
| QUID SI COELUM RUAT? | What if the heavens fall? 56 Sq., RAF. |
| QUID UTILIS | Something useful. Goldie. |
| QUID VERUM ATQUE DECENS | What is true is also befitting. Ricketts, Trevor. |
| QUID VERUM ATQUE DECENS CURO ET ROGO | I care for and ask what is true and befitting (Horace, *Epistles* I. ii.). La Touche. |
| QUIETUM NEMO ME IMPUNE LACESSIT | No one provokes me with impunity when I am at rest. Francesco Sforza, d. 1466, took possession of Milan. |
| QUINQUE IN UNO | Five in one. West Midlands Police Authority, 1967. |
| QUIS AUDEAT LUCI AGGREDII | Who would dare to go against the light. Prior. |
| QUIS ERIPET DENTES | Who will draw my teeth. HMS *Tiger* (tiger's head as badge). |
| QUIS METUIT | Who feared. Sturminster (Dorset) RDC, 1961. |
| QUIS NOS SEPARABIT | Who shall separate us. Peninsular and Orient Steam Navigation Co., 1937. |
| QUIS OCCURSABIT? | Who will encounter me? Lords Hamilton of Dalzell. |
| QUIS SEPARABIT? | Who shall separate? Pope Boniface IX, 1389–1404, a Neapolitan, 88th Foot – Connaught Rangers, Order of St Patrick (Order founded in 1783 by George III in order to reward distinguished Irish noblemen and gentlemen; the question was answered in 1921 when the 26 counties of Southern Ireland were granted independence from Britain and became Eire, now the Republic of Ireland; since 1921 no fresh appointments have been made to the Order, which is therefore obsolescent), Connaught Rangers, 4th (Royal Irish) Dragoon Guards (the words of the motto are followed by MDCCLXXXIII, date of cr. of Order of St Patrick; regimental badge includes the Cross of St Patrick), 4th and 7th Dragoon Guards (words of motto followed by MCMXXII, date of amalgamation of the regts.), Irish Guards, formed 1900, 5th (Royal Irish) Lancers, Royal Irish Rifles, Sligo Rifles (Militia). |
| QUIS TIMET? | Who fears? Price of Saintfield. |
| QUIS UT DEUS? | Who is there like God? Order of St Michael (Bavaria). St Michael's Coll., Leeds. |
| QUISQUE FABER FORTUNAE SUAE | Everyone smith of his own fortune. Faber. |
| QUISQUE TENAX | Each tenacious. 99 Sq., RAF. |
| QUO CERTIOR EO TUTIOR | The more fully informed, the safer. Aeronautical Information Documents Unit, RAF. |
| QUO DEUS VULT | Whither God wills. Wills of Hazelwood, Bts. |
| QUO FAS ET GLORIA | Whither law and glory (lead). Robertson-Glasgow. |
| QUO FAS ET GLORIA DUCUNT | Whither destiny and glory lead us. 97th Foot (Queen's Own), Roy. West Kent Regt. One of two mottoes granted 1832 Royal Regt. of Artillery, the other being Ubique. |

| | |
|---|---|
| QUO FATA VOCANT | Whither the fates call. Adlercron, Bland, Cowell, Lords de Lisle (Sidney), Jackson, co. Beds., Russell of Handsworth, Sidney, Bts., Lords Thurlow (Cumming-Bruce). 5th Foot – Northumberland Fusiliers, 7th (The Princess Royal's) Dragoon Guards, Tyneside Scottish (raised in 1914–18). |
| QUO FATA VOCENT | Whither the fates may call. 500 Co. of Kent (B) Sq., RAF, formed 1931 at Manston, Kent (badge the White Horse of Kent – a horse forcene). |
| QUO HONESTIOR EO TUTIOR | By how much the more honest, so much the safer. Guise, Bts. |
| QUO JE SURMONTE | By which I rise. Chancellor of Shieldhill, co. Lanark. |
| QUO LUX DUCIT | Where the light leads. Lords Dulverton (Wills), Rendcomb Coll., Glos., 1920 (Whither light leads). |
| QUO JUSSA JOVIS | Whither Jove orders. Maximilien de Béthune, Duc de Sully, 1560–1641, Finance Minister of Henri IV of France. |
| QUO ME CUMQUE VOCAT PATRIA | Wherever my country calls me. Arden of Longcroft, Staffs. Only English family with a proven pre-Conquest pedigree, and the family of Shakespeare's mother, Mary Arden (B.L.G., 1952). |
| QUO NON ASCENDAM? | Whither shall I not rise? Nicolas Fouquet, 1615–80(?), Finance Minister before Colbert, his fall gave the lie to his motto which was begotten of his earlier success. Representation of him is in A. Dumas, *Vicomte de Bragellonne*. |
| QUO NON QUANDO NON? | Whither not? When not? 159 Sq., RAF. |
| QUO VADIS SEQUIMUR | Whither Thou goest we follow. Didsbury Coll., Bristol. |
| QUO VIRTUS DUCIT SCANDO | I climb where virtue leads. Follet. |
| QUOAD POTERO PERFERAM | I endure as much as I can. Lord Hurcomb. |
| QUOCUMQUE | Whithersoever. 173 Sq., RAF. |
| QUOCUMQUE QUID VEHERE VELITIS | Wherever you may wish to carry something. No. 2 Mechanical Transport Sq., RAF. |
| QUOCUMQUE FERAR | Wherever I may be carried. King Peter III of Aragon, 1276–85, who conquered Sicily, 1282. |
| QUOCUNQUE JECERIS STABIT | Wherever you may cast it, it will stand. Macleod of Cadboll, Isle of Man (all. to the arms, three legs conjoined), Isle of Man Rifle Volunteers. |
| QUOD ADEST | That which is present. Marsham. |
| QUOD ADEST GRATUM JUVAT | What is pleasant and present helps. Worsley. |
| QUOD CAEPIO PERSEQUOR | What I take I follow through. Jones of Treeton, Bts. |
| QUOD DEUS VULT | What God wills. Mallaby-Deeley, Bts. |
| QUOD DEUS VULT FIAT | God's will be done. Chetwynd, Bts., Dimsdale, Bts. |
| QUOD DIXI DIXI | What I have said, I have said. Dixie, Bts. (also with addition Deo gratia grata, Grace pleasing to God), Dixey, Dixon Holman (formerly Dixon). |
| QUOD EORUM MINIMIS MIHI | What you did to the least of these, ye did to me (St Matthew 25:40). Corp. of Sons of the Clergy (arms grant 1685). |

| | |
|---|---|
| QUOD ERO SPERO | What I shall be I hope. Barton, Booth, Gore-Booth, Bts., Gowans, Haworth. |
| QUOD FACIO VALDE FACIO | What I do I do with energy. Reardon-Smith, Bts., Sikes, Sykes. |
| QUOD HONESTUM UTILE | What is honest is useful. Annand of Annandale, Lawson, Bts. |
| QUOD IMPROBUM TERRET PROBO PRODEST | What terrifies the wicked is of service to the just. Penzance (Cornwall), Bor. of. |
| QUOD JUSTUM NON QUOD UTILE | What is just, not what is expedient. Phillips of Garendon Park. |
| QUOD MARE NON NOVIT | What the sea did not know. Furness Withy & Co. Ltd. |
| QUOD NON ES NOLIS | Do not want what you are not. Jones of Borth, co. Cardigan. |
| QUOD PETIS HIC EST | Here is what you seek (Horace, *Epistles* I. xi. 29). Inst. of British Engineers. |
| QUOD POTERO ENITAR | What I can, I will try. Ivory. |
| QUOD POTUI PERFECI | I have done what I could do. Viscount Melville (Dundas). |
| QUOD TIBI HOC ALTERI | Do to another what thou wouldst have done to thee (St Luke 6:31). Crawfurd, Fleetwood, Fleetwood-Hesketh, Hesketh, Terry of Middlethorpe Hall. |
| QUOD TIBI ID ALII | Do that to another which thou wouldst have done to thee. Lopes, Lords Ludlow (Lopes) *(NEP)*, Lords Roborough (Lopes). |
| QUOD TIBI VIS FIERI FAC ALTERI | Do to another what you wish done to yourself. Ram. |
| QUOD VERUM TUTUM | What is safe is true. Courtenay, Earls of Devon (Courtenay), Reynolds. |
| QUOD VULT, VALDE VULT | What he wishes, he wishes fervently. Holt, Horton, Mansel, Bts., Maunsell, Porter. |
| QUONDAM HIS VICIMUS ARMIS | Formerly we conquered with these arms. Bowman of Holmbury St Mary, Bts., Carleton, Lords Dorchester (Carleton *NEP*). |
| QUONIAM SUMUS IN VICEM MEMBRA | Since we are members one of another. UK Temperance & General Provident Inst., 1940. |
| QUORSUM VIVERE MORI? MORI VITA | Wherefore live or die? To die is life. Blencowe, Tillard. |
| QUOS BRUMA LEGEBAT | Which winter bequeathed. Italian Academy of Rinovati. |
| QUOVIS NOCTE INTERDIU | Anywhere by day or night. 2nd Tactical Air Force Communications Sq., RAF. |
| QUOVIS PER ARDUA | Everywhere through difficulties. 669 Sq., RAF. |

# R

| RADIO MAXIMO ARVO | I radiate in the greatest field. Radio Manufacturers' Assn. |
|---|---|
| RAG MATERN APOW | For king and country (Cornish). Polkinghorne. |
| RAG Y MATERNHA Y POBEL | For king and people (Cornish). Grylls. |
| RAISED AGAIN | Hunter (formerly of Crighton Dean). |
| RAJAWALI RAJA LANGIT | Eagle King of the sky (Malayan). 36 Sq., RAF (eagle badge). |
| RAMIS MICAT RADIX | The root glisters in its branches. Robertson. |
| RAMOSA CORNUA CERVI | The branching horns of the stag. Woodstock (Oxon.), Bor. of, 1949. |
| RAPIDE | E. Signals Centre, RAF. |
| RATIO ATQUE USUS | Reason and use. Royal Inst. of Chemistry. |
| RATIO MIHI SUFFICIT | The reason is sufficient for me. Graham of Drumgoon. |
| RATIONE DIRIGE CURSUM | Direct thy course by reason. Univ. Coll. Hosp. (or North London Hosp.). |
| RATIONE ET CONCILIO | By reason and counsel. Magistrates' Assn., Lords Trefgarne. |
| RATIONE NON VI | By reason not force. McTaggart, Bt. |
| RE DEU | By God (Cornish). Bolitho. |
| RE ET (E) MERITO | By reality and merit. Bagnell, Clarke, Dobbin, Gildea, Hebden, Turpin, Vassal-Fox. |
| READINESS | Metropolitan Communications Sq., RAF. |
| READY | RAF Levies, Iraq. |
| READY ALL APPEAR | Market Harborough (Leics.) RDC. |
| READY AND FAITHFUL | Walker of Oakley House, Bts. |
| READY AYE READY | Johnston, Merchiston Castle Sch., Edinburgh, 1833, Lords Napier and Ettrick, Sir John Scott of Thirlestaine (given motto and a crest (a sheaf of spears) by James V of Scotland because he was only one of Scots nobles willing to follow the king to war), 1st Brigade Glamorgan Artillery Volunteers. |
| READY TO FIGHT | 404 Sq., RCAF. |
| READY TO SERVE | Ulster Maritime Support Unit, RAAF. |
| READY TO STRIKE | 453 Sq., RAAF. |
| REASON CONTENTS ME | Graham of Esk, Bts., Graham of Netherby, Bts., Graham of Norton Conyers, Bts. |

REBUS ANGUSTIS FORTIS | Brave in adversity. Cobbold.

RECIPIENT FOEMINAE SUSTENTACUTO NOBIS | From us women receive support. Pattenmakers' Co., inc. 1670 (makers of footwear, hence the motto, reference to benefits of pattens (a raised shoe) for wet and muddy roads).

RECTA SURSUM | Right upward. Graham of Duntroun, Reckitt, Bts.

RECTAM VIAM SEQUI | To follow the right way. North Kesteven (Lincs.) RDC.

RECTE AD ARDUA | Honourably throughout difficulties. Muir Mackenzie of Delvine, Bts.

RECTE COLLINEO | I rightly hit the mark. Ashbolt.

RECTE ET CELERITER | Accurately and quickly. RAF Communication Centre, Germany.

RECTE ET SUAVITER | Rightly and agreeably. Curzon, Marquesses of Curzon (NEP), Scarsdale, Wyborn.

RECTE FAC NOLI TIMERE | Do right, do not fear. Prestwick (Lancs.), Bor. of, 1939, Rea Bros. Ltd., 1958.

RECTE FACIENDO SECURUS | Safe in acting justly. Inglis, Bts., Lawrence of Wimbledon Park.

RECTE MONTEM ASCENDAM | I will rightly ascend the mountain. Bowen-Jones, Bt.

RECTE NUMERARE | Rightly to number. Inst. of Chartered Accountants.

RECTE OMNIA DUCE DEO | God being my guide all things will be rightly done. Lords Rennell (Rodd), Rodd.

RECTE QUOD HONESTE | That is rightly which is honestly done. Anderson of Glasgow, Burney, Bts.

RECTE VOLARE | To fly straight. RAF Sch. of Air Navigation.

RECUPERARE ET RENOVARE | To retrieve and restore. No. 63 Maintenance Unit, RAF.

REDDE CUIQUE SUUM | Render to each his own. Pope Eugenius IV, 1431–47, Cardinal Eugenius Gabriel Condolmieri of Venice.

REDDIMUS TAMQUAM NOVA | We restore as new. No. 9 Maintenance Unit, RAF.

REDDITE DEO | Give (thanks) to God. Redditch (Worcs.) UDC 1943 (skilful pun on the name).

REFLECT AND RESOLVE | Lord Fleck (NEP).

REFUGIUM REBUS ADVERSIS | A refuge in adversity. Refuge Assurance Co. Ltd., 1951.

REFULGENT IN TENEBRIS | They glitter in the dark. Studdert.

REFULGET LABORES NOSTROS COELUM | Heaven reflects our labours. Scunthorpe (Lincs.), Bor. of.

REGARDE À LA MORT | Look to the death. Minchin, co. Tipperary.

REGARDEZ MON DROIT | Respect my right. Middleton of Crowfield, Bts.

REGEM DEFENDERE VICTUM | To defend the conquered king. Whitgreave. In B.L.G., 1952, is following entry on Whitgreave pedigree: 'Thomas Whitgreave of Moseley Old Hall, Capt. in the army of Charles I, served at Naseby where he was wounded, and was greatly instrumental in saving the life of Charles II by sheltering him for 2 nights after

Worcester 1651. He was subsequently rewarded by the grant of a pension and was Gentleman Usher to Queen Catherine of Braganza.' He also received an honourable augmentation to the family arms, this being a chief argent thereon a rose gules irradiated gold within a wreath of oak ppr. There is another augmentation to the crest, viz. out of a ducal coronet a sceptre in pale or, surmounted by a branch of oak ppr. and a rose gules slipped in saltire also ppr.

REGI AUSUMAS COLONI — Colonials venture for the king. King Edward's Horse (The King's Overseas Dominions Regt.).

REGI ET PATRIAE FIDELIS — Faithful to king and country. Earls of Norbury (Graham-Toler).

REGI FIDELIS PATRIAEQUE — Faithful to king and country. Scott of Great Barr, Bts.

REGI REGNOQUE FIDELIS — Faithful to king and kingdom. Pochin, Pocock, Bts., Simpson.

REGI SEMPER FIDELIS — Ever faithful to the king. Smyth, Bts.

REGNANT QUI SERVIUNT — They rule who serve. Chesterfield (Derbys.) RDC, Finchley, London Bor. of.

REI CUSTOS TUAE — Guardian of thy property. Fourth Post Office Bldg. Soc.

RELIANCE — Reliance Marine Insurance Co. Ltd., 1947.

RELIGION, INDEPENDENCIA, UNION — Religion, independence, union. Order of Our Lady of Guadaloupe (Mexico).

RELIGIONE AC BONIS ARTIBUS — By religion and good arts. Cotton Coll., co. Staffs., 1762–3.

REM ACU TANGERE — To touch a thing with a needle. 10 Bomber Sq., RAF.

REMEMBER — Allen, Gavin, Home of Wedderburn, Falmouth (Cornwall), Bor. of.

REMEMBER AND FORGET NOT — Hall, co. Monaghan.

REMEMBER YOUR OATH — Haulton, Poulters' Co., inc. 1665.

REMEMBREZ — Remember. Lord Portsea (Falle) (*NEP*).

RENASCENTUR — They will rise again. Viscount Avonmore (Yelverton) (*NEP*), Foster, co. Hants., Goring, Bts., Skiffington.

RENOVATA REDDIMUS — We return it restored. No. 24 Maintenance Unit, RAF.

RENOVATE ANIMOS — Renew your minds. Alliston, Drummond, Hay, Earls of Kinnoull (Hay).

REPAIR — No. 103 Maintenance Unit, RAF.

REPAIR AND PREPARE — No. 390 Maintenance Unit, RAF.

REPARABIT CORNUA PHOEBE — The moon will replenish her horns (from Ovid, *Metamorphoses*). Constable-Maxwell-Scott (descended in the female line from Sir Walter Scott), Lord Polwarth (Hepburn-Scott), Scott of Abbotsford, Scott of Raeburn and Harden (family from which Sir Walter descended).

REPETUNT PROPRIOS QUAQUE RECESSUS — Each seek their own retreats. Herbert of Upper Hemsley.

| | |
|---|---|
| RERUM COGNOSCERE CAUSAS | To know the causes of things (Virgil, *Georgics* ii. 490; quotation starts 'Felix qui potuit'). Inst. of Brewing, Univ. of Sheffield, 168 Sq., RAF. |
| RERUM PRUDENTIA CUSTOS | Prudence the guardian of affairs. Marguerite de France, Duchess of Berry and Savoy, dau. of Francis I. |
| RES ET SPES | Matter and hope. Pyke-Nott. |
| RES MIHI NON ME REBUS | Things yield to me, not I to things. Aitken, Lords Beaverbrook (Aitken). |
| RES NON VERBA | Facts, not words. Crisp, Bts., Duberly, Jackson, Jarret, McMicking, McRorie, Wilson. |
| RES NON VERBA QUAESO | I seek things, not words. Morris, co. Derbys. |
| RESOLUTE | 76 Sq., RAF. |
| RESOLUTE AND FIRM | Milbanke, Bts. |
| RESPICE | Look back. Nepean, Bts. |
| RESPICE, ASPICE, PROSPICE | Look back, look at, look forward. Bootle (Lancs.), Co. Bor. of, Halesowen (Worcs.), Bor. of, Viscount Knutsford (Holland-Hibbert), Knutsford (Ches.) UDC. |
| RESPICE FINEM | Regard the end. Dickson of Corstorphine, Fisher, Homerton Coll., Camb., Lucas, Newmarket (Suffolk) UDC, 285 Sq., RAF. |
| RESPICE PROSPICE | Look backward and forward. Ealing, London Bor. of, Lloyd of Gloster, Stoke Newington, London Bor. of, Trowbridge (Wilts.) UDC, Worcester Royal Gram. Sch., 1961. |
| RESPICIENS PROSPICIENS | Looking backward and forward. Lords Tennyson. |
| RESPONDETE NATALIBUS | Answer to your birth. Truro Cathedral Sch. (orig. medieval known from 1549 as Truro Gram. Sch.). |
| RESTORED TO FIGHT AGAIN | No. 160 Maintenance Unit, RAF. |
| RESURGAM | I shall rise again (saying is found on memorials in seventeenth-century English churches). Pope Clement IX, 1667–9, Cardinal Giulio Rospigliosi. Blake of Tillmouth, Bts., Crosly, Stewart of New Hall. |
| RETINENS VESTIGIA FAMAE | Still treading in the footsteps of an honourable ancestry. Lister, Lloyd of Leaton Knoll, Lords Masham (Cunliffe-Lister) *(NEP)*, Lords Riblesdale (Lister). |
| RETRIEVE | 276 Sq., RAF (badge a retriever's head; unit on air/sea rescue). |
| RETRIEVE, REPAIR, RESTORE | No. 49 Maintenance Unit, RAF. |
| REVENGE | Logan-Home. |
| REVERA PRO REGE | In truth for the king. Reeve, co. Leics. |
| REVIRESCAM | I shall flourish again. Dalgleish, co. Fife. |
| REVIRESCAT | He revives in vigour. Heron-Maxwell, Bts. |
| REVIRESCO | I flourish again. Clarke, Clark-Maxwell, Farran, McEwen, Mackenan, Maconochie-Welwood, Maxwell of Maxwell, Rushton, Rushton UDC, Wedderburn-Maxwell. |

| | |
|---|---|
| REWARD OF INTEGRITY | Cree, co. Dorset. |
| REX DEDIT BENEDICAT DEUS | The king gave, God blessed. King's Sch., Chester, founded 1541 by Henry VIII. |
| REX ET NOSTRA JURA | The king and our rights. Great Yarmouth (Norfolk), Bor. of. |
| RHAGWELEDIAD A DIWYDRWDD | Foresight and diligence. Sayce. |
| RHYDDID GWERIN FFYNIANT GWLAD | The people's freedom, the country's prosperity. Carmarthenshire CC. |
| RHYDDID HEDD A LLWYDDIANT | Freedom, peace and success. Carmarthen, Bor. of. |
| RIDE ON | Lord Helsey (Life Baron). |
| RIDE THROUGH | Lords Belhaven and Stenton (Hamilton). |
| RIDENT FLORENTIA PRATA | The flowery meadows laugh. Downham (Cambs.) RDC, Pratt of Ryston. |
| RIEN SANS DIEU | Nothing without God. Kerrison, Bts., Peters. |
| RIEN SCET QUI NE VA HORS | He learns nought who goes not forth. Storrs. |
| RIGHT AND MIGHT AND ALL USED TRULY | Rambaut. |
| RIGHT IS MIGHT | Colthup of Hopebourne, Kent. |
| RINASCO PIU GLORIOSA | I rise again more glorious. Earls of Rosslyn (St Clair-Erskine). |
| RING TRUE | Ritchie. |
| RIPAE ULTERIORIS AMORE | By love of the further bank. (Virgil, *Aeneid* vi. 314). Mersey Tunnel Joint Cttee, 1952. |
| RISE FROM THE EAST | 247 Sq., RAF (sq. was gift from British Communities in China, 1918; badge is a demi-lion holding a scroll on which, in Chinese characters, are the words Chu Feng 'fierce wind'). |
| RO AN MOR | (spelling possibly archaic; untranslatable at present). Newquay (Cornwall) UDC. |
| ROBUR DURABIT | Strength will endure. No. 211 Flying Training Sch., RAF. |
| ROI JE NE PEUX, DUC JE NE VEUX, ROHAN JE SUIS (*or* ROI NE PUIS, DUC NE DAIGNE, ROHAN SUIS) | King I cannot be, duke I disdain, Rohan I am. This magnificently aristocratic boast, almost as of a noble caveman, noble *ab initio*, was that of great Breton house of Rohan, who descended from junior line of the Dukes of Brittany, at one time independent princes; the earliest date in the pedigree is 1120. As the Rohans acquired dukedoms, the motto had to be given up. For a full account see *Encyclopedia Britannica*, 14th ed., and *Royalty, Peerage and Nobility of the World*, Annuaire de France, n.d., where details are given of Prince Rohan, 13th Duke of Montbazon and of Bouillon, also 13th Duke of Rohan-Chabot. |

ROLCIA, VIMIERA, MARTINIQUE, TALAVERA, ALBUHERA, BADAJOZ, VITTORIA, FUENTES D'ONOR, SALAMANCA, PYRENEES, NIVELLE, NIVE, CIUDAD RODRIGO, TOULOUSE, ORTHES, DELHI, PUNJAUB, MOOLTAN, GOOJERAT, TAKU FORTS, PEKIN
: Not a motto, for one is not needed with such a list of honours. 60th Regt., KRRC.

ROSA CONCORDIA SIGNUM
: The rose is a sign of concord. Northamptonshire CC.

ROSA SINE SPINA
: A rose without a thorn. Used by Henry VIII on some of his coinage, and by Elizabeth I.

ROSAM QUI MERUIT FERAT
: Let him bear the rose who has deserved it. Price of Ardingly, Bt.

ROUSE AND WAKEN
: Rowse.

ROY, FOY, LOY
: King, faith, law. Aylwen, Bt.

ROY JE NE SUIS, PRINCE NI, CONTE AUSSI. JE SUIS LE SIRE DE COUCY.
: King I am not, nor prince or count, I am the Sire de Coucy. Very similar to 'Roi je ne peux . . .' of Rohan (q.v.). Motto quoted by J. H. Round in *Peerage and Pedigree*, vol. 2, 1970, p. 342. 'The proud boast . . . and which has bequeathed us in its stronghold the noblest tower in France.' In a conspiracy against Louis IX, the crown was offered to the Sire de Coucy, Enguerrand III, who declined in the words of the motto.

ROYALE ET LOYALE
: Royal and loyal. Launceston (alias Dunheved) (Cornwall), Bor. of. Ref. to fact that the Prince of Wales is Duke of Cornwall under a Charter of Edward III, 1337, this being the first use of the ducal title in England.

RUBET AGNUS ARIS
: The lamb reddens at the altars. René de Birague (Italian, Renato Birago of Milan), Cardinal and Chancellor of France, said to have been an adviser of the massacre of Huguenots on 24 August 1572, St Bartholomew's Day.

RURA MIHI PLACENT
: Country things please me. Congleton (Ches.) RDC.

RUGBEIA FLOREAT UBIQUE
: Let Rugby (football) flourish everywhere. Rugby Football Union.

RURIS ARTES FOVERE
: To cherish country arts. Ringwood and Fordingbridge (Hants.) RDC.

RUS DILIGENTER CURATE
: Diligently care for the country. East Kesteven (Lincs.) RDC.

RUS GRATUS MUSISQUE DIGNUM
: The country is worthy of the pleasing muses. Bathavon (Som.) RDC.

RUTHEK HA YAGH
: Ruddy and hearty (Cornish). Ruddle.

RUPTO ROBORE NATI
: Born from the broken oak. Aikenhead (formerly of Otterington Hall) all. to acorns in the arms and chaplet of oak in the crest.

RURA DILIGERE CONSILIO ADJUVARE
: To love rural things, to help with counsel. Rural District Councils Assn.

RYENS MIEUX                          Smiling more. Anne of Cleves, dau. of Philip the Good, Duke of Burgundy, and 2nd wife of Adolphus, Duke of Cleves.

RYTHSYS                              Freedom (Cornish). Stephens.

# S

**SACRARIUM REGIS CUNABULA LEGIS**
The shrine of kings and the cradle of the law. Bury St Edmunds (Suffolk), Bor. of. Refers to St Edmund King and Martyr, last king of the East Angles. Killed by the Danes (slain by arrows, then beheaded) in 870, on refusing to renounce Christ. From his death began King Alfred's (Edmund's close friend) recovery from the heathen invaders. Hence magnificent abbey built over St Edmund's tomb. Reference is also to association of the barons before Runnymede who vowed in the abbey to uphold principles set out in Magna Carta.

**SAEVITER AD LUCEM**
Fiercely to the light. 432 Sq., RCAF.

**SAEVUMQUE TRIDENTEM SERVAMUS**
We keep the fierce trident. Broke-Middleton, Bt. (the 1st Bt. of this creation, Admiral Sir Philip Vere Broke, commanded HMS *Shannon* when after 15 minutes' battle he captured the USS *Chesapeake*, 1 June 1812; hence motto commemorates the British victory), Loraine, Bts.

**SAFE AND SOUND**
Leeds Perm. Bldg. Soc.

**SAFE GUARD**
British Insurance Assn., No. 44 Maintenance Unit, RAF.

**SAFELY TO EARTH**
Parachute Test Unit, RAF.

**SAINT-MALO AU RICHE DUC**
Saint Malo for the rich duke. Saint-Malo in Brittany.

**ST VINCENT**
(Derived from defeat of Spanish fleet, 14 February 1797, off Cape St Vincent by Admiral Sir William Waldegrave, cr. 1st Lord Radstock, 1800). Lords Radstock (Waldegrave) *(NEP)*.

**SAL EST VITA**
Salt is life (refers to local salt industry). Northwich (Ches.) UDC.

**SAL SAPIT OMNIA**
Salt makes all things taste. Salters' Co., charter 1558.

**SALO EXTENDERE SCIENTIAM**
To extend knowledge by the (salt) sea. Seafarers' Education Service.

**SALUBRITAS ET AMOENITAS**
Healthiness and amenity. Folkestone (Kent), Bor. of.

**SALUBRITAS ET ERUDITIO**
Health and learning. Cheltenham (Glos.), Bor. of.

**SALUBRITAS ET INDUSTRIA**
Health and industry. Swindon (Wilts.), Bor. of.

**SALUBRITAS PER INDUSTRIAM**
Health through work. Princess Alexandra Hosp., RAF, Wroughton.

**SALUM ET CARINAE PIGNORA VITAE**
Keels and the open sea are the pledges of life. Inst. of Naval Architects.

**SALUS ET FELICITAS**
Health and happiness. Royal Acad. of Dancing, Sale (Ches.), Bor. of, Torbay (Devon), Co. Bor. of, Torquay (Devon), Bor. of.

**SALUS GENERIS HUMANI**
The health of mankind. Roy. Sanitary Inst., 1949.

**SALUS IN ARDUIS**
Salvation in lofty things. Wellingborough Sch., 1478.

| | |
|---|---|
| SALUS IN FIDE | Salvation through faith. Lord Armaghdale (Lonsdale) *(NEP)*, Magrath. |
| SALUS INFIRMORUM | The health of the infirm, Barnsley Hosp. Management Cttee. |
| SALUS NAUFRAGIS SALUS AEGRIS | Safety to the shipwrecked, health to the sick. Ramsgate (Kent), Bor. of. |
| SALUS PATRIAE SALIS DOMINATIO | The domination of the salt (sea) is the safety of the country. Chamber of Shipping of UK. |
| SALUS PER CHRISTUM | Salvation through Christ. Abernethy, Christian of Stonerwood Park, Hants. (it was to this Manx family that Fletcher Christian belonged, involved in mutiny on the *Bounty*, settled on Pitcairn Island), Forbes of Culloden, Gordon, Hare of Docking, Norfolk, Leith of Whitehaugh, Stewart of Banchory-Devenick. |
| SALUS PER CHRISTUM REDEMPTOREM | Salvation through Christ the Redeemer. Earls of Moray (Stuart), Stuart of Duncarn, Viscount Stuart of Findhorn. |
| SALUS PER PRUDENTIAM | Safety through prudence. Eastbourne Bldg. Soc. |
| SALUS PER SAPIENTIAM | Safety through wisdom. No. 38 Group Examining Unit, RAF. |
| SALUS POPULI | The welfare of the people. Southport (Lancs.), Co. Bor. of, Southport Volunteers, 1914. |
| SALUS POPULI CURANDA | The safety of the people must be our care. Salford Hosp. Management Cttee, 1968. |
| SALUS POPULI NOSTRA MERCES | The safety of the people is our reward. Nottinghamshire Combined Police Authority. |
| SALUS POPULI SUPREMA LEX | The welfare of the people is the highest law (from Cicero, *De Legibus* III. iii. 8). Eastleigh (Hants.), Bor. of, Harrow, London Bor. of, Holborn Law Soc., Lewisham, London Bor. of, Lytham St Annes (Lancs.), Bor. of, Swinton and Pendlebury (Lancs.), Bor. of, Tonbridge (Kent) UDC, Urmston (Lancs.) UDC, 1942. |
| SALUTEM ALERE MORBUM LEVARE | To cherish health, to alleviate sickness. Inst. of Community Medicine, RAF, Inst. of Health and Medical Training, RAF, Medical Training Establishment and Depot, RAF. |
| SALUTIFER ORBI | Health-bearer to the world. Sch. of Pharmacy (London Univ.). |
| SALVE MAGNA PARENS | Hail, great parent. Lichfield (Staffs.), City of. |
| SALVET ME DEUS | May God help me. Spiers. |
| SALVETE PORTUM INVECTI | Rejoice, having been drawn to the port. Bristol Airports Auth. |
| SAMHOLD I STUD | Together in battle. 332 Sq., RAF (Norwegian), 1942. |
| SAMNITICO NON CAPITUR AURO | Not captured by Samnite gold. Fabrizio Colonna, *c.*1520, celebrated Italian soldier. |
| SANCTA CLAVIS COELI FIDES | Faith is the sacred key to heaven. Hadfield, Bt., Sankey. |
| SANCTAE NOMINE CRUCIS | In the name of the Holy Cross. Waltham Holy Cross (Essex) UDC 1956 (Abbey founded by Harold II, killed at Hastings, 1066; his body was ultimately buried there; modern sculpture in his memory is in the church). |

| | |
|---|---|
| SANCTAS CLAVIS FORES APERIT | The key opens the sacred out of doors. Bury Gram. Sch., Lancs., endowed 1634 by Henry Bury but previously existing. |
| SANCTE ET SAPIENTER | Holily and wisely. King's Coll., London Univ., 1829, King's Coll. Sch., Wimbledon Common, London, 1829. |
| SANCTUS BOSCUS | Holy wood. Holywood (co. Down) UDC. |
| SANITATE CRESCAMUS | May we grow in health. Croydon, London Bor. of. |
| SANITATI PERDUCERE | To lead to sanity. Lancaster Moor Hosp. Management Cttee. |
| SANS AUTRE GUIDE | Without other guide. The Dukes of Gueldres, motto supposed to be derived from the heaps of stone erected by pilgrims to mark their journey. |
| SANS BRUIT | Without noise. Kenworthy. Lords Strabolgi (Kenworthy). |
| SANS CHANGER | Without changing. Lords Baillieu, Clarke of Ashgate, Earls of Derby (Stanley), Viscount Eversley (Shaw-Lefevre), Musgrave, Bts., Muspratt, Bt., Lords Sheffield (Stanley), Stanley, co. Cumb., Wykeham-Musgrave. |
| SANS CHANGER MA VERITÉ | Without changing my truth. L'Estrange, Barons of Knokin, Strange of Knokin. |
| SANS CRAINTE | Without fear. Gordon-Cumming, Miles, Petre, Privett, Sanderson, Tyrell, Bts., Lord Tyrell of Avon (NEP). |
| SANS DIEU JE NE PUIS | Without God I cannot do it. Skipworth. |
| SANS DIEU RIEN | Without God nothing. Ashby de la Zouch (Leics.) UDC, Lords Furnivall (in abeyance), Godley, co. Leitrim, Hodgkinson, Jarvis of Toronto, Lords Kilbraken (Godley), Peter of Harlyn, Peter-Hoblyn, Lords Petre, Sanderson, Bts., Saunderson, Worksop (Notts.), Bor. of, 1932. |
| SANS MAL | Without evil. Hornyhold-Strickland, Lord Strickland. |
| SANS PEUR | Without fear. Hagart-Alexander, Bts., Hoggart, Karr, Sutherland, Countess of Sutherland (Janson), 5th Bn. Territorials, Sutherland and Caithness Highlanders. |
| SANS RECULLER JAMAIS | Without ever receding. Brackenbury, ancient co. Durham family. |
| SANS REGRET | Without regret. Lazarus. |
| SANS TACHE | Without stain. Viscount Gormanston (Preston), Hurry, Le Blanc, Martin, Michell, Moray, Napier, Napier, Bt., Preston, Ure, Urie. |
| SANS TRAVAIL RIEN | Nothing without work. Ryan, Bts., |
| SANS VARIANCE TERME DE MA VIE | Without change all my life. Sir George Bowes, temp. Elizabeth I, ancestor of Earls of Strathmore, badge being the canting device of arrows. |
| SANS VARIER | Without changing. Anne (formerly Charlton), Charlton of Lea Hall. |
| SAPERE AUDE | Dare to be wise (Horace, Epistles I. ii. 40). Amos, Caldwell, Bt., Cooper, Leeson-Marshall, Earls of |

Macclesfield (Parker), Manchester Gram. Sch., 1515, Oldham (Lancs.), Bor. of, Oxfordshire CC, Lord Redcliffe-Maud (Life Baron), Townley-Parker, Wise of Ford House, Wyse, Vyvyan, Bts.

| | |
|---|---|
| SAPIENS INCIPIT A FINE | The wise man begins from the end. Bartlett (formerly Holwell). |
| SAPIENS QUI ASSIDUUS | He is wise who is industrious. Drinkwater, Hansler, Mitchell, Sperling, Sykes, Bts. |
| SAPIENS QUI PROSPICIT | He is wise who looks forward. Dudley (Worcs.), Co. Bor. of, Malvern Coll., Worcs., 1862, Thompson of Reculver, Bts. |
| SAPIENS QUI VIGILAT | He is wise who watches. Bagshot, Fowler of Braemore, Bts. |
| SAPIENTER ET AUDACTER | Wisely and boldly. Koch de Gooreynd. |
| SAPIENTER ET FORTITER FERRE | To bear wisely and bravely. Porritt, Bts. |
| SAPIENTER ET SINCERE | Wisely and sincerely. Inderwick. |
| SAPIENTER SI SINCERE | Wisely if sincerely. Davidson. |
| SAPIENTES SIMUS | Let us be wise. Cambridgeshire and Isle of Ely CC. |
| SAPIENTIA | Wisdom. Stevenson. |
| SAPIENTIA AEDIFICATUR DOMUS | A house is built of wisdom. West Bromwich Bldg. Soc., 1955. |
| SAPIENTIA DONUM DEI | Wisdom is the gift of God. Lord Field *(NEP)*. |
| SAPIENTIA ET VERITAS | Wisdom and truth. Akers-Douglas, Viscount Chilston (Akers-Douglas), Douglas of Baads. |
| SAPIENTIA PROFICIENS | Advancing by wisdom. Nottinghamshire CC. |
| SAPIENTIS TUTUS | Safe by wisdom. Crewdson. |
| SAPIENTIA URBS CONDITUR | A city is founded by wisdom. Nottingham Univ. |
| SARANG SERTA SENGAT | The nest with the sting. RAF station, Butterworth. |
| SARANG TEBUAN JANGAN DIJOLOK | Never stir up a hornet's nest (Malayan). 100 Sq., RAF. |
| SAT CITO SAT BENE | If well done it is swiftly enough. Colman, Bts., Colman, co. Norfolk, Harrison of Wychnor Park. |
| SATIS EST PROSTRASSE LEONI | It is enough to a lion to have lain low. Salisbury, Salisbury-Jones, Salusbury, Bts. |
| SAVE | RAF Hosp., Ely. |
| SAVE AND PROSPER | Save and Prosper Group Ltd., 1962. |
| SAXIS CONDITE | Build with stones. Chubb of Stonehenge, Bt. |
| SAY AND DO | Everard, co. Leics. |
| SCIENCE AND THE USEFUL ARTS | Lord Penney (Life Baron). |
| SCIENCE CONQUERS | Aircraft Torpedo Development Unit, RAF. |
| SCIENCIAS, LETRAS E ARTES | Science, letters arts. Order of St James of the Sword (Portugal). |
| SCIENTIA COLORIS MINISTRA | Science is the handmaid of colour. Soc. of Dyers and Colourists. |

| | |
|---|---|
| SCIENTIA COMMUNE BONUM | Science is the common good. Assn. of Commonwealth Univs. |
| SCIENTIA DABIT ALAS | Knowledge will give us wings. Birmingham Univ. Air Sq., RAFVR. |
| SCIENTIA DIRIGIT | Knowledge guides us. Sch. of General Reconnaissance, RAF. |
| SCIENTIA ET ARMIS | By knowledge and arms. Coastal Cmd. Development Unit, RAF. |
| SCIENTIA ET INGENIO | By knowledge and intellect. Inst. of Civil Engineers. |
| SCIENTIA ET LABORE | By knowledge and labour. Manchester Coll. of Science and Technology. |
| SCIENTIA IMPERII DECUS EST TUTAMEN | The knowledge of empire is ornament and defence. Imperial Coll. (London Univ.), founded 1851. |
| SCIENTIA IN ALTO | Knowledge in the sky. Manchester Univ. Air Sq., RAFVR. |
| SCIENTIA PRO HOMINIBUS | Science is for men. British Inst. of Radio Engineers, 1956. |
| SCIENTIA UNITATE | Science in unity. British Assn. of Oral Surgeons, 1962. |
| SCIENTIA VIS AUGETUR | By science strength is increased. Nat. Gas Turbine Establishment. |
| SCIENTIAE ET LABORI DETUR | Due to knowledge and labour. Luton (Beds.), Bor. of. |
| SCIENTIAM INGENIUM ARTES | Cultivate science, intellect, the arts. Univ. of Wales, 1910. |
| SCIO CUI CREDIDI | I know whom I have believed. Gaskell, Milnes, St Martin's Coll., Lancaster, 1966. |
| SCIRE SUADERE SEQUI | To know, to advise, to follow. No. 27 Group HQ, RAF. |
| SCITE, CITO, CERTE | Skilfully, swiftly, certainly. Carmens' Co., inc. 1946, though centuries earlier licences for carmen were issued by Christ's Hospital. Arms have two wheels in the shield, two dray horses as supporters; crest is a demi-carthorse resting sinister hoof on a wheel. |
| SCORPIONES PUNGENT | Scorpions sting. 84 Sq., RAF (badge a scorpion). |
| SCRIBITE SCIENTES | Write skilfully. Scriveners' Co., inc. 1617 (also given in form 'Scribere scientes' (Knowing how to write). Additional motto is 'Littera scripta manet' (The written word remains). |
| SCUTO FIDEI | By the shield of faith. Morris, Bts., Morris, co. Lancs. |
| SCUTUM AMORIS DIVINI | The shield of divine love. Scudamore. |
| SE INSERIT ASTRIS | He places himself among the stars. Crosse, Hamilton of Fyne Court. |
| SEA AND AIR | No. 235 Operation Conversion Unit, RAF. |
| SEARCH AND RESEARCH | Bombing Trials Unit, RAF. |
| SEARCH BY DAY AND NIGHT | No. 724 Signals Unit, RAF. |
| SECRET ET HARDI | Secret and bold. Lords Dynevor (Rhys), Rice. |
| SECUNDIS DUBIISQUE RECTUS | Upright both in prosperity and in perils. Earls Camperdown (Haldane-Duncan) (NEP), Dukes of Cleveland (Fitzroy), Lippincott. |

| | |
|---|---|
| SECUNDIS REBUS CAVE | In well, beware. Wombwell (W.R. Yorks.) UDC. |
| SECUNDUM TAMESIM QUOVIS GENTIUM | Following the Thames for what you will of races. Thurrock (Essex) UDC, 1957. |
| SECUNDUS SED NULLI SECUNDUS | Second but second to none. No. 2 Maintenance Unit, RAF. |
| SECURE VIVERE MORS EST | To live securely (i.e. without caution) is death. Dayrell. |
| SECURI TRANSEANT | Let them go safely on the way. Central Air Traffic Control Sch., RAF. |
| SECURIOR QUO PARATIOR | More secure by how much one is more prepared. Portman Bldg. Soc. |
| SECURIS FECIT SECURUM | My axe saved me. Luxmoore. |
| SECURITAS IN COELO | Safety in the sky. Air Traffic Control Centre, RAF, Watnall. |
| SECURITY AND SERVICE | London and Lancashire Insurance Co. Ltd., 1949, S. Staffs. Bldg. Soc. |
| SECURITY THROUGH THRIFT | Bristol and West Bldg. Soc. |
| SECUS RIVOS AQUARUM | By rivers of waters. Rivers, Bts. |
| SED OMNIA DISPOSUISTI | But Thou hast disposed all things. British Assn. for the Advancement of Science. |
| SEDES INVENIRE ET CAUSAS MORBORUM | To find out the seat and causes of disease. Coll. of Pathologists. |
| SEDULUS ET AUDAX | Diligent and bold. Rutherford, Bt. |
| SEEK AGREEMENT | Dickinson, Bts. |
| SEEK AND DESTROY | 41 Sq., RAF. |
| SEEK HEAR AND GUIDE | RAF station, Wythall. |
| SEEK QUIET | Deacon. |
| SEEK, STRIVE, ATTAIN | Seaton (Devon) UDC, 1967. |
| SEEK THE TRUTH | Leon, Bts. |
| SEEK THE WAY | No. 1 Air Navigation Sch., RAF. |
| SEGUO ED INSEGUO | It follows and is noted. Lords Caccia. |
| SELECT | Officers and Aircrew Selection Centre, RAF. |
| SELITO TENETO SI LETO | Choose, hold, even if to death. Sillitoe. |
| SEMEL ET SEMPER | Once and always. Allcard, Swinburne, Bts. |
| SEMEL ET SIMUL | Once and simultaneously. RAF station, Bicester. |
| SEMNI NE SEMNI | (Untranslateable). Dering, Bts., extinct 1975. Before using the above, Derings used 'Dering andraedath ne dering', which is not really Anglo-Saxon (or Old English). Family then adopted the above, which was supposed to mean 'I can do nothing without God's help.' 'On this, Mr. Stevenson comments, How *semni* can mean I can do nothing and God's help, in any conceivable language, except Chinese, is beyond me' (quoted in J. H. Round, *Peerage and Pedigree*, vol. 2, 1970, p. 116. |

| | |
|---|---|
| SEMPER | Always. Lorenzo de Medici, 'the Magnificent'. The word is supposed to abbreviate the thought that everything should be done for the love of God. |
| SEMPER AD COELESTIA | Always to the celestial things. Worksop Coll., Nottingham, founded 1890 by Canon Woodward. |
| SEMPER ADAMAS | Always adamant. Col. Antonio Caracciolo, Marquis of Vico. |
| SEMPER ADAMAS IN POENIS | Always adamant in punishment. Cosimo de Medici, 1st Grand Duke of Tuscany, d. 1574. |
| SEMPER AGGRESSUS | Always aggressive. 23 Sq., RAF (badge an eagle preying on falcon). |
| SEMPER ALACER | Always alert. No. 7 Air Gunners' Sch., RAF. |
| SEMPER ALIQUID NOVI | Always something new (proverbial motto from Pliny, *Historia Naturalis* II. viii. 42, starting 'Ex Africa'). Aircraft Depot, India (Lahore), RAF, Commission for the New Towns. |
| SEMPER AUDAX | Always bold. Lord Dalziel of Kirkcaldy *(NEP)*. |
| SEMPER CIVIBUS MEIS SERVIO | I always serve my citizens. Lord Heycock (Life Baron). |
| SEMPER CONSTANS ET FIDELIS | Ever constant and faithful. Irton, Lynch, Spoor. |
| SEMPER CONTENDO | I always contend. Crewe (Ches.), Bor. of, 261 Sq., RAF (I strive continually). |
| SEMPER EADEM | Always the same. Collmore, Cullimore, Elizabeth Coll., Guernsey, Fairbairn, Bts., Forrester, Bts., Harvey, Hewitt, Bts., Hollingsworth, Hornsey, Ipswich Sch., Suffolk (founded *c.*1390 by Ipswich Merchant Guild of Corpus Christi), Leicester, City of, Lloyd-Kirk, Morley, Ovey, Panton, Reid, Whitehead, Henry III, King of Castile 1390–1406. A favourite with Elizabeth I, 'our glorious *semper eadem*, the banner of our pride' (Lord Macaulay, *Spanish Armada*). |
| SEMPER FIDELIS | Always faithful. Abraham, Arding, Athletes' Volunteer Force (City of Exeter), 1914, Berridge, Bonner, Broadmead, Bruce, Burrows, Chesterman, Devonshire Regt., Dick, East Devon Militia, Edge, Firth of the Flush, Bts., Formby, Exeter (Devon), City of, Garret, Houlton, Hughes-Onslow, Ievers, Lacey, Lomax, Lombard Marcroft Ltd., Lynch, Bts., Marriott, Lea, Bts., Mitton, Molteno, Lords Morris, Newill, Nicholas, Bts., Polhill-Drabble, Viscount Radcliffe, Reliance Mutual Life Insurance Soc. Ltd., 1951, Richardson, Lords Sanderson of Ayot, Smith-Marriot, Steuart, Stewart, Stirling of Glorat, Bts. (dormant), Sturdy, Taylor, Thomson of Old Nunthorpe, Bts., Webb, Weigall, Bt. |
| SEMPER FIDELIS MUTARE SPERNO | Ever faithful, I scorn to change. Worcester, City of. |
| SEMPER FLOREAT | May it always flourish. Inverarity of Forfar. |
| SEMPER IN EXCUBITU VIGILANS | Constantly alert and on the watch. No. 500 Signals Unit, RAF. |
| SEMPER INTER PRIMOS | Always among the first. RAF station, Old Sarum. |

| | |
|---|---|
| SEMPER PARARE | Always be ready. Hanson, Bts. |
| SEMPER PARATI | Always ready. 613 City of Manchester Sq., AAF. |
| SEMPER PARATUS | Always prepared. Armytage, Bts., Lords Cadman, Clifford, Constable, Cottrell-Dormer, Dallas, Elphinstone of Sowerby, Bts., Glover, Johnstone, Knowles, Bts., Lancaster, Leckey of Londonderry, Viscount Marchwood (Penny), Mounsey, Phillpotts, Royds, Stewart of Inchbrock, Studholme, Upton of Ingmire, Usticke, Welles, Wells of Grebly Hall, 207 Sq., RAF. |
| SEMPER PARATUS PUGNARE PRO PATRIA | Always ready to fight for my country. Lockhart of Lee, Bts., Macdonald of Largie. |
| SEMPER PARATUS, SEMPER TUTUS | Always prepared, always safe. Tregoning. |
| SEMPER PLACIDUS | Always placid. Wells of Hove, Bts. |
| SEMPER PRAEBEBIMUS | We will always supply. Newport and Monmouthshire Water Bd. |
| SEMPER PRAECINCTUS | Ever ready, girt up. Lords Dunleath (Mulholland), Mulholland, Bts. |
| SEMPER PROCEDENS | Always going forth. Lancaster RDC. |
| SEMPER PROFICIMUS | Always we progress. Leyland (Lancs.) UDC. |
| SEMPER PRORSUM | Always forward. Aylesbury (Bucks.), Bor. of. |
| SEMPER RESURGENS | Always rising again. No. 22 Group HQ, RAF. |
| SEMPER SERIO | Always in earnest. Hatfield (Herts.) RDC. |
| SEMPER SITIENS | Always thirsty. Drought (all. to the name). |
| SEMPER SPERANS, SEMPER LABORANS | Always hoping, always working. Charles, Bts. |
| SEMPER SURSUM | Always upwards. Barrow-in-Furness (Lancs.), Co. Bor. of. |
| SEMPER VERUS | Always true. Home of Kames, Howe, Upton. |
| SEMPER VICTOR | Always conqueror. Ramsay of Whitehill, Bts. |
| SEMPER VIGILANS | Always on the look out. Alexander of Sundridge Park, Bts., Érik Boheman (b. 1895), a Kt. of the great Swedish Order of the Seraphim, Bourne, Eagle Oil and Shipping Co. Ltd., England, Hughes-Hughes, Todd, Williams of Shernfold Park, Wilson, Wilson-Todd, Bts. |
| SEMPER VIGILANS REGE ADJUVANTE | Always vigilant, the king helping. Chartered Inst. of Secretaries. |
| SEMPER VIGILATE | Be always vigilant. 202 Sq., RAF. |
| SEMPER VIRENS | Always flourishing. Broadwood of Lyne. |
| SEMPER VIRESCIT VIRTUS | Virtue always flourishes. Lind. |
| SEMPER VIRET | It always flourishes. Holmden. |
| SEN MYGHAL AGAN GWYTH | Saint Michael our protection (Cornish). Mitchell. |
| SEN PETROC AGAIN GWYTH | Saint Petroc our protection (Cornish). Pethick. |

| | |
|---|---|
| SEN PERRAN AGAN GWYTH | Saint Piran our protection (Cornish). Fudge. Whetta. (Saint Piran is one of the very numerous Cornish saints. As can be seen from place-names, the latter attest to very strong pre-Reformation Cornish Catholicism.) |
| SPQR (SENATUS POPULUSQUE ROMANUS) | The Senate and the people of Rome. Motto of the Roman Republic; abbreviation appears on shield of the City of Rome. Used apparently as symbol of Julius Caesar or of later emperors who ruled Britain, it is on the very elaborate coat of arms of Elizabeth I (Sir Thomas Kendrick, *British Antiquity*). |
| SEPTEM IN UNO SURGENT | Seven shall rise in one. Newtown Abbey (co. Antrim) UDC. |
| SEPULTO VIRESCO | I revive from my burial. Hamond-Graeme, Bts. The great Marquess of Montrose was done to death by the Presbyterians and his head set on the tolbooth of Edinburgh, whence it was removed in 1650 by the maternal line ancestor of this family. The second crest shows two hands holding a man's skull, ref. to exploit and to motto. |
| SEQUAMUR | Let us follow. Estcourt–Oswald. |
| SEQUAR ET ATTINGAM | I will follow and touch. Burne-Jones, Bt. |
| SEQUERE DEUM | Follow God. Cardinal Spelman, Archbishop of New York, d. 1967. |
| SEQUITANDO SI GUINGE | By following he comes up. Lambert, Bts. |
| SEQUITUR VICTORIA FORTEIS | Victory follows the brave. Campbell of Aberuchill, Bts. |
| SEQUOR NEC INFERIOR | I follow, but am not inferior. Marquesses of Crewe (Crewe-Milnes, originally Offley) *(NEP)*. |
| SERAY COME A DIEU PLAIRA | I shall be as God pleases. Sir Reginald (or Reynold) Bray, KG, *c*.1485. For an account of his rise see Oswald Barron, 'The Brays of Shere', in *The Ancestor*, vol. VI, 1903. |
| SERIO SERVIRE | In earnest to serve. Wimborne and Cranborne (Dorset) RDC. |
| SERIT ARBORES QUAE ALTEM SECULO PROSUNT | It sows trees which will reach their height in a century. Royal Forestry Soc., 1963. |
| SERMONI CONSONA FACTA | Deeds agreeing with words. Collins, Salusbury-Trelawny, Bts., Trelawney. |
| SERO SED SERIO | Slow but sure. Lords Brockley (Cecil), Viscount Cecil of Chelwood, Gayre, Ker, Kerr, Marquesses of Lothian (Kerr), Lord Nairn, Lord Quickswood (Gascoyne-Cecil), Marquesses of Salisbury (Cecil), Lords Teviot (Kerr). |
| SERPENTES VELUT ET COLUMBAE | As serpents and doves (ref. to Christ's saying (St Matthew 10:16): Be ye therefore wise as serpents, and harmless as doves). Enys. |
| SERVA FIDEM | Keep faith. Blackburn (Lancs.) RDC, Corfield of Chatwall Hall, Salop, Glasgow Academy, 1845. |
| SERVA JUGUM | Keep the yoke. Dalrymple-Hay, Bts., Earls of Erroll (Hay), Hay, Nuttall, O'Hea. |
| SERVABO FIDEM | I shall keep the faith. Dutton, Lord Evans *(NEP)*, Johnson of Runcorn, Lords Sherborne (Dutton). |

| | |
|---|---|
| SERVANDO RURSUS VOLAMUS | By storing we fly again. No. 8 Maintenance Unit, RAF (unit's function to store aircraft). |
| SERVARE ET SANARE | To serve and make sound. Newcastle Regional Hosp. Bd. |
| SERVARE MODUM | To keep the mean. Earle, Bts., Folke, Herne. |
| SERVARE MUNIA VITAE | To keep to the duties of life. Oglander, Bts. |
| SERVAT ET ABSTINET | He serves and abstains. Jean Baptiste Colbert, 1619–83, Chief Minister of Louis XIV. |
| SERVATA FIDES CINERI | The promise made to the ashes has been kept. Earls of Harrowby (Ryder) (adopted by 1st Lord Harrowby in ref. to his father having died before he could be made a peer, in 1756; promise not fulfilled to the son until 1776), Verney of Claydon House, Bts. |
| SERVATE ET SERVITE | Save and serve. Leeds & Holbeck Bldg. Soc. |
| SERVATUM CINERI | Keep faithfully. Prevost, Bts. *B.P.* 1970 records that the supporters and the motto were granted by royal sign manual, October 1816, to 2nd Bt. (a clergyman). The supporters are two grenadiers of the Bedfordshire Regt. and motto presumably refers to the 2nd Bt.'s respect for his father and forebears. |
| SERVAVI PATRIAM SINE CLADE | I have served my country without destruction. Judkin-Fitzgerald. |
| SERVE ALL SLIGHT NONE | Sleight, Bts. |
| SERVE AND OBEY | Haberdashers' Co., charter 1510. Haberdashers Aske's Sch. (founded 1690, income from estate left in trust by Robert Aske, liveryman of Haberdashers' Co.), Monmouth Hill Sch., Monmouth (founded 1614 by William Jones of Haberdashers' Co.). |
| SERVE AND SHARE | Riddell-Webster. |
| SERVE AND SUPPORT | RAF station, Medmenham. |
| SERVE BY SEA | HMAFV *Bridport* RAF (trans. from RN to RAF). |
| SERVE HUMANITY | The London Clinic. |
| SERVE LAND AND AIR | No. 278 Maintenance Unit, RAF. |
| SERVE ONE ANOTHER | Chesham (Bucks.) UDC. |
| SERVE THE HIGHEST | Harvie-Watt, Bts. |
| SERVE TO UNITE | RAF station, Negombo, Ceylon. |
| SERVE WISELY WITH FAITH | Young of Partick, Bts. |
| SERVI BALLISTAE | Servants of the gun. 595 Sq., RAF. |
| SERVICE | Maintenance Cmd., RAF. |
| SERVICE AND EFFICIENCY | Stretford (Lancs.), Bor. of and UDC. |
| SERVICE AND FORTITUDE | British Limbless Ex-servicemens' Assn. |
| SERVICE AND SECURITY | Newcastle & Gateshead Bldg. Soc. |
| SERVICE IN PEACE AND WAR | Vickers Ltd., 1963. |
| SERVICE LINKS ALL | Leatherhead (Surrey) UDC, Parts of Lindsey (Lincolns.) CC. |

| | |
|---|---|
| SERVICE TO ALL | 122 Airfield HQ, RAF. |
| SERVICE TO MANY | RAF station, Hullavington. |
| SERVIENDO | By serving. Hawkey, Bts., Simeon, Bts. |
| SERVIENDO FIDEM TENEMUS | By serving we keep faith. Roy, Berkshire Hosp., 1937. |
| SERVIMUS | We serve. Falmouth Docks & Engineering Co. |
| SERVIMUS ET SERVAMUS | We serve and we save. No. 43 Group HQ, RAF. |
| SERVIR DE BON GRE | Serve with good success. Lord Grey of Nauton (Life Baron). |
| SERVIR LE ROY | Serve the king. Bennett, Bts. |
| SERVIRE CONTENDIMUS | We strive to serve. Chertsey (Surrey) UDC. |
| SERVIRE DEO SAPERE | To serve God is to be wise. Sadlier. |
| SERVIRE DEO REGNARI EST | To serve is to be ruled by God. Sevenoaks Sch., Kent, founded 1418 by Sir William Sevenoke, Warden of the Grocers' Co. and Lord Mayor of London, as thankoffering for his share in victory of Agincourt. Friend of Henry V, Sir William derived his surname from the fact that he had as a baby been found abandoned by the side of a road leading to Sevenoaks. |
| SERVIRE EST VIVERE | To serve is to live. Viscount Addison. |
| SERVIRE ET SERVARE | To serve and to keep. Lords Altrincham (Grigg); present peer disclaimed the peerage 1963 under Peerage Act, 1963. |
| SERVIRE POPULO | To serve the people. Bromley, London Bor. of. |
| SERVIRE SINE TIMORE | To serve without fear. Taylor, Bt. |
| SERVYAF AN RY GWYR | I serve the true king (Cornish). Penderil. |
| SERVYEUGH AN GWYR | Follow the truth (Cornish). Grigg. |
| SET ON AND WIN | Seton. |
| SEUL LE PREMIER PAS COÛTE | Only the beginning is difficult. RAF station, Cosford. |
| SHANET A BOO | Shanet to victory (or defying). Fitzgerald, Knight of Glin (hereditary knighthood cr. by King John), Foster-Vesey-Fitzgerald. |
| SHIELD AND DETER | RAF station, Middleton St George. |
| SHIPSHAPE | No. 238 Maintenance Unit, RAF. |
| SHUPAVU NA THABITI | Tough and strong. RAF station, Eastleigh, Hants. |
| SI CELERES QUATIT PENNAS | If he shakes the swift wings. Lord Carlingford (Parkinson-Fortescue) (NEP). |
| SI DEUS EST PRO NOBIS, QUIS CONTRA NOS? | If God is for us, who is against us? Eyton, Morris, co. Galway. |
| SI DEUS NOBISCUM, QUIS CONTRA NOS? | If God be with us, who can be against us? Brenan, Lords Killanin (Morris), Lloyd of Dinas, Mairis, Lord Morris (NEP), Mountmorris, Otway, Order of Philip the Magnanimous (Hesse), Viscount Tredegar (Morgan). |
| SI DEUS QUIS CONTRA? | If God be with us, who can be against us? Benson, Lords Charnwood (Benson) (NEP), Spence, Spens. |

| | |
|---|---|
| SI DILIGENS HONORABILIS | If diligent, then honourably. Kenyon. |
| SI IN VIRIDI QUID IN ARIDO? | If they do these things in a green tree, what shall be done in the dry? (motto from St Luke 23:31). Caldora family. |
| SI JE PENSE | If I think. Paston, co. Norfolk (well known from *Paston Letters*, family now represented by Paston-Bedingfeld, Bts. (Francis Blomfield, *History of Norfolk*). |
| SI JE PUIS | If I can. Cahun, Colquhoun, Bts., Eyre, Lord Fairhaven (Broughton) *(NEP)*, Radcliffe. |
| SI NEMO SEQUITUR SOLUS IBO | If no one follows, I will go alone. Riley, co. Yorks. |
| SI PLACET NECAMUS | We destroy at will. 139 Sq., RAF. |
| SI POSSIM | If I could. Livingstone. |
| SI SIT PRUDENTIA | If there be prudence. Lords Auckland (Eden), Brown, Earls of Avon (Eden), Eden, Bts., Lords Henley (Eden). |
| SI TARDIOR SPLENDIDIOR | The slower the more brilliant. Prospero Colonna, *c.*1463, cr. Cardinal, by his uncle Pope Martin V. |
| SI TE FATA VOCANT | If the fates call. Cardinal Pietro Bembo, Sec. to Pope Leo X (1513–21), mentioned with respect by Ariosto. |
| SI VIS PACEM PARA BELLUM | If you want peace, prepare for war. 604 Sq., Co. of Middlesex AAF (Roman motto). |
| SIBI CONSTAT | Agree with thyself. Lords Walpole. |
| SIBIMET MERCES INDUSTRIA | Industry is a recompense in itself. Miller, co. Lancs. |
| SIC BENE MERENTI PALMA | Thus the palm goes to him who deserves well. Palmer of Castle Lackin, Bts. |
| SIC CREDE | Thus believe. Bernardo Accolti of Arezzo. *See* Unam aspicit. |
| SIC DIVA LUX MIHI | Such is the divine light to me. Ferdinand Carafa, Marquis of Santo Lucito, sixteenth century. |
| SIC DONEC | Thus until. Lords Egerton of Tatton *(NEP)*, Dukes of Sutherland (Egerton). |
| SIC ERAT IN FATIS | So it was (written) in the fates. King Christian II of Denmark. |
| SIC FIDEM SERVAMUS | Thus we keep faith. 196 Sq., RAF. |
| SIC FIDEM TENEO | Thus I keep my faith. Molesworth. |
| SIC ITUR AD ASTRA | Thus is the path to the stars, *or* Such is the way to immortality. Barker, Carnac, Bts., Davies, Day, Lord Evershed *(NEP)*, Herts. and Essex Girls' High Sch., Kerry, Mackensie of Glen Muick, Bts., Martin, Pugh. |
| SIC ITUR IN ALTUM | This is the way to heaven. Cowan of the Baltic, Bts. |
| SIC LUCEAT LUX | Thus may light shine. Lett, Bt. |
| SIC NOBIS JUSTICIA | Thus justice is for us. Jackson. |
| SIC NOS NON NOBIS | Thus we are not for ourselves. Equitable Life Assurance Soc. |
| SIC ROS NON NOBIS LABORAMUS | Thus we toil not for ourselves. Pocklington (Yorks.) RDC, 1958. |

| | |
|---|---|
| SIC NOS SIC SACRA TUEMUR | Thus we defend sacred things. McMahon, Bts. |
| SIC PARVIS MAGNA | Thus great things arise from small. Drake. |
| SIC STAMINA FATI | Such are the threads of fate. Caird of Belmont Castle. |
| SIC TUTUS | Thus safe. Gordon of Park, Bts. |
| SIC VIRESCIT INDUSTRIA | Thus industry flourishes. Rotherham (Yorks.), Bor. of. |
| SIC VIRESCIT LUX | Thus light flourishes, Sheffield and Rotherham Police Authority. |
| SIC VIRESCO | Thus I shall flourish. Christie, Christy. |
| SIC VOS NON VOBIS | Thus not for ourselves. Baldock (Herts.) UDC. Antonio de Leyva, d. 1537 (general of Emperor Charles V, did not consider himself properly requited for his service, hence motto, part of verse which Virgil pasted on gates of Augustus' palace when Bathyllus had claimed authorship of some of his work), Van Mildert Coll., Durham Univ., Lords Waleran (Walrond), RAF station, Idris (We labour to serve others). |
| SIC VOS NON VOBIS MELLIFICATIS APES | If you do not make honey for yourselves (part of famous verse, purposely left unfinished, which Virgil wrote on doorpost of Augustus's palace. Franks, Lords Hives. |
| SICUT AQUILA JUVENESCAM | I will renew my youth as the eagle. Barlow of London, Bts. (ref. to eagle in shield and crest and to false natural history of eagle renewing its youth). |
| SICUT COLUMBAE | As the doves. St Columba's Coll., Dublin, 1843. |
| SICUT LILIUM | As the lily. Magdalen Coll. Sch., Oxford, founded 1478 by William Waynflete, possibly all. to Lily, distinguished grammarian who, with many other notable men, was at the school. |
| SICUT OLIVA VIRENS LAETOR IN AEDE DEI | As the flourishing olive, I rejoice in the house of God. Oliver, Olivier (coat of arms of Lord Olivier, of cr. 1924, now ext. *(NEP)*, and of cr. 1970 – that of Sir Laurence Olivier later Lord Olivier includes olive tree, as representing the name of Lord Olivier the famous actor, and a plough, which is all. to name of his wife, Joan Plowright; motto is described as a family one). |
| SICUT QUERCUS VIRESCIT INDUSTRIA | Industry flourishes like the oak. Mansfield (Notts.), Bor. of. |
| SICUT QUI MINISTRANT | (We are) as they who serve. RAF Hosp., Nocton Hall. |
| SICUT SERPENTES SICUT COLUMBAE | As serpents, as doves (from St Matthew 10:16) (motto also occurs in Greek). Radley Coll., Oxon., 1847. |
| SIDUS ADSIT AMICUM | Let my propitious star be present. Bateman. |
| SIGNAL SERVICE | No. 7 Radio Sch., RAF. |
| SIGNUM PACIS AMOR | Love is the sign of peace. Bell of Glasgow, Bts., Bell of Mynthurst, Bts. |
| SIGNUM QUAERENS IN VELLERE | Seeking a sign in wool. Clarke of Rupertswood, Bts. |
| SILENT WE STRIKE | 298 Sq., RAF. |
| SILENTER IN MEDIAS RES | Silently into the midst of things. 177 Sq., RAF. |

| | |
|---|---|
| SILENTIO ET SPE | In silence and hope. Brander. |
| SILENTLY WE SERVE | 527 Sq., RAF. |
| SIMILI FRONDESCIT VIRGE METALLO | The twig bears leaves of similar metal. Calmady. |
| SIMPLEX MUNDITIIS | Plain with neatness (Horace, *Odes* I. v. 1). Philips, Viscount Simonds, Symonds of Pilsdon. |
| SIMPLICES SICUT PUERI, SAGACES SICUT SERPENTES | Harmless as boys, wise as serpents. Vaughan of Courtfield. |
| SINCERE ET CONSTANTER | Sincerely and steadfastly. Order of the Red Eagle (Prussia). |
| SINCERITATE | By sincerity. Francklin. |
| SINCERITY | Southam (Warwicks.) RDC, 1955. |
| SINE CLADE STERNO | I spread out without disaster. Thicknesse. |
| SINE CONSILIO NIHIL | Nothing without counsel. County Coll., Lancaster Univ. |
| SINE CRIMINE FIAT | Be it done without reproach. Innes. |
| SINE DEO FRUSTRA | All in vain without God. Gull, Bts. |
| SINE ERRORE SINE TARDORE | Without error, without delay. Communication Centre, RAF Rudloe Manor, SW Signals Centre, RAF. |
| SINE LABE DECUS | Honour without stain. Wimbledon, London Bor. of. |
| SINE LABE NOTA | Known to be without a stain. Craufurd, Bts., Crawford, Crawfurd-Pollok, Bt., McKenzie, Pile, Bts. |
| SINE MACLA | Without a mascle. Piccolomini, noble Italian family from Siena. |
| SINE MACULA | Without spot. Cary, Flint, Mackenzie of Scatwell, Bts., McCulloch, Mount St Mary's Coll., Derbys. (founded 1842 by Soc. of Jesus), Norcliffe, Synnot. |
| SINE MACULA MACLA | The mascle without a stain. Lord Asquith of Bishopstone (*NEP*), Clough, Earls of Oxford and Asquith. |
| SINE METU | Without fear. Jameson. |
| SINE MORA | Without delay. 267 Sq., RAF. |
| SINE NOBIS SCIENTIA LANGUET | Without us science languishes. Scientific Instrument Makers. |
| SINE PAVORE SINE FAVORE | Without trembling, without favour. Penrith RDC, 1961. |
| SINE PERICULO IN ORIENTE | Without peril in the East. RAF Eastern Radar. |
| SINE PHOEBO LUX | Light without the sun. Lords Kinnaird. |
| SINE PRAEJUDICIO | Without prejudice. Lloyd's Register of Shipping. |
| SINE QUA NON | Indispensable. 540 Sq., RAF. |
| SINGULARITER IN SPE | Specially in hope. Lescher. |
| SIOTHCHAIN AGUS FAIRSINGE | Peace and plenty. Kavanagh. |
| SIR IS SATH | Seek out and thrust. 3510 Co. of Inverness Fighter Control Unit, RAAF. |
| SIS FORTIS | Be thou brave. Lindley. |

| | |
|---|---|
| SIS MEMOR ET PERSTA | Be mindful and persist. Harrison. |
| SIS PIUS IN PRIMIS | Be pious among the first. Barlow, Bts. |
| SIS UT LEONES | Be like the lions. HMS *Sea Lion* (a submarine). |
| SIT FORSTER FELIX | Let Forster be happy. Forster of Lysways, Bt. |
| SIT SINE LABE DECUS | Let ornament be without stain. Earls of Eldon (Scott). |
| SIT TIBI SANCTA COHORS COMITUM | To Thee be the band of comrades dedicated. Congleton Boro. of. |
| SITU EXORITUR SEGEDUNI | Arose on the site of Segedunum. Wallsend (Northumb.), Bor. of, 1902. Arms of the borough show a golden eagle standing on a wall, all. to the fact that town arose at the end of Hadrian's Wall on site of Roman settlement of Segedunum. |
| SIVE AERE SIVE CAMPO | In the air and in the field. 652 Sq., RAF. |
| SJO VORDUR LOPT VORDUR | Guardian of the sea and air (Icelandic). 240 Sq., RAF, served over northern waters; badge a Viking winged helmet. |
| SKAGH MAC-EN-CHROE | The bush (*or* sign) of McEnchroe. Crowe of Dromore, co. Clare (according to an Irish scholar the motto should read Skagh McEbchroe). |
| SKOAL | (Norse drinking salutation). Linkletter. |
| SNELL HA LETL | Swift and loyal (Cornish). Snell (play on the surname). |
| SO FARRE NO FARTHER | Fothergill. |
| SO RUN THAT YE MAY OBTAIN | (1 Corinthians 9:24). Baker of Bayfordbury, co. Herts. |
| SOBRIE, JUSTE, PIE | Soberly, justly, piously. Coales. |
| SOCIETAS FLOREBIT | The society will flourish, Benfleet (Essex) UDC. |
| SOIES FERME | Be firm. Sir Marmaduke Constable, *c.*1520, Maxwell. |
| SOIS JUSTE ET FORT | Be just and strong. Joly de Lotbinière. |
| SOL ET PASTOR DEUS | The sun and God our shepherd. Sunbury-on-Thames (Middx.), 1948. |
| SOL ET SALUBRITAS | Sun and healthiness. Bexhill-on-Sea (Sussex), Bor. of. |
| SOL ET SCUTUM DEUS | God is our sun and shield. Nicholson, Pearson. |
| SOL MEA TESTIS | The sun is my witness. Boteler (formerly Boehm), Bt. |
| SOLA BONA QUAE HONESTA | Those things only are good which are honest. Archer, Lords Colebrooke *(NEP)*, Leamington Spa (Warwicks.), Roy. Bor. of. |
| SOLA CRUCE | With the Cross alone. Best, Best-Shaw of Eltham, Bts. |
| SOLA FACTA, SOLUM DEUM SEQUOR | I follow God alone, as I have been made solitary. Bona of Savoy, wife of Galeazzo Maria Sforza (d. 1476), all. to her widowhood. |
| SOLA IN DEO SALUS | Safety alone in God. Mayhew, Robinson, Rokeby. |
| SOLA NOBILITAS VIRTUS | Virtue is the only nobility. Apsey, Marquesses of Abercorn (Hamilton), Blake of Menlo, Bt., Hamilton, Standish. |

| | |
|---|---|
| SOLA PROBA QUAE HONESTA | Those things only are good which are honourable. Neave, Bts. |
| SOLA SALUS SERVIRE DEO | The only safe course is to serve God. Gore, Bts., Magenis, Ware of Edinburgh. |
| SOLA VERITAS INVICTA | Truth alone is unconquered. Apsley (formerly Meeking). |
| SOLA VIRTUS INVICTA | Virtue alone invincible. Collis, Viscount Fitzalan of Derwent (Fitzalan-Howard), Goff of Goff's Oak, Bt., Haige, Hanson, Harris, Howard, Dukes of Norfolk (Fitzalan-Howard), Teeling. |
| SOLA VIRTUS NOBILITAT | Virtue alone ennobles. Enraght-Mooney, Lords Faringdon (Henderson), Henderson, Pelly. |
| SOLA VIVAT IN ILLO | She lives only in him. Diane de Poitiers, Duchesse de Valentinois, d. 1560. |
| SOLEM FERO | I bear the sun. Aubrey, Bt. |
| SOLERTIA DITAT | Prudence enriches. Whitelaw. |
| SOLERTIA VINCAT | Let cleverness conquer. Clarke. |
| SOLI DEO | To God alone. Ullathorne Gram. Sch., Coventry, 1934. |
| SOLI DEO GLORIA | Glory be to God alone. Bishop's Stortford Coll., Herts., founded 1868 mainly for Nonconformists, Bonteine, Eustace, Glovers' and Skinners' Co., Lesly. *See also* To God only. |
| SOLI DEO HONOR | Honour to God alone. Stewart of Shambellie. |
| SOLI DEO HONOR ET GLORIA | Huddleston of Sawston, Leathersellers' Co., inc. 1444. Queen Mary Coll. (London Univ.) has this motto as inscription on a book, one of the charges in the arms. |
| SOLIS ORTUM CONSPICERE | To behold the sunrise. East Riding Yorks. CC, 1945. |
| SOLO DEO SALUS | Salvation from God alone. Lords Rokeby (Robinson) *(NEP)*. Rokeby in N.R. Yorks. was the estate of the Rokebys associated with the poem of that name by Sir Walter Scott; estate bought by William Robinson, whose descendant became 1st Lord Rokeby in Irish Peerage. |
| SOLUM PATRIAE | Only to my country. Lord Hungarton (Crawford) *(NEP)*. |
| SOLVITUR AMBULANDO | It is solved by walking (saying of Greek philosopher to those who denied validity of movement). Lord Pearson. |
| SORIA PUR CABEZA DE ESTREMADURA | Soria is simply the head of Estremadura (province). City of Soria in Spain. |
| SORTE SUA CONTENTUS | Content with his lot. Hartwell, Bts. |
| SOUVERAIGNE | Duchy of Lancaster. Dukedom was merged with the Crown in 1399, when Henry Bolingbroke, Duke of Lancaster, usurped English throne as Henry IV. Subsequent sovereigns, male and female, remain Dukes of Lancaster; both George VI and Elizabeth II have acknowledged this as a loyal toast when in Lancashire. |
| SOW FOR PROSPERITY | Longridge (Lancs.) UDC. |
| SOYEZ FERME | Be firm. Earls of Carrick (Butler), Foljambe, Holt-Needham, Hyde, Insole, Earls of Liverpool (Foljambe), Skerrin, Snow. |

| | |
|---|---|
| SOYEZ JUSTE | Be just. Sismey. |
| SOYEZ SAGE | Be wise. Eliot of Stobs, Bts. |
| SOYEZ SAGE ET SIMPLE | Be wise and simple. Spry. |
| SPAIR NOUGHT | Brisbane, Bts., Hay, Marquesses of Tweeddale (Hay), Yester. |
| SPARE AND THOU HAST NOUGHT | Haworth, Bts. |
| SPARE NOT | Gifford. |
| SPARSA ET NEGLECTA COLGI | I have gathered the scattered and neglected. Claude Fauchet, 1530–1601, who collected the old French Chronicles. |
| SPARTAM NACTUS ES: HANC EXORNA | Thou hast met (come to) Sparta, adorn it. Loretto Sch., Musselburgh, E. Lothian. |
| SPE | By hope. Horrocks, Lovett. |
| SPE ET LABORE | By hope and exertion. Lords Gladwyn (Jebb), Jebb. |
| SPE EXPECTO | I expect in hope. Forbes, Forbes-Leith, Livingstone. |
| SPE LABOR LEVIS | Labour is light from hope. Hill, co. Norfolk, Ochterlony of that Ilk, Price. |
| SPE NEMO RUET | No one will fall by hope. Spennymoor UDC, 1952. |
| SPE POSTERI TEMPORIS | In the hope of after time. Atcherley, co. Salop. |
| SPE TUTIORES ARMIS | Safer by hope than by arms. Lewis of Parwich. |
| SPE VIRES AUGENTUR | Powers are increased by hope. Critchley, Hope, Scott of Dunninald, Bts., Scott of Silwood Park, Bts. |
| SPE VITAE MELIORIS | In hope of a better life. Lea. |
| SPE VIVIMUS | We live in hope. Weir. |
| SPE VIVITUR | One lives in hope. Dobree. |
| SPECTAMUR AGENDO | We are viewed by our actions. Royal Dublin Fus., 1st Bn., 102nd Royal Madras Fus., 30th Foot – East Lancashire Regt. |
| SPECTEMUR AGENDO | Let us be viewed by our actions. Agar-Roberts, Barnsley, Co. Bor. of, Brown, Browne, Chorley (Lancs.) RDC, Drumson, Duckett, Ellis, Elvin of E. Dereham, Foster, Hammersmith, London Bor. of, Hartley, Jones, Lambeth, London Bor. of, Levy, co. Leics., Lloyd, McLeur, Bt., Montagu-Pollock, Bts., Montague, Moore, Morris, Mott, Reid, Bts., Reynolds, Rutson, Earls of Shannon (Boyle), Vigors, RAF station, Benson. |
| SPECULATE NUNTIATE | Having watched, bring word. 236 Sq., RAF. |
| SPECULATUM ASCENDAMUS | We ascend to observe. 666 Scottish Sq., RAAF. |
| SPEED, STRENGTH AND TRUTH UNITED | Framework Knitters' Co., inc. 1657. The dexter supporter of the arms is a student of the Univ. of Cambridge, who is meant to commemorate the Rev. William Lee of St John's Coll., Cambridge, who in 1589 invented machine for knitting woollen stockings and later silk hose; he got no support and died in France a poor man. |

| | |
|---|---|
| SPEED WELL | Speid, Lord Stokes (Life Baron). |
| SPEED WITH ACCURACY | Supply Control Centre, RAF. |
| SPEM FORTUNA ALIT | Fortune nourishes hope. Balfour-Kinnear, Lord Kinnear, Petree. |
| SPEM SUCCESSUS ALIT | Success nourishes hope. Lockhart of Carstairs, Bts., Ross of Balnagowan, Bt. |
| SPEM VIGILANTIA FIRMAT | Vigilance strengthens hope. Dunbar of Northfield, Bts. |
| SPERANDUM EST | It is to be hoped for. Wallace. |
| SPERANS PERGO | I advance hoping. Fletcher, Tomkinson, co. Worcs. |
| SPERAREM | I would have hoped. Lords Southborough (Hopwood). |
| SPERAT IN DEO | He hopes in God. Beale-Brown. |
| SPERATE INFESTIS | Having hoped in adversity. Colborne, Lords Seaton (Colborne-Vivian) *(NEP)*. |
| SPERATUM ET COMPLETUM | Hoped for and completed. Arnet, Arnott, Bts., Arnut. |
| SPERNIT PERICULA VIRTUS | Virtue despises dangers. Carpenter-Garnier, Forrester, Ramsay of Banff, Bts. |
| SPERO | I hope. Allan, Annard, Briscoe, Chalmers, Calderwood, Dolling, Douglas, co. Dumfries, Douglas-Cooper, Gib, Gordon, Hutton, Langlands, Learmouth, Leveson, Makepeace, Menzies, Sparrow, Shank, Toole, Wakefield, Warner, Bts., Waters. |
| SPERO AVANZAR CON LA VIGILIA IL SONNO | I hope to surpass (time of sleep) by watching. Italian Academy of Sonnachiosi of Bologna. |
| SPERO ET CAPTIVUS NITOR | I hope, and though a captive I strive. Devenish, Devonsheere. |
| SPERO MELIORA | I hope for better things. Ainsworth, Blyth, Carrington, Cazalet, co. Kent, Darby, Douglas, Fairholme, Grigg-Strode, Hill-Lowe, Lord Hobhouse *(NEP)*, Laird, Marindin, Maxwell, Moffat, Murray, Phillips, Rait, Rhet, Rodie, Sanderlands, Scopholine, Shaw, Bts., Shaw-Stewart, Bts., Smith, Sparkes, Stewart, Lords Turphichen (Sandilands), Watson, Wignall. |
| SPERO UT FIDELIS | I hope as being faithful. Baskerville, Mynors. |
| SPES | Hope. Lords Aldington (Law), Gaskell. |
| SPES ALTERA | Another hope. Maxwell-Gumbleton. |
| SPES ANCHORA TUTA | Hope is a safe anchor. Dunmure, Priestman, Bt. |
| SPES ASPERA LEVAT | Hope raises hard things. Ross of Dunboyne, Bts. |
| SPES DABIT AUXILIUM | Hope will lend aid. Dunbar of Durn, Bts. |
| SPES DECUS ET ROBUR | Hope is our ornament and strength. Eardley-Smith, Bts. |
| SPES DURAT AVORUM | The hope of my ancestors remains. Kimbolton Sch., Cambs., 1600, Anne de Rohan, Princess de Guemene, d. 1685 (married her cousin, Louis VIII (1598–1667), who became Duke of Montbazon in 1654), Rochfors, Walmesley. |
| SPES EST IN DEO | My hope is in God. Bagge. |

| | |
|---|---|
| SPES ET AUDAX | Hope and daring. Bland-Sutton, Bt. |
| SPES ET FIDES | Hope and faith. Chamberlain, Bts., Lord Clauson (NEP), Lucas, Whitaker. |
| SPES ET FORTUNA | Hope and fortune. Viscount Chelmsford (Thesiger). |
| SPES FORTI VIRO | Hope for a strong man. Forbes-Leith, Bts. |
| SPES IN DEO | Hope in God. Boultbee, Lords Piercy. |
| SPES IN FUTURA | Hope in the future. Wadge. |
| SPES MEA CHRISTUS | Christ is my hope. Bingham of Melcombe, Lords Clanmorris (Bingham), Earls of Lucan (Bingham), Smith-Bingham. |
| SPES MEA COPIA FECIT | My hope made my store. Bell of Thirsk, co. Yorks. |
| SPES MEA DEUS | God is my hope. Brooke, De Capel Brooke, Bts., Foot of Holly Park, Hackett, O'Farrell. |
| SPES MEA EST IN DEO | My hope is in God. Threlfall. |
| SPES MEA IN DEO | My hope is in God. Ambrose, Lord Ardilaun (Guiness) (NEP), Boxall, Bt., Brooke, Dewhurst, Gaskell, Gosker, Greaves, Guiness, Guinness, Earls of Iveagh (Guinness), Kingsford-Lethbridge, Kirkwood, Lethbridge, Bts., Lewin, Player, Richards, Roper, Ryle, Saunders, Lords Teynham (Roper-Curzon), Wainwright. |
| SPES MEA IN FUTURO EST | My hope is in the future. Robinson, Bts. |
| SPES MEA NON FRACTA | My hope is not broken. Lords Glendevon (Hope). |
| SPES MEA VERITAS | Truth is my hope. Farnham. |
| SPES NOSTRA DEUS | God is our hope. Curriers' Co., inc. 1606, but from 1415 autonomous apart from Cordwainers. |
| SPES PATRIAE RUS | The country is the hope of our country. Strood (Kent) RDC, 1953. |
| SPES SIBI QUISQUE | Each man's hope of himself. Ebden, Penn. |
| SPES TUTISSIMA COELIS | The surest hope is in heaven. Burman, King, Earls of Kingston (King-Tenison), Price of Glanwilly, Stafford-King-Harman, Bts. |
| SPES VITAE MELIORIS | Hope for a better life. Lord Broughton (Hobhouse) (NEP), Hobhouse, Bts. |
| SPIANDACT TAPEIR NEILL | See Griandacht. |
| SPIRAT IN DEO | It breathes in God. Northleach (Glos.) RDC. |
| SPIRITUS DURISSIMA COQUIT | Courage digests the hardest things. Girolamo Mattei, Capt. of Guard to Pope Clement VII, killed a Cardinal's nephew; took device of ostrich swallowing an iron nail (i.e. time would enable him to overcome great injuries); secured pardon from the Pope. |
| SPIRITUS GLADIUS | The sword of the spirit. Hutton of Marske. |
| SPIRITUS INTUS ALIT | The spirit within nourishes. Clifton Coll., Bristol, 1862. |
| SPLENDIO TRITUS | I shine though worn. Ferrers. |
| SPOLIATIS ARMA SUPERSUNT | Arms still remain to the despoiled. Emmanuel Philibert, Duke of Savoy 1528–80, because although the French had despoiled his territories, he continued to wage war. |

| | |
|---|---|
| SPONTE FAVOS, AEGRE SPICULA | Honeycombs, willingly, stings unwillingly. Pope Urban VIII, Maffeo Barberini (*see also* Exercet sub sole laborem). |
| S'RIOGHAL MO DHREAM | My clan is loyal. MacGregor, McGregor. |
| STA SALDO | Stand! Lord Forster *(NEP)*. The word *saldo* must have had some significance in this anciently recorded family; it does not occur in classical Latin. |
| STABILE BONUM | A stable good. Lang of Renfrew. |
| STABILIS | Stable, Hardcastle. |
| STABILITY | Anglia Bldg. Soc. |
| STABIT CONSCIOUS AEQUI | Conscious of the just he will stand. Charlton, Chirnside, Grant-Dalton. |
| STABIT SAXUM, FLUET AMNIS | The stone will stand, the river will flow. Clitheroe (Lancs.), Bor. of. |
| STABO | I shall stand. Kinmond. |
| STALK AND STRIKE | 403 Sq., RCAF, 1943. |
| STAND FAST | Black of Highfield Park, Hants., Grant of Frenchie, Grant-Duff, Marriott-Dodington, Earls of Seafield (Grant), Lords Strathspey (Grant). |
| STAND FAST IN HONOUR AND STRENGTH | Merton, London Bor. of. |
| STAND ON | Saunders of Dolphington House, Sykes. |
| STAND SURE | Adson, Airderbeck, Anderson, Grant of Burnside, Grant of Forres, Bts., Grant of Lichborough, Grant-Ives, Ponton. |
| STAND UNITED | National Defence Coll., Latimer, Bucks. |
| STANT INNIXA DEO | They stand upheld by God. Harrison-Crawfurd. |
| STAT FORTUNA DOMUS VIRTUTE | The fortune of our house stands by virtue. Molyneux of Castle Dillon, Bts. |
| STAT RELIGIONE PARENTUM | He continues in the religion of his forefathers. De Grey, Lucas. |
| STAT VERITAS | Truth endures. Sandeman, Stavert, Stewart-Sandeman, Bt. |
| STEADFAST | Lords Gretton, Lords Sandhurst (Mansfield), Welchman, RAF station, Cerney, Glos. (badge of Roman helmet indicates location nr. Cirencester and that town's early Roman association). |
| STEADFAST AND FAITHFUL | Axminster (Devon) Parish Council. |
| STEADFAST IN DIFFICULTIES | Tottenham UDC. |
| STEADY | Lords Aylmer, Aylmer, Bts., Viscount Bridport (Hood), Hood, Hood Bn. (Royal Naval Div.), M'Adam, Neill, Norris, Northen, Northey, Tonge, Verelst, Weller. |
| STEDFAST | Beazley of Warborough, co. Oxon. |
| STELLA MARIS | Star of the sea. Broadstairs (Kent) UDC (motto is title frequently given to the B.V. Mary). |
| STEP BY STEP | Nationwide Bldg. Soc. |

| | |
|---|---|
| STET CAPITOLIUM FULGENS | Let the capital stand shining. North Thames Gas Bd. |
| STET FORTUNA DOMUS | May the fortune of our house endure. Harrow Sch., Lippitt, John Lyons Sch., Harrow, Tiarks. |
| STETIT IN EXIDO PRO PATRIA FIDES | Faith stood in disaster on behalf of the country. Cazenove of Cottesbrooke, Northants. |
| STILTE BAART WIJSHEID | Silence engenders wisdom. RAF station, Eindhoven, Netherlands. |
| STIMULAT SED ORNAT | It stimulates but adorns. Macartney, Bts. |
| STIMULIS MAJORIBUS ARDENS | Burning with greater hopes. Hamilton of Silverton Hill, Bts. |
| STO PERSTOQUE | I stand and stand firm. McQuitty. |
| STO PRO VERITATE | I stand for the truth. Guthrie. |
| STOP AT NOTHING | 175 Sq., RAF. |
| STORE IN READINESS | No. 39 Maintenance Unit, RAF. |
| STRAIGHT AND STRONG | Furniture Makers' Guild. |
| STRAIGHT AND TRUE | RAF station, Leeming. |
| STRENGTH | Stamford Mutual Insurance Co. Ltd., 1965. |
| STRENGTH IN RESERVE | E. Midlands Univ. Air Sq., RAFVR. |
| STRENGTH IN UNITY | 158 Sq., RAF. |
| STRENGTH IS FREEDOM | RAF station, Wittering, W. Sussex. |
| STRENGTH THROUGH MOBILITY | RAF station, El Hamra. |
| STRENUE CONSTANTER ET RECTE | Earnestly, constantly and rightly. Frickley, Healey, Warde-Adlam. |
| STRENUE ET HONESTE | Strenuously and honestly. Jackson of Fairburn. |
| STRENUE ET PROSPERE | Earnestly and successfully. Johnson. |
| STRENUE INSEQUOR | Follow quickly. Luke. |
| STRENUIS ARDUA CEDUNT | Difficulties give way to efforts. Univ. of Southampton. |
| STREPITUS NON TERRET OVANTEM | Loud noises do not frighten one who is rejoicing. Dorington, Bts. |
| STRIKE | Lords Hawke, 232 Sq., RAF. |
| STRIKE AND RETURN | 460 Sq., RAF. |
| STRIKE AND STRIKE AGAIN | 455 Sq., RAAF. |
| STRIKE AND SUPPORT | RAF station, Labuan, Borneo. |
| STRIKE FAST | Royal Australian Air Force. |
| STRIKE HARD | 104 Sq., RAF (badge a thunderbolt). |
| STRIKE HARD, STRIKE HOME | 349 Sq., RAF (Belgian), 1943. |
| STRIKE HARD, STRIKE SURE | Bomber Cmd., RAF. |
| STRIKE SURE | Central Bomber Establishment, RAF, Greig, 14th Co. of London Bn. (London Scottish) Territorials. |
| STRIKE TO DEFEND | 83 Sq., RAF. |

| | |
|---|---|
| STRIKE TRUE | 80 Sq., RAF. |
| STRIKE WITH ACCURACY | Strike Cmd. Bombing Sch. (Bomber Cmd. Bombing Sch.), RAF. |
| STRINGE MA NON CONSTRINGE | It binds without constraining. Thomas I, d. 1233, Count of Savoy, whose device was a lover's knot. |
| STRIVE | Anderson, Bt., Cary, Bt. |
| STRIVE AND ENDURE | Caird of Glenfarquhar, Bt. |
| STRIVE FOR THE GAIN OF ALL | Gainsborough (Lincs.) UDC. |
| STRIVE FOR THE RIGHT | Poole, Bts. |
| STRIVE, PROBE, APPLY | Lords Marks of Broughton, Marks & Spencer Ltd., 1968. |
| STRIVE TO HEAL | Princess Mary's RAF Hosp., Akrotiri, Cyprus. |
| STRIVE WITHOUT STRIFE | Ashton (formerly of Darwen, Lancs.). |
| STRONG AND FIRM | Wolrige-Gordon. |
| STRONG FOUNDATIONS | RAF station, Driffield. |
| STRONG TO ENDURE | No. 85 Op. Training Unit, RAF. |
| STRONG TO SERVE | 130 Sq., RAF (Punjaub.). |
| STRUGGLE | Ruggles-Brise, Bts. |
| STUDEO ESSE UTILIS | I study to be useful. Lord Brooke (De Capell Brooke) (NEP). |
| STUDIIS DIVISI VOLANDO SOCIATI | In their studies they are divided, flying they are united. Univ. of Liverpool Air Sq., RAFVR. |
| STUDIO FIDE ANIMIS | By study, faith and spirits. St Faith's and Aylsham RDC. |
| STUDIO FLOREMUS | We flourish by study. Witney Gram. Sch., Oxon., 1959. |
| STUDIO SAPIENTIA CRESCIT | Wisdom grows by study. Framlingham Coll., Suffolk, 1864. |
| STUDY QUIET | Head, Patrick. |
| SUA ALIENAQUE PIGNORA NUTRIT | He nourishes his own and other pledges of love. Mattias Corvinus, 1458–90, King of Hungary. |
| SUA DEXTRA CUIQUE | Under the right for each. Oates, co. Yorks. |
| SUA GRACIA PARVIS | Small in our own favour. Little. |
| SUAVE | Suavely (or Easily) (word is part of the Vulgate version (St Matthew 11:30) of Christ's words 'Jugum meum suave est . . .' ('My yoke is easy'). Giovanni de Medici, Pope Leo X, 1513–21; his suavity occasioned the Protestant Reformation. |
| SUAVITER ET FORTITER | Mildly and firmly. Daubeney, Earls of Minto (Elliot-Murray-Kynynmound), Rathbone. |
| SUAVITER IN MODO, FORTITER IN RE | Gentle in manner, firm in act. Beevor, Bts., Harris, Lords Newborough (Wynn), Nunn, Wynn, 180 Sq., RAF. |
| SUAVITER SED FORTITER | Mildly but firmly. Busk, Chapman, Bts., Dennis, Smith of Barnes Hall, Williams of Lee. |
| SUB ALIS | Under the wings. Radcliffe. |

| | |
|---|---|
| SUB CRUCE CANDIDA | Under the white cross. Arden, Earls of Egmont (Perceval), Perceval, co. Sligo. |
| SUB CRUCE COPIA | Plenty under the Cross. Cross of Marchbankwood, Bt. |
| SUB CRUCE FLOREAMUS | May we flourish under the Cross. Poulton le Fylde (Lancs.) UDC. |
| SUB CRUCE GLORIOR | I glory under the Cross. Astell, co. Bedfords. |
| SUB CRUCE SALUS | Salvation under the Cross. Crosse of Shaw Hill, co. Lancs., Viscount Bangor (Ward), Fletcher, co. Staffs., Nelson-Ward, Ward of Wilbraham Place, Bt., Ward of Willey. |
| SUB CRUCE VERITAS | Truth under the Cross. Crosse, Woollcombe-Adams. |
| SUB HOC SIGNO VINCES | Under this sign thou shalt conquer. Hartley, co. Staffs., Viscount De Vesci, Vaizey. |
| SUB LIBERTATE QUIETEM | Rest under liberty. Burrell, Cay, Carter, Hoblyn, Kay, Keay, Parker, Peter, Stephenson, Walsham, Bts. |
| SUB PACE COPIA | Under peace, plenty. France, Franco, Lords Ludlow (Lopes, previously Franco) (NEP). |
| SUB ROBORE VIRTUS | Manhood under the oak (all. to oak in arms crest). Aikin of Liverpool, Robertson-Aikman. |
| SUB SOLE NIHIL | I seek nothing beneath the sun. Monteith, Stuart-Menteth, Bts. |
| SUB SOLE SUB UMBRA VIRENS | Flourishing alike under sun and shade. Irvine, Irvine-Fortescue. |
| SUB SPE | Under hope. Cairns, Coutts-Duffus, Dunbar, Duffas. |
| SUB TEGMINE FAGI | Under the shelter of the beech. Beech of Brandon Hall, Coventry (beech tree in shield). |
| SUB UMBRA ALARUM | Under the shadow of His wings (from Psalm 17:8). Jones. |
| SUB UMBRA ALARUM TUARUM | Under the shadow of Thy wings (Psalm 17:8). Lawder, King Peter II of Aragon, 1196–1213. |
| SUBDITUS FIDELIS REGIS EST SALUS REGNI | A faithful subject of the king is the salvation of the kingdom. Carlos (formerly of Broomhall). Col. William Carlos was present at Battle of Worcester, 3 September 1651, and saved Charles II in the Royal Oak at Boscobel. He received grant of arms dated 21 May 1658 in which the main charge was an oak tree (family pedigree B.L.G., 1952). |
| SUBLIMIORA PETAMUS | Let us seek higher things. Biddulph, Stonhouse, Bts. |
| SUBLIMIORA PETO | I seek higher things. Jackson of Glasgow. |
| SUBLIMIORA SPECTEMUS | Let us regard loftier things. Warren. |
| SUBLIMIS AB UNDA | Aloft from the wave. King Edward VII Sch., Lytham, Lancs., 1908. |
| SUBMARINE MINERS | Royal Engineers Submarine Miners (raised 1863, abolished 1907). |
| SUDORE NON SOPORE | By sweat not sleep. Pearson, co. Notts., St Ives, Bor. of. |

| | |
|---|---|
| SUDORE QUAM SANGUINE | By sweat and by blood. 52 Sq., RAF. |
| SUFFER | Earls of Camperdown (Haldane-Duncan) *(NEP)*, Chinnery-Haldane of Gleneagles, Haldane, Halden, Oswald. |
| SUFFIBULATUS MAJORES SEQUOR | I follow my ancestors, having been buckled (i.e. armed). Hathorn, Johnston Stewart, MacTaggart Stewart, Bts. |
| SUFFICIT MERUISSE | It is enough to have deserved well. Hunter-Rodwell, Plumptre. |
| SUI MEMORES MERENDO | Mindful of oneself in deserving. Earls Jellicoe. |
| SUIS STAT VIRIBUS | He stands by his own powers. Lords Abinger (Scarlett). |
| SUIVANT ST PIERRE | Following St Peter. Knight. |
| SUIVEZ MOI | Follow me. Borough, Bt. |
| SUIVEZ RAISON | Follow reason. Barberrie, Browne of Elsing Hall, co. Norfolk, Critchett, Bts., Dixon of Unthank Hall, Gardner-Brown, Gore-Browne, Hillasdon, Lords Kilmaine (Browne), Viscount Montague, Marquesses of Sligo (Browne), Stanyforth, Wyatt. |
| SUM QUOD SUM | I am what I am. Butt, Bts., Coldicott, Foresight. |
| SUM TALBOTI PRO VINCERE INIMICOS | I belong to Talbot to conquer his enemies. On sword of John Talbot, 1st Earl of Shrewsbury, killed at Battle of Chastillon, 1453, at age of 80. |
| SUME SUPERBIAM QUAESITAM MERITIS | Assume the pride of mind which you have acquired by your merits. Seaver. |
| SUMMA PETO | I seek the highest. Lord Winterbottom (Life Baron). |
| SUMMA PETUNT IUVENES | Youth strives for the highest. Edinburgh Univ. Air Sq., RAFVR. |
| SUMMUM NEC METUAM DIEM NEC OPTEM | May I not dread nor desire the last day. Tighe. |
| SUMORSAETE EALLE | All for Somerset. Somerset CC. |
| SUO SE ROBORE FIRMAT | He establishes himself by his own strength. Grant of Carron, Grant-Sturgis. |
| SUO STAT ROBORE VIRTUS | Virtue stands by its own strength. Mowbray, Bts. |
| SUPER ACCRA AD SIDERA | Over the maples to the stars. No. 33 Air Navigation Sch., RAF (badge is the maple leaf of Canada, where sch. was located). |
| SUPER AETHERA VIRTUS | Virtue is above the heavens. Speke of Jordans. |
| SUPER ANTIQUAS VIAS | Upon the ancient tracks. St Peter's Sch., York, 1953, Thorp. |
| SUPER ARDUA | Above the difficulties. Roy. Coll. of. Obstetricians and Gynaecologists. |
| SUPER FUNDAMENTIS CERTIS | Over certain foundations. St Aidan's Soc. (Durham Univ.), 1957. |
| SUPER OMNIA UBIQUE | Over all everywhere. 82 Sq., RAF. |
| SUPER SIDERA VOTUM | My wishes are above the stars. Rattray. |
| SUPERA MORAS | Overcome delays. Bolton (Lancs.), Co. Bor. of. |

| | |
|---|---|
| SUPERAT TELLUS SIDERA DONAT | Earth conquers yet bestows the heavens. Academy of Elevati of Ferrara. |
| SUPERATA TELLUS SIDERA DONAT | Earth conquered gives the stars. Leeds Univ. Air Sq., RAFVR. |
| SUPERNA PETIMUS | We seek high things. RAF College, Cranwell. |
| SUPERO | I overcome. 274 Sq., RAF. |
| SUPPLIES FOR HEALTH | No. 248 Maintenance Unit, RAF (previously known as Medical Stores Depot). |
| SUPPLY ALL | No. 113 Maintenance Unit, RAF. |
| SUPPORT | Home Cmd., RAF. |
| SUPPORT, SAVE, SUPPLY | RAF station, Lyneham. |
| SUPPORT TO THE WINGS | No. 206 Group HQ, RAF. |
| SUPRA MARE SUPRA TERRAMQUE | Above the sea and the land. RAF station, Wattisham, formed April 1939. From where squadrons carried out first operation in World War II, attacking German ship off Wilhelmshaven. |
| SUPRA MONTEM POSITA | Placed above the mountain. St Hilda's College, Durham, 1902. |
| SUPRA URBEM ALAE NOSTRAE VOLANT | Our wings rise over the city. RAF station, Castle Bromwich. |
| SUR ESPÉRANCE | Upon hope. Graver-Browne, Moir, Moncreiff. |
| SUR ET LOYAL | Sure and loyal. Bagnall-Wild. |
| SURE AND STEADFAST | Martin of Anstey Pastures, Martin of Norton, Stewart-Clark, Bts. |
| SURELY AND QUICKLY | 511 Sq., RAF. |
| SURGAM | I shall rise. Hutchision of Rossie, Bts. |
| SURGAMUS ERGO STRENUE | Let us therefore rise strenuously. Baildon (W.R. Yorks.) UDC. |
| SURGE ET FULGE | Rise and shine. Lawson of Weetwood Grange, Bts. |
| SURGET ALAUDA | Let the lark rise. Larken. |
| SURGIMUS | We rise. Saltburn (N.R. Yorks.) UDC. |
| SURGIT POST NUBILA PHOEBUS | The sun rises after clouds. Coachmakers' and Coach Harness Makers' Co., inc. 1677, Constable, Bts. |
| SURGITE LUMEN ADEST | Arise, the day is at hand. Glover, Bt. |
| SURGIT NOX ADEST | Arise, night is at hand. 215 Sq., RAF. |
| SURGUNT COMMERCIA GENTES | Nations rise by commerce. National and Grindlays Bank Ltd. (arms granted 1954 to Nat. Bank of India Ltd.). |
| SURRIGERE COLLIGERE | To arise and to pick up. 194 Sq., RAF. |
| SURSUM | Upwards. Calandrine, Douglas, Hutchinson, Pringle, Scott of Gala, Stephens, Bts., Wills. |
| SURSUM CORDA | Lift up your hearts (exhortation in 1662 Book of Common Prayer, Holy Communion Service). Howison, Langton, McGillycuddy. |

| | |
|---|---|
| SURSUM CORDA HABEMUS AD DOMINUM | Lift up your hearts, we lift them up unto the Lord. St Margaret's Sch., Bushey, Herts., 1957. |
| SURTOUT LOYAL | Loyal above all. HMS *Royalist*. |
| SUSCIPERE ET FINIRE | To undertake and accomplish. Motion. |
| SUSTENTET NOS DEUS | Let God uphold us. Roy. London Mutual Assurance Soc., 1934. |
| SUSTENTO SANGUINE SIGNA | I support the standard with my blood. Seton. |
| SUSTINE ET ABSTINE | Sustain and abstain. Benedetto Arbusani (Podesta (administrative head of a commune) of Padua, sixteenth century), Kearney, co. Limerick. |
| SUSTINE BONA SUSTINEATUR | Uphold good things. Upholders of the City of London, cr. 1963. |
| SUSTINEATUR | Let it be sustained. Cullum of Hasted (or Hawstead), Bt. (crest of Cullum was a lion holding between the paws a column). |
| SUSTINERE | To sustain, support, maintain. No. 5 Maintenance Unit, RAF. |
| SUSTINET NEC FATISCIT | He sustains and does not grow weary. Andrea Gutti, Doge of Venice, d. 1539; ref. to his device of Atlas, mythical upholder of the world. |
| SUUM CUIQUE | To every man his own Lord Bayford (Sanders) *(NEP)*, Don of Spittal, Every, Bts., Grant of Monymusk and Cullen, Bts., Grant of Holborn House, Barbados, Milne, Order of Black Eagle of Prussia, Thomson of Banchory. |
| SUUM CUIQUE TRIBUERE | Render to each his due. Wrexham (Denbighs.) RDC, 1948. |
| SWIFT | 72 Sq., RAF (badge a swift volant). |
| SWIFT AND SECURE | No. 12 Signals Unit, RAF. |
| SWIFT AND SUDDEN | (cuneiform). No. 1 Armoured Car. Co., RAF (formed 1922 at Heliopolis, Egypt). |
| SWIFT AND SURE | 51 Sq., RAF. |
| SWIFT AND TRUE | Fust, Readett-Bayley (formerly of Lenton Abbey co. Notts.). |
| SWIFT IN DESTRUCTION | 112 Sq., RAF (badge a black cat; unit was stationed at Helwan, nr. Memphis, the cat being worshipped in ancient Egypt). |
| SWIFT IN PURSUIT | 243 Sq., RAF. |
| SWIFT TO ATTACK | No. 1 Group HQ, RAF. |
| SWIFT TO DEFEND | RAF station, Amman. |
| SWIFT TO MOVE | UK Mobile Air Movements Sq., RAF. |
| SWIFT TO REPLY | RAF station, North Luffenham. |
| SWIFT TO RESPOND | No. 1 Co. of Hertford Maritime Headquarters Unit, RAAF. |
| SWIFT TO SERVE | Suffolk and Ipswich Fire Authority, 1950. |
| SWIFT TO STRIKE | 123 Sq., RAF (East Indian). |
| SWIFT YET SURE | Lords Swaythling (Montagu). |

# T

| | |
|---|---|
| TACE AUT FAC(E) | Say naught or do. Scott of Ancrum, Scott of Dunninald, Bts., Burges. |
| TACENT SATIS LAUDANT | Their silence is praise enough. No. 72 Maintenance Unit, RAF. |
| TÂCHE SANS TACHE | Strive without reproach. Carnegy of Lour, co. Angus, Earls of Northesk (Carnegie). |
| TACITURNUS TURDUS | A silent thrush ('turdus' thus used by Horace, but in Pliny the Elder meant a kind of fish). Italian Literary Academy of the Occulti. |
| TAK THOCHT | Fairlie. |
| TAKE THE BULL BY THE HORNS | RAF station, Hereford. |
| TAKE UP THE CHALLENGE | Evans of Rottingdean, Bt. |
| TALLY HO! | 609 Sq., AAF (hunting horns part of badge; words frequently used when RAF was hot on enemy's trail). |
| TAM ARIS QUAM ARATRIS | As well by altars as by ploughs. Oxley. |
| TAM ARTE QUAM MARTE | As much by art as strength. MacQuaker, Wright. |
| TAM CRAS QUAM HODIE | As much tomorrow as today. Wellingborough (Northants.) RDC. |
| TAM INTERNA QUAM EXTERNA | As well internal as external. Arbuthnot, co. Kincardineshire. |
| TAM LABORE QUAM ARTE | As much by labour as by art. Lords Brock. |
| TAM MARTE QUAM ARTE | As much by Mars as by art. Milne of Inveresk, Bts. |
| TAM NOCTE QUAM DIE SAPERE | To be wise as well by night as by day. Ludlow-Hewitt. |
| TANDEM FIT SURCULUS ARBOR | The twig will yet grow into a tree. Bush, Burnet, Douglas, Maurice of Nassau, Prince of Orange. |
| TANGNEFEDD Y'R-TY | Peace be to the house. Guest-Williams. |
| TANNAN ARIAN GEIRIAN ARIAN | Silver chords, silver words. Caerwyn Parish Council, Flints. |
| TANT QUE JE PUIS | As much as I can. De Cardonnell, Hilton, Lords Hylton (Jolliffe), Jolliffe, Lawson of Cramlington, Williams of Woolland House. |
| TANTO MONTA | Virtually untranslateable, since second word is not Latin; has been rendered 'tantamount', as it was used by Ferdinand II the Catholic King of Aragon, 1479–1516, who by marriage with Isabella of Castile and conquest of Granada and Navarre became King of all Spain; word 'tantamount' referred to Ferdinand's desire to be equal to his Queen. Used also by Ferdinand's dau., Queen Catherine of Aragon, wife of Henry VIII. |

| | |
|---|---|
| TANTUM IN SUPERBOS | Only against the proud. Jacob. |
| TANTUM VOLITUR UMBRA | Only the shadow revolves. |
| TE DIGNA SEQUERE | Follow thou worthy things. Borlase, Lords Congleton (Parnell). |
| TE FAVENTE VIREBO | Under Thy favour I shall flourish. Grant of Dalvey, Bts. |
| TE GUBERNATORE | Thou the pilot. Ferdinand III the Saint, King of Castile and Leon, 1217–50. |
| TE IPSUM NOSCE | Know thyself (famous motto of Delphic Oracle). Shaw of Cobbe Place. |
| TE SPLENDENTE | Whilst Thou art shining. Lawson, co. Fife. |
| TE STANTE VIREBO | With you standing I shall flourish. Charles de Guise, Cardinal de Lorraine, d. 1574 (used device of a pyramid, probably in ref. to King Henry II, whose favour he sought), Temple. |
| TEACH WELL | No. 241 Operational Conversion Unit, RAF. |
| TEAGAISG SEALGAIR NA FAIRGE | Teach the hunter of the sea (Gaelic). Maritime Operational Training Unit, RAF. |
| TEG YW HEDDWCH | Peace is beautiful. Davies-Gilbert. |
| TEMPER THE SWORD | No. 230 Operational Conversion Unit, RAF. |
| TEMPERANS ET CONSTANS | Temperate and constant. Verschoyle. |
| TEMPLA QUAM DILECTA | Temples how beloved. Dukes of Buckingham and Chandos (Chandos-Grenville) (NEP), Lords Nugent, Temple. |
| TEMPORE UTIMUR | We use time. Greenwich, London Bor. of. |
| TEMPORI PARENDUM | The time must be served. Stockton (Durham) RDC, 1958. |
| TEMPUS FUIT EST ET ERIT | Time was, is and will be. The Times Publishing Co., 1929. |
| TEMPUS RERUM IMPERATOR | Time the ruler of (all) things. Clockmakers' Co., inc. 1631; a clock in the shield, Old Father Time as one of the supporters. |
| TENACITY | 166 Sq., RAF (badge, a bulldog affrontée). |
| TENATE ET PERFICITE | Attempt and achieve. 102 Sq., RAF. |
| TENAX ET AUDAX | Tenacious and audacious. 25th Co. of London (Cyclist Bn.), the London Regt. |
| TENAX ET FIDE | Persevering and with faith. Lords Carrington, Smith of East Stoke, Bts. |
| TENAX ET FIDELIS | Tenacious and faithful. Abdy, Coombe Tennant, Dartford (Kent), Bor. of, Lane, co. Worcs., Earl Jowitt (NEP). |
| TENAX IN FIDE | Steadfast in faith. Lords Bicester (Smith), Marquesses of Lincolnshire (Wynn-Carrington) (NEP), Smith-Bosanquet. |

| | |
|---|---|
| TENAX PROPOSITI | Firm of purpose. Lords Aldenham and Hunsden (Gibbs), Ballymena Academy, co. Antrim, HMS *Caroline*, Elgood, Gibbes, Gilbert of Cantley Hall, Gilbert of Chedgrave, Lords Hollenden (Hope-Morley), Markham, Morley, Osborne-Gibbs, Bts., Poole, Roundell, Lords Rayleigh (Strutt), Stapleton-Bretherton, Lords Wraxall (Gibbs), 64 Sq., RAF. |
| TEND AND MEND | Inst. of Accident Surgery. |
| TENDIMUS | We advance. British & Commonwealth Shipping Co. Ltd., Craik, Bt. |
| TENDIMUS AD COELUM | We reach to heaven. McCowan, Bts. |
| TENDIT AD ASTRA FIDES | Faith reaches towards heaven. Burns, Burns-Callander, Burns-Murdoch. |
| TENDIT IN ARDUA VIRTUS | Virtue reaches the heights. Lloyd of Loddett. |
| TENEBO | I will hold. Gray of Wheatfield, Lords De Tabley (Leicester, previously Byrne), Warren. |
| TENEBRAS EXPELLIT ET HOSTES | He drives out darkness and the enemy. O'Gowan. |
| TENEBRAS MEAS | (Lighten) my darkness. Lords Donington (Clifton-Hastings-Campbell) *(NEP)*. |
| TENEO | I retain. Staples, Bts. |
| TENEO ET CREDO | I hold and I believe. Carson. |
| TENEO TENEBO | I hold, I will hold. No. 30 Balloon Barrage Group, RAF. |
| TENES LE VRAIE | Keep the truth. Lord Emmott *(NEP)*. |
| TENEZ LE DROIT | Hold the right. Clifton, Wilkinson. |
| TENEZ LE VRAYE | Keep the truth. Green-Emmott, Townley of Townley. |
| TENTANDA VIA EST | The way must be tried. Peckham of Nyton, Stronge, Bts., Wildman of Newstead Abbey. |
| TERAR DUM PROSIM | May I be worn out provided I do good. Merriman, Merrman. |
| TERRA CAELOQUE DOCEMUS | We teach on land and in the air. Training Cmd., RAF. |
| TERRA, MARE, FIDE | With faith by sea and land. Campbell of Islay. |
| TERRA MARIQUE | By land and sea. Newport, (Mon.), co. Bor. of, Sutton, Bt., Thornton Cleveleys (Lancs.) UDC, 1950. |
| TERRA MARIQUE AD CAELUM | By land and sea to the sky. No. 1 Training Sch., RAF. |
| TERRA MARIQUE POTENS | Powerful by land and sea. O'Malley. |
| TERRAM AUTEM FILIIS HOMINEM | But the earth hath He given to the sons of men (from Psalm 115:16: 'The heaven, even the heavens are the Lord's: but the earth . . .'; passage frequently quoted, especially in USA by opponents of space travel). Inst. of Quarrying, 1958. |
| TERRANA PERICULA SPERNO | I despise earthly dangers. Hulton-Harrop, Ogilvy, Bts. |
| TERRENA PER VICES SUNT ALIENA | All earthly things by turns are foreign to us. Fust. |
| TERRERE NOLO, TIMERE NESCIO | I wish not to intimidate, and know not how to fear. Dering, Bt., Dyer. |

| | |
|---|---|
| TERTIUS PRIMUS ERIT | The third will be first. No. 3 Fighter Sq., RAF. |
| TEST AND PROVE | RAF station, Norton. |
| TESTIMONIUM PERHIBERE VERITATI | Bear witness to the truth. All Hallows R.C. Sch., Farnham, Surrey. |
| THA AN LUCHAIR AGAINN NE | We hold the key. 518 Sq., RAF (badge, a hand holding a key; a meteorological sq.). |
| THANKE GOD FOR ALL | Keele University (arms grant 1950 to Univ. Coll. of N. Staffs. has for crest a representation of Rodin's 'The Thinker'). |
| THANKFUL | Stevenson-Hamilton. |
| THAT THE PAST MAY SERVE | Trustees of the Imperial War Museum. |
| THAY MYAY GYEE SHIN SHIVE HTI | Death or glory. 257 Sq., RAF Burma (badge a chinthe or lion, Burma being donor of the sq.). |
| THE AIR IS OUR PATH | 575 Sq., RAF. |
| THE CROSS ME SPEDE | Stamford Sch., Lincs., *ante* 1552. |
| THE FEAR OF GOD AND NO OTHER | Tylee. |
| THE GOOD EARTH PROVIDES | Viscount Lambert. |
| THE HEART OF A TOWN LIES IN ITS PEOPLE | Stevenage (Herts.) UDC, 1958. |
| THE KNOT UNITES | Staffordshire CC (knot is in the arms of De Stafford). |
| THE LORD OF HOSTS | On the first English military medal, showing a charge of the Ironsides at Dunbar, 1650, Cromwell having used this as his watchword at that great victory. |
| THE LORD WILL PROVIDE | Garnett-Botfield. |
| THE LOVE OF LIBERTY BROUGHT US HERE | Order of African Redemption (Liberia). |
| THE NOBLEST MOTIVE IS THE PUBLIC GOOD | Earls of Bantry (White) *(NEP)*, White. |
| THE PAST IS BUT THE PROLOGUE | Electricity Council. |
| THE SAME TO ALL MEN | Castlereagh (co. Down) RDC. |
| THE STRONGEST LINK | RAF station, Biggin Hill, Kent. |
| THE SUN MY COMPASS | Crompton-Inglefield. |
| THE SUN NEVER SETS | Far East Communication Sq., RAF. |
| THE VOICE OF THE STARS – THE VOICE OF GOD | Murray of Dinmore Manor (this is how the motto is given, *as a translation*, in *B.L.G.*, 1952, but on the arms block the words on the scroll appear as 'Jus nan regultan jus aide'. |
| THE WISE ARE AWAKE | 3502 Ulster Fighter Control Unit, RAAF. |
| THERE REMAINETH A REST | (From Hebrews 4:9, the rest of the line being 'to the people of God'). Stewart of Stewartby, Bts. |
| THESAUROS IN AGRO | Treasures in the field. Wisbech (Cambs.) RDC, 1954. |
| THEY RYGHT DEFEND | Southwold (Suffolk), Bor. of. |

| | |
|---|---|
| THEY SAY – QUHAT SAY THAY – THAY HAIF SAYD – LAT THAME SAY | Earls of Kintore (Keith). |
| THEY SEWED FIG LEAVES TOGETHER AND MADE THEMSELVES APRONS | (Genesis 3:7). Needlemakers' Co., charter 1656 from Cromwell; reincorp., 1664. Supporters of the Co.'s arms are Adam and Eve. |
| THEY SHALL NOT PASS UNSEEN | 461 Sq., RAAF. |
| THINK AND ACT | Smith of Keighley, Bts. |
| THINK AND THANK | The Marquesses of Ailesbury (Brudenell-Bruce). Montefiore ext. Bts., ref. Tate of Bruleigh Park, Bts., where it is put in what was thought to be 'ye olde Englishe', *thinke and thanke.* |
| THINK ON | MacClellan, Maxwell of Cardoness, Bts., Ross. |
| THINK RIGHT AND DO RIGHT | Holderness (E.R. Yorks.) RDC. |
| THINK WELL | Erskine of Sheffield, Erskine-Hill, Bts. |
| THINK WELL AND PREVAIL | Erskine-Hill, Bts. |
| THINKE AND THANKE | Tate of Bruleigh Park, Bts. |
| THIS ALSO DEFENDING | Macfarlane of Carlung. |
| THIS ARM SHALL DO IT | 422 Sq., RCAF. |
| THIS I'LL DEFEND | Durand, Macfarlan, McFarland, Bts., Macfarlane, MacPharlin. |
| THIS IS OUR CHARTER | Chartres, Earls of Wemyss and March (Charteris). |
| THOIR AN AIRE | Take care. RAF station, Lossiemouth, Moray. |
| THOROUGH | Fraser of Ledeclune, Bts., Hood, Bts., Earls Kitchener of Khartoum, Lamplugh, Electrical and Wireless Sch., RAF. |
| THOUGHT THE HARDER, HEART THE KEENER | (derived from Old English poem quoted, e.g., in Hope Muntz's novel of the Norman Conquest, *The Golden Warrior*). University of Essex. |
| THOURNIB CREVE'TH | I give you the bush (i.e. laurel). Creagh. |
| THROUGH | Dukes of Hamilton. Hamilton. |
| THROUGH COURAGE | Earls of Orkney (Fitz Maurice). |
| THROUGH DARKNESS TO LIGHT | 205 Group HQ, RAF. |
| THROUGH SCIENCE TO SERVICE | Radio Introduction Unit, RAF. |
| THRUGSCRYSSOUGH NE DEU A NEF | Do not disbelieve the God of Heaven (Cornish). Tremenheere. |
| THRUST ON | Thruston, Thurston. |
| THUS | Jervis. Viscount St Vincent (Jervis). |
| THY CARE I SHARE | Jackson. |
| TI A MI E MI A TI | Thou to me and I to thee. Beatrice d'Este, wife of Ludovico Sforza, 'Il Moro' (the Moor) from his colour. |
| TIBI CREDITUM DEBES | You owe credit to yourself. Mathematical Assn. |
| TIBI SOLI | To thee alone. Kyle. |

| | |
|---|---|
| TICASIMBA NEZANA | Strength will come to us through our fledglings. Rhodesian Air Training Group, RAF. |
| TIDAK AKAN UNDOR | (In Malayan script) Never retreat. RAF Regt., Malaya. |
| TIEN LE DROICT | Hold the right. Soc. of Clerks of the Peace of Counties and of Clerks of County Councils. |
| TIEN TA FOY | Keep thy faith. Earls Bathurst, Viscount Bledisloe (Bathurst), Hervey-Bathurst, Bts., Kemp, Mignon. |
| TIENS A LA VERITÉ | Keep the truth. Lords Blaquiere, Courtauld of Halstead, co. Essex, Courtland, Bt., Lords De Blaquiere (NEP), Hoffman, Lewthwait. |
| TIENS FOI | Keep faith. James of Western Australia. |
| TIENS LA FOI | Keep the faith. Helbert, Wagg & Co. Ltd., 1960. |
| TILL THEN THUS | Longueville, Willding-Jones. |
| TILL TIME CEASES | Richardson of Eccleshall, Bt. |
| TIME TRIES THE TRUTH IN EVERYTHING | Essex Inst. of Agriculture. |
| TIME TRIETH TRUTH | Lords Hungerford (the Hungerford barony was called out of abeyance in 1921 and is now (1983) held by 2nd Viscount St Davids; name is commemorated in Hungerford Bridge in London), Trevelyan, Bts. (with variant 'troth'), Tyrwhitt-Wilson, Bts. Frome (Som.) UDC. |
| TIMEANT DANAEIOS | Let them fear those belonging to Danae. HMS *Danae*, named after Danae, dau. of Acrisius, king of Argos, who imprisoned her in a tower (hence ship's badge of a tower). |
| TIMERE SPERNO | I scorn to fear. Jackson. |
| TIMET PUDOREM | He dreads shame. Viscount Downe (Dawnay). |
| TIMOR DOMINI FONS VITAE | The fear of the Lord is the fountain of life. Arcedeckne-Butler, Butler, Lords Dunboyne (Butler). |
| TIMOR DOMINI INITIUM SAPIENTIAE | The fear of the Lord is the beginning of wisdom (from Proverbs 1:7). Tettenhall Coll., Wolverhampton, 1863. |
| TIMOR OMNIS ABEST | All fear is gone. Craigie of Cairsay. |
| TIMOR OMNIS ABESTO | All fear be absent. Macnab, Bt. |
| TINGIJUB AKKARVINGA | Landing place of the large bird. RAF Unit, Goose Bay, Labrador. |
| TO CONQUER OR DIE | Purcell. |
| TO GOD ONLY BE ALL GLORY | Skinners' Co. (additional to main motto *In Christo fratres*), Goldsmiths' Co. |
| TO HOLD ON HIGH | 407 Sq., RCAF. |
| TO HUNT AND TO KILL | No. 236 Operational Conversion Unit, RAF. |
| TO LEARN, TO DO, TO SERVE | Dunstable Coll., Beds. |
| TO MNIES BOLI | Counts Zamoyski of Poland. |
| TO MY UTMOST | Lords Wrenbury (Buckley). |
| TO SEE AND BE SEEN | 279 Sq., RAF (air/sea rescue, hence motto). |

| | |
|---|---|
| TO SEEK AND STRIKE | RAF station, Bruggen. |
| TO SERVE AND TO HOLD | No. 51 Maintenance Unit, RAF. |
| TO SERVE MANKIND | The City University, London. |
| TO STRIVE AND NOT TO YIELD | 626 Sq., RAF. Motto taken from last line of Lord Tennyson's poem 'Ulysses', badge being an ancient ship, with seven oars representing the number of the crew of Lancaster bomber. |
| TO THE CORE | Howard, Bts. |
| TO THE HILLS | Lord Amulree (Mackenzie). |
| TO THINE OWN SELF BE TRUE | (part of Polonius' advice to Laertes in *Hamlet*). Lord Leatherhead (Life Baron), Wiggin, Bts. |
| TOGAIDH MI MO SHUILEAN CHUM NAM BEANN | Lord Drumalbyn (Macpherson). |
| TOGETHER | Burrows of Long Crendon, co. Bucks. |
| TOGETHER IN ENTERPRISE | Milk Marketing Bd. |
| TOKNYS COLONNEKTER | Emblems of bravery (Cornish). Geach. |
| TOLLE LEGE | Take, read. These words formed part of game played by children in Italy *c*.AD400. St Augustine, in *Confessions*, describes his perplexed state, wondering if he should be converted to Christianity. He tells us that on hearing these words, he took them as a sign from God. He went into his house and took up the first book of the Bible available to him ,which was Epistle to the Romans, and opening it at random he read therein; this led him to his conversion. Legg. |
| TOMORROW'S WEATHER TODAY | 520 Sq., RAF (meteorological reconnaisance). |
| TONNERE | Thunder. Tunnard. |
| TOT PRAEMIA VITAE | So many rewards in life. Sullivan, Bts. |
| TOTI CONTERMINUS ORBI | Coterminous with the whole world. British Internal Combustion Engine Manufacturers' Assn. |
| TOTIS VIRIBUS | With all our powers. Goode, Durrant & Murray (Consolidated) Ltd. |
| TOUCH NOT THE CAT BUT (BOT) A GLOVE | Motto of famous Highland clan of Macphersons, who have the wild cat as their crest. Cheyne-Macpherson, Gillespie, Grant, McBean, McCrombie, McIntosh, Mackintosh of Clan Chattan, Macpherson. |
| TOUCH NOT GLOVELES | Lords Catto. |
| TOUCHE Y SI TU L'OSES | Touch if you dare. Gaston, Comte de Foix, *c*.1391, called 'Phoebus' from his beauty, being like Apollo. Most of his life spent in hunting, on which he wrote illustrated book. Details in L. G. Pine, *History of Hunting*. |
| TOUJOURS À PROPOS | Always at the right moment. 211 Sq., RAF. |
| TOUJOURS DE BONNE HEURE | Always in good time. Lapage. |
| TOUJOURS FIDÈLE | Always faithful. Beauchamp of Grosvenor Place, Bts., Bladen, Fenwick, Hairstanes, Hickman, Holford, Mercier, Mill, Ogilvie, Proctor-Beauchamp, Bts., Wallington, Waters. |

| | |
|---|---|
| TOUJOURS FIRME | Always firm. Cathcart-Walker-Heneage, Lords Heneage. |
| TOUJOURS L'AUDACE | Always audacious. Strachan-Audas. |
| TOUJOURS PRÊT (or PREST) | Always ready. Abbott, Anstruther of Elie, Armstrong-Macdonnell, Lord Brampton (Hawkins), Broadhurst, Bt., Carmichael, Bt., Earls of Clanwilliam (Meade), Crawfurd, Daniel, Dayman, Dease, Donald, Gibon, Hawkins, Knight, Lingard, McConell, MacDonnell, Meade, Ogilvie, Petty, Phelps, Prescott, Prideaux-Brune, Nixon, Bts., Sitwell, Smyth, Bts., Sutton, Bts., Tyssen, 242 Sq., RAF. |
| TOUJOURS PROPICE | Always fortunate. Earls of Dartrey (Dawson) (NEP). |
| TOUJOURS SANS TACHE | Always without stain. Baring-Gould. |
| TOUS JOURS LOYAL | Always loyal. Fenwick, Howards, Earls of Surrey c.1520, Winford. |
| TOUS PREST | All ready. Dukes of Atholl (as Chief of the Name and Arms of Murray). |
| TOUT BIEN OU RIEN | All well or nothing. Barham, Ellison, Earls of Gainsborough (Noel), Hicks, Montgomery of Skelmorlie, Bts., Noel. |
| TOUT COMPRENDRE C'EST TOUT PARDONNER | To know all is to pardon all. Newsum. |
| TOUT D'EN HAUT | All from above. Bellew, Grattan-Bellew. |
| TOUT DROIT | All right. Carling, Carr, Ker, Le Mottée. |
| TOUT EN BON HEURE | All in good time. Beach of Oakley Hall, Hicks, Earls of St Aldwyn (Hicks Beach). |
| TOUT EST DE DIEU | All is from God. Rokewode-Gage, Bts. |
| TOUT EST D'EN HAULT | All is from above. Whitefoord. |
| TOUT(E) FOYS PREST | Always ready. Pigot, Bts., Pigott Brown of Doddershall Park. |
| TOUT JOUR | Always. Browne of Callaly Castle, Ogilvie, Lords Strathspey (Ogilvie Grant). |
| TOUT JOURS PREST (PRET) | Always ready. Earls of Antrim (McDonnell), Carmichael, Lady Macdonald of Earnscliffe (NEP), Mansergh, Sutton, Bts. |
| TOUT OU RIEN CONTENT, MELUN | All or nothing satisfies Melun. Melun. |
| TOUT POUR DIEU ET MA PATRIE | Wholly for God and my country. Lords St Oswald (Winn), Winn. |
| TOUT POUR L'ÉGLISE | All for the Church. Marris, Wandesford, Winston-Davis-De-Marris. |
| TOUT PREST | Quite ready. Murray, Younger of Auchen Castle, Bts. |
| TOUT SANS FAILLIR ET SANS LUCRE | All without failing and without greed. Wakeman, Bts. |
| TOUT VIEN(T) DE DIEU | All comes from God. Lords Clinton, Collinson-Cooper, Leahy, co. Cork, Lords Leigh, Leigh of Bro Castle, co. Glam., Pinchard, Trefusis. |

| | |
|---|---|
| TOUT VIENT D'EN HAUT | All comes from on high. Trollope-Bellew. |
| TOUTES POUR UNE, LÀ ET NON PLUS | All for one, there and no more. Claude de Lorraine, Duc de Guise, 1496–1550. |
| TOWARDS UNDERSTANDING | Lord Jackson of Burnley *(NEP)*. |
| TRA(E) ANADL GOBAITH | While there is breath there is hope. Lords Clwyd (Roberts). |
| TRA MOR TRA MEIRION | While the sea lasts, so shall Merioneth. Merionethshire CC. Trans. is paraphrase, as local authority stated that motto would not stand translation (Scott-Giles, *Civic Heraldry*, p. 85). |
| TRADE AND NAVIGATION | Royal Exchange Assurance Co. |
| TRADITUM AB ANTIQUIS | Handed down from the ancients. Frere of Wimbledon, Bts. |
| TRAIN FOR BATTLE | No. 240 Operations Conversion Unit, RAF. |
| TRAIN TO TRIUMPH | No. 20 Operational Training Unit, RAF. |
| TRAMITE RECTA | By a direct path. Roe, Bts. |
| TRANQUILLUS ET CONSTANS | Tranquil and constant. Pacific Steam Navigation Co., 1957. |
| TRANS MARE EXIVI | I went out across the sea. 95 Sq., RAF. |
| TRANSFIGAM | I will transfix. Colt, Coult, Coutts-Duffus. |
| TRANSIBUNT MULTI | Many shall pass through. No. 41 Movements Unit, RAF. |
| TRANSIRE CONFIDENTER | Pass through confidently. RAF station, Brize Norton, Oxon. |
| TRANSPORTATIO CULTUM SIGNIFICAT | Transport signifies culture. Ulster Transport Authority, 1959. |
| TRE GHRASTA DE GACH AON RUD | Everything through the grace of God. McLoughlin (Maelseachlainn). |
| TRE NAW MEN | The homestead of the nine stones (Cornish). Triniman. |
| TRE RES | The homestead of the ford (Cornish). Treace. |
| TRECHYN CED NAC ARFAETH | Ellis Griffith, Bts. |
| TREGORYON AN ENYS | Dwellers of the island (Cornish). Inch. |
| TREMERE NESCIT VIRTUS | Virtue knows not how to fear. Tremlett. |
| TREU UND FEST | True and faithful. The Prince Consort, Tylden-Wright, 11th (Prince Albert's Own) Hussars. |
| TRIA JUNCTA IN UNO | Three joined in one (i.e. Faith, Hope and Charity; 1 Corinthians 13:13). Order of the Bath. |
| TRIAL BY AIR AND SEA | Marine Aircraft Experimental Establishment, RAF. |
| TRIES-A-WELL | Treasawell. |
| TRINIS CATENIS VINCTUS | Bound by threefold chains. Dawley (Salop) UDC. |
| TRINITAS IN UNITATE | Trinity in unity. Trinity House Guild of Fraternity. |
| TRIUMPHO MORTE TAM VITA | I triumph in death as in life. Allen. |
| TROFAST | True fast. Hall, co. Antrim. |
| TRUE | Bruce of Pittarthie. Home, Bts. |

| | |
|---|---|
| TRUE AND SURE | Fletchers' Co. – in 1371 separated by agreement with City from Bowyers, but no charter of corp. Needless to record, arrows occur in both shield and crest; Co.'s function being to make arrows (fletcher = arrow-maker). |
| TRUE FAITH, TRUE POLICY | Metropolitan Life Assurance Soc. |
| TRUE HEARTS AND WARM HANDS | Glovers' Co., inc. 1639. |
| TRUE TO THE END | Atkinson (formerly of Morland, Westmorland), Binning, Campbell of Powis, Bts., Ferguson, Foreman, Earls of Home. Hume, Logan-Home, Orr, Lords Polwarth (Hepburne-Scott), Powell, co. Hereford. |
| TRUE TO YOU | Darell. |
| TRUE WORTH NEVER FAILS | Failsworth UDC. |
| TRUST AND FEAR NOT | Hertfordshire CC, RAF station, Bovingdon, Herts. |
| TRUST AND TRIUMPH | Gainsborough (Lincs.) RDC. |
| TRUST IN GOD AND HE WILL GIVE STRENGTH | Austin, Bts., Davis, Hardness, Hasdell. |
| TRUSTIE TO THE END | Forbes-Leith, Bts. |
| TRUSTY | 148 Sq., RAF. |
| TRUSTY TO THE END | Lords Burgh (Willoughby Leith), Leith Buchanan, Bts., Lumsden. |
| TRUTH | RAF Chaplains' Sch. |
| TRUTH AND BEAUTY | Viscount Eccles. |
| TRUTH AND JUSTICE | Hills of Hills court, Bt. |
| TRUTH IS THE LIGHT | Wax Chandlers' Co., charter 1483. |
| TRUTH IS LIGHT | Joseph of Stoke-on-Trent, Bts. |
| TRUTH WILL TRIUMPH | British Council. |
| TRWYR ARWYDD HWN UNOLYDYM | By this sign we are united. No. 31 Maintenance Unit, RAF. |
| TRY | Gethin, Bts., O'Hara, Parker, Bts. |
| TRY AGAIN | Lord Craigton (Browne) (Life Baron). |
| TRYGG HAVET | Guarding the seas. 330 Sq., RAF (Norwegian), formed 1941 in Iceland. |
| TU NE CEDE MALIS | Do not yield to misfortunes (Virgil, *Aeneid* ix. 95). Amery, Bradshaw of Lifton Park, Devon, Damer, De Neuron, Pietro Gonzago, Cardinal, of Mantua (helped to secure release of Pope Clement VII after sack of Rome 1527), Lindsay-Smith, Parry, Bt., Riddock, Steere, Turner. |
| TU NIDUM SERVAS | You keep the nest. Neath (Glam.), Bor. of. |
| TU VINCULA FRANGE | Do Thou break the chains. Lords Napier of Magdala (possibly all. to 1st Lord Napier's expedition to Ethiopia in 1867 when he stormed Magdala and set free mad King Theodore's captives). |

| | |
|---|---|
| TUEOR | I will defend. Viscount Byng *(NEP)*, Cranmer-Byng, Earls of Strafford (Byng). Viscount Torrington (Byng). |
| TURN NOT ASIDE | Viscount Samuel. |
| TURN NOT SWERVE | Turnor. |
| TURPE NESCIRE | Disgraceful to be ignorant. Queen Elizabeth Gram. Sch., Wakefield, 1591, Wolsey Hall, Oxford, correspondence coll., 1894. |
| TURRIS FORTIS MIHI DEUS | God is a strong tower to me. Clugstone, Kelly, Macquarie, O'Kelly, Peter. |
| TURRIS FORTISSIMA DEUS | God is the strongest tower. Torr. |
| TURRIS FORTISSIMA EST NOMEN JEHOVAH | The name of Jehovah is the strongest tower. Plymouth City and Co. Bor. of, 1931. |
| TURRIS FORTITUDINIS | A tower of strength. Mansfield. |
| TURRIS FORTITUDINIS TU, DOMINE | Thou O Lord art a tower of strength. De Sausmarez, Bt. |
| TURRIS MEA DEUS | My tower is God. Towers-Clark of Western Moffat, co. Lanark. |
| TURRIS PRUDENTIA CUSTOS | Prudence is the safeguard of the tower Dick-Lauder, Bts. This family is thought *(see B.P.)* to be descended from Lauder of that Ilk; crest is a tower, portcullis down, and a sentinel head and shoulders above the battlement. Reason assigned for this crest is that when in 1333, at Halidon Hill, Edward III crushed the Scots and avenged Bannockburn, Sir Robert Lauder held one of the few places (Castle Urquhart, Loch Ness) that Edward III could not capture. |
| TURRIS TUTISSIMA VIRTUS | Virtue is the safest fortress. Carlyon of Tregrehan, Cornwall. |
| TUTA SILENTIO MERCES | From silence is a sure wage. Lord Normanbrook (Brook) *(NEP)*. |
| TUTA TIMENS | Fearing safe things. Leadbetter. |
| TUTA VELUT COR ANGLIAE | Safe as the heart of England. Hinckley & Country Bldg. Soc. |
| TUTAMEN | A defence. Skrine. |
| TUTAMEN PULCHRIS | A defence for the fair. Chambre. |
| TUTANTUR TELA CORONAM | Weapons guard the crown. Tisdall. |
| TUTELA | A defence. Lyell. |
| TUTELA CORDIS | Guardian of the heart. No. 11 Group HQ, RAF. |
| TUTI VOLENT | Let them fly in safety. No. 24 Group HQ, RAF. |
| TUTIOR QUO PARATIOR | The safer by how much more prepared. Cheshire Police Authority, 1965. |
| TUTOR ET ULTOR | Teacher and avenger. 73 Sq., RAF (badge a demi-talbot with maple leaf on shoulder to commemorate Canadian personnel). |
| TUTUM REFUGIUM | A safe refuge. Gillon. |

| | |
|---|---|
| TUTUS IN UNDIS | Safe on the waves. Lord Lambourne (Lockwood) *(NEP)*. |
| TUTUS PER SUPREMA PER IMA | Safe above and below. (Italian) Affidati Academy, ref. to the nautilus, creature credited by fabulous ancient natural history with swimming on its back. |
| TUTUS PER UNDAS | Safe through the waters. Marescaux. |
| TUTUS SI FORTIS | Safe if strong. Raeburn, Bts. |
| TUUM EST | It is thine. Cooper of Toddington, Earls Cowper *(NEP)*. |
| TWENTY FINISHED | Twentyman. |
| 'TWIXT SEVERN AND WYE | Lydney (Glos.) RDC. |
| TYDE WHAT MAY | Haig. Part of Thomas Rhymer's ancient saying: 'Tyde what may, Haig shall have Bemersyde.' |
| TYME TRYETH TROTH (TRUTH) | Trevelelyan, Tyrwhitt. |
| TYNCTUS CRUORE SARACENO | Tinged with Saracen's blood. Tynte. Motto has a most interesting sociological quality. The following explanation is given in *B.L.G.*, 1846, p. 1449, *sub* Kemeys-Tynte. 'The family of Tynte has maintained for centuries a leading position in the west of England; of its surname tradition handed down the following derivation. In the year 1192, at the celebrated battle of Ascalon, a young knight of the noble house of Arundel, clad all in white, with his horse's housings of the same colour, so gallantly distinguished himself on that memorable field that Richard Coeur de Lion remarked publicly after the victory "that the maiden knight hath borne himself as a lion and done deeds equal to those of 6 Croises of Crusaders", whereupon he conferred on him for arms a lion argent on a field gules between six crosslets of the first and for motto as above. His descendants thence assumed the surname of Tynte.' Richard I (1189–99) was first English sovereign to assume a coat of arms – heraldry had become widespread from *c.*1150. Some families like the above ascribe their arms to this king. The Mountains who bear 3 cross crosslets in their arms have tradition that Sir John Mountain received these arms from Coeur de Lion for his valour against the Saracens. These traditions may be true but, as Charles Kingsley remarked in another context, 'let every man believe what he will.' |

# U

**UBERIMMA FIDES**

The most perfect faith. Victory Insurance Co. Ltd., 1944. (This is a legal expression denoting the most perfect frankness. 'This is essential to the validity of certain contracts between persons bearing a particular relationship to one another, e.g. guardian and ward, solicitor and client, insurer and insured', *Mozley & Whiteley's Law Dictionary*).

**UBI AMOR IBI FIDES**

Where there is love there is faith. Aubrey, co. Hereford, Duckinfield, Bt., Garratt, Inge, Lord Mamhead (Newman) *(NEP)*, Newman, co. Devon.

**UBI FIDES IBI LUX ET ROBOR**

Where there is faith there is light and strength. Birkenhead (Ches.), Co. Bor. of.

**UBI LAPSUS QUID FECI?**

Whither fallen, what have I done? Courtenay, Earls of Devon. This great family had added distinction of having Edward Gibbon as their historian. In note at end of chapter LXI of *The Decline and Fall*, he states of above motto that it was probably adopted by the Powderham branch after loss of earldom of Devonshire. (This really refers to the earldom of Devon, which was supposed to have become ext. in 1556. It was not until 1831 that the head of the Courtenays established his right to the earldom of Devon, cr. 1553. For full story, *see B.P.*, 1970.)

**UBI NUNC SAPIENTIS ODDA MERLINI?**

Where now are the bones of the wise Merlin? Marlborough (Wilts.), Bor. of. (Merlin is the wizard in the Arthurian romances, the adviser of King Arthur, but eventually becoming enamoured of a young woman, Vivian, he lets her know how he can be put to sleep by a spell. It is said that he sleeps in the forest of Brocéliande in Brittany.)

**UBI SPIRITUS IBI LIBERTAS**

Where the Spirit is, there is liberty (from 2 Corinthians 3:17). Hartley Victoria Methodist Coll., Manchester.

**UBI VOLUNTAS IBI PISCAMUR**

Where there is the will, there we fish. Williams-Fisher.

**UBICUMQUE SUMUS DOMI SUMUS**

Wherever we are, we are at home. HMAFV *Adastral* (RAF depot ship for flying boats).

**UBIQUE**

Everywhere. O'Brien-Twohig, Corps of Royal Engineers, 1832, Royal Regt. of Artillery, 1832.

**UBIQUE FECUNDAT IMBER**

Everywhere the rain fertilises. Higgingbottom, Imbert-Terry.

**UBIQUE LOQUIMUR**

Everywhere we speak. No. 38 Group Tactical Communications Wing, RAF.

**UBIQUE NAVIGAMUS**

We sail everywhere. Royal Overseas League.

**UBIQUE PATRIAM REMINISCI**

Everywhere to remember one's country. Cass, Harris, Earls of Malmesbury (Harris).

| | |
|---|---|
| UBIQUE SINE MORA | Everywhere without delay. 167 Sq., RAF (ferrying aircraft). |
| UBIQUE SPECULABUNDUS | Watching everywhere. 653 Sq., RAF. |
| UBIQUE VIDEO | I see everywhere. Royal Radar Establishment. |
| UCHIEL Y GORING | Whyte. |
| ULTOR IN UMBRIS | Avenging (avenger) in the shadows. 214 Sq., RAF. |
| ULTRA FERT ANIMUS | The mind bears onwards. Durham. |
| ULTRA TELLUREM DICO | I speak above the earth. RAF station, Oakhanger, Glos. |
| UN DIEU UN ROI | One God, one king. D'Arcy, Lyttleton. |
| UN DIEU, UN ROI, UN COEUR | One God, one king, one heart. Lake, Bts., Lakin. |
| UN DURANT MA VIE | The same while I live. Barrington, Johnston-Gerrard. |
| UN TOUT SEUL | Only one. Verney. |
| UNA SALUS | The only salvation. St Charles Borromeo, Cardinal and Archbishop of Milan, 1538–84, nephew of Pope Pius IV. |
| UNAM ASPICIT | It beholds one only. Bernardo Accolti of Arezzo, poet of the time of Pope Leo X. Motto all. to Accolti's device of an eagle, and the superstition that the eagle gazed directly at the sun. Another motto of Accolti was *Sic crede* (Thus believe). |
| UNDAS DOMARE CONAMUR | We strive to master the waves. No. 10 Radio Sch., RAF. |
| UNDAUNTED | Alexander of Inverness. Ball (formerly of Veryan, Cornwall), No. 5 Group HQ, RAF. |
| UNDAUNTED BY WEATHER | 510 Sq., RAF (meteorological sq.). |
| UNDEB | Union. Morgan of Whitehall Court, Bt., Vaughan-Morgan, Bts. |
| UNDEB, HEDD, LLWYDDIANT | Unity, peace, prosperity. Breckonshire CC. |
| UNDEBB SYDD NERTH | Union is strength. Pembrokeshire CC. |
| UNG DIEU ET UNG ROY | One God and one king. Daray, Lords Hatherton (Littleton). |
| UNG DIEU UNG ROY | One God, one king. Bingham of Melcome Bingham, Dorset, Bradford of Mawddwy, Bt., Viscount Cobham (Lyttelton), Sir William Conyers, 1st Baron Conyers (barony in abeyance) *(NEP)*, D'Arcy, Gell, Lyttleton. |
| UNG DURANT MA VIE | One during my life. Barrington, Bts., Gerrard, Poe-Domvile, Bts. |
| UNG JE SERVIRAI (*or* SERVIRAY) | One will I serve. Earls of Carnarvon (Herbert), Lords Darcy De Knayth, Fitzherbert, Herbert, The Baroness Lucas (Palmer), Earls of Pembroke & Montgomery (Herbert), Earls of Powis (Herbert), Lords Stafford (Fitzherbert). |
| UNG NOUS SERVONS | One we serve. Pembroke, Bor. of, 1950. |
| UNG ROY, UNG FOY, UNG LOY | One king, one faith, one law. Burke, Marquesses of Clanricard (DeBurgh-Canning) *(NEP)*, DeBurgo, Bts., Jenings, Owen of Clongowna, Rush. |
| UNG SENT UNG SOL | One sense one ground. Verney of Claydon House, Bts. |

| | |
|---|---|
| UNG SENT UNG SOLEIL | One sense one sun. Verney of Eaton Square, Bts. |
| UNGUIBUS ET ROSTRO ATQUE ALIS ARMATUS IN HOSTEM | Armed against the enemy with talons, beak and wings. Gian Paolo Baglione, tyrant of Perugia, beheaded 1520. Pope Leo X tricked him with a safe conduct, then when he came to Rome, had him tortured and killed. |
| UNI AEQUUS VIRTUTI | Friendly to virtue alone. Earls of Mansfield (Murray). |
| UNICUS | Unparalleled. 48 Sq., RAF Regt. |
| UNICUS EST | He is the only one. Uniacke. |
| UNIONE FORTITER | Stronger by union. Earls of Mar and Kellie (Erskine). |
| UNITAS ET QUIES | Unity and quiet. Atkinson of Wellington, NZ. |
| UNITAS EFFICIT MINISTERIUM | Unity brings service. Barnet, London Bor. of. |
| UNITAS SOCIETATIS STABILITAS | Unity is the stability of society. Parish Clerks' Co., inc. 1441. |
| UNITATE FORTIOR | Stronger by union. Army and Navy Club, Building Societies' Assn., Heston and Isleworth (Middx.), Bor of. |
| UNITATE PRAESTANS | Standing forth in unity. Preston (Lancs.) RDC, 1948. |
| UNITE | Brodie. |
| UNITE TO FLOURISH | Aldridge and Brownhills (Staffs.) UDC. |
| UNITED IN EFFORT | 53 Sq., RAF (part of badge a thistle as officer from Cameron Highlanders had once commanded sq.). |
| UNITED TO SERVE | Southwark, London Bor. of. |
| UNITED WE ADVANCE | Huntingdon and Godmanchester, Bor. of. |
| UNITED WE ENDEAVOUR | RAF station, Episkopi, Cyprus. |
| UNITED WE LEARN | Empire Radio Sch., RAF. |
| UNITED WE PREPARE | Sch. of Air Support, RAF. |
| UNITED WE SERVE | Southwark Volunteer Bn. (later 1/11th Bn.), 1914. |
| UNITED WE STRIKE | RAF station, Binbrook, Lincs. |
| UNITER | Central Signals Area, RAF. |
| UNITY | No. 281 Maintenance Unit, RAF. |
| UNITY AND PROGRESS | Melksham (Wilts.) UDC, Warley (Worcs.), Co. Bor. of, 1966. |
| UNITY AND SERVICE | Silsden (W.R. Yorks.) UDC, 1954. |
| UNITY IS STRENGTH | Nat. Fed. of Fruit and Potato Trades, Salisbury and Wilton (Wilts.) RDC, 1959, No. 33 Service Flying Training Sch., RAF. |
| UNIUS COLORIS | Of one colour. Luigi d'Aquino, Lord of Castiglione in Naples. |
| UNIVERSAL UNDERSTANDING | Inst. of Linguists. |
| UNIVERSITATE SUBLIMIS | Sublime in university. York Univ. Air Sq. |
| UNLEASH FOR COMBAT | 3619 Co. of Suffolk Fighter Control Unit, RAAF. |
| UNO ANIMO AGIMUS | We act with one mind. 35 (bomber) Sq., RAF. |

| | |
|---|---|
| UNSWERVING | RAF station, Sylt, Germany (formed July 1945). |
| UNTO GOD ONLY BE HONOUR AND GLORY | Bancroft Sch., Woodford Green, Essex, founded 1727 by Francis Bancroft of Drapers' Co., Drapers' Co., inc. 1438, but with charter of monopoly, 1364. |
| UNUM E PLURIBUS | One from many. Wokingham (Berks.) RDC, 1962. |
| UNUS ET IDEM | One and the same. Liddell. Lords Ravensworth (Liddell). |
| UNUS NON SUFFICIT ORBIS | One world is not enough (from Juvenal). Philip II of Spain, sentence exemplifies the king's hope of universal empire. |
| UP KILLIK | Killik. |
| UPRIGHT AND STRONG | No. 11 Sch. of Recruit Training, RAF. |
| UPTON SUPER SABRINAM | Upton upon Severn. (Worcs.) RDC, 1948. |
| UPWARD | Lorimer. |
| UPWARD AND ONWARD | HMS *Rocket* (ship's badge was Stevenson's famous steam engine). |
| UPWARDS AND ONWARDS | Davies-Colley of Newfold, Chester. |
| URBS IN RURE | City in country. Solihull (Warwicks.), Co. Bor. of, 1948. |
| URGET MAJORA | He urges the greater. James V, King of Scotland, d. 1542, after defeat at Solway Moss (ref. to his device of whale led by little fish). |
| USE WELL YOUR TALENT | Barker of Clare Priory. |
| USPIAM ET PASSIM | Everywhere unbounded. 8 Sq., RAF. |
| USQUAM | Anywhere. 70 Sq., RAF (bomber transport). |
| USQUE AD COELUM FINES | Extending as far as the sky. RAF station, Finningley, Notts. |
| USQUE AD FINEM | As far as the end. Kilburn, 428 Sq., RCAF (Right to the end). |
| USQUE AD MORTEM FIDUS | Faithful even to death. Ward of Salhouse. |
| USQUE ADARAS AMICUS | A friend as far as the altars. Copland-Griffiths. |
| USQUE CONABOR | Thus far I will try. Nairn, Bts., Spencer-Nairn, Bts. |
| USQUE FIDELIS | Always faithful. Melles, Napier of Balwhaple. |
| UT AQUILAE VOLENT | That eagles may fly. Support Cmd., RAF. |
| UT ET ALIOS INSTRUAM | That I may instruct others. Coll. of the Ven. Bede, Durham. |
| UT HOMINES LIBERI SINT | That men may be free. Egham (Surrey) UDC (Runnymede is near Egham). |
| UT IPSE FINIAM | That I myself may complete (it). Pope Adrian VI, 1522–3, Cardinal Adrian Dedel of Utrecht, last non-Italian Pope before election of Pope John Paul II in 1978. All. is to Adrian's device of pyramid in course of erection, i.e. that he might raise the Church to a high point. |
| UT LIBERATI SERVIAMUS | Let us serve as having been freed. Lord Courtney of Penwith *(NEP)*. |

| | |
|---|---|
| UT MIGRATURUS HABITA | Dwell here as one about to depart. Dick-Lauder, Bts., Lauder. |
| UT NIHIL DESIT | That nothing may be wanting. Donna Geronima Colonna (ancient Roman family). |
| UT OLIM INGENII NECNON VIRTUTIS CULTORES | As formerly cultivators of intellect but also virtue. Liverpool Collegiate Sch. |
| UT PALMA JUSTUS | The righteous is like the palm. Palmes. |
| UT POSSIM | As I can. Lords Foley, Livingston of Glentarran. |
| UT PROAVI IN DEO CONFIDEMUS | As our ancestors (did) we confide in God. Enniskillen (co. Fermanagh), Bor. of. |
| UT PROSIM | That I may be of use. Ryde Sch., I. of W., 1921. |
| UT PROSIM ALIIS | That I may be of use to others. Fergusson of Kilkerran, Bts., Greenwood, Jennings. |
| UT PRUDENTIA VIVAM | That I may live with prudence. Alessandro d'Alessandri, Italian lawyer, d. 1523. |
| UT QUIESCAT ATLAS | That Atlas may repose. Philip II of Spain, when his father Charles V, 'the weary Titan', had abdicated and retired into a monastery, where he supervised the rehearsal of his own funeral. |
| UT QUOCUMQUE PARATUS | That I may be prepared on every side. Campbell-Lambert, Earls of Cavan (Lambart), Lambart, Lambert. |
| UT SECURE VOLENT | That they may fly free from care. Inst. of Aviation Medicine, RAF. |
| UT SIBI SIC ALTERI | As to thyself, so to another. Letchworth. |
| UT SURSUM DESUPER | I swoop down to rise again. Rumbold, Trevor-Cox, Worseley, Worsley. |
| UT TIBI SIC ALIIS | To thyself as to others. Bicester (Oxon.) UDC. |
| UT TIBI SIC ALTERI | As to thyself so to another. Boles, Bts., Lords Kingsdon, Leith Pemberton. |
| UT VITAM HABEANT | That they may have life (quotation from Christ, St John's Gospel 10:10). University of Leicester. |
| UT VIVAS VIGILA | Watch that you may live. Coape-Arnold. |
| UT VIVAT | That it may live. Cristoforo Mandruccio, Cardinal Trent, d. 1578. Emblem was a phoenix on the funeral pyre, ref. to ancient belief that the phoenix incinerated itself previous to its resurrection. Taken as a type of Christ (St Clement, 4th Bishop of Rome, *c.* AD 95, *First Epistle to the Corinthians*). |
| UTERE DUM POTES | Use while you can. Benson, co. Westmorland. |
| UTILE ET DULCE | Useful and pleasant. Riddell, Bts. |
| UTILE SECERNERE HONESTUM | To sever the honourable from the useful. Davis of Hollywood, Bts. |
| UTITUR ANTE QUAESITIS | It is used before you seek. Drughorn, Bt. |
| UTQUE SOLES CUSTOS ADSIS | That you may be present as guardian as you are wont. Barcroft. |

| | |
|---|---|
| UTRAQUE FORTUNA CONTENTUS | Content with either fortune. Vosper. |
| UTRAQUE PALLADE | With both Pallas. Bendyshe (formerly of Barrington Hall). Ref. to Pallas as goddess of wisdom and of war; i.e. with skill in war. |
| UTRIQUE FIDELIS | Faithful to both. Monmouthshire CC. |
| UTRUMQUE | (literally) And whether? Henry II of England, 1154–89, allegedly ref. to badge of sword and olive branch in saltire, meaning that either war or diplomacy would be used. |
| UTRUMQUE | On both sides. James IV, King of Scotland, killed at Flodden 9 September 1513; m. Margaret, dau. of Henry VII of England. |
| UYANIK | Watchful (Turkish). 264 Signals Unit, RAF (Cyprus). |

| | |
|---|---|
| VADE ET TU FAC SIMILITER | Go thou and do likewise (from parable of Good Samaritan, St Luke 10:37). No. 2 Flying Instructors' Sch., RAF. |
| VAE TIMIDO | Woe to the timid. Maddison. |
| VAE VICTIS | Woe to the conquered (famous saying attributed by Livy (*History* V.xiviii. 9) to the Gallic conqueror, Brennus, when he cast his sword into the scale against the ransom money paid by the besieged Romans). Senhouse. |
| VAE VISO | I've espied it, woe betide it. 664 Sq., RAAF. |
| VAILLANCE AVANSE L'HOMME | Valour advances the man. Acton of Wolverton, co. Worcs. |
| VAILLANT ET VEILLANT | Valiant and watching. Viscount Cardwell *(NEP)*. |
| VALDE ET SAPIENTER | Strongly and wisely. Sagar-Musgrave. |
| VALE SAPE | Farewell, be wise. Northwick (Ches.) UDC. |
| VALENS ET VOLENS | Able and willing. Fetherstonhaugh of Kirkoswald. |
| VALET ANCHORA VIRTUS | Virtue our anchor is strong. Lord Burghclere (Gardner), Lords Gardner *(NEP)*. |
| VALIANT AND VIGILANT | 543 Sq., RAF. |
| VALLIS VESPERIS | The western ramparts. RAF station, Gütersloh. |
| VALOR LEALDADE E MERITO | Valour, loyalty and merit. 247 Group HQ, RAF. |
| VALORE ET VIRTUTE | By valour and virtue. Huggins. |
| VALOUR, LEALDADE E MERITO | Valour, loyalty and merit. Order of the Tower and Sword (Portugal). |
| VALUE WITH INTEGRITY | Incorp. Soc. of Valuers and Auctioneers, Ltd., 1968. |
| VANA SPES VITAE | Vain is the confidence of life. Paul of Paulville, Bts. |
| VANITAS VANITATUM ET OMNIA VANITAS | Vanity of vanities and all things are vanity (from Ecclesiastes 1:2). Robert II of Scotland, d. 1390. |
| VANUS EST HONOR | Honour is vain. Butler-Bowden of Pleasington. |
| VECTORAS MINISTRO | Service by transport. No. 236 Maintenance Unit, RAF. |
| VEILLANT ET VAILLANT | Watchful and valiant. Erskine of Cambo, Bts. |
| VEL CUM PONDERE | Even with weight. Italian Academy of Insensati of Perugia. |
| VELIS PLENIS | With full sails. Elliot of Harwood. |
| VELLE QUOD DEUS VULT | To wish what God wills. Bankes, Banks. |
| VELLERA FIANT AUREA | May the fleece be golden. Nat. Wool Textile Export Corp., Bradford. (Ref. derived from Golden Fleece of Greek legend sought by Jason and the Argonauts.) |

| | |
|---|---|
| VELOCITATE FORTIS | Strong by speed. 195 Sq., RAF. |
| VELOCITER ET SECURITER | Swiftly and securely. British Railways Bd. |
| VELOX ET VINDEX | Swift to vengeance (Swift and avenger). 113 Sq., RAF. |
| VELUM VENTIS | The sail to the winds. Alfonso IV, King of Portugal, 1325–57. |
| VELUT SILVA FLOREAT | May it flourish as a wood. East Dean (Glos.) RDC. |
| VENALE NEC AURO | Not bought with gold (part of a line in Horace, *Carmina* II, 16). Jervis-White-Jervis, Bts. |
| VENANTES DIRIGAMUS | We guide those who hunt. RAF station, Hartland Point, Devon, No. 405 Signals Unit, RAF. |
| VENENA PELLO | I expel poisons. Bartolomeo D'Alviano of Orvieto, general engaged in wars of sixteenth century in Italy. |
| VENI CREATOR | Come, O Creator (words are the opening of the classic hymn to the Holy Ghost, *Veni Creator Spiritus*). Commonwealth Development Corp. |
| VENIENDO RESTITUIT REM | By coming he restored the state. William III of Orange. |
| VENIENTI OCCURRERE CASU | To meet the occasion when it arises. No. 6 Maintenance Unit, RAF. |
| VENIT HORA | The hour comes. Hoare of Annabella, Bts., Hoare, co. Cork. |
| VENTIS SECUNDIS | By favourable winds. Viscount Hood, Rowley, Bts., HMS *Hood* (world's most powerful warship, destroyed by a shell from the German battleship *Bismarck*, 24 May 1941; only 3 survivors out of *Hood*'s crew of 1,418). |
| VENTO FAVENTE | With favouring wind. HMS *Boreas*. |
| VENTRE À TERRE | All out. 30 Bomber Sq., RAF. |
| VENTURE AND PROSPER | Birmingham Chamber of Commerce. |
| VENTUS SECUNDET | Let the wind be favourable. Pritchard-Jones, Bts. |
| VER NON SEMPER VIRET | Spring does not always bring forth spring. Vernon. |
| VERA FICTIS LIBENTIUS | True things are better than fiction. Trevelyan Coll., Durham. |
| VERA TROPHOEA FIDES | Faith is our true trophy. Swabey of Langley Marish. |
| VERAX ATQUE PROBUS | Trustworthy and honest. Ruttledge. |
| VERBO ET FACTO | By word and deed. Dawson. |
| VERBUM DEI LUCERNA | The word of God is a lamp (reminiscent of Psalm 109:115: 'Thy word is a lamp unto my feet'). Dean Close Sch., Cheltenham, 1884. |
| VERBUM DOMINI MANET IN AETERNUM | The Word of the Lord endures for ever. Stationers' and Newspaper Makers' Co., former inc. 1557, and in 1937 charter of amalgamation with newly formed Company of Newspaper Makers. |
| VERBUM NOSTRUM SATIS | Our word is sufficient. Gerard and Reid, Ltd., 1961. |
| VERBUM SAT SAPIENTI | A word (is enough) to the wise. No. 2 Flying Training Sch., RAF. |

| | |
|---|---|
| VERITAS | Truth. Hutchesons' Gram. Sch., Glasgow (founded 1641 by brothers George and Thomas Hutcheson), Stuart-French. |
| VERITAS AD FINEM | Truth to the end. Leith, Bt. |
| VERITAS ET HONESTAS | Truth and honesty. Austin of Shelford, Cambs. |
| VERITAS ET VIRTUS VINCUNT | Truth and virtue prevail. Lords Ormathwaite (Walsh), Walsh. |
| VERITAS IN VIRTUTE | Truth in virtue. Red House Sch., Ltd., Stockton-on-Tees. |
| VERITAS LIBERABIT | Truth will liberate. Adams of New Jersey, USA, Bodenham. |
| VERITAS LIBERAVIT | Truth has freed me. Slingsby. |
| VERITAS LIBERTAS | Truth, liberty. Abraham. |
| VERITAS, LIBERTAS, PIETAS | Truth, liberty, piety. Manchester Coll., Oxford. |
| VERITAS MAGNA EST | Truth is great (from 1 Esdras 4:35, continues, 'et praevalebit'). Jephson, Bts. |
| VERITAS ME DIRIGIT | Truth directs me. Brocklehurst, Bts., Lord Ranksborough (Brocklehurst) (NEP). |
| VERITAS ODIUM PARIT | Truth brings forth hate. Kennedy of Ellerslie. |
| VERITAS OMNIA VINCIT | Truth conquers all things. Kedslie, Waterhouse, Wrightson, Bts. |
| VERITAS PRAEVALEBIT | Truth shall prevail. Paul, Thomson of Corstorphine. |
| VERITAS PURITAS | Truth, purity. Lords Alverstone (Webster) (NEP). |
| VERITAS SEMPER MAGNA EST | Truth is always great. Kenny. |
| VERITAS SUPERABIT | Truth will conquer. Hill (formerly Hanbury). |
| VERITAS TEMPORIS FILIA | Truth is the daughter of time. Mary I (Bloody Mary), 1553–8 (also used 'Pro ara et regni custodia' for the altar and defence of the kingdom. |
| VERITAS VICTRIX | Truth the victor. Lord Penzance (Wilde) (NEP). |
| VERITAS VINCET | Truth will conquer. Orpen. |
| VERITAS VINCIT | Truth conquers. Barratt, French, Keith, Earls of Kintore (Keith), Laslo de Lombos, Parker, co. Cork, Phillips, Bts., Troup, Wilson-Wright, Wright. |
| VERITATE SCIENTIA HABERE | To have the knowledge in truth. Loughborough University of Technology. |
| VERITATE SCIENTIA LABORE | By truth, knowledge, labour. Loughborough Technical Coll. |
| VERITATEM EME ET NOLI VENDE | Buy the truth and do not will to sell it. Belfast Presbyterian Coll. |
| VERITATEM PETIMUS | We seek the truth. Inst. of Work Study, 1960. |
| VÉRITÉ SANS PEUR | Truth without fear. Abrahams, Bedford, Gunning, Lords Middleton (Willoughby), Ward of Brynhir, Willoughby, Bts. |
| VERNON SEMPER VIRET | Vernon always flourishes. Lords Lyveden (Vernon), Vernon. |

| | |
|---|---|
| VERO NIL VERIUS | Nothing truer than truth. De Vere, Bts., Hope-Vere. Play on the name of Vere, one of the most famous medieval families, holders of the now extinct (or possibly dormant) earldom of Oxford, to which an heir may well exist. |
| VERRIMUS CAELUM | We sweep the skies. RAF station, Duxford, Cambs. |
| VERSA EST IN CINERES | It is turned into ashes. Margaret of Austria, Duchess of Florence and Parma, d. 1588, natural dau. of Emperor Charles V. Twice a widow, hence emblem (and motto) of an arm issuing from clouds and threatening an oak. |
| VERSATILE | 187 Sq., RAF. |
| VERSATILIS | Versatile. 37 Sq., RAF Regt. |
| VERSATILITY | 183 Sq., RAF. |
| VERTUE VAUNCETH | Virtue advances. Verney, Lords Willoughby de Broke (Verney). |
| VERUM EXQUIRO | Seek the truth. RAF station, Wyton, Hunts. |
| VERUM NOBILISSIMUM EST | The true is the most noble. Urwick Orr & Partners Ltd., 1957. 'A new departure [i.e. in arms grants] is in the case of a company like Urwick Orr & Partners Ltd., who are business consultants in management . . . [they] are rather a professional than a business concern and it is on the score of their professional standing and regard for professional etiquette that they have been accorded the privilege of a coat of arms. It must follow that many other semi-professional bodies and associations will seek to emulate them' (L. G. Pine, *Teach Yourself Heraldry and Genealogy*, p. 131). The prophecy has proved most true, as many entries in this book testify. |
| VERUS AMOR PATRIAE | The true love of country. Hughes, co. Wexford. |
| VERUS ET FIDELIS | True and faithful. Kirk of Cardiff. |
| VERUS ET FIDELIS SEMPER | True and faithful ever. Aylward. |
| VESCITUR CHRISTO | He feeds on Christ. Rous. |
| VESTIGA NULLA RETRORSUM | No steps backwards. Baily, Earls of Buckinghamshire (Hobart-Hampden), Buckinghamshire CC, Coninsby, Hampden, Levinge, Bts., Trevor, 5th (Princess Charlotte of Wales) Dragoon Guards, Leicestershire Militia. |
| VETERA NOVAQUE TUERI | To guard old and new. Malton (N.R. Yorks.) UDC. |
| VETERI FRONDESCIT HONORE | It flourishes in ancient honour. 3rd Foot (The Buffs, East Kent Regt.). |
| VETERUM NON IMMEMOR | Not unmindful of old things. Adamson. |
| VETUSTAS DIGNITATEM GENERAT | Age generates dignity. East Retford (Notts.), Bor. of. |
| VI ATTAMEN HONORE | By force yet by honour. Wyatt. |
| VI DEFENDUM ARS PROTECTUM | Art protected and defended by force. Keyworth. |
| VI DEI TERRAEQUE | By the strength of God and of the earth. Richmond (N.R. Yorks.) RDC, 1955. |
| VI ET ANIMO | By strength and courage. Hankinson. McCulloch. |

| | |
|---|---|
| VI ET ARMIS | By force and arms. Armstrong Bts., Heaton-Armstrong (ancient Scottish border family, one of whom was famous Johnnie Armstrong, the victim with 30 of his men of 'Armstrong's Last Goodnight'), 65 Sq., RAF. |
| VI ET ARTE | By strength and will. Colyer-Fergusson, Bts., Ferguson, Stevens. |
| VI ET ICTU | By force and impact. Balloon Cmd., RAF. |
| VI ET PRUDENTIA | By force and prudence. Maple, Bt. |
| VI ET VIRTUTE | By strength and valour. Lords Annaly (White), Bairds, Bts., Beard (formerly of Grayshott Hall), Bibby, Bt., Farriers Co., inc. 1673, Hull, Hunt of Logie, Maturin-Baird, Nash, Ogle, Pooler, Spraight. |
| VI MARTIALI DEO ADJUVANTE | With martial strength, God helping. Marshall, co. Northumb. |
| VI NULLA INVERTITUR ORDO | The order is not inverted by any force. King Stephen of Blois, 1135–54 (responsible for the anarchy in England, supposed to be ref. to his badge of ostrich feathers), Cordwainers' Co., inc. 1439. |
| VI PARVA NON INVERTITUR | Is not overthrown by a small force. Rodolph, Duke of Suabia (Swabia), d. 1307, son of Rodolph of Hapsburg (or Habsburg) (castle in Switzerland) from whose time, c.1273, the Holy Roman Empire became virtually hereditary in the Habsburg family. |
| VI VICTUS NON COACTUS | Overcome by force, not compelled. Warter. |
| VI VIVO ET ARMIS | I live by force and arms. Lords Windlesham (Hennessy). |
| VIA AD SALUTEM | The road to health. RAF Hosp., Cosford, Warwicks. |
| VIS CRUCIS VIA LUCIS | The way of the Cross is the way of life. King's Sch., Gloucester (founded by Henry VIII, 1541–7), Sinclair, Counts Sinclair of Sweden (branch of Scottish Sinclairs), Dr Bengt Sundkler, Bishop of Bokuba in Swedish Evangelical Church of NW Tanganyika, 1961. |
| VIA LABORIS VIA HONORIS | The road of hard work is the road of honour. No. 9 Sch. of Technical Training, RAF. |
| VIA MEDIA EXEMPLI GRATIA | A middle way for the sake of example. Building Surveyors Inst. |
| VIA TRITA VIA TUTA | The beaten road is the safe road. Agar, Laprimandaye, Earls of Normanton (Agar). |
| VIA TUTA VIRTUS | Virtue is a safe path. Dick. |
| VIA VI | A way by force. Lord Haversham (Hayter) (NEP), Hayter. |
| VIA VIRTUTIS VIA HONORIS | The way of virtue, the way of honour. Oddin-Taylor. |
| VIAM DEMONSTRAMUS | We show the way. RAF station, Middle Wallop, Hants. |
| VIAM INVENIAM AUT FACIAM | I will find a way or make one. Peterlee Development Corp. |
| VIAS TUAS DOMINE DEMO(N)STRA MIHI | Show me Thy ways O Lord. Andrea Doria, 1468–1560, famous admiral and statesman, set up aristocratic regime in Genoa. |

| | |
|---|---|
| VIATORES CAELI TUTARE | To guard the travellers of the sky. London Air Traffic Control Centre (Military), RAF. |
| VICI MUS | I Mus have conquered. Viscount Esher (Brett). Ref. must be to two Romans, P. Decimus Mus and his son of the same name, both of whom devoted themselves to death to gain victory for their country. |
| VICINAS URBES ALIT | It nourishes neighbouring cities. Spalding (Lincs.) UDC, 1950. |
| VICISTI ET VIVIMUS | Thou hast conquered and we survive. Johnson of Bath, Bts. All. to victory gained by 1st Bt., Sir Henry Johnson, over Irish rebels at New Ross, 5 June 1798, by which lives of many Protestants were saved. Johnson Bts. also bear the motto 'Nunquam non paratus'. One of the supporters of the Johnson arms has a banner with the words 'New Ross' upon it. |
| VICTIMA DEO | A victim for God. Malet-Veale. |
| VICTO DOLORE | Sorrow having been conquered. Simpson, Bts. |
| VICTOR IN ARDUIS | Conqueror in difficult things. McConnell, Bts. |
| VICTOR SE TOLLIT AD AURAS | The victor raises himself to the sky. Academy of Eterea of Padua. |
| VICTORIA | Victory. La Beaume, Locock Bts., Luckock. |
| VICTORIA GLORIA MERCES | Glory is the reward of victory. Berwick-upon-Tweed (Northumb.), Bor. of (in Scotland geographically, but after changing hands 14 times was ceded to England 1482). |
| VICTRIX FORTUNAE SAPIENTIA | Wisdom the conqueror of fortune. Geach. |
| VICTURI VOLAMUS | We fly to conquer. 122 Sq., RAF. |
| VICTURUS | About to conquer. Vick. |
| VIDEO VINCAM | I see, I shall conquer. Yorkshire Residential Sch. for the Deaf, Doncaster, 1952. |
| VIDEMUS, DELEMUS | We see, we destroy. 658 Sq., RAF. |
| VIDENDA | Things to be seen.Joint Sch. of Photographic Interpretation, RAF. |
| VIDERE NON VIDERI | To see and not be seen. 170 Sq., RAF. |
| VIDI VICI | I came, I conquered. 191 Sq., RAF (part of Julius Caesar's report after his victory in Asia, 'Veni, vidi, vici'). |
| VIGET IN CINERE VIRTUS | Virtue flourishes after death. Davidson. |
| VIGIL ET FORTIS | Wakeful and brave. Ivrea. |
| VIGILA | Keep watch. RAF station, St Mawgan, Cornwall. |
| VIGILA ET AUDE | Watch and hear. Fox of Liverpool, Bts. |
| VIGILA ET ORA | Watch and pray. Croxwell, Rogers of Dowdeswell, Waechter, Bts., Wake, Bts. |
| VIGILA PROFLIGA OCCUPA | Keep watch, strike down, take possession. No. 84 Group HQ, RAF. |
| VIGILAMUS | We watch. RAF station, Fylingdales, N.R. Yorks. |

| | |
|---|---|
| VIGILAMUS ET DEFENDIMUS | We watch and defend. RAF station, Stanton Wood. |
| VIGILANCE | RAF Hosp., Halton, Bucks. |
| VIGILANCE AND KNOWLEDGE | RAF station, Catterick, N.R. Yorks. |
| VIGILANDO | By watching. Campbell, Bts., Campbell of Dunstaffnage, Argylls, McLeod. |
| VIGILANDO ASCENDIMUS | We rise by being vigilant. Order of the White Falcon (Saxe-Weimar). |
| VIGILANDO CUSTODIMUS | We guard by watching. 612 Sq., RAF. |
| VIGILANS | Watchful. Burton, Johnson, Kadwell, Leadbitter-Smith, McCullagh, Bts., Taylor, No. 60 Group HQ, RAF. |
| VIGILANS ET AUDAX | Vigilant and bold. Bradley, co. Worcs., Campbell, Cockburn, Bts., Corrie, Corry, Dunn, Everard, co. Som., Union Castle Mail Steamship Co. Ltd., 1956, Viscount Wakefield (NEP). |
| VIGILANS ET CERTUS | Vigilant and sure. Anderson of Little Harle Tower, Newcastle-upon-Tyne. |
| VIGILANS ET PRUDENS | Vigilant and prudent. Morris of Bryn Myrddin. |
| VIGILANS ET UTILIS | Vigilant and useful. Manchester Chamber of Commerce. |
| VIGILANS IN DEFENDO | Watchful in defence. 3509 Co. of Stafford Fighter Control Unit, RAAF. |
| VIGILANS NON CADET | Vigilance will not fail. Calder, Vigilant Assurance Co. Ltd. |
| VIGILANT | 208 Sq., RAF. |
| VIGILANT AND RESOLUTE | Lords Harding. |
| VIGILANTE | Watching. Leigh-Clare. |
| VIGILANTER | Watchfully (Vigilantly). Gregory, Hill of Good-a-Meavy, Stawell, Wegg, No. 591 Signals Unit, RAF. |
| VIGILANTES | Watching. Cleethorpes (Lincs.), Bor. of. |
| VIGILANTI SALUS | Safety for the vigilant. Rickards. |
| VIGILANTIA | Vigilance. Aird Bts., British Horological Instruments Ltd., Carfrea, Harrison of Maer, Bt. |
| VIGILANTIA NON CADET | Vigilance will not miscarry. Cadell, co. Linlithgow. |
| VIGILANTIA, ROBUR, VOLUPTAS | Vigilance, strength, pleasure. Arundell, Hunter, Hunter Blair, Bts. |
| VIGILANTIBUS | While they watch. Acheson, Achison, Aitchison, Earls of Gosford (Acheson), Porter. |
| VIGILAT SACRI THESAURI CUSTOS | The guardian of the sacred treasure is vigilant. Pope Sixtus V, 1585–90, Cardinal Felice Peretti, son of a vineyard labourer and in his youth a swineherd. He left papal treasury full of gold, hence relevance of his motto. |
| VIGILATE | Watch. Alcock, Allcock, Cruwys, Fell, Leeds, Bts., Longstaff, Touche, Bts., Tucker, Walkey. |
| VIGILATE ET ORATE | Watch and pray. Capron, Lords Castlemaine (Handcock), Clevedon (Som.) UDC, Handcock, Law of Marble Hill, Shuckburgh. |

| | |
|---|---|
| VIGILO | I watch. Desse, Geikie, Gregson of Murton, Machado. |
| VIGILO ET ARCEO | I watch and ward. 63 Sq., RAF Regt. |
| VIGILO ET SPERO | I watch and hope. Daunt, Galbraith. |
| VIGORE | With vigour. Vickers. |
| VIGUEUR DE DESSUS | Strength is from above. Braidwood, Lords Inchiquin (O'Brien), O'Brien, O'Bryen, Marquesses of Thomond (O'Brien), Willington. |
| VIL GOD I ZAL | Kay-Menzies. Menzies, Bts. |
| VILA DE ARGAUIL | Town of Argauil, Portugal. |
| VILIUS VIRTUTIBUS AURUM | Gold is viler than virtues. Soames. |
| VIM PROMOVET INSITAM | It moves the innate force. Bristol University, 1909. |
| VIM VI REPELLERE LICET | It is lawful to repel force by force. Gwyn-Hulford, Lord James of Hereford (NEP), Moore-Gwyn. |
| VINCAM VEL MORIAR | I will conquer or die. Benyon of Englefield, Berks., Caton, McDougall, McDowall. |
| VINCE MALUM PATIENTIA | Overcome evil with patience. Lee, Townshend. |
| VINCEMUS | We will conquer. No. 2 Group HQ, RAF. |
| VINCENDO VICTUS | Conquered in conquering. Ley. |
| VINCENTI DABITUR | It shall be given to the conqueror. Vincent. |
| VINCERE EST VIVERE | To conquer is to live. Holt of Cheetham, Bts., Smyth, 143 Sq., RAF. |
| VINCERE VEL MORI | To conquer or die. Eyre, MacDowall of Garthland, Maclaine, Maclean of Dochgarroch, MacNeil, O'Morchoe. |
| VINCET VERITAS | Truth will conquer. Allison, Schroder, Bt. |
| VINCIENDO VINCIMUS | We link together to conquer. 525 Sq., RAF (transport). |
| VINCIT AMOR PATRIAE | Love of my country exceeds everything. Anderson-Ashton, Anderson-Pelham, Archbishop Holgate's Sch., York, 1546, Earls of Chichester (Pelham), Cooper, Gunn, Hargreaves, James, Viscount Molesworth, Lords Muncaster (Pennington) (NEP), Pennington, Earls of Yarborough (Pelham), Thursby-Pelham. |
| VINCIT OMNIA INDUSTRIA | Industry overcomes all things. Bury (Lancs.), Co. Bor. of. |
| VINCIT OMNIA PERSEVERANTIA | Perseverance conquers all. Inst. of Bookkeepers and Related Data Processing Ltd. |
| VINCIT OMNIA VERITAS | Truth conquers all things. Clayton, Courcy, Eaton, Gillett, Bts., Goodchild, Lords Kingsale (De Courcy), Laffan, Bts., Moon, Bts., Savory, Bt. |
| VINCIT OMNIA VIRTUS | Virtue conquers all. White of Aspley Guise. |
| VINCIT PERICULA VIRTUS | Virtue overcomes dangers. Brady, Bt., Maine, Thornton. |
| VINCIT PERSEVERANTIA | Perseverance conquers. Lords Michelham (Stern), Stern, Lord Wandsworth (Stern) (NEP), Lord Wandsworth Coll., Basingstoke, Hants, 1912. |

| | |
|---|---|
| VINCIT QUI PATITUR | He conquers who endures. Ackworth, Addenbrooke, Amphlett, Ashhurst, Best-Shaw of Eltham, Bts., Chester, Colt, Bts., Dalgety, Dancer, Bts., Disney of the Hyde, Hamfrey, Harrison, Inglesby, Prescott of Godmanchester, Bts., Ruck Keens, Shaw, Bts., Smerdon, Stockport Gram. Sch., Cheshire, 1487, Stone, Trinity Sch., Croydon (founded by Archbishop John Whitgift, 1596), Turberville, Whitgift, Whitgift Sch., South Croydon, 1596, Wise, RAF station, El Adem. |
| VINCIT QUI SE VINCIT | He conquers who conquers himself. Ellis, Holland, Jones of Sanderstead, Pilditch, Bts., Wilson, co. Yorks. |
| VINCIT SEMPER VERITAS | Truth always conquers. Tabor. |
| VINCIT VERITAS | Truth conquers. Alison, Bts., Allix, Archer-Shee, Baxter, Boddington, Coote, Bts., Ewbank, O'Shee, Paget-Tomlinson, Peacocke, Bts., Presten, Pretyman, Rodd, Shaw, Shee, Bts. |
| VINCIT VIM VIRTUS | Virtue conquers force. Kennedy of Underwood, Ayrshire. |
| VINCTUS NON VICTUS | Bound not conquered. Lord Pirbright (De Worms) *(NEP)*. |
| VINCTUS SED NON VICTUS | Chained but not conquered. Gallwey. |
| VINCULA TEMNO | I despise bonds. Sinclair of Longformacus, Bts. |
| VINDICAT IN VENTIS | It avenges in the winds. 504 Co. of Nottingham Sq., AAF. |
| VINUM EXHILARAT ANIMUM | Wine exhilarates the spirit. Vintners' Co., charter 1437. |
| VIR SAPIENS FORTIS EST | The wise man is strong. Dewey, Bts. |
| VIR TUTUS ET FIDELIS | A man safe and faithful. North-Bomford. |
| VIRES ACQUIRIT EUNDO | It acquires powers by going. Inst. of Fuel, Loughborough Gram. Sch., Leics., 1495, RAF station, Feltwell (Even gathering new strength in our course). |
| VIRES ACQUIRINT EUNDO | They acquire power in (*or* by) going (verb is usually *acquirunt*). Inst. of Production Engineers, 1939, Officer Cadets, Sandhurst. |
| VIRES AGMINIS UNUS HABET | One has the strength of an army. Grylls. |
| VIRES ANIMAT VIRTUS | Virtue animates our powers. Garden. |
| VIRES CONTERAMUS ARTI | We connect strength to art. Castle Donnington (Leics.) RDC. |
| VIRES DE CAELO | Strength from the sky. RAF station, Stradishall, Suffolk. |
| VIRES VERITAS | Truth gives powers. Kennedy of Clowburn, Bts. |
| VIRESCIT VULNERE VIRTUS | Her virtue flourishes by her wound. Brownrigg, Bts., Burnett, Bts., Burnett-Stuart, Dopping-Hepenstal, Foot, Earls of Galloway (Stewart), Green, Ker, Lord Seaforth (Stewart-Mackensie), Webb. |
| VIRESCO | I flourish. Greenless, Greenwell, Bts., Monteath, Smellet, Stewart, Tailefer. |
| VIRET IN AETERNUM | It flowers for ever. 13th Hussars, 13th Light Dragoons. |
| VIRIBUS AUDAX | Bold in strength. RAF Sch. of Physical Training. |

| | |
|---|---|
| VIRIBUS CONTACTIS | With gathered strength. 108 Sq., RAF. |
| VIRIBUS UNITIS | With forces united. South African administered territory of South West Africa (Namibia), 1961. |
| VIRIBUS VIGEAMUS | Let us flourish through strength. RAF station, Gaydon, Warwicks. |
| VIRIBUS VINCIMUS | We conquer by our strength. 21 Sq., RAF. |
| VIRIBUS VIRTUS | Virtue from powers. Smyly. |
| VIRILITER | Manly. Birrell. |
| VIRILITER AGITE ESTOTE FORTES | Quit yourselves like men, be strong (from 1 Samuel 4:9). Culford Sch., Bury St Edmunds, 1881, South West London College, Barnes, 1920. |
| VIRTUE HAVE VIRTUE | Leith-Ross. |
| VIRTUE, LEARNING, MANNERS | Brentwood Sch., Essex, founded in 1557 by Chief Justice of Common Pleas, Sir Antony Browne (both his judicial position and knighthood came after 1557). |
| VIRTUE MINE HONOUR | Lean, Maclean, Bts., Maclean of Dochgarroch. |
| VIRTUE VIA VIRTUS | Virtue, the way, manhood. Mountain, a family traced in Bristol to 1592 as far as records have been searched. Arms – barry lozengy or and azure, on a chief gules 3 cross crosslets or, assigned 1613 to George Mountain, Dean of Westminster, who d. shortly after installation as Archbishop of York. In *DNB* he is described as a member of the Mountains of Westow in Yorkshire. Motto has distinction of being in English (one word) and Latin (two words). |
| VIRTUS AD AETHERA TENDIT | Virtue reaches to heaven. Lewthwaite, Bts., The Earls of Balfour, Balfour of Balbirnie, Fife, Cairns. |
| VIRTUS AD SIDERA TOLLIT | Virtue raises to the stars. Wilson. Lord Winmarleigh (Patten Wilson) *(NEP)*. |
| VIRTUS ARIETE FORTIOR | Virtue is stronger than a battering ram. Earls of Abingdon (Bertie), Bertie, Harman. |
| VIRTUS ASTRA PETIT | Virtue seeks the stars. Flamank, Vandeleur. |
| VIRTUS AUGET HONOREM | Virtue increases honour. Edmonstone, Bts. |
| VIRTUS AURO PRAEFERENDI | Virtue is preferred rather than gold. Allen. |
| VIRTUS BASIS VITAE | Virtue is the basis of life. Jerningham. |
| VIRTUS CASTELLUM MEUM | Virtue is my castle. Bailey, Bts., Bruce of Thorington. |
| VIRTUS DEPRESSA RESURGET | Virtue, though depressed, shall rise again. Kendall. |
| VIRTUS DIFFICILIA VINCIT | Virtue overcomes difficulties. Whitburn. |
| VIRTUS EST DEI | Virtue is of God. Briggs, Brooke (formerly of Haughton Hall). |
| VIRTUS EST DEO | Virtue is from God. Briggs, Bts. |
| VIRTUS EST VENERABILIS | Virtue is venerable. Leech. |
| VIRTUS EST VITIUM FUGERE | It is virtue to flee from vice. Reynardson. |
| VIRTUS ET HONOS | Virtue and honour. Order of Merit of the Bavarian Crown. |

| | |
|---|---|
| VIRTUS IN ACTIONE CONSISTIT | Virtue consists in action. Lords Broughshane (Davison), Clayton, Bts., Earls Craven, Everard, Bts., Halford, Sier. |
| VIRTUS IN ARDUA | Courage against difficulties. Pottinger, Bts. |
| VIRTUS IN ARDUIS | Courage in difficulties. Lords Ashburton (Baring), Bradish, Cockain, Cockane, Lords Cullen of Ashbourne, Dorman, Bts., Gamon, MacQueen, Woodhouse. |
| VIRTÚS IMMORTALIS | Immortal virtue. Hodges of Dorchester. |
| VIRTUS INSIGNIT AUDENTES | Virtue marks the bold. Beamish. |
| VIRTUS INVICTA | Virtue unconquered. MacCarthy-Morrogh. Morrough Bernard. |
| VIRTUS INVICTA GLORIOSA | Unconquered virtue is glorious. Bentham of Lincoln's Inn, Thomas of Wenvoe, Bts. |
| VIRTUS INVIDIAE SCOPUS | Virtue is the mark of envy. Lords Methuen, Methuen (formerly of Stratton Lodge). |
| VIRTUS LAUDATA CRESCIT | Virtue which is praised grows. Berkhamsted Sch., Herts., founded 1541. |
| VIRTUS MILLE SCUTA | Virtue equals a thousand shields. Armitage, Clifford, Bts., Dayrell, Earls of Effingham (Howard), Howard, Sadler, Vyse. |
| VIRTUS NOBILITAT | Virtue ennobles. Order of the Netherlands Lion, 1815. |
| VIRTUS NON STEMMA | Virtue not pedigree. Lords Ebury (Grosvenor), Grosvenor London, Lords Stalbridge (Grosvenor), Dukes of Westminster (Grosvenor). |
| VIRTUS PARET ROBUR | Virtue begets strength. Richardson-Bunbury, Bts. |
| VIRTUS PATIENTIA VERITAS | Virtue, patience, truth. Johnson of Derby. |
| VIRTUS PRAESTANTIOR AURO | Virtue is more excellent than gold. Severne, Whieldon. |
| VIRTUS PROBATA FLORESCIT | Tried virtue flourishes. Viscount Bangor (Ward), Cologan. |
| VIRTUS PROPTER SE | Virtue for its own sake. A'Court-Repington, Bosville-MacDonald of Sleat, Bts., Radcliffe, Bts., Reppington. |
| VIRTUS REPULSAE NESCIA SORDIDAE | Virtue unconscious of base repulse. Earls of Desart (Cuffe). |
| VIRTUS SALUS DUCUM | Virtue is the health of leaders. Leader of Sheffield. |
| VIRTUS SEMPER VINCIT | Virtue always conquers. White of Donegal. |
| VIRTUS SEMPER VIRIDIS | Virtue is always green. Earls of Belmore (Lowry-Corry), Cory of Llantarnam Abbey, Bt., France, Gorry, Laurie, Lowrie, Rollason. |
| VIRTUS SIBI MUNUS | Virtue is its own reward. Dalrymple-White, Bts. |
| VIRTUS SINE METU | Virtue without fear. Howard of Broughton Hall. |
| VIRTUS SOLA INVICTA | Virtue alone is invincible. Eyre. |
| VIRTUS SOLA NOBILITAS | Virtue is the only nobility. Blake of Menlo, Bts., Blake, co. Galway, Ffrench-Blake, Throckmorton, Bts. |

| | |
|---|---|
| VIRTUS SOLA NOBILITAT | Virtue alone ennobles. Blake, Caddle, Henrison, Henryson-Caird, McCausland, Nicholson, Bts., Lords Wallscourt (Blake) *(NEP)*, Watson. |
| VIRTUS SUB CRUCE CRESCIT | Virtue increases under the Cross. Bury. |
| VIRTUS SUB PONDERE CRESCIT | Virtue grows under the load. Hickey. |
| VIRTUS SUI IPSIUS PRAEMIUM | Virtue is its own reward. Preston. |
| VIRTUS SURGIT IN ALTUM | Virtue rises to the height. Whitcombe. |
| VIRTUS TUTISSIMA CASSIS | Virtue is the safest helmet. Barker, co. Warwicks., Bellairs, Finch, Hatton, Raymond-Barker, Stephenson, Williams, Willis. |
| VIRTUS TUTISSIMA TURRIS | Virtue is the safest tower. Grayson, Bts. |
| VIRTUS VERA NOBILITAS | Virtue is true nobility. Elborne, Henville. |
| VIRTUS VERITAS LIBERTAS | Virtue, truth, and freedom. Glossop (Derbys.), Bor. of. |
| VIRTUS VIGET IN ARDUIS | Virtue flourishes in difficulties. Gurdon. |
| VIRTUS VINCIT INVIDIAM | Virtue overcomes envy. Clibborn, Lords Cornwallis, Mann. |
| VIRTUTE | By virtue. Brymer of Ilsington, co. Dorset, Church, Couper, Bts., Dick, Ferguson of Pitfour, Keane, Kirk, Lord Overtoun (White), Order of Adolf of Nassau – Luxembourg, 1858. |
| VIRTUTE ACQUIRITUR HONOR | Honour is acquired by virtue. Gill, Richardson, Richie, Ritchie, Spence. |
| VIRTUTE ACQUIRITUR HONOS | Honour is acquired by virtue. Richardson, Ritchie, Bts., Stewart-Richardson, Bts. |
| VIRTUTE ADEPTA | Acquired by virtue. Lords Keyes. |
| VIRTUTE DIGNUS AVORUM | Worthy of the virtue of his ancestors. Worthington. |
| VIRTUTE DUCE | With virtue for guide. Elder, Shand, Shannon. |
| VIRTUTE ET ASTUTIA | By virtue and cleverness. Pirie-Gordon of Buthlaw. |
| VIRTUTE ET CLARITATE | By virtue and clearness. O'Hara. |
| VIRTUTE ET CONSTANTIA | By virtue and constancy. Auld, D'Engelbronner. |
| VIRTUTE ET FIDE | By valour and faith. Collins, Fisher of Helme Hall, Harley, Lamb, Marriot. Westminster Coll., Oxford, 1956. |
| VIRTUTE ET FIDELITATE | By valour and fidelity. Blaikie, Crofts, Goodsir, Lyons, Order of the Golden Lion of Hesse-Cassel, Reeves, Wilkin. |
| VIRTUTE ET FORTITUDINE | By virtue and fortitude. Cooper of Hursley, Bt. |
| VIRTUTE ET FORTUNA | By valour and good fortune. Andrews. |
| VIRTUTE ET INDUSTRIA | By virtue and industry. Boord, Bts., Bristol, City of (cr. a county by Edward III in 1373), Watney. |
| VIRTUTE ET INGENIO | By virtue and ability. Chester-Master. |
| VIRTUTE ET JUSTITIA | By virtue and justice. Keeling, co. Staffs. |

| | |
|---|---|
| VIRTUTE ET LABORE | By valour and exertion. Allan, Chichester-Clark, Clark, Cochran, Lords Cochrane of Cults, Cochrane of Woodbrook, Bts., Earls of Dundonald (Cochrane), Foster of Norwich, Bt., Lords Headley (Allanson-Winn), Heddle, Hilder, Hill of Stockbridge, Bt., Knight, Lord, M'Clintock, McLintock, Bts., McKenzie, Malcolmson, Profumo, Rig, Rigg, Wethered, Whitehead, Winn, Wood, Bts. |
| VIRTUTE ET NUMINE | By virtue and providence. Lords Cloncurry (Lawless) *(NEP)*, Creagh, Lawless. |
| VIRTUTE ET OPERA | By virtue and work. Bennie, Behrens, co. Yorks., Benzie, Bernie, Devas, Duff, Fife, Dukes of Fife (Carnegie), Fifeshire Artillery Volunteers, Grant-Duff, Harris, MacDuff, Scott-Duff. |
| VIRTUTE ET PROBITATE | By virtue and honesty. Magan. |
| VIRTUTE ET ROBORE | By virtue and strength. Chetwynd (Salop), Bor. of, Pellans. |
| VIRTUTE ET VALORE | By virtue and valour. Batt. C. in C.'s Yeomanry Escort (Imperial Yeo.), Ennis, Bts., Goulding, Bts., Herdman, Lord Kirkley (Noble) *(NEP)*, Leech, Mackensie of Ganloch, Bt., M'Kenzie, Noble of Ardmore, Bts., Peppard, Earls Roberts (Roberts, later Lewin), Stamer, Bts., Waldron-Hamilton. |
| VIRTUTE ET VERITATE | By virtue and truth. Blathwayt, co. Glos., Pocklington Sch., York, 1514. |
| VIRTUTE ET VIGILANTIA | By virtue and vigilance. Buddicom, Dorking (Surrey) UDC. |
| VIRTUTE EXCERPTAE | Plucked by valour. Cary of Torre Abbey, co. Devon. |
| VIRTUTE FIDEQUE | By virtue and faith. Viscount Elibank (Murray) *(NEP)*, McMurray, Murray, Royal Free Hosp. Sch. of Medicine. |
| VIRTUTE FORTUNAM DOMARE | To rule fortune by virtue. Leycester. |
| VIRTUTE GLADI PARI | Obey by virtue of the sword. Buchanan-Jardine, Bts. |
| VIRTUTE IN FACTIS | By virtue in deeds. Calne and Chippenham (Wilts.) RDC. |
| VIRTUTE MOENIA CEDANT | Let walls yield to valour. Wilder. |
| VIRTUTE NON ALITER | By virtue not otherwise. Moir, Bts. |
| VIRTUTE NON ARMIS FIDO | I confide in virtue, not in arms. Earls of Wilton (Egerton). |
| VIRTUTE NON ASTUTIA | By courage not by craft. Earls of Limerick (Pery), Thomas, Whitbread. |
| VIRTUTE NON VERBIS | By valour not by boasting. Baxter, Coulthart, Lord Fitzmaurice, Fitzmaurice of Duagh, Fitz-Morris, Marquesses of Lansdowne (Fitzmaurice), Petty, Robinson, Sawers. |
| VIRTUTE NON VI | By virtue not by force. Barneby, Bradstreet, Bt., Chivas, Coppinger, Derrick, Hawkes, Rumsey, Shivez. |
| VIRTUTE OFFICII | By virtue of office. Corp. of Secretaries, 1954. |

| | |
|---|---|
| VIRTUTE QUAM ASTUTIA | By character as by cleverness. Browell. |
| VIRTUTE QUIES | Repose through valour. Marquesses of Normanby (Phipps), Phipps. |
| VIRTUTE SECURUM | Secure in virtue. Earl De Montalt (Maude) *(NEP)* (arms shown in Brettenham and Thorpe Morieux churches, Suffolk, being impaled by Warner, Bts.). |
| VIRTUTE SECURUS | Safe by virtue. Viscount Hawarden (Maude). |
| VIRTUTE TUTUS | By virtue safe. Blair, Marshall, Nutchinson, Bt., Phayre. |
| VIRTUTE VICI | By valour I conquered. Ingram, Meynell of Meynell Langley. |
| VIRTUTE VINCES | By virtue thou shalt conquer. Leatham. |
| VIRTUTEM CORONAT HONOS | Honour crowns virtue. Earls of Perth (Drummond). |
| VIRTUTI ET MERITO | To virtue and merit. Papal Order of Pius IX, 1847. |
| VIRTUTI FORTUNA COMES | Fortune is companion of valour. Lang. |
| VIRTUTI GLADII PARAVI | I have prepared for virtue of the sword. Murray-Buchanan. |
| VIRTUTI IN BELLO | To bravery in war. Order of St Henry (Saxony), 1736. |
| VIRTUTI MIHI INVIUM | Impenetrable to me, in virtue. Hillary, Bts. |
| VIRTUTI NIHIL INVIUM | Nothing is impervious to valour. Chamberlayne, Dashwood of Kirtlington Park, Bts., Hillary, Bts. |
| VIRTUTI NON ARMIS FIDO | I trust to virtue not to arms. Grey Egerton, Bts., Twiss of Kerry, Earls of Wilton (Egerton). |
| VIRTUTI PRO PATRIA | For valour on behalf of our country. Order of Maximilian Joseph (Bavaria), 1797. |
| VIRTUTIS ALIMENTUM HONOS | Honour is the food of valour. Parker, co. Cumb. |
| VIRTUTIS AMORE | By love of virtue. Earls of Annesley, Stephens, Viscount Valentia (Annesley). |
| VIRTUTIS AVORUM PRAEMIUM | The reward of my ancestors' valour. Viscount Templetown (Upton), Upton. |
| VIRTUTIS COMES INVIDIA | Envy is the companion of valour. Viscount Hereford (Devereux). |
| VIRTUTIS FORTUNA COMES | Fortune the companion of virtue. Lords Ashtown (French), Brook, Ferguson of Raith, Fox, co. Cornwall, Viscount Harberton (Pomeroy), Hughes, Jason Maino, d. 1519 (celebrated jurisconsult in France), Viscount Novar (Munro-Ferguson) *(NEP)*, Rothwell, Dukes of Wellington (Wellesley), The Duke of Wellington's W.R. Regt. |
| VIRTUTIS GLORIA MERCES | Glory is the reward of valour. Deuchar, Gyll, Lorimer, McDonagh, Macgregor, Mackeson-Sandbach, MacRobert, Bts., Lord Robertson (Life Baron), Robertson of Struan. |
| VIRTUTIS IN BELLO PRAEMIUM | The reward of valour in war. Seton-Stewart (or Steuart), Bts. |
| VIRTUTIS LAUS ACTIO | The praise of virtue is action. Corbet, Bts., Rumbold, Bts., Tansley. |

| | |
|---|---|
| VIRTUTIS NAMURCENSIS PRAEMIUM | Reward of virtue at Namur. 18th Foot (Royal Irish Regt.). |
| VIRTUTIS PRAEMIUM | The reward of virtue. Myrton of Cogar, Bt., Stewart of Overton, Thoms. |
| VIRTUTIS PRAEMIUM HONOR | Honour is the reward of virtue. Earls of Denbigh and Desmond (Feilding), Fielden, Feniscowles, Millington. |
| VIRTUTIS PRAEMIUM LAUS | Praise is the prize of virtue. Jervoise. |
| VIS CELATA | Hidden strength. No. 63 (Western and Welsh) Group HQ, RAF. |
| VIS ET UNITAS | Strength and unity. Lords Casey. |
| VIS EX ARMIS CONSILIOQUE ORTA | Power derived from arms and knowledge. RAF station, Andover, Hants. |
| VIS FORTIBUS ARMA | Strength is arms to the brave. Cruikshank. More, Nisbett. |
| VIS IN CONSILIO | Strength in counsel. Glyn of Berbice, Bts. |
| VIS TUTA VIRTUTIS | The strength of virtue is safe. |
| VIS UNITA FORTIOR | Strength united is the more powerful. Brook, Brooke, Crosby (Lancs.), Bor. of, Derby Co. and Bor. Police Authority, Flood, Hales, Hoskin, Lidwell, Midland Bank Ltd., Moore, Earls Mountcashell (Moore) *(NEP)*, Pulteney, Lords Rathdonnell (McClintock-Bunbury), Retail Fruit Trade Federation Ltd., Royal Coll. of Veterinary Surgeons, Stoke-on-Trent, City and Co. Bor. of, Lords Wrottesley. |
| VISE À LA FIN | Look to the end. Calder. Home, Bts. |
| VISU ET NISU | By sight and by step. RAF Staff Coll., Bracknell, Berks. (By vision and effort). |
| VITA CARA CARIOR LIBERTAS | Life is dear, liberty dearer. Leese, Bts. |
| VITA DONUM DEI | Life is the gift of God. Royal Coll. of Midwives. |
| VITA EX AQUA VENIT | Life comes from water. Mersey and River Weaver Authority, 1965 (all. to physical science view that life originated in the sea). |
| VITA EX UNDIS ABREPTA | Life snatched from the waves. 294 Sq., RAF (air/sea rescue). |
| VITA MUSIS GRATIOR | Life is more pleasing with the Muses. Haslemere (Surrey) UDC. |
| VITA PERIT LABOR NON MORITUR | Life dies, labour does not die. Alexander of Edgehill, Bts. |
| VITA POSSE PRIORE FRUI | To be able to enjoy the recollections of a former life (Martial, *Epigrammata*, X. xxiii). Colley Cibber, actor and dramatist, used as prefix to his celebrated autobiography, *An Apology for the Life of Colley Cibber, Comedian*, 1740 (he was appointed Poet Laureate 1730; his poems were very bad, and he also erred in adapting Shakespeare's language; of his poetry Dr Johnson said, 'For nature formed the poet for the King' (i.e. George II); Cibber's trans. of the motto was, 'When years no more active life retain/'Tis youth renew'd to laugh them o'er again'), Tickell (the poet), Townsend. |

| | |
|---|---|
| VITA SINE LITTERIS MORS | Life without letters is death. Derby Sch., Derby. |
| VITA VERITAS VICTORIA | Life, truth, victory. Londonderry, City of. |
| VITAE VIA VIRTUS | Virtue is the way of life. Dawson, Earls of Portarlington (Dawson-Damer), Rust, Vaughan, Watkins, Weeks. |
| VITAM DIRIGAT | He directs my life. Christison, Bts. |
| VITAM DUCE BONAM | Lead a good life. Bonham. |
| VIVAT REX | Long live the King. McCorkell, McCorquodale. |
| VIVAT VERITAS | Let truth endure. Duncan, Bts. |
| VIVE ANIMA DEI | Live soul of God. Lord Swansea (Vivian). |
| VIVE BENE | Live well. Mander, Bts. |
| VIVE DEO ET VIVES | Live unto God and you will live. Craig, Bts. |
| VIVE DEO UT VIVAS | Live to God that you may live. Craig, Bts. |
| VIVE HODIE | Live for today. Green-Price, Bts. |
| VIVE MEMOR LETHI | Live mindful of death. Dixon-Hartland, Bts. |
| VIVE REVICTURUS | Live as if about to live again. Lords Vivian. |
| VIVE UT POSTEA VIVAS | So live that you may live hereafter. Frazer, James, Johnston of Caskieben, Bts. |
| VIVE UT VIVAS | Live that you may live. Abercrombie, Abercromby, Alford, Bathgate, Falconar-Stewart, Faulkner, Lords Falconer (dormant, *NEP*), Fawkner-Corbett, Hall of Hall Park, Hartley, Hosken, Ilife, Lord Iliffe, Johnston of Belfast, Keith-Falconer, Lanyon, M'Kenzie, Rugge-Price, Bts., Scott-Chad, Vivian, Sladen. |
| VIVE VIVANT ALII | Live, let others live. Phillips of Cilyblaidd. |
| VIVERE NEC OBLIVISCI | To live not to be forgotten. Norman, Bts. |
| VIVERE SAT VINCERE | To conquer is to live enough (sometimes given with *est* in place of *sat*). Attwood, De Molines, Molyneux, Bts., Earls of Sefton (Molyneux), Lords Ventry (De Moleyns). |
| VIVERE VIRTUTE | To live by virtue. Lord Hartwell (Berry), Viscount Camrose (Berry). |
| VIVIMUS IN SPE | We live in hope. Thorburn. |
| VIVIS SPERANDUM | Where there is life there is hope. Neven, Niven. |
| VIVIT POST FUNERA VIRTUS | Virtue lives after death. Boyle, Craig, Nottingham, City of, Earls of Shannon (Boyle). |
| VIVITE FORTES | Live ye brave. Pennefather. |
| VIVUNT DUM VIRENT | The forests live while the trees are green. Forrest, Bts. (oak trees in shield and crest). |
| VIX EA NOSTRA | Scarcely our own. Lambert of West Bridgford. |
| VIX EA NOSTRA VOCO | I scarce call these things our own. Campbell, co. Norfolk, Copeman, co. Norfolk, Fountain, Fountaine, Gamble, Bts., Lords Grenville, Hussey, Pechell, Bts., Earls of Warwick (Greville). |
| VIXI LIBER ET MORIAR | I have lived a freeman and will die one. Gray, Lord Rookwood (Selwyn-Ibbetson) *(NEP)*. |

| | |
|---|---|
| VOCATUS OBEDIVI | Having been called I have followed. Gell. |
| VOLAMUS SERVATURI | We fly to save. 281 Sq., RAF (air/sea rescue; badge is head of St Bernard dog). |
| VOLAMUS UT SERVIAMUS | We fly to serve. 691 Sq., RAF. |
| VOLANS ET VIDENS | Flying and seeing. 656 Sq., RAF. |
| VOLANT PER AETHERA VERBA | Words fly through the ether. RAF Communications Centre, Malta. |
| VOLAT AD AETHERA VIRTUS | Virtue flies to heaven. Hon. Soc. of the Inner Temple. Ref. derived from the arms, which are azure a pegasus salient argent. As the Hon. Soc. succeeded to the land formerly held by the Order of Knights Templars, the winged horse (Pegasus) is thought to be derived from the early emblem of the Templars, of two knights riding on one horse, denoting their (original) poverty. |
| VOLENS ET POTENS | Willing and able. RAF station, Long Benton, Northumb. |
| VOLENS ET VALENS | Willing and able. Fetherston, Bts., Rowcliffe. |
| VOLO NON VALEO | I am willing but unable. Earls of Carlisle (Howard), Greystock, Howard. |
| VOLUNTATE ET LABORE | By will and labour. Sven Hedin, Swedish explorer of Central Asia; last Swede to be ennobled, 1903. |
| VOM FELS ZUM MEER | From crag to sea. Royal Order of Hohenzollern (Prussia), 1841. |
| VOOR MOED BELEID TROUW | For courage, prudence and fidelity. Order of Wilhelm (Netherlands). |
| VOS COLLOCASTIS NOS CUSTODIEMUS | Do you collect, we will guard. Chester, Wrexham and N. Wales Savings Bank. |
| VOTA VITA MEA | Vows (are) my life. Lords Brabazon of Tara (Moore-Brabazon), Gibon-Brabazon, Lindsey-Brabazon, Earls of Meath (Brabazon). |
| VRAI À LA FIN | True to the end. Pike. |
| VRAYE FOY | True faith. Boswell (formerly of Auchinleck). |
| VULNERATI NON VICTI | Wounded not conquered. Cooks' Co., inc. 1482. |
| VULNERATUS NON VICTUS | Wounded not conquered. Viscount Guillamore (O'Grady) (NEP), Hartigan, O'Grady. |
| VULNERE VIRTUS | Virtue from a wound. Synnott. |
| VULTUS IN HOSTEM | The countenance against the enemy. Codrington, Bts. |
| VYKETH | Enduring (Cornish). Nance. |
| VZDY PRIPRAVEN | Always ready (Czech.). 68 Sq., RAF, formed 1941 (many Czechoslovak members). |

| | |
|---|---|
| WACHSAM UND GLÜCKLICH | Vigilant and fortunate. Wagner. |
| WACHSTUM UND STETIGKEIT | Wakefulness and steadiness. Lord Walston (Life Baron). |
| WAGTER IN DIE LUG | A guard in the sky (Afrikaans). 26 Sq., RAF (orig. formed in S. Africa). |
| WALK IN THE FEAR OF GOD | Cathcart-Walker-Heneage, Walker-Heneage. |
| WASTE NOT | Green of Wakefield, Bts. |
| WATCH | Forbes, Gordon of Haddo, Otter, Pakenham-Walsh, Lords Sempill (Forbes-Sempill). |
| WATCH AND WARD | Adamson of Linden Hall, Northumb. |
| WATCH WEIL | 2 City of Edinburgh Maritime HQ Unit, RAAF. |
| WATCH WELL | Lord Haliburton, Halyburton, Scott of Abbotsford, Bts. |
| WATCHFUL AND BOLD | Coates of Haypark, Bts. |
| WATCHFUL AND SURE | No. 1 Air Gunners' Sch., RAF. |
| WATCHING EVER FAITHFUL | 3512 Co. of Devon Fighter Control Unit, RAAF. |
| WAUR AND DAUR | War and dare. Mackie, Bt. |
| WAYS AND MEANS | Selby-Lowndes. A member of this family, William Lowndes, was chairman of Ways and Means in the House of Commons (hence the motto). 'To whom the nation is indebted for originating the funding system' (B.L.G., 1952). |
| WE ARE ONE | Armourers' and Braziers' Co. (i.e. the union of a number of crafts). There are two coats of arms, dexter the Armourers, sinister the Braziers. Also over the crest of man in armour is the motto 'Make all sure'. |
| WE AVENGE | 625 Sq., RAF. |
| WE BRING FREEDOM AND ASSISTANCE | 356 Sq., RAF. |
| WE DEFY | 264 Sq., RAF. |
| WE EXERCISE THEIR ARMS | 695 Sq., RAF (badge 3 arms to denote 3 services). |
| WE FIGHT TO DEFEND | No. 12 Group HQ, RAF. |
| WE FIGHT TO REBUILD | 310 Sq., RAF (Czechoslovak), 1940. |
| WE FLY FOR THE GUNS | 663 Sq., RAAF. |
| WE FORGE THE WEAPON | No. 92 Group HQ, RAF. |
| WE GOVERN BY SERVING | Greenwich, London Bor. of. |
| WE GROW BY INDUSTRY | Blyth (Northumb.), Bor. of. |
| WE GUIDE THE SWORD | 225 Sq., RAF (Army Co-op). |

| | |
|---|---|
| WE GUIDE THOSE WHO GUIDE | No. 10 Air Navigation Sch., RAF. |
| WE GUIDE TO STRIKE | No. 8 Group HQ, RAF. |
| WE HAVE SERVED AND EVER SHALL | No. 35 Maintenance Unit, RAF. |
| WE LEARN BY TEACHING | No. 41 Service Flying Training Sch., RAF. |
| WE LIGHT THE WAY | 156 Sq., RAF (Pathfinders, hence motto and badge of Mercury holding torch). |
| WE LONG ENDURE | Colne (Lancs.), Bor. of. |
| WE PREPARE FEARING NOUGHT | No. 12 Service Flying Training Sch., RAF. |
| WE RISE TO CONQUER | 46 Sq., RAF. |
| WE RISE TO OUR OBSTACLES | RAF station, Cottesmore, Rutland. |
| WE SEEK ALONE | 91 Sq., RAF. |
| WE SEEK TO STRIKE | No. 16 Group HQ, RAF. |
| WE SERVE | East Surrey Regt., 13th (Wandsworth) Bn., 1914–18, Dartford (Kent) RDC, Wandsworth, London Bor. of, Wandsworth Volunteer Training Corps (later 14th Bn.), 1914, No. 25 Maintenance Unit, RAF. |
| WE SERVE AND STRIKE | RAF West Africa. |
| WE SERVE INDUSTRY | British Steel Piling Industries Ltd. |
| WE SERVE THE LAND | Country Landowners' Assn. |
| WE SERVED | Victoria (ex-services) Assn. Ltd., 1958. |
| WE SHALL BE THERE | 280 Sq., RAF (air sea rescue). |
| WE STOOP NOT | Anderton of Euxton, anciently recorded family of landed gentry in Lancashire, firm in adherence to Roman Church in sixteenth and seventeenth centuries, hence the above. |
| WE SUSTAIN | No. 226 Operational Conversion Unit, RAF. |
| WE TAKE OUR TOLL | RAF station, Sandwich, Kent. |
| WE TRAVEL THE HORIZONS | Middle East Communications Sq., RAF. |
| WE WATCH ALL AROUND | RAF station, Seletar, Straits Settlements. |
| WE'LL PUT IT TO A VENTURE | Johnston of Coubister. |
| WEAVE TRUTH WITH TRUST | Weavers' Co., first charter from Henry II c.1155. (In some versions, Weave trust with trust.) |
| WELD WELL WIELD WELL | No. 84 Operational Training Unit, RAF. |
| WELFARE | Welfare Insurance Co. Ltd., 1956. |
| WELL WE DO | Lord Tayside (Urquhart, Life Baron). |
| WELL WIN, WELL WERR | Hort, Bts. |
| WHAR DAUR MEDDLE WI' ME | Border Mounted Rifles. |
| WHAT IS THERE NOT POSSIBLE TO AN ENERGETIC MAN | (in Sinhalese). Air HQ, RAF, Ceylon. |
| WHATEVER MEN DARE THEY CAN DO | Lords Kirkwood. |

| | |
|---|---|
| WHATEVER YOU UNDERTAKE DO WELL | Waring, Bts. |
| WHATSOEVER THY HAND FINDETH TO DO, DO IT WITH THY MIGHT | (Ecclesiastes 9:10) Buxton of Shadwell Lodge, Bts. |
| WHEARE VERTUE LYS LOVE NEVER DIES | Thompson of Guiseley, Bts. |
| WHERE JUSTICE RULES THE VIRTUE FLOWS | Leominster (Herefords.), Bor. of. |
| WHO DARES, WINS | Lords Alvingham (Yerburgh), Special Air Service (SAS), successful in saving the hostages at Iranian Embassy, Prince's Gate, London, May 1980. |
| WHO LEADS SERVES | Lords Nelson of Stafford. |
| WHO SHALL STOP US? | 144 Sq., RAF (bomber). |
| WHO STOPS | Jackson-Stops. |
| WHO'S AFEAR'D? | Dorset CC. |
| WHY NOT? | Lord Braintree (Critall) *(NEP)*. |
| WIL SONE WIL | Lords Wilson. |
| WILL GOD AND I SHALL | Lords Ashburnham, Earls of Ashburnham (ext.), also used 'Le roy et l'estat' (The king and the state). |
| WILL GOD I SHALL | Menzies. |
| WILL WELL | Urquhart, Lord Willis (Life Baron). |
| WIN | Wingate, Bts. |
| WINGS IN THE SUN | Middle East Air Force (changed to Near East Air Force, RAF, 1961, and to Air Headquarters, Cyprus, 1976). |
| WINGS OF MERCY | RAF Hosp., Changi. |
| WISDOM'S BEGINNING IS GOD'S FEAR | Campbell of Skerrington. |
| WISE WITHOUT EYES | 37 Sq., RAF (badge, hawk hooded – indicative of duties of 'blind flying'). |
| WITH FORT AND FLEET FOR HOME AND ENGLAND | Gillingham (Kent), Bor. of. |
| WITH GOD'S HELP | Lords Burgh (Willoughby Leith). |
| WITH HEAD AND HEART AND HAND | British Medical Assn., 1832. |
| WITH MIND AND HANDS | National Council for Technical Awards. |
| WITH OR ON | 252 Sq., RAF (badge is a spartan shield, hence motto taken from words of the Spartan mother: 'Return with your shield or upon it.'). |
| WITH SPEED I STRIKE | 114 Sq., RAF. |
| WITH SPEED TO THE MARK | RAF station, Church Fenton, Yorks. |
| WITH THESE KEYS | Hayling Island Co. Secondary Sch., Hants. |
| WITH THY MIGHT | Smyth of Duneira, Worsley-Taylor, Bts. |
| WITH TRUTH AND HONOUR | De Chair. |

| | |
|---|---|
| WITH VIGILANCE WE SERVE | 69 Sq., RAF. |
| WITH WINGS ALONE | No. 3 Glider Training Sch., RAF. |
| WITHIN THE ARK SAFE FOR EVER | Shipwrights' Co., inc. 1605. |
| WITHOUT BLOOD NO VICTORY | Lord Redmayne (Life Baron). |
| WITHOUT FEAR | Campbell of Achalader, co. Perth, Cockburn-Campbell, Lords Duffus, Sutherland. |
| WITHOUT FEAR OR FAVOUR | HQ, Provost and Security Services (UK), RAF. |
| WITHOUT HASTE, WITHOUT REST | Birchenough, Bt., Lees of Lytchet Manor, Bts. |
| WOE TO THE UNWARY | 217 Sq., RAF. |
| WORK WINS | Knights. |
| WORK SUPPORTS ALL | Worksop (Notts.) RDC, 1952. |
| WORKERS OF THE WORLD UNITE | Soviet Union, 1917 – 'the phrase is printed in gold lettering on the ribbon (of the Soviet arms) in the 15 official languages of the Soviet Union, now only 14' (C. A. von Vorlborth, *Heraldry of the World*, 1973, where it is added that the Soviet design (and presumably the motto) became the model for the arms of most other Communist countries and even for some non-Communist, such as the Republic of Italy). |

# Y

| | |
|---|---|
| Y-DDIODDEFWS-Y-ORVY | He suffered to conquer. Morgan, Williams of Aberpergwm. |
| Y DDRAIG GOCH DDYYY GYCHWYN | The Red Dragon shall lead. Prestatyn (Flint) UDC, 2nd Royal Cheshire Militia, The Welsh Regt., 16th Bn., City of Cardiff, 1914–18. |
| Y FATELYAF ABARTH RYTHSIS | I fight for freedom (Cornish). Plummer. |
| Y FFYNNO DUW Y FYDD | What God willeth shall be. Viscount Llandaff (Matthews) (NEP). |
| Y GWIR YN ERBYN Y BYD | The truth against the world. Edwards of Garth, Bt., Earls Lloyd George of Dwyfor, Viscount Tenby (Lloyd George). |
| Y SIAFFT I FLAEN Y BICELL | Shaft for the spearhead. RAF station, St Athan. |
| YANG PERTAMA DI MANA MANA | 15 Sq., RAF Regt. |
| YEOMEN OF BUCKS STRIKE HOME | The Royal Buckinghamshire (Yeomanry) Hussars. |
| YET HIGHER | Kinloch of Gourdie. |
| YMA'N YDHYOW WHATH OW CLASA | The ivy still flourishes (Cornish). Ivey. |
| YMDRECH I DRECHU | James, co. Monmouth. |
| YMLAEN | Forward. Lewis, No. 233 Operational Conversion Unit, RAF. |
| YMLAEN LLANELLI | Forward Llanelli. Llanelly (Carm.), Bor. of. |
| YN DAN AN ROSEN Y WHRAF SOWYNY | I prosper under the rose (Cornish). Roseveare. |
| YN TON KYN NYJYAF | In a wave I swim (Cornish). Tonkin. |
| YN Y NWYFRE YN HEDFAN | Hovering in the heavens. 210 Sq., RAF. |
| YORK AND LANCASTER | 84th Foot, York and Lancaster Regt. |
| YR HAFAN DEG AR FIN Y DON | A fair haven by the wave. Rhyl (Flint) UDC, 1967. |
| YR IOR YUIN (YWN) HANGOR HI | Our anchor is the Lord. Jones, co. Radnor. |

# Z

| | |
|---|---|
| ZA VITEZSTVI | Order of the White Lion (Czechoslovakia), 1922. |
| ZEAL AND HONOUR | Bloomfield, Bts. |
| ZEALOUS | Lords St Audries (Fuller-Acland-Hood) *(NEP)*, Lord Hood of Avalon *(NEP)*. |
| ZEALOUS IN SUPPORT | RAF station, Rheindahlen (formerly RAF Munchengladbach). |

# GREEK MOTTOES

ἀιεὶ φθάνομενον — Always ahead. 150 Sq., RAF (unit formed in Greece at Salonika 1918).

αἰέν ἀριστεύειν — Always to be best (or to excel). Broadbent, Bts., Kelvinside Acad., Glasgow, 1878.

ἀεροβατέω καὶ περιφρονέω τὸν ἥλιον — I will walk the sky and keep my thoughts on the sun. Oxford Univ. Air Sq., RAFVR.

ἅμα ὀρετόμενοι — Pulling together. Italian Literary Acad., Catenati of Macerata.

ἀνδρεῖα — Manly. St Andrew's Sch., Eastbourne.

ἀνδρίζεσθη — Behave like a man. Selwyn Coll., Cambridge, 1964.

ἀπλανής — Fixed. Montmorency (celebrated French family).

βαδίζε τὴν εὐήθειαν — Walk the straight way. Ralli, Bts.

βάλλ᾽ οὕτως — Throw thus. Cardinal Alessando Farnese, grandson of Pope Paul III; alluding to his singleness of purpose.

ἕν Κυριοῦ εὐχαριστία — In the Lord is thanksgiving. Alberigo Malaspina, Marchese di Massa, ca. 1623.

εὕρηκα — Eureka (the famous cry of Archimedes when solving the problem in his bath). Robinson of Hawthornden, Bts.

ἡ παιδειά καὶ τῆς σοφίας καὶ τῆς ἀρετής μήτηρ — Childhood is the mother of both wisdom and virtue. The Edinburgh Academy. Sir Walter Scott presided at opening ceremony 1824.

ἡμεις δ᾽ οἴατε φύμα — But we who are like the leaves (thought to be from the Homeric Hymns). The family of the late Lord Stow Hill (Soskice).

θάλασσα καύξει πάντα τ᾽ἀνθρώπων κακὰ — The sea removes all the ills of men. Tenby (Pembroke), Bor. of.

θάρσει — Be of good courage. Isaacson.

καθόρομεν ἀίστοι — Looking down unseen. 220 Sq., RAF (formed at Imbros, 1918).

μελέτη τὸ πᾶν — Meditation is all. Godlee, Bt.

ὀλέθριον ὄμμα — Death-dealing eye. 662 Sq., RAF (662 Army Aviation Sq.).

οὐρανόθεν — From heaven. Italian Literary Academy of the Ardenti of Naples.

πάθηματα μάθηματα — All experience is knowledge. Rodgers, Bts. Sufferings bring knowledge. Watson of London, Bts.

πραῶς καὶ ἰσχυρῶς — Gently and strongly. Demetrios, Metropolitan of Aleppo, Patriarch of the Greek Orthodox Church.

| | |
|---|---|
| σπεῦδε βραδέως | Hasten slowly (festina lente). Argenti of Picts Hill, co. Bedford, a family of Italian and later of Byzantine descent. |
| το δ' εὐ νικάτω | Thus, conquer well. Brighton Coll., founded 1845 by a few prominent residents in the town (primarily on C. of E. principles). |
| χρυσὸς ἀρετῆς οὐκ ἀντάξιος | Gold is not the equivalent of virtue. Exeter Sch., 1633. |
| ὡς ἀεὶ ἐνώπιον τοῦ θεοῦ | As always in the presence of God. Londonderry High Sch. |
| ὥς ἴδον ὥς ἐμάνην | As I saw, so I learned. Pierre de Ronsard, 1524–85, great French poet, the chief of the Pléiade. |

# INDEX